LEARNING ABOUT DRINKING

International Center for Alcohol Policies
Series on Alcohol in Society

Grant—*Alcohol and Emerging Markets: Patterns, Problems, and Responses*
Grant & Litvak—*Drinking Patterns and Their Consequences*
Heath—*Drinking Occasions: Comparative Perspectives on Alcohol and Culture*
Houghton and Roche—*Learning About Drinking*
Peele & Grant—*Alcohol and Pleasure: A Health Perspective*

LEARNING ABOUT DRINKING

Edited by

Eleni Houghton
International Center for Alcohol Policies

and

Ann M. Roche
National Centre for Education and Training on Addiction,
Flinders University of South Australia

BRUNNER-ROUTLEDGE
Taylor & Francis Group

USA	Publishing Office:	BRUNNER-ROUTLEDGE *A member of the Taylor & Francis Group* 325 Chestnut Street Philadelphia, PA 19106 Tel: (215) 625-8900 Fax: (215) 625-2940
	Distribution Center:	BRUNNER-ROUTLEDGE *A member of the Taylor & Francis Group* 7625 Empire Drive Florence, KY 41042 Tel: 1-800-634-7064 Fax: 1-800-248-4724
UK		BRUNNER-ROUTLEDGE *A member of the Taylor & Francis Group* 27 Church Road Hove E. Sussex, BN3 2FA Tel: +44 (0) 1273 207411 Fax: +44 (0) 1273 205612

LEARNING ABOUT DRINKING

1 2 3 4 5 6 7 8 9 0

Printed by Edwards Brothers, Lillington, NC, 2001

A CIP catalog record for this book is available from the British Library.
♾ The paper in this publication meets the requirements of the ANSI Standard Z39.48-1984 (Permanence of Paper)

Library of Congress Cataloging-in-Publication Data

Learning about drinking / edited by Eleni Houghton, Ann M. Roche.
p. cm.
Includes bibliographical references and index.
ISBN: 1-58391-316-5 (alk. paper)
1. Drinking of alcoholic beverages--Social aspects. 2. Drinking of alcoholic beverages--Psychological aspects. 3. Learning, Psychology of. I. Houghton, Eleni, II. Roche, Ann.
HV5035 .L44 2001
362.292--dc21

CIP
00-051296

ISBN: 1-58391-316-5 (case)

Contents

Editors' Biographies

Eleni Houghton is the Director of Social Policy at the International Center for Alcohol Policies. She has published and presented papers on a range of topics concerning alcohol education and international alcohol policy. Ms. Houghton received a B.A. from Vassar College and an M.Sc. in International Relations from the London School of Economics.

Ann M. Roche is Professor and Director of the National Centre for Education and Training on Addiction (NCETA) at Flinders University of South Australia. She has over 25 years experience as a researcher, educator, policy analyst, and as a consultant for government and nongovernment bodies including the World Health Organization.

Contributors

MARCUS GRANT
President
International Center for Alcohol Policies
Washington, D.C., U.S.A.

ANN M. ROCHE
National Centre for Education and Training on Addiction
Flinders University of South Australia
Adelaide, Australia

GERARD M. SCHIPPERS
Amsterdam Institute for Addiction Research
Amsterdam, The Netherlands

MARCEL A. G. VAN AKEN
University of Nijmegen
Nijmegen, The Netherlands

SYLVIA M. M. LAMMERS
University of Nijmegen
Nijmegen, The Netherlands

LAURA DE FEUNTES MERILLAS
Amsterdam Institute for Addiction Research
Amsterdam, The Netherlands

JUAN JOSÉ SANCHEZ-SOSA
Postgraduate Division of Psychology
National University of Mexico
Mexico City, Mexico

FLAVIO POLDRUGO
Office for Research and Innovative Projects on Alcohol, Other Addictions, and Mental Health
University of Trieste
Trieste, Italy

GAIL GLEASON MILGRAM
Center of Alcohol Studies
Rutgers University
Piscataway, New Jersey, USA

SHOSHANA WEISS
Alcohol Researcher
Karmiel, Israel

MARTIN PLANT
Alcohol & Health Research Centre
Edinburgh, Scotland, United Kingdom

RUTH CLIFFORD ENGS
School of Health, Physical Education, and Recreation
Indiana University
Bloomington, Indiana, USA

IAN NEWMAN
Nebraska Prevention Center for Alcohol
Lincoln, Nebraska, USA

DAVID J. HANSON
Department of Sociology
State University of New York—College of Potsdam
Potsdam, New York, USA

JANET E. STOCKDALE
Department of Social Psychology
London School of Economics
London, United Kingdom

KEITH R. EVANS
Alcohol, Tobacco, and Other Drug Services
Brisbane, Australia

GARY MAX
Gary Max and Associates
Bentleigh, Victoria, Australia

GRAHAM WILLERSDORF
Fosters Brewing Group
Southbank, Victoria, Australia

ELENI HOUGHTON
International Center for Alcohol Policies
Washington, D.C., USA

Foreword

The International Center for Alcohol Policies (ICAP) was established in 1995 with the goal of facilitating understanding and dialogue among all those with an interest in the development of alcohol policy. It is a not-for-profit organization, based in Washington, D.C., USA, and supported by major international drinks producers.

This is the fifth book in the ICAP Series on Alcohol and Society. Each book is intended to promote a fresh and more balanced perspective on a key alcohol policy issue. The first book, *Drinking Patterns and Their Consequences* (Grant & Litvak, 1997), argued that drinking patterns are more important than level of consumption in predicting positive and negative drinking outcomes. The second, *Alcohol and Emerging Markets: Patterns, Problems and Responses* (Grant, 1998), presented evidence suggesting that developing countries urgently require balanced alcohol policies based on partnerships between the public and private sectors. The third, *Alcohol and Pleasure: A Health Perspective* (Peele & Grant, 1999), is based on an international conference which explored the notion that for most people, most of the time, alcohol can confer considerable benefits although it carries some risks. The fourth book, *Drinking Occasions: Comparative Perspectives on Alcohol and Culture* (Heath, 2000), is an anthropological review of global drinking habits which concludes that most drinking occasions are normal parts of daily life and not associated with problems or excess.

The purpose of the current book is to gain a better understanding of the major influences that come to bear on a young person's decision to drink alcohol or not and, if so, how to drink. The book takes as its basic assumption that drinking is a learned behavior. In many ways, it is much like learning to drive or ski. It entails instruction, modeling, and even some experimentation, as part of the process of learning how to undertake the activity efficiently and without problems. If we can better understand what influences this learning, programs that seek to reduce harm are likely to be more effective.

This book is thus conceived as helping to lay the intellectual foundation for the concept of drinking alcohol as a learned behavior. It seeks to understand single influences—such as family, peers, the media, and religion—on young people as well as how these influences interact with one another and operate synergistically to influence drinking patterns and behaviors. In doing so, it is hoped that a better understanding of how nonproblematic drinking patterns may be facilitated. Since most young people are likely to experiment with alcohol, this book argues that it is better that they should be taught about it safely rather than having to learn in riskier settings. Since it is hoped to have a real world impact, each chapter has practical applications that can quickly be translated into better practice.

The book is the result of a careful process of international consultation. In 1997, ICAP commissioned four papers by social scientists from Latin America, Australasia, South Africa, and Europe to capture their perceptions of how youth in those cultures learned about drinking alcohol. Each consultant was asked to focus particularly on the informal social mechanisms that influenced young people, such as the role of family, peers, culture, and religion. They were also asked to consider the effect more formal policies and programs have on learning about alcohol. These papers were discussed at a meeting held at ICAP in February 1998, which the four consultants attended, together with other education specialists and a representative from the alcohol beverage industry. Shortly after the meeting, a fifth paper on China was also commissioned.

The main findings from the five very different commissioned papers can best be summarized in four points: (1) very little is actually known about how young people learn about drinking; (2) alcohol is an integral part of most cultures; (3) parents and peers (generally in that order) are the main influences on a young person's decision to drink or not; and (4) there are very few programs in formal settings that address the issue of learning about drinking, except in some parts of Europe. It became clear from the papers that knowledge about alcohol, whether intentionally or not, is transferred to the young person, but that our understanding is still lacking on how this transference takes place in different cultures. This conclusion is further corroborated in the literature (Boys et al., 1999).

Following the recommendations of the meeting, experts in relevant fields were invited to contribute chapters to this book. The five commissioned papers were made available to them all as source material and remained an important anchor point during the process of drafting, revising, and finalizing the chapters. Our intention is to have a book that represents the most innovative thinking in this area but never loses sight of the joys and sorrows of young people's drinking around the world. In maintaining this balance between innovation and reality, I believe that the editors—Eleni Houghton (Director of Social Policy at ICAP) and Ann Roche (Professor of Addictive Behaviors at Flinders University of South Australia in Adelaide)—have succeeded admirably.

Of course, the views expressed in this book are those of the contributing authors and do not necessarily reflect the views of ICAP or its sponsors. No effort was made to direct the views of individual authors, who expressed themselves as freely as they saw fit.

Marcus Grant
President
International Center for Alcohol Policies

REFERENCES

Boys, A., Marsden, J., Fountain, J., Griffiths, P., Stillwell, G., & Strang, J. (1999). What influences young people's use of drugs? A qualitative study of decision-making. *Drugs: Education, Prevention and Policy, 6*(3), 373–387.

Grant, M. (Ed.). (1998). *Alcohol and emerging markets: Patterns, problem, and responses*. Philadelphia: Brunner/Mazel.

Grant, M., & Litvak, J. (Eds.). (1997). *Drinking patterns and their consequences*. Washington, DC: Taylor & Francis.

Heath, D. (2000). *Drinking occasions: Comparative perspectives on alcohol and culture*. Philadelphia: Brunner/Mazel.

Peele, S., & Grant, M. (Eds.). (1999). *Alcohol and pleasure: A health perspective*. Philadelphia: Brunner/Mazel.

Acknowledgments

The editors wish to acknowledge the invaluable contribution of Linda Schmidt whose research and editing skills greatly improved the manuscript. We are also grateful to David Thompson who provided superb technical editing and to Marcus Grant for vision and ongoing support. Marjana Martinic, David Chamowitz, Ashely McClendon, and Meredith Mulhern all provided much appreciated advice and support along the way. Last, but not least, we are grateful to the chapter authors for their conscientious efforts in producing rigorous and critical examinations of complex areas and for providing new insight and meaning in this challenging area.

Chapter 1

Drinking Behavior: A Multifaceted and Multiphasic Phenomenon

Ann M. Roche

The central premise of this book is that drinking[1] behaviors are primarily learned behaviors. As such, they are subject to a range of processes and forces that influence learning experiences. To date, relatively little emphasis has been placed on the learning experiences of young persons in relation to the way they develop drinking behaviors, styles, and patterns.

Most research about this ubiquitous form of human activity has been developed from a problems-based perspective. Comparatively little has been published about alcohol that has not been written from the perspective of its negative consequences (Douglas, 1987). Much of the research on alcohol and family life has been conducted on abnormal populations, where one or more family members are in contact with a service because of an identified drink problem (Wright, 1999).

[1]Terms such as "drinking," "consumption," and "alcohol use" mean substantially different things in different contexts and are not necessarily synonymous. For instance, "to use alcohol" implies a much wider range of contextual, setting, behavioral and symbolic factors than does the term "to drink." To illustrate this point further, we can *use* alcohol (or food, clothes, cars, or a range of other commodities) to impress (this can be achieved through a variety of means including excessive consumption), to convey status (offering only the most expensive or better-quality alcohol beverages, as is often the case among Japanese businessmen), to signify an important event (e.g., the breaking of a champagne bottle over the bow of a newly launched boat), to signify success (as seen in the spraying of the winners of rally car driving events with champagne), or to show support or comradeship. These behaviors involve the use of alcohol, and are not essentially about the consumption of the product. Hence, it is important to recognize the significantly different ways in which language pertaining to alcohol is used. Wherever possible, the more accurate and precise terms have been employed in the relevant chapters throughout this book.

In general, there has been a preoccupation with alcohol-related problems, while nonpathological drinking patterns, practices, and behaviors have been largely ignored (Pittman, 1967). Overall, we know considerably more about drinking problems than we do about the development of low-risk drinking behaviors. More importantly, we know relatively little about resilience, protective factors, and their acquisition (Doll & Lyon, 1998). There is great scope for gaining a better understanding of how we can be more effective in minimizing problems associated with alcohol.

This book will explore the multifaceted phenomenon of learning about drinking. It will explore the various ways in which people learn about alcohol and drinking. In doing so, it will traverse encounters with alcohol at various life stages. Examination of the individual's experience of alcohol and drinking will be located within a social and cultural context. Our experiences of learning about drinking are a function of a multitude of factors, not the least of which is the place and position alcohol holds in any given society and social structure.

Decisions to drink, or not to drink, are shaped to some extent by observation of others around us, and especially by those we value most, e.g., parents, friends, and peers. The groups of individuals we value most and are the more influential members of our social sphere change over time and throughout the life span. Throughout this chapter we will examine some of these influential social forces and the manner in which their influence operates at different points in a person's life.

An examination of the ways in which different people at different points in their life learn to incorporate drinking in their day-to-day routine may help to inform us how to better use alcohol in nonproblematic ways in the future.

It is also noted at the outset that many people across all societies choose, for a variety of reasons, not to drink. This option is fully acknowledged, respected, and valued throughout all chapters of this book as a valid and appropriate life choice. Nothing in this book should be interpreted as implying anything other than validation of this position. Hence, the book is not predicated on the notion that people *should* drink. Rather it stems from a position that many people in most societies do so and that learning to do so in the most low-risk manner possible is an intrinsically valuable thing to seek to achieve.

PATTERNS OF DRINKING

In recent years, the individual's *pattern* of drinking has increasingly been held to be more important than the sheer volume of alcohol consumed. In some ways this book provides a companion volume to an earlier publication *Patterns of Drinking* (Litvak & Grant, 1998). Patterns of alcohol consumption vary greatly and comprise a remarkably varied set of drinking terrains. It has been argued that to know *how* any group of individuals drinks is as necessary for an understanding of the times as to know *how much* they drink. The manner in which particular patterns of drinking are acquired reflects our social and individual experiences with alcohol.

The terms "patterns" is taken to include the biomedical and psychosocial factors that may contribute to consequences of specific drinking patterns and may serve as predictors of risk or benefits associated with drinking. "Patterns" also refers to several aspects of drinking behavior, including temporal variations in drinking, the number and characteristics of heavy drinking occasions, the setting where drinking takes place, the activities associated with drinking, the personal characteristics of the drinkers and their drinking confederates, the types of beverages consumed, and the clusters of drinking norms and behaviors often referred to as drinking cultures (Single & Leino, 1998).

To examine lifetime drinking patterns requires us to comprehend shared understandings, values, and beliefs surrounding the place and role of alcohol in a given society. It requires a broad investigative sweep allowing for the inclusion of the culturally and socially constructed meanings attached to alcohol. That is, when examining drinking and the way we learn about drinking, we are also examining our own cultural complexity. Heterogeneity is the overriding characteristic of drinking patterns. They vary across different countries, cultures, communities, and individual life spans. Specific experiences with and exposure to drinking are equally varied, but the mechanisms and pathways by which we learn about drinking tend to be universal in nature.

In this introductory chapter, four separate, but overlapping, sections are presented. They cover

- **(a)** aspects of learning in general,
- **(b)** the sociocultural dimensions of learning about drinking,
- **(c)** the impact of an individual's beliefs and expectations on his or her drinking behaviors,
- **(d)** drinking across the life span.

Each of these sections offers an overview rather than an exhaustive exploration, as later chapters will also address some of these issues in more detail. This chapter therefore sets the scene for much of what follows in subsequent chapters.

LEARNING DEFINITIONS AND THEORIES

It is useful to commence with a clarification of what is meant here by the term "learning." In the current context, the term "learning" is used in its widest sense. It encompasses a broad range of factors and experiences that shape human behavior, and it should not be interpreted as referring just to formal education. Indeed, the process of learning about drinking has very little to do with formal education and training programs. The question whether drinking behavior is amenable to formal education will be addressed later.

Every experience of being in the world is a "learning experience." Every aspect of our social or personal world conveys messages, either covertly or overtly, and it is the receiving, interpreting, and interacting that occurs which forms our learning experiences. Learning has been defined as changes in behavior resulting from experience (Lefrancois, 1972). In this sense, the terms "learning" and "behavior" are seen to be, if not synonymous, then symbiotic.

Much effort has been directed at explaining, predicting, and controlling behavior, and in particular, drinking behavior. It is assumed from this perspective that behavior is subject to certain rules, that it is affected in certain predictable ways by experience, and is generally not subject to erratic, random forces. Many of these same assumptions underpin the work presented here on learning and drinking. That is, drinking behaviors will occur in a reasonably predictable fashion that reflects sets of social, environmental, and individual characteristics and circumstances.

It has been observed for some time that many patterns of behavior within a given culture or community are collective in nature. It is the group that establishes the norms for acceptable behavior and, by and large, individuals comply with these group norms. Changes that occur usually occur on a collective basis. While on one level this is an incomplete view of human behavior, it is nonetheless important in this context to recognize the social and cultural nature of most alcohol consumption and the complex array of external forces that operate to influence patterns of consumption.

There is a well-established view among social psychologists that an individual operates within a social field which includes both the physical environment and other people. In the early 1950's, Kurt Lewin (1951) proposed that behavior is a function of the interaction between the person and the environment. It is this interaction between the person and his or her environment that is of fundamental importance in the learning process. Aspects of the individual, the group, and the environment have an impact on the way we learn about drinking.

Sargent (1979), in her book *Drinking and Alcoholism in Australia*, which provided a sociological analysis of drinking there, called one chapter "Making the Drinker: Learning Drinking Patterns." Her title underscores the role that learning has in the acquisition of our knowledge and understanding about what alcohol is and how it can be used. Sargent goes on to illustrate this point by contrasting Irish and Jewish styles of drinking, and in doing so highlights the role of learning:

> Differences between the two cultural patterns [which] include vastly different attitudes, beliefs, customs, and socialization methods. While Jewish children learn a 'ritual' attitude centred on sobriety as a semi-religious value, Irish children learn a 'utilitarian' attitude which holds that almost any individual, self-centered reason for drinking is socially acceptable, even when it means getting drunk now and then (Sargent, 1979, p. 21).

Ten Assumptions About Learning

1. Human beings have a natural potentiality for learning.
2. Significant learning takes place when the subject matter is perceived by the subject as having relevance for his or her own purposes.
3. Learning that involves a change in self-organization—in the perception of one's self—is threatening and tends to be resisted.
4. Learning that is threatening to the self is more easily perceived and assimilated when external threats are at a minimum.
5. Students learn better when not threatened.
6. Students learn better by doing.
7. Learning is facilitated when the student participates responsibly in the learning process.
8. Self-initiated learning which involves the whole person of the learner—feelings as well as intellect—is the most lasting and persuasive.
9. Independence, creativity, and self-reliance are all facilitated when self-criticism and self-evaluation are basic and evaluation by others is of secondary importance.
10. The most socially useful learning in the modern world is the learning of the process of learning.

Source: Carl Rogers (1983).

In addition to the learning that occurs in the group context, there is also learning at the personal or individual level. The text box, which summarizes Carl Rogers' well-known principles of learning, highlights some of the key characteristics of learning at the individual level. In an overview of the impact of learned behavior on an individual's conditioned responses to the use of various psychoactive substances, Siegal (1999) has recently highlighted the extent to which "It has become increasingly apparent that learning contributes to many effects of drugs" (p. 1121). For instance, certain responses to alcohol, such as tolerance, vary considerably according to where we usually drink and under what circumstances, and the extent to which we have learnt to associate certain responses to drinking with particular settings and circumstances. Such responses to alcohol are not fixed in a formulaic sense (i.e., dose x = response y); rather there is a complex interaction that occurs which determines the outcome for each individual and on each specific occasion. The outcomes of these interactions also change not just with context but over time. The learning process is thus both complex, subjective and highly variable.

How we learn to know, internalize, understand, and exhibit the values and behaviors of our specific culture in relation to alcohol requires closer attention and explication. To examine how people learn about drinking, it is necessary to review selected models, and to consider what people/things/factors act as reinforcers. The first step in this process involves consideration of relevant theories and explanatory models.

Social Learning Theory

One of the better known and widely accepted explanatory frameworks for alcohol use, especially in relation to young people, is social learning theory (Bandura, 1977). Social learning theory is one of the dominant theoretical models that operates in learning any new behavior. Its fundamental premise is that people behave in the way they do largely because they *learn* to behave in that way. Learning can take place on a number of levels and in a multitude of ways. Social learning theory attempts to encapsulate the range of ways in which people learn—it incorporates conditioning at one extreme through to reflection at the other.

This theory holds that we learn about alcohol largely by observing and modeling the attitudes and behaviors of parents and friends, and through being rewarded or punished by these socializing agents. Bandura (1977) maintains that people learn through a process of observation and imitation of role models, and that role models and adolescents' perceptions of alcohol norms serve as social influences for drinking alcohol. Further, family members, friends, peers, and other adults also serve as role models for adolescents.

Lord Chesterfield is reputed to have stated that "We are, in truth, more than half what we are by imitation." Heather and Robertson (1989) ask why we imitate others so often, so thoroughly, and sometimes with apparent negative consequences. They suggest that the answer may be that, in evolutionary terms, doing as others do (i.e., modeling) has been the best way of surviving. Young members of the species copied their parents or died; they ran when their peers ran on the assumption that they knew something that the young did not; they found where food was by watching where others went. Children learn a huge part of their behavioral repertoire by observing parents.

Observational learning, or imitation, is central to the processes of socialization. Bandura (1969) argues that one of the fundamental means by which new modes of behavior are acquired and existing patterns modified is through observational learning. Social learning involves the acquisition of behavior patterns which society expects. Socially acceptable behavior varies from culture to culture, and also from person to person within a culture, the latter largely being determined by role or occupation, gender, age, status, and position in society. Hence, individuals undergo constant exposure to socially accepted or expected behavior throughout their life course.

One depiction of social learning theory is that children learn "cultural recipes" which present ways to use alcohol such that the desired result may be achieved. Cultural recipes also describe the where, when, what, and how of alcohol use that is socially sanctioned (Maloff, Becker, Fonaroff, & Rodin, 1979). The acquisition of these cultural recipes occurs through modelling and reinforcement by people who are of significance in a person's life. Once in school, the child becomes oriented more to its peer group; a vast amount of modeling takes place among children. Television, advertisements and videos too are major sources of observational learning. Crazes and fads, such as tattoos, skin piercing, hair sculpting, skateboards and rollerblades, are all modeling phenomena. While some modeling is quite conscious, at other times it takes place without either person being aware of what is happening. In general terms *people learn simply by watching others.*

Other Theories of Relevance

While social learning theory is one of the most useful concepts to aid our understanding of drinking behavior, it is not the only theory of relevance. The fact that different consumption patterns have emerged in different ethnic and cultural groupings has intrigued researchers and other observers of human behavior for many years. Theories abound regarding the underlying factors that contribute to the emergence of different forms of drinking. Some of the more important of these theories are noted below.

Normative Theory In the late 1960's two Scottish researchers, MacAndrew and Edgerton (1969), developed an interesting formulation of the way people learn to drink, as outlined in their classic tome *Drunken Comportment*. They suggested that much drinking and consequent behaviour was fashioned from social expectation. They saw the consumption of alcohol to the point of inebriation as deriving from the integration of drunkenness into the social order. Their "normative hypothesis" suggested a new comprehensive view and explanation of culturally derived variations in the use of alcohol. Moreover, it was a hypothesis fully consistent with a social learning theory of drinking.

Anxiety Hypothesis Prior to the emergence of normative theory, Horton's (1943) anxiety hypothesis had held sway as a dominant explanatory theory for the consumption of alcohol, particularly where alcohol was consumed to excess. Horton argued that the primary function of alcoholic beverages in all societies is the reduction of anxiety. Various researchers, noting that alcohol is a disinhibitor, have posited that its major functions are to reduce anxiety and to alleviate stress and, therefore, that alcohol can have positive social and psychological benefits for its users. The notion that alcohol reduces tension and anxiety, mitigates pain, and even reduces fear (i.e., "Dutch courage") is widely held (Ragland, 1996). However, others hold that the relationship between tension and alcohol is a complex interaction of learning and psychological processes and only one of a myriad of potential reinforcers (Stockwell et al., 1984).

The Power Hypothesis The limitations of the anxiety theory have been well illustrated for some decades. An alternative postulated by McClelland et al. (1972) was the power hypothesis, which maintained that people drink in order to feel powerful. While it was seen by some as a refinement of the anxiety theory of alcohol use and was consistent with a normative interpretation of use, the power theory also appeared to explain all types of drinking in all cultural contexts. Moreover, it provided an explanatory model that did not focus on alcoholism or deviancy, and accommodated the internationally observed phenomenon that men tend to drink more and more often than women. For a time, the power theory was held to contain considerable utility.

Aspects of these various explanatory models will be referred to throughout the book. The next section of this chapter will address various sociocultural aspects of drinking, and in particular, how they relate to the manner in which we learn about drinking and their potential role in future intervention programs.

SOCIOCULTURAL DIMENSIONS

"The act of drinking alcohol cannot be understood solely from within the context of the individual; it is an act infused with meaning that derives from socially determined conventions and consequences. But because individuals are socialized within different sociocultural niches, this meaning can vary dramatically from one individual and group to another."

(Johnson & Johnson, 1999; p. 79)

Cultural Context and Cultural Variation

The consumption of alcohol beverages is commonplace in most human societies, but the act of consumption holds different functions for different consumers (Pittman, 1996). And just as there is great variability in the manner in which individuals use alcohol, so too there are enormous cultural differences across different countries and within countries, and between different groups of people. Drinking and drinking mores are functions of ideologies, customs, and social processes (Rorabaugh (1979, p. 246).

When we examine drinking behavior, and the use of alcohol in general, it is essential to address cultural practices that facilitate or encourage moderate or excessive consumption (Moore, 1990). Drinking derives its meaning from its social context and setting. Defining who eats what, and with whom, is one of the most powerful ways of defining and differentiating groups (Iossofides, 1992). Alcohol serves to create, mediate and unite different categories while in no way dissolving those categories (Gefou-Madianou, 1992). Drinking together, even more than eating together, serves to bind members of a group in ways that other joint activities do not. It is one of the more potent ways in which we learn about our position in society. In this sense, alcohol can act as a metaphor for social relationships (Sherratt, 1995a, p. 6).

The meaning and interpretation given to alcoholic beverages, their uses, and even the consequences of drinking vary over time and place. The timing, frequency, and, above all, company of drinkers can tell us a great deal about sociability and shared values (Barrows & Room, 1991). To consume a certain substance, and especially alcohol, in a certain way can be seen as a statement (Sherratt, 1995b). Choice and combination of particular items of food and drink embody notions of status, value, identity, and belonging. The choice of foods and drinks, therefore, and their manner of preparation and serving, is fundamental to the definition, and indeed the creation, of social groups and classes. In this sense, it is the social, rather than the biological, interpretation that makes sense of Ludwig Feuerbach's old aphorism—*der Mensch ist, was er isst* (man is what he eats) (Sherratt, 1995b, p. 12).

The psychological experience of alcohol is also culturally constructed to a large extent. Peele (1997) raises a little addressed question regarding how culture fits into models of alcohol consumption and its consequences. In those Western nations where alcohol is consumed more often in integrated social settings than in settings devoted exclusively to drinking alcohol, use tends to be behaviorally benign (Peele, 1997; Single, 1993).

Psychoactive substances, such as alcohol, frequently form the focus of specific social occasions, both in their cultures of origin and (in rather different manifestations) in societies to which they have been introduced (Sherratt, 1995a, p. 4). Alcohol is partaken of in religious ceremonies, at celebratory occasions, for medicinal purposes, and also for its utilitarian value. "Alcohol comes into people's lives at every turn. Friends give each other bottles of liquor as holiday gifts. Airlines sell drinks in flight and placate passengers with free drinks . . . on billboards and in magazines the pleasures of drinking are everywhere extolled" (Weil & Rosen, 1993). But overall, sociability is the primary reason many people give when asked why they drink (Heath, 1995).

For most people in the world, drinking is a social act, and one that conforms to known and shared norms (Heath, 1987). To breach the social strictures that surround drinking is an act of deviance in some cultures. For instance:

> In many Mediterranean societies drinking excessively is not always associated with drunkenness, whereas drinking alone, even in lesser quantities, is. To drink and eat are by definition acts which imply commensal relations. They cannot, or rather should not, take place alone, individually. They are enmeshed within the collectivity. (Gefou-Madianou, 1992, p. 1)

In many countries, alcohol holds a unique place within a given culture as a psychoactive substance that is widely accepted and extensively integrated within the lifestyle of many, if not most, inhabitants. Certain features of social structure and organization constitute environmental factors that interact with genetic and biomedical factors in shaping how, when, with whom, and for what reason people drink (Heath, 1989).

The Functions of Drinking

Reasons for drinking have varied little throughout history. Alcohol is mostly used to enhance social interaction and to help people relax especially at the end of the working day. People also commonly use it to get high, feel exhilarated, and at times of religious and lay celebration, as well as to signal "time out" behavior. Drinking as "time out" has also been described as a means by which to loosen the responsibilities and strictures of everyday life (Driessen, 1992). Similarly, Joseph Gusfield (1987), a symbolic interactionist, treats alcohol and coffee as two opposing pointers. Coffee cues the shifts from play to work and alcohol, among its many functions, can cue the transition from work to play.

It is common knowledge that alcohol can also be used inappropriately or with negative consequences on either a shorter- or longer-term basis. Many of the specific consequences of drinking have been known for centuries, while others have only in more recent times become known to the scientific and wider community. The patterns of consumption that confer most benefit and least harm remain ill-defined for many communities (Roche, 1998).

Heterogeneity of Drinking Patterns

Although alcoholic beverages are consumed in virtually all societies, certain socioeconomic, cultural, and biobehavioral factors and ethnic and gender differences are among the strongest determinants of drinking patterns in a society (deLint, 1976). There is considerable variation in the proportion of drinkers in any given population when assessed by ethnicity, gender, age, religious affiliation, and socioeconomic status (Agarwal, 1996). What happens at a social and individual level that produces such different outcomes? Moreover, as individuals pass from infancy to childhood, adolescence, adulthood, and into older age, what factors impinge on their level and patterns of drinking such that it is likely to change over time? Some of these questions will be explored in the following sections, and in subsequent chapters.

Epidemiological Profiles

Differences in patterns of consumption will first be examined from a broad epidemiological perspective. Four select culture-specific case illustrations are highlighted below. These examples are included here to illustrate the wide variability of drinking styles and patterns, and to flag some of the issues and factors that contribute to the emergence of such different patterns. It is self-evident that the experiences of learning about drinking in each of these distinct cultural contexts will be quite different.

Cultural Case Illustrations

Northern Vs. Southern European Drinking Patterns Many Northern European countries have a tradition of spirit drinking, where alcohol is thrown back rather than sipped and is not usually taken with meals, and where drinking to intoxication is viewed as the probable outcome when a group of friends gets together with a bottle or two of spirits. In contrast, toward the south of Europe, where wine is the traditional beverage, alcohol will often be taken with food or around the family table, and may be regarded as a beneficial component of the diet rather than an intoxicant. It has been argued that the Italian pattern of high consumption of wine combined with rare inebriation reflects an Italian belief that wine is a food. Nearly all meals in Italy are usually accompanied by wine, but wine by the same token is usually only drunk at mealtime. Conversely, the British tend to consume most of their alcohol outside mealtimes. Italians traditionally have drunk very little alcohol in the form of spirits, because it is not recognized as a food, although this pattern is now changing. It is interesting to note that the Italian use of wine also contrasts with the patterns of the French, who consumed not only large amounts of wine but also distilled spirits in the form of brandy or liqueurs.

Australian Drinking—Traditionally a Male Domain Until the late 1970's most publicly consumed alcohol in Australia was drunk in male-only drinking establishments that were reminiscent of butcher's shops or lavatory blocks. They were sterile and cavernous, containing only the most functional items of furniture—a bar and a limited number of bar stools; a narrow shelf (just wide enough to precariously balance a beer glass) ran around the room, and the floors and the walls were tiled. Tiled surfaces allowed the whole establishment to be hosed out at the end of each day's trading. Sterile tiles also minimized any potential damage from spilt drinks and vomit, of which there were often prodigious amounts. Until the 1960's all licensed premises were also required to close by 6 p.m. each evening. This resulted in what was known as "the six o'clock swill." As closing time approached a bell would be rung by the publican and orders shouted for last drinks to be purchased. At this point, most customers would rush the already heavily crowded bar, purchase several drinks per person, and then proceed to consume them in rapid succession (hence the "swill"). This was often followed by involuntary regurgitation as the drinker's stomach had difficulty accommodating such an influx of liquid. This ritual would then be repeated on the next, and subsequent, evenings as men returned home enroute from their place of work.

Asian Settings In other cultural settings the experience of drinking is substantially different. For instance, among the Chinese moderate and infrequent consumption is stressed, and intoxication is only permissible at certain social occasions such as weddings, banquets, and special family gatherings. Koreans have been reported as likely to fall into one of two extremes, either abstainers or heavy drinkers (Lubben et al., 1989). Japanese society, in contrast, has seen a rapid spread of alcohol consumption over the past 20–30 years since postwar reconstruction. Consumption of large volumes of high-quality spirits is now often an integral part of Japanese business affairs. For the Japanese, sharing drinking and getting drunk without overstepping societal norms is an important aspect of appropriate drinking behavior. But the Japanese person who becomes violent or obnoxious because of drunkenness is reviled and labeled as a *shuran* (a pathological drinker) (Shimizu, 1985). Tolerance towards drinking by the Japanese in Japan is selective and does not extend to all drinking situations. The use of social cues to monitor self-regulation of drinking appears to reflect the Japanese emphasis on group-oriented behavior (Akutsu, 1989). In Japan, as in most other cultures, an understanding of socially acceptable drinking behaviors is learned in the family through socialization and is reflected in adolescents' drinking behavior (Shimizu, 1985). However, in other Asian countries, as well as many parts of the Middle East, use of alcohol is strongly mediated through religious beliefs such as Islam, which act as a deterrent to drinking and counsel either extreme moderation or total abstinence.

Drinking and Indigenous Peoples An interesting phenomenon occurring in many developing countries around the world is the adoption of more westernized forms and patterns of drinking. Among immigrant populations, indigenous cultural styles coupled with assimilation and acculturation to the so-called Western societies have made a powerful impact on the use of alcohol. Such patterns are often adopted to emulate the dominant cultures. Unfortunately, history is replete with examples of the difficulties that groups encounter when patterns of alcohol use are adopted without an established tradition for safely managing that use. Examples of this phenomenon include the Australian Aborigines, the Canadian Inuits, the North American Indians and so on. Such lessons of history painfully underscore the role of learning in the acquisition of low-risk drinking patterns.

For instance, Aboriginal Australians, who have among the highest consumption levels of any group, learned to drink in an environment where alcohol was a prominent part of colonial life. Patterns of consumption were influenced by the hardships and isolation of frontier life, availability of alcohol, social pressures to consume, and legal constraints. Alcohol consumption among people of European origin in remote Australia retained features of frontier drinking, and alcohol was used at times as a reward for station workers, and in payment, or as an inducement for sex (Hunter, 1993).

Hunter (1993) also reported that prohibition among Aboriginal groups influenced emerging consumption patterns and encouraged secretive binge-drinking. Those who lived on reserves had to obtain their alcohol surreptitiously, and drink it away from European observation. The freedom to consume alcohol was the symbolic offer of equal status with Europeans. Immediate confirmation of full citizenship was to be able to walk into a pub and drink with, and like a "white-fella" (Healy et al., 1985). A possible explanation why very few (indigenous) women drank might be that they were not exposed to drinking role models to the same extent as men; they had not been "taught" to drink (Watson, Fleming, and Alexander, 1991; p. 64).

Latin America and Sub-Saharan Africa In Latin America, drinking was originally based on privately brewed fermented beverages. Almost all consumption was limited to ceremonial situations, as intoxication was seen as an impediment to military readiness, among other things. During colonization, the use of alcohol increased, possibly to calm the tension and fears of an invaded society (Madrigal, 1998). The Europeans saw alcohol as the source of misbehavior and debauchery among the indigenous people, while in some places it was used instead of salary to pay laborers' wages. The convergence of these two uses of alcohol pointed directly at the lower classes as being most associated with drink, tainting its image in the eyes of both the elites and the missionaries. Later, as the region caught on to sugar cane as a cash-crop used for alcohol manufacture, laws governing all aspects of the industry and its products' use grew stronger and were more effectively enforced. Thus, alcohol use decreased to levels similar to precolonial times, though now they were legally, not culturally, mandated.

In sub-Saharan Africa beer was an important part of tribal culture, playing a role in many day-to-day situations. It was supplied as a good-faith drink during tribal councils, as a celebratory indulgence following success in hunting or agriculture, and as ceremonial wedding gifts or dowries for newlyweds. Alcohol was also used to promote merriment during flush times. Its use was important in many arenas of normal socialization, and the villager who did not offer drink to his fellows through parties, or who abstained completely, was treated with suspicion and could lose his social standing.

Due to the rapid sociocultural changes that have taken place in this region, drinking patterns have changed substantially in many regions, most notably in urban areas (Haworth & Acuda, 1998). Today, most beverage alcohol consumed in sub-Saharan Africa is commercially produced, though homebrew still exists and informal beer halls, known as shebeens, are still quite popular. However, drinking in the rural areas in some countries has become less of a social activity and often falls outside of customary roles (Muokolo, 1990).

Gender and Drinking

Finally, in this section brief mention is made of gender and drinking, with emphasis on changing patterns of women's drinking. For women in most societies, there are fewer obviously defined social roles regarding alcohol and substantial proscriptions. A notable change is now occurring in many developed countries in relation to the patterns of drinking among women, especially young women (Plant, 1997). Young women with increasing frequency have equal employment opportunities and comparable roles to men, and have unstructured leisure time and expendable income to use. For some time it was speculated that the convergence of social roles would result in a concomitant convergence of drinking levels and patterns among males and females (Wilsnack & Wilsnack, 1997; Neve, Lemmens, & Drop, 1997). But it has only been in relatively recent times that this pattern has become apparent.

For most of recorded history and in most societies, women have been precluded from or allowed only restricted access to public places where alcohol was either sold and/or consumed. Driessen (1992) maintains that certain drinking patterns point to the importance of gender in drinking. Traditionally, men have drunk to mark their identity as true males. Indeed, alcohol has long been identified as a demarcator of class and sex:

> Men drinking together in homosocial gatherings reach a state of methy—spiritual intoxication—through drunkenness which is highly valued because it stresses sharing and egalitarianism. It facilitates 'transcendence' and is contrasted with the intoxication of the lonely drinker, or the habitual drunkard of the community, who are both condemned (Gefou-Madianou, 1992, p. 12).

In Euro-Mediterranean cultures a distinct differentiation is made between male and female domains in relation to drinking alcohol. This holds true for both Northwestern European countries, and for Southern European ones (Gefou-Madianou, 1992; p. 7). The when, where, and how of male drinking of alcohol in coffeehouses and bars in some communities have served to constitute their identity as men independently from household relations and to the exclusion of women. Cross-culturally, there is a high degree of consistency with regard to greater acceptance of drinking among young adults compared to teenagers. There is great variability around attitudes towards drinking by women. For example, almost two-thirds of Swedes believe that 16-year-old females should be allowed to drink, but in Zambia only 5% share this view (Callan et al., 1991).

The universal ideal of femininity discouraged drinking, and women were mostly required to demonstrate restraint. There is speculation that these restrictions on the consumption of alcoholic beverages by women led to the use of alcohol-based medicines for "health" purposes. In most societies there was also a high level of intolerance towards women consuming alcohol in taverns or public houses, a view that has held sway until relatively recently. Even in contemporary Western society this view has not totally eroded, although most hotels and licensed drinking premises are vastly more "women-friendly" than in the past.

In contemporary Western society it is interesting to note the increase in alcohol consumption among women that has occurred in parallel with their changing roles and positions within society (Park, 1990). While there is evidence that traditionally women have succumbed less to social pressure to drink than do males, (Wilks, Callan, & Austin, 1989) the way women acquire particular drinking patterns and styles—so far neglected—will become an area of greater focus in the future (Plant, 1997).

Hence, not only do experiences of learning about drinking vary substantially from one cultural setting to another, they also vary greatly between the genders within those cultural settings. Such is the rich diversity of experiences that help shape an individual's drinking behavior. In the following section, emphasis will be placed on the development of internal belief systems and expectancies regarding drinking.

BELIEFS, EXPECTATIONS, AND BEHAVIORS

> "I know *something* interesting is sure to happen," she said to herself, "whenever I eat or drink anything: so I'll just see what this bottle does."
>
> Alice, in Lewis Carroll's *Alice's Adventures in Wonderland*

Beyond the sociocultural dimensions of learning about drinking, a theme running throughout this book is the extent to which our use of, and our views about, alcohol are colored and shaped by our personal beliefs and expectations surrounding the substance. Important questions that arise therefore are: How do we obtain our beliefs? At what age do we acquire these beliefs? And, how do such beliefs change as we age, and acquire different life experiences and different experiences of drinking?

Beliefs about alcohol are far from consistent, although there is some degree of concordance within groups. The extent of alcohol's effects on human behaviors and emotions varies widely and is highly irregular (Steel & Josephs, 1990). This is well illustrated by MacAndrew and Edgerton (1969) who described how:

> The same man, in the same bar, drinking approximately the same amount of alcohol may, on three nights running, be, say, surly and belligerent on the first evening, the spirit of amiability on the second, and morose and withdrawn on the third (p. 15).

Research has shown that many of the behavioral effects of alcohol are due, not to pharmacological actions, but to the beliefs held by the drinker (Critchlow, 1986; Siegal, 1999). Expectancy effects must be considered in addition to the pharmacological properties of alcohol (Marlatt & Rohsenow, 1980). That is, having prior beliefs or expectations about what might happen when you drink can strongly influence what you actually experience when you do drink. Thus, "the effects of alcohol on social behavior are not physiologically bound but are instead learned" (Critchlow, 1986; p. 751). Placebo experiments have shown that merely believing that one has had a "drink" leads people to act in ways that they would normally expect to behave when under the influence of alcohol.

The concept of expectancies is essentially that people often drink alcohol to get the effects they assume it will directly cause: relaxation, a better mood, courage, social ease, and so on (Goldman et al., 1987; Leigh, 1989). Nonetheless, alcohol is also known to have profound social and psychological effects that are independent of expectancy effects (Steel & Josephs, 1990). It is now believed that alcohol has relatively consistent effects on nonsocial behaviors (e.g., cognition and motor performance), but that drinking expectancies affect social behavior.

The alcohol expectancies of the young and very young are especially important. Novice drinkers will experience certain effects which combine with their observations of what happens to parents and peers when they drink to form drinking expectations or expectancies. Both negative and positive expectancies are held about alcohol (McMahon, Jones, & O'Donnell, 1994). Critchlow (1986; p. 751) has highlighted how "our social institutions create and maintain the reputation of alcohol as an agent that can transform its users in both prosocial and antisocial ways."

The types of positive expectancies (Brown et al., 1980) that young people develop about drinking include appearing adult, disinhibition, reduced sexual tension, enhanced sexuality and social interaction, and increased assertiveness; while negative expectancies (McMahon et al., 1994) can include impaired speech and thinking, reduced physical coordination, facilitation of aggression, and hangovers and sickness the day after drinking.

Once an expectancy is confirmed by experience, and is valued by the young drinker, a behavior pattern begins to be established, which may in turn be reinforced by the behavior of the young drinker's companions (Wright, 1999). Expectancies are also predictive of the amount of alcohol that may be consumed by a young person. Studies have found, for instance, that young people holding more positive expectancies drink at higher levels and in potentially more risky or hazardous ways (Wiers, Hoogeveen, Sergeant, & Gunning, 1997).

In general, research indicates that if young people expect to enjoy themselves more if they drink, they do. Correspondingly, if young people expect alcohol to reduce nervousness or to enhance their sexual experiences then they are more likely to drink. Moreover, those young people who believe that alcohol will enhance or facilitate their sexual experiences will drink larger amounts of alcohol (Leigh, 1990). Expectancies about alcohol also impinge on other behaviors. For example, young men who expect alcohol to disinhibit them sexually are more likely to hold negative attitudes to condom use and they are less likely to use condoms (Gordon, Carey, & Carey, 1997).

The issue of expectancies will be explored further by other authors in subsequent chapters, but it is noted that changes in expectancies are held to be an important aspect of changes in drinking patterns over the life span.

CHANGES IN DRINKING ACROSS THE LIFE SPAN

"Time present and time past
Are both perhaps present in time future,
And time future contained in time past."

T.S. Eliot, in *Four Quarters*, 1944

Throughout one's life important changes occur in relation to alcohol. A brief overview of the major lifetime changes that are commonly experienced is outlined below. As illustrated in the previous section, an individual's experience of alcohol will vary greatly according to his or her social and cultural context. While there is substantial variation between and within different cultures regarding what is considered acceptable and appropriate drinking behavior, it is nonetheless the case that what we are exposed to will largely shape our behavior as young people and impact on us in a variety of ways throughout the course of our life.

Childhood

There is a saying among New Zealand Maori that "We enter the world facing backwards." That is, it is the values of the previous generations that will strongly influence our own development. It is by observing those around us that we learn about ourselves, our communities, and our place in that community. We learn what types of behaviors are rewarded, endorsed, and supported and those that are not. We also learn from whom to take our social and cultural cues. These influential shaping forces will vary and broaden throughout our life, but for young children they will primarily be the immediate family. It is not surprising, therefore, to discover that much of the way that adolescents and young adults drink is very often a direct reflection of the drinking patterns within their own homes.

Learning about the role and location of alcohol begins in early childhood as part of the developmental process. Almost universally, the strongest influences on very young children are the family and home environment. When children are first exposed to drinking the behavior has no intrinsic meaning. The meaning of the act exists in the surrounding social world, which provides the raw material or data that the child uses to construct a working model of drinking and its effects on behavior. And, with repeated exposure to the behavior and its social consequences, its meaning emerges and is internalized (Johnson & Johnson, 1999; p. 79).

The following depiction of a young man's early recollection of his first encounter with alcohol during his pre-teenage years nicely illustrates the subtlety with which we learn about drinking in a familial context:

> His parents owned a drink's cabinet which contained various decanters of alcoholic drinks. He did not know what they were, presumably whisky, sherry, and port, but he recalled the special status they were given within the home. In his reminiscence he recalled that they were invested with an almost magical status; they were not to be touched except by his parents, who seemed to value the contents highly. They were to him also, at that time, beautiful to look at. He described the deep colors and the shining glass formed into attractive shapes. Thus, for him they assumed high

> status shrouded in mystery and became extremely desirable. So alcohol acquired an exotic and desirable image; it became something which once attained would be a passport into the mysterious and pleasurable world of his parents . . . this led to a preoccupation with intoxication which was informed by a pursuit of the forbidden (Dean, 1997).

Cultures that incorporate drinking within regular day-to-day functions and where alcohol is commonly taken with meals have tended to report fewer problems involving young people and intoxication (Heath, 1987). Having been exposed to frequent low doses of alcohol within the family context is thought to lessen difficulties with teenagers "discovering" the thrill of intoxication. Moreover, alcohol in these contexts tends not to be used as an integral part of rites of passage from youth to adulthood, as occurs in some cultures.

From the time of birth (an event that is often celebrated with alcohol in many cultures), the effects of adults' drinking on children and young people are both direct and indirect, mediated through other aspects of family life and the wider social environment (Wright, 1999). Parental attitudes and behavior play an important part in the development of their children's behavior. It is increasingly held that appropriate modeling of safe, low-risk drinking by parents and other significant adults in a child's life is an important, yet often overlooked, feature of developing low-risk drinking patterns.

Familial influences are complex. It is relevant to note that both abstainers and heavy drinkers are more likely to have heavy-drinking children (McKechnie, Cameron, Cameron, & Drewery, 1977; Orford, 1990). The possible mechanisms operating in each case, however, are different. With heavy-drinking parents, a combination of both modeling and potential genetic influences is likely to be at play. In the case of parents who are abstainers, on the other hand, it is thought that young children lack sufficient exposure to role models who adequately display appropriate low-risk drinking behaviors, so that these skills are not acquired. Moreover, excessively negative views about alcohol may actually make it particularly attractive to children.

In most industrialized countries young people have had some, usually limited, experience of drinking by the time they are 12 years of age. In many instances, they are weaned into consumption by taking small amounts of diluted drinks. In some cultures this weaning process occurs at the age of 8–12 years, while in other cultures with "drier" drinking norms it may not happen until the age of 12–16. In Japan, as a case in point, youngsters are introduced to alcohol at an early age and are gradually socialized into the adult drinking culture. By the age of 12, more than 75% of Japanese adolescents are reported to have tried alcohol, usually in the family or traditional settings such as a ceremonial occasion or after a bath. The majority of high school students also agreed that drinking by minors was acceptable in particular circumstances (Wada, et al., 1998; p. 381).

Drinking and Youth

Drinking for many young people is inextricably linked with their social development. Major socializing locations are also often key drinking locations. For instance, in many countries young people's initial forays into the adult world involve spending time at pubs, clubs, discos, and sporting venues. The reasons reported by young people for going to pubs are most commonly to socialize, to meet people, and to drink alcohol (Wright, 1999).

In many cultures today, adolescents perceive drinking in a public house as a mark of manhood. Men are perceived to encourage youthful drinking and fathers to glow proudly when their son becomes old enough to accompany them to the tavern where they can drink as equals from the same glass. Wilks and Callan (1984) found that while young Australian males develop similar positive attitudes towards drinking as their fathers, this was less true of young females and their mothers. However, as noted above, the failure to find corresponding attitudes echoed by daughters may be shifting in response to the intergenerational changes in the roles of women, increased equity, and better job and employment opportunities.

Drinking is largely perceived to be a positive experience by most young people. The most common short-term negative experiences reported tend to be physiological in nature—hangover, nausea, falls and minor trauma, etc. Young women tend to report more emotional experiences or negative social consequences, while young men are more likely to report involvement in criminal activity (Wright, 1999).

There is a substantial body of research data that indicates that adolescents initially adopt the drinking behaviors of their parents and peers (e.g., Barnes & Welte, 1986). Young people themselves have identified the negative influence that poor family relationships and inappropriate parental drinking can have on their later drinking patterns (Foxcroft, Lowe, & May, 1994). But as they progress through adolescence it is the drinking behavior of their peers that is more influential. Epstein, Botvin, Baker, and Diaz (1999) have emphasized that it is the *perception* of peer norms that is the strongest predictor of alcohol use.

Research has illustrated the extent to which family influence, parental consent, and appropriate parental and family drinking are key factors in the development of sensible drinking patterns later in life. For instance, African-American and Hispanic family structures, parent-child interaction patterns, and value orientations function to maintain negative belief schemas, thereby minimizing the involvement of children and adolescents with alcohol (Johnson & Johnson, 1999, p. 79). Black and Hispanic women are both groups with high rates of abstention and relatively low rates of per capita consumption (Gilbert, 1985), which may deter their children from initiation into alcohol use. Not surprisingly, it has been suggested that alcohol use (or nonuse) is a function of an adolescent's identification with his or her ethnic group (Blane, 1993).

Young people are also the heaviest drinkers in most cultures, and the age of heavy drinking is decreasing in many countries, although it is important to note that young people do not necessarily see themselves in this light. The majority of young people in some studies report themselves to be moderate drinkers and few actually worry about their drinking (Wright, 1999). Beyond one's initiation into drinking is the experience of excess or intoxication. Getting drunk or becoming intoxicated for the first time is often a highly significant, symbolic, and memorable part of a young person's life.

> I was sixteen when I first got drunk. It was a revelation, more fun than a barrel of monkeys. I screamed and hollered and carried on and did somersaults and hugged my friends (who were also drunk) and just had a blast. Naturally, I kept wanting to repeat the experience.
>
> (Weil & Rosen, 1993, pp. 194–195)

In some cultures many "Young people, especially heavier drinkers, drink to get drunk" (Wright, 1999, p. 79). The centrality of intoxication in young people's drinking styles is an increasingly common phenomenon in some developed countries (Gillespie, Davey, Sheehan, & Stedson, 1991; Roche & Watt, 1999). In many settings, it is also more socially acceptable to get drunk than to take illegal drugs (Wright, 1999). This view is illustrated in the following quote from Mathrani's (1998) British study on young drinkers (as cited in Wright, 1999) which found that:

> Young people drink in order to reach an altered state of mind and the idea of having one or two 'social' drinks is an alien concept. The young experimenters (13–15 year olds), in particular, were seeking a personal 'buzz' or 'hit,' a heady, drug-like sensation. This was also true of heavy drinking 16–20 year olds, especially males.

Heavy-drinking bouts are often colocated with other major life milestones, such as going to college or university, joining the workforce or the armed forces, or first independent social experiences (large parties, going to a night club or pub). As noted earlier, drinking behaviors and drunken comportment usually conform to known and shared norms (Heath, 1987), and drunkenness can also serve as an explanation of bad behavior (Room, 1996). Heavy-drinking sessions are often highly tolerated among older teenagers and young adults. This level of tolerance can sometimes be quite extreme, as the following colorful illustration from a prestigious Australian university college highlights:

> At a typical Victory Dinner there is a constant traffic of students departing and returning to relieve themselves or to vomit. Gradually, the journey becomes too daunting and they make use of the windows instead, using the long sleeves of their academic gowns to wipe their mouths afterwards. For one or two at the table the prospect of getting even as far as the windows is too much and they vomit where

they sit... No one pays any attention. When they finish they replenish their glasses (Cameron, 1997).

While drinking patterns of the new initiate are often characterized by bouts of excess, these patterns are usually short-lived and normally superseded by other and more important things in life. The transience of this type of drinking is illustrated in the recent work of Roche and Watt (1999), which found that over 70% of 17-year-old Australian university students reported drinking to intoxication at least once a week. This level dropped substantially among the slightly older students aged 18–19, of whom 40% drank to intoxication each week.

Hence, the mid to late teenage years are a time in many cultural settings when experimentation with alcohol is very common. Moreover, drinking heavily becomes the norm for many young people. But (as seen in the case of Australian university students) heavy drinking tends to be self-regulated as young people become more accustomed to their new-found freedoms and emerging adult identity, and other aspects of their life take precedence over the initial thrill of getting drunk. However, there is also evidence that hazardous drinking patterns established early in life can persist for decades, well into adulthood (Chasin & DeLucia, 1996; Kandel & Logan, 1984; Schuckit, 1995).

Adolescence is, therefore, commonly a time when young people are at elevated risk from harms associated with attempts to explore and stretch boundaries in many areas of their lives, not the least of which may be their exploration of drinking. Special attention is needed to ensure a safe passage for young people during this time of unparalleled experimentation, limit-testing, and risk-taking.

Learning to Drink Within "Safe" Limits In most Western countries, drinking is generally viewed as appropriate by the community at large, as long as the drinking is not excessive and does not transgress important social norms or lead to dangerous behavior (Callan et al., 1991). In settings where drinking to get drunk is the norm among young people, learning to exercise control and restraint over consumption levels is sometimes difficult. Wright (1999) reports that for many young people the most acceptable excuse for refusing drinks is to say "I'm driving" but overall little is known of the self-control strategies that young people adopt. Using alternatives to avoid drinking, such as taking nonalcoholic drinks, leaving the situation, getting involved in other activities, or stating that "they had had enough," was more common among females than males.

Young people are still in the process of clarifying their values, discovering their own personal codes of behavior, and learning self-control. As these behaviors are not as well established as in older people; the young are more easily affected by alcohol (Wright, 1999). Young people's lack of experience in how to behave when intoxicated and in handling the effects of alcohol also exposes them to increased risks.

lack of experience

Wright (1999) reports that young people indicated in relation to influences on their drinking that teachers had virtually no influence at all on attitudes or behavior. Rather, information was mediated through peer groups, with choices being made that were favored or approved by immediate circles of friends. Prevailing health education messages appeared to be interpreted by young people as telling them that drinking was wrong, naughty, or bad; furthermore, most young people did not want school-based subjects on the matter (Wright, 1999). It is ironic that there remains a strongly held belief that school-based programs or formal educational input can have a significant impact on young people's drinking behavior. These views persist in spite of extensive literature which illustrates their limited effectiveness (Paglia & Room, 1998; Roche, 1999). Encouragingly, some recent work has been undertaken from a harm minimization perspective which has shown positive results (McBride, Midford, Farringdon, & Phillips, 2000).

Perception of Risk Among Young People Various concepts of risk are applied to alcohol use. Teenagers often underestimate the negative effects of alcohol, especially on their performance in driving motor vehicles (Wilks, 1985). They acquire more accurate perceptions of risk and better motor coordination over time, largely as a function of maturation processes and the development of skills and tolerance to the physiological effects of alcohol (Julien, 1995).

There are positive and negative aspects to risk-taking. Leigh (1999) has recently examined ways in which young people develop knowledge of the probability of harm (in the sense of risk versus certainty) and objective and subjective risk. In exploring the relationship between alcohol and risky behavior, Leigh highlighted the following models:

- One model groups together drinking and sensation-seeking, risk-taking behavior and problem behavior. A "problem-behavior" approach views alcohol use and risk-taking as manifestations of a single underlying dimension of deviance or unconventionality.
- An alternative model argues that people take risks not because they feel like it but because they do not perceive the risks correctly. For instance, there is evidence that heavier drinkers underestimate risks in some situations.
- A further view is that alcohol use, driving, crime and violent behavior, and sexual activity all peak at the same stage of life. In addition, various situations encourage both alcohol use and risky behavior.
- Last, according to a social learning model of alcohol effects, alcohol has an "expectancies and excuse" function.

The model of risk behavior and alcohol assumed will color the types of strategies that may be considered appropriate to reduce harm. It is relevant to note the patterns that emerge from both the sociological and treatment literatures about factors in a person's life and the way they learn about drinking that appear to be associated with the fewest problems. In her book, *The Young Drinkers*,

O'Connor (1978) reported the following summation of factors contributing to lowest levels of alcohol problems in "wet" cultures:

1 The children are exposed to alcohol early in life, within a strong family or religious group.
2 Whatever the beverage, it is served in a very diluted form and in small quantities, with consequent low blood-alcohol levels.
3 The beverage commonly, although not invariably used by the groups are those containing relatively large amounts of nonalcoholic components, which also give low blood-alcohol levels.
4 The beverage is considered mainly as a food and usually consumed with meals, again with consequent low blood-alcohol levels.
5 Parents present a constant example of moderate drinking.
6 No moral importance is attached to drinking.
7 Drinking is not viewed as a proof of adulthood or virility.
8 Abstinence is not socially acceptable.
9 Excessive drinking or intoxication is not socially acceptable. It is not considered stylish, comical, or tolerable.
10 Finally, and perhaps most important, there is wide and usually complete agreement among members of the group on what might be called the ground rules of drinking. (O'Connor, 1978, pp. 7–8)

The Adult Years

When people reach the adult years (defined here as over 25), a number of important changes have usually occurred in relation to their use of alcohol. Adulthood represents a time in a person's life when new responsibilities are taken on such as marriage, child-rearing, and expanded work roles, and leisure activities also sometimes change. The position and significance that alcohol has held as an agent of socialization, self-discovery, and experimentation during one's youth tend to change in the adult years in concert with broader lifestyle changes.

While adult drinking is considered a societal norm in most Western societies, particularly among men, the heaviest periods of consumption tend to occur in the early 20's. After that age, drinking levels and patterns usually alter quite substantially for most individuals. These changes partly reflect the level of expendable income, the time available for the social activities that are often associated with drinking, and changing priorities in one's life.

More drinking occurs in private homes than in public settings among adults than among younger drinkers (Commonwealth Department of Health and Human Services, 1996). For example, in Australia, 65% of 20- to 34-year-olds reported their preferred drinking location to be pubs, clubs, and wine bars, whereas only 39% of the over-35-year-olds shared this preference. The first preference for a drinking location for 80% of over 35-year-olds was their own home. Again, this is a reflection of a range of factors, including family responsibilities (i.e., the need to care for children), a preference for different styles of socializing (e.g., dinner parties and barbecues rather than discos and beach parties), and less expendable income (drinking at home is generally cheaper than purchasing drinks at licensed premises).

Following the Second World War alcohol consumption in most developed countries increased steadily over the preceding decades reaching a peak in the late 1970's. Since that time adult alcohol consumption has steadily declined, in contrast to patterns among younger people, where over the same period there has been a gradual, and in some countries a dramatic, increase in consumption. The reason for the change in adult drinking patterns is not entirely clear. These shifts, recorded over decades, are consistent with Room's (1974) historical depiction of "long waves" in consumption patterns.

During the adult years, drinking patterns are increasingly dictated by relations and roles in the working world (rather than those exclusively within the social and familial worlds). For instance, in some settings drinking is more than just part of the social routine; it is also integrally woven into the working life of some communities. As an example of this phenomenon, Mars (1989) identified two distinct groups of workers among longshoremen in the Canadian province of Newfoundland: the "regular men" and the "outside men." The regular men were frequently hired and rehired to work on the docks at the port of St. John's. One of the requirements to be a "regular man" was to learn the proper drinking behavior for members of that group. Not to do so resulted not only in social exclusion but also in loss of income.

In Japan, there is a saying that "alcohol is the lubricating oil for society." At home, drinking alcohol after bathing is part of the traditional way of life among Japanese men, as is drinking alcohol with their coworkers and bosses after work (Wada et al., 1998, p. 381).

The influence of one's work or professional occupation cannot be underestimated in relation to levels and patterns of drinking. There is good evidence to illustrate the adoption of particular drinking styles among those who join given occupational groupings. One of the clearest illustrations of this phenomenon is the data on standardized mortality rates for cirrhosis of the liver. The risk of incurring this serious disease is strongly correlated with the amount of alcohol consumed.[2] Particular occupational groups known to be at elevated risk include groups such as publicans, people in the hotel and restaurant industry, those in shipping and engineering, the armed forces and police, and writers and journalists (Favazzi, 1981). Clearly, occupational characteristics (rather than individual propensities) act as strong factors in influencing drinking patterns. Such factors include availability, social isolation, lack of alternative recreational options, irregular working hours, and established socializing patterns.

A further shift noted in the consumption patterns of adults is towards a preference for better-quality alcohol beverages. While this is partly a function

[2]It is noted that hepatitis C is an increasingly important causal factor in the development of cirrhosis of the liver.

of expendable income, it also reflects tastes acquired as people mature. Hence, some changes in drinking pattern are somewhat more difficult to discern, as they are not necessarily reflected in prevalence data that measure only the volume consumed. Rather, they are more subtle changes that are found in measures of quality, and not just quantity, of alcohol consumed.

Alcohol and Leisure Drinking has often been underrated as a leisure-related activity (Simpura, 1985), although the two are clearly strongly associated. The alcohol and leisure relationship is an important but complex area that is riddled with ambiguities and inconsistencies. In situations where there is a clear boundary between work and nonwork, drinking can often serve as a symbolic marker to set one world off from the other. Kunz (1997) holds that leisure and drinking share several common characteristics. Both are social creations carried out in nonwork hours and both have the potential to serve as a means of self-expression and stress reduction. Both are also highly regulated by social organizations, subject to the influence of the market economy and capable of generating profits. Kunz recently undertook a review of the literature associating alcohol with leisure and noted the dearth of research in this area. She identified four distinct themes:

1. alcohol as an integral part of leisure experience;
2. drinking as an impediment to leisure;
3. participation in active leisure reducing alcohol use/abuse;
4. drinking and leisure as unrelated.

Tourists and holiday-makers are specifically known to be heavy, and heavier than usual, consumers of alcohol because of increased socializing, and the absence of work responsibilities, and the symbolism of alcohol as a mechanism to wind down and take time out; in addition, particular holiday destinations may be more conducive to increased consumption than others (Crundall, 1996). Crundall maintains that the relationship between holidays and alcohol is complex and has received relatively little attention or detailed analysis to date.

Sexual Enhancement Alcohol is also commonly associated not only with the social motivations of individuals, but also with their sexual motivation. This is equally true for drinkers of all ages. Beyond social lubrication, alcohol has long been reputed to act as a facilitator of sexual relations and an enhancer of sexual performance. However, the research literature fails to directly confirm alcohol's overall beneficial rôle in this area of keen interest, and there is difficulty in separating out expectancy effects (Julien, 1995; Leigh, 1990). Furthermore, the effects of alcohol on the various phases and stages of sexual encounters are equally complex and largely dependent on the biphasic actions of alcohol. It has been found, however, that alcohol is associated with an increased likelihood of engaging in sexual activity. This likelihood is even greater if a new, rather than established, partner is involved (Norris, 1994).

Mental Health There have long been claims of the role of moderate drinking in improved mood, social adjustment, and even cognitive functioning but very little definitive work has been undertaken in this area. Over a decade ago, Baum-Baicker (1985) reviewed the psychological benefits of moderate alcohol consumption in the areas of stress reduction, cognitive performance, "affect-state," and short-term memory. Few published works since Baum-Baicker's have systematically examined the psychological effects of moderate alcohol consumption.

At an epidemiological level, some of the areas of benefit have begun to be established in population studies of drinking and mental health, particularly the association of moderate alcohol consumption with lower depression levels, and superior functioning and cognitive acuity among the elderly who drink moderately. Alcohol's role in reducing clinical depression has also been reported (Neff & Husaini, 1982; White & Moesbergen, 1989), and it is valued as a stress reliever (Hall, 1995; Lipton, 1994).

Adverse Life Events Although drinking during the adult years tends to be more moderate than that engaged in during the more turbulent time of youth, for some people the adult years are also pitted with painful and distressing experiences, where relief is sought through the use of alcohol. Negative life changes such as divorce, bereavement, job loss, work-related stress (including demotion/promotion), and mental health problems can all act as precipitating factors for changes in drinking patterns that are less than positive (Schuckit, 1995). Moderate-and low-risk drinking patterns established earlier in adult life can change dramatically in the face of changed life circumstances. In such instances, individuals may be reluctant to seek assistance. Fluctuations in patterns of drinking over the life span highlight the importance of both vigilance in regard to using alcohol safely and wisely and the continuing acquisition of skills to manage alcohol well. That is, the learning processes involved in using alcohol to maximize potential gains and minimize potential problems accompany us throughout our lifetime.

Older People

Future generations of people over 70 and 80 years of age will not only be increasingly common, they will also be increasingly healthy and vital. This has important implications for possible changes in their patterns of drinking. Most data so far suggest that people tend to drink less as they age (Adams et al., 1990; Fillmore et al., 1991). However, there is some speculation that this may be a cohort effect and that in future years this may change.

Weil and Rosen (1993, p. 194) cite the following example of the way alcohol is viewed by some users who are well into their adult years, and who have a lifetime of experience with alcohol:

> I like alcohol. It is a powerful drug and God knows, for some people a hellish one, but if used carefully it can give great pleasure. After a long, hard day, the splendid warm glow that strong drink provides is one of my favorite feelings; it starts in the pit of my stomach, then spreads to my limbs and brain. I know that alcohol is a depressant, but it acts and feels like a gentle relaxant—of the spirit as well as of the physical body. Just notice the increased vivacity and noise level at a cocktail party after a drink has been served to see how alcohol can put people at ease emotionally. Aside from the pleasureful intoxication of strong drink, I also enjoy tasting other forms of alcohol. Few sensations are more delightful than the wet but dry taste of cold beer to a parched throat. The subtle, taste-enhancing, enriching relationship of wine to food is a subject that has inspired many poets and writers far more capable than I of putting words together, but I can tell you that what they say is true. The fascinating, complex flavor of good wine can be profoundly sensual (a 62-year-old male psychoanalyst).

In some studies, drinking has been found to be positively associated with social activities rather than with isolation or the stresses of aging. Alexander and Duff (1988) found that drinking among retirement village residents was substantially greater than among older people generally in the U.S. Drinking was an integral part of the leisure subculture in these communities. Their data suggested that people who moved into the retirement community and participated in its social life learned to consume alcohol as a consequence of that participation. Support was found for the position that the social life of the community encouraged residents to drink as part of the process of integration into the leisure subculture (Alexander & Duff, 1988).

Alcohol and Pleasure Not specific or exclusive to older people, but certainly very relevant to them, is the issue of the pleasure derived from the use of alcohol. In recent times, not only has increasing attention been focused on the potential benefits of alcohol (usually measured in terms of morbidity and mortality, such as cardiovascular disease), but there is growing interest in the "pleasures" derived from alcohol (Peele & Grant, 1999).

Lowe and Taylor (1993), for instance, have demonstrated a significant relationship between the amount that people drink and how much they laugh. They suggest that somewhat heavier drinkers use humor or laughter more in their everyday lives than do lighter drinkers. Chick (1997a) has also highlighted how anxious, shy young British people use drinking occasions to negotiate the passage to independence and identity. He speculates that in such a cultural milieu to avoid the pub or party might harm an individual's sense of belonging. The emotional effects of alcohol are highly dependent on factors related to the setting, such as social atmosphere (Sher, 1985), and pharmacological mechanisms alone cannot produce emotional changes irrespective of setting (Gustafson, 1991), although it is interesting to note the more recent work on alcohol reinforcement and neuropharmacology (Lewis, 1996). Overall, Lewis cites alcohol's euphoric and anxiolytic properties and its association with other reinforcers as its principal rewards and motivators—some of which are beneficial to the consumer. These positive reward effects of alcohol do not seem subject to tolerance, as other effects of alcohol have been found to be (Julien, 1995).

SUMMARY

In the complex and diverse processes involved in learning about drinking, only some of which have been briefly touched on in this chapter, it is evident that powerful positive and negative forces are at work. And while social pressures and expectations about appropriate behavior in regard to drinking are clearly at work in most settings, they are often not sufficient to counterbalance the need within some young people to experiment and take risks. An obvious question is this: If drinking is a learned behavior, is there not considerable untapped scope for influencing the way in which individuals and groups learn to drink such that its pleasurable and positive aspects can be achieved while minimizing potential hazards?

Up to the present, comparatively little effort has been consciously directed towards influencing the way in which people learn to drink. Efforts to assist young people to learn to drink wisely, if they should choose to drink, have traditionally been minimal. But it is well established that low-risk alcohol consumption occurs primarily where it is part of the established cultural life of a group or society, and where clearly prescribed guidelines and powerful (if sometimes subtle) sanctions operate to ensure compliance with certain forms and patterns of consumption. In recent years it has been argued that:

> Unless you are a Muslim or a Mormon or belong to some other group that refuses its use altogether, you will have to learn how to refuse alcohol if you don't want to drink or know how to drink it intelligently and not let your use get out of control (Weil & Rosen, 1993, p. 67).

If an assumption is made that in many, if not most, cultures the cultural norm is for young people to be exposed to alcohol, and that many will start to drink at a relatively early stage of life, an emphasis on enhancing positive experiences and minimizing negative consequences, among young people especially, becomes a prime consideration. A better understanding of how we learn about drinking and what are the risk and resilience factors in the development of safe or problematic patterns of use may be helpful in minimizing harms in the future.

For many societies around the world alcohol is the social drug of choice. It is used extensively by all age groups, especially young people, and in many and varied social, religious, and sometimes professional settings. It is widely available, usually extensively advertised, and often consumed excessively or inappropriately. Used wisely, it can bestow a wide range of benefits on consumers and their associates. However, used inappropriately or excessively it can result in acute and long-term problems for individuals, their families, and the community at large. Individuals learn to drink in a manner that is largely socially ordained. Ensuring that the learning process is as productive and the outcome is as low-risk as possible warrants our close attention.

REFERENCES

Adams, W. L., Garry, P. J., Rhyne, R., Hunt, W. C., Goodwin, J. S. (1990). Alcohol intake in the healthy elderly: Changes with age in a cross-sectional and longitudinal study. *Journal of the American Geriatric Society, 38*, 211–216.

Agarwal, D. P. (1996). Racial/ethnic and gender differences in alcohol use and misuse. In T. J. Peters (Ed.), *Alcohol misuse: A European perspective* (pp. 23–40). Amsterdam, The Netherlands: Harwood Academic Publishers.

Akutsu, P. D., Stanley, S., Zane, N. W., & Nakamura, C. Y. (1989). Ethnic differences in alcohol consumption among Asians and Caucasians in the United States: An investigation of cultural and physiological factors. *Journal of Studies on Alcohol, 50*(3), 261–267.

Alexander, F., & Duff, R. (1998). Social interaction and alcohol use in retirement communities. *The Gerontologist, 28*(5), 632–636.

Bandura, A. (1969). *Principles of behavior modification*. New York: Holt, Rinehart, and Winston.

Bandura, A. (1977). *Social learning theory*. London: Prentice–Hall.

Barnes, G. M., & Welte, J. W. (1986). Adolescent alcohol abuse: Subgroup differences and relationships to other problem behaviors. *Journal of Adolescent Research, 1*(1), 79–94.

Barrows, S., & Room, R. (1991). *Drinking Behavior and Belief in Modern History*. Berkley and Los Angeles: University of California Press.

Blane, H. T. (1993). Ethnicity. In M. Galanter (Ed.), *Recent Developments in Alcoholism, Vol. 11, Ten Years of Progress* (pp. 109–122). New York: Plenum Press.

Brown, S., Goldman, M., Inn, A., & Anderson, L. (1980). Expectations of reinforcement from alcohol: Their domain and relation to drinking patterns. *Journal of Consulting and Clinical Psychology, 48*(4), 419–426.

Callan, V. J., Gallois, C., Noller, P., & Kashima, Y. (1991). *Social psychology*. (2nd ed.). Sydney, Australia: Harcourt, Brace Jovanovich.

Cameron, P. (1997). *Animal House*. Sydney, Australia: Allen and Unwin.

Chasin, L., & DeLucia, C. (1996). Drinking during adolescence. *Alcohol Health and Research World, 20*, 175–176.

Chick, J. (1997). *Possible benefits to mental health of drinking: A review*. Unpublished manuscript.

Commonwealth Department of Health and Family Services. (1996). National Drug Strategy Household Survey. Survey Report Australian Government Publishing Service (AGPS), Canberra, Australia.

Critchlow, B. (1986). The powers of John Barleycorn. *American Psychologist, 41*(7), 751–764.

Crundall, I. (1996). Interstate tourists and the estimation of per capita alcohol consumption. *Drug and Alcohol Review, 15*, 21–28.

Dean, A. (1997). *Chaos and intoxication*. London: Routledge.

Delint, J. (1976). Epidemiological aspects of alcoholism. *International Journal of Mental Health, 5*, 29–51.

Doll, B., & Lyon, M. A. (1998). Risk and resilience: implications for the delivery of educational and mental health in schools. *School Psychology Review, 27*, 248–363.

Douglas, M. (Ed.) (1987). *Constructive Drinking: Perspectives on Drink from Anthropology*. Cambridge, UK: Cambridge University Press.

Driessen, H. (1992). Drinking on masculinity: Alcohol and gender in Andalusia. In D. Gefou-Madianou (Ed.), *Alcohol, culture and gender* (p. 71–79). London and New York: Routledge.

Edwards, G., Anderson, P., Balsor, T., Casswell, S., Ferrence, R., Giesbrecht, N., Godfrey, C., Holder, H., Lemmons, P., Makela, K., Norstrom, T., Osterberg, E., Romelsjo, A., Room, R., Simpura, J., & Skog, O. J. (1994). *Alcohol policy and the public good*. Oxford: Oxford University Press.

Epstein, J., Botvin, G., Baker, E., & Diaz, T. (1999). Impact of social influences and problem behavior on alcohol use among inner-city Hispanic and Black adolescents. *Journal of Studies on Alcohol, 60*, 595–604.

Favazzi, A. (1981). Alcohol and special populations. *Journal of Studies on Alcohol, 9* (Suppl.), 87–98.

Fillmore, K. M., Hartka, E., Johnstone, B. M., Leino, E. V., Motoyoshi, M., & Temple, M. T. (1991). A meta-analysis of life course variation in drinking: The Collaborative Alcohol-Related Longitudinal Project. *British Journal of Addiction, 86*, 1221–1268.

Foxcroft, D., Lowe, G., & May, C. (1994). Adolescent alcohol use and family influences: Attributive statements by teenage drinkers. *Drugs: Education, Prevention and Policy, 1*, 63–69.

Gefou-Madianou, D. (1992). Introduction: Alcohol commensality, identity transformations and transcendence. In D. Gefou-Madianou (Ed.), *Alcohol, gender and culture* (pp. 1–34). London: Routledge.

Gilbert, M. J. (1985). Mexican-Americans in California: Intercultural variation in attitudes and behaviour related to alcohol. In L. A. Bennett & G. M. Ames (Eds.), *The American Experience with Alcohol: Contrasting Cultural Perspectives* (pp. 255–277). New York: Plenum Press.

Gillespie, A., Davey, J., Sheehan, M., & Stedson, D. (1991). Thrills without spills: The educational implications of research into adolescent binge drinking for a school based intervention. *Drug Education Journal of Australia, 5*, 121–127.

Goldman, M. S., Brown, S. A., & Christiansen, B. A. (1987). Expectancy theory: thinking and drinking. In H. Blane and K. Leonard (Eds.), *Psychological theories of drinking and alcoholism*. New York: Guilford Press.

Gordon, C., Carey, M., & Carey, K. (1997). Effects of a drinking event on behavioural skills and condom attitudes in men: implications for HIV risk from a controlled experiment. *Health Psychology, 16*, 490–495.

Grant, M., & Litvak, J. (Eds.) (1988). Drinking patterns and their consequences. Washington, DC: Taylor & Francis.

Gusfield, J. (1987). Passage to play: Rituals of drinking time in American society. In M. Grant (Ed.), *Constructive drinking: Perspectives on drink from anthropology*. Cambridge: Cambridge University Press.

Gustafson, R. (1991). Effect of alcohol on quantity of creative production using the Purdue Tests. *Psychological Reports, 69*, 83–90.

Hall, W. (1995). Changes in the public perception of the health benefits of alcohol use, 1989 to 1994. *Australia and New Zealand, 20*, 93–95.

Haworth, A., & Acuda, W. (1998). Sub-Saharan Africa. In M. Grant (Ed.), *Alcohol and emerging markets: Patterns, problems and responses* (pp. 19–90). Philadelphia: Brunner/Mazel.

Healy, B., Turpin, T., & Hamilton, M. (1985). Aboriginal drinking: A case study in inequity and disadvantage. *Australian Journal of Social Issues, 20*, 191–208.

Heath, D. B. (1995). Some generalizations about alcohol and culture. In D. B. Heath (Ed.), *International handbook on alcohol and culture* (pp. 348–361). Westport, CT: Greenwood Press.

Heath, D. B. (1989). Environmental factors in alcohol use and its outcomes. In H. W. Goedde & D. P. Agarwal (Eds.), *Alcoholism: Biomedical and genetic aspects* (pp. 312–324). New York: Pergamon Press.

Heath, D. B. (1987). Anthropology and alcohol studies: Current issues. *Annual Review of Anthropology, 120*, 16–99.

Heather, N., & Robertson, I. (1989). *Problem drinking* (2nd ed.). Oxford: Oxford University Press.

Horton, D. J. (1943). The functions of alcohol in primitive societies: A cross cultural study. *Quarterly Journal of Studies on Alcohol, 4*, 199–320.

Hunter, E. (1993). *Aboriginal health and history: Power and prejudice in remote Australia*. Cambridge: Cambridge University Press.

Iossofides (1991). Sisters in Christ: Metaphors of kinship among Greek nuns. In P. Loizos & E. Papataxiarchis (Eds.), *Contested Identities*. Princeton, New Jersey: Princeton University Press.

Johnson, P., & Johnson, H. (1999). Cultural and familial influences that maintain the negative meaning of alcohol. *Journal of Studies on Alcohol, 13* (Suppl.), 79–83.

Julien, R. (1995). *A primer of drug action.* (7th ed.). New York: Freeman and Co.

Kandel, D. B., & Logan, J. A. (1984). Patterns of drug use from adolescents to young adulthood: Periods of risk for initiation, continued use, and discontinuation. *American Journal of Public Health, 74*, 660–669.

Kunz, J. L. (1997). Associating leisure with drinking: current research and future directions. *Drug and Alcohol Review, 16*, 69–76.

Langford, P. (1989). *Educational psychology: An Australian perspective.* Melbourne, Australia: Longman Cheshire.

Lefrancois, G. R. (1972). *Psychology for teachers: A bear always faces the front.* Belmont, CA: Wadsworth Publishing Co.

Leigh, B. C. (1989). In search of the seven dwarfs: Issues of measurement and meaning in alcohol expectancy research. *Psychological Bulletin, 105*, 361–373.

Leigh, B. C. (1999). Peril, chance, adventure: concepts of risk, alcohol use and risky behaviour in young adults. *Addiction, 94*, 371–383.

Leigh, B. C. (1990). The relationship of sex-related alcohol expectancies to alcohol consumption and sexual behaviour. *British Journal of Addiction, 85*, 919–928.

Lewin, K. (1951). *Field theory in social science.* New York: Harper & Row.

Lewis, M. J. (1996). Alcohol reinforcement and neuropharmacological therapeutics. *Alcohol and Alcoholism, 31* (Suppl. 1), 17–25.

Lipton, R. I. (1994). The effect of moderate alcohol use on the relationship between stress and depression. *American Journal of Public Health, 84*, 1913–1917.

Litvak, J., & Grant, M. (Eds.) (1998). *Drinking patterns and their consequences.* Washington, DC: Taylor and Francis.

Lowe, G., & Taylor, S. B. (1993). Relationship between laughter and weekly alcohol consumption. *Psychological Reports, 72*, 1210.

Lubben, J. E., Chi, I., & Kitano, H. H. L. (1989). Relative influence of selected social factors on Korean drinking behavior in Los Angeles. *Advances in Alcohol and Substance Abuse, 8*, 1–17.

MacAndrew, C., & Edgerton, R. B. (1969). *Drunken comportment: A social explanation.* London: Thomas Nelson & Sons.

Madrigal, E. (1998). Sub-Saharan Africa. In M. Grant (Ed.), *Alcohol and emerging markets: Patterns, problems and responses.* Philadelphia: Brunner/Mazel.

Maloff, D., Becker, H. S., Fonaroff, A., & Rodin, J. (1979). Informal social controls and their influence on substance misuse. *Journal of Drug Issues, 9*, 161–184.

Marlatt, G. A., & Rohsenow, D. J. (1980). Cognitive processes in alcohol use: Expectancy and the balanced placebo design. In N. Mello (Ed.), *Advances in substance abuse: Behavioral and biological research.* Greenwich, CT: Jai Press Inc.

Mars, G. (1989). Longshore drinking, economic security and union politics in Newfoundland. In M. Douglas (Ed.), *Constructive drinking: Perspectives on drink from anthropology* (pp. 91–101). Cambridge: Cambridge University Press.

Mathrani, S. (1998). *Young drinkers: A qualitative study.* Report to the Health Education Authority, London.

McBride, N., Midford, R., Farringdon, F., & Phillips, M. (2000). Early results from a school alcohol harm minimisation study: The School Health and Alcohol Harm Reduction Project. *Addiction, 95*, 1021–1042.

McClelland, D. C., Davis, W. N., & Kalin, R. (1972). *Drinking man: Alcohol and human motivation.* New York: Free Press.

McKechnie, R., Cameron, D., Cameron, I., & Drewery, J. (1977). Teenage drinking in South west Scotland. *British Journal of Addiction, 72*, 287–295.

McMahon, J., Jones, B. T., & O'Donnell, P. (1994). Comparing positive and negative alcohol expectancies in male and female social drinkers. *Addiction Research, 1*, 349–365.

Moore, D. (1990). Anthropological reflections on youth drug use research in Australia: What we don't know and how we should find out. *Drug and Alcohol Review, 9*, 333–342.

Muokolo, A. (1990). Alcohol and its main functions in the Congo. In J. Maula, M. Lindblad, C. Tigerstedt, & L. Green-Rutanen (Eds.), *Alcohol in developing countries: Proceedings from a meeting in Oslo, Norway, August 7–9, 1988* (pp. 127–133). Helsinki: Nordic Council for Alcohol and Drug Research.

Neff, J. A., & Husaini, B. A. (1982). Life events, drinking patterns and depressive symptomatology. *Journal of Studies on Alcohol, 43*, 301–318.

Neve, R. J. M., Lemmens, P. H., & Drop, M. J. (1997). Gender differences in alcohol use and alcohol problems: Mediation by social roles and gender role attitudes. *Substance Use and Misuse, 32*, 1439–1459.

Norris, J. (1994). Alcohol and female sexuality: A look at expectancies and risks. *Alcohol Health and Research World, 18*, 197–201.

O'Connor, J. (1978). *The young drinkers: A cross-national study of social and cultural influences*. London: Tavistock.

Orford, J. (1990). Alcohol and the family. In L. T. Koslowski (Ed.), *Research advances in alcohol and drug problems* (pp. 81–155). New York: Plenum.

Paglia, A., & Room, R. (1998). Preventing substance use problems among youth: A literature review and recommendations. ARF Research Document Series No. 142. Toronto, Canada: Addiction Research Foundation.

Park, J. (1990). Only 'those' women: women and the control of alcohol in New Zealand. *Contemporary Drug Problems, 17*, 2.

Peele, S. (1997). Utilising culture and behaviour in epidemiological models of alcohol consumption and consequences for Western countries. *Alcohol and Alcoholism, 32*, 51–64.

Peele. S., & Grant, M. (Eds.). (1999). *Alcohol and pleasure: A health perspective*. Washington: Taylor and Francis.

Pittman, D. J. (1996). What do we know about beneficial consequences of moderate alcohol consumption on social and physical well-being? A critical review of the recent literature. *Contemporary Drug Problems, 23*, 389–406.

Pittman, D. (Ed.). (1967). *Alcoholism*. New York: Harper & Row.

Plant, M. (1997). *Women and alcohol: Contemporary and historical perspectives*. London: Free Association Books.

Poole, M. (1989). Adolescent transitions: A life-course perspective. In K. Hurrelman (Ed.), *Social world of adolescents: International perspectives* (pp. 66–85). Berlin: Walter de Gruyter.

Ragland, D. R. (1996). Current developments in the study of stress and alcohol consumption. *Alcoholism Clinical and Experimental Research, 20*, 51A–52A.

Roche, A. M. (1998, February). Patterns, paradoxes and ambiguities of consumption. Paper presented at the International Conference on Drinking Patterns and Their Consequences, Perth, Australia.

Roche, A. M., & Watt, K. (1999). Drinking and university students: from celebration to inebriation. *Drug and Alcohol Review, 18*, 625–632.

Rogers, C. (1983). *Freedom to Learn for the 80s*. Columbus, Ohio: C.E. Merrill Publishing Company.

Room, R. (1974). Minimising alcohol problems. *Alcohol Health and Research World* (Preview Issue), 12–17.

Room, R. (1996). Alcohol consumption and social harm—conceptual issues and historical perspectives. *Contemporary Drug Problems, 23*, 373–388.

Rorabaugh, W. J. (1979). *The alcoholic republic: An American tradition*. New York: Oxford University Press.

Sargent, M. (1979). *Drinking and alcoholism in Australia*. Melbourne, Australia: Longman Cheshire.

Schuckit, M. A. (1995). *Drug and alcohol abuse: A clinical guide to diagnosis and treatment*. New York: Plenum.

Sher, K. J. (1985). Subjective effects of alcohol: the influence of setting and individual differences in alcohol expectancies. *Journal of Studies on Alcohol, 46*, 137–146.

Sherratt, A. (1995a). Peculiar substances. In J. Goodman, P. Lovejoy, & A. Sherratt (Eds.), *Consuming habits: Drugs in history and anthropology* (pp. 1–10). New York: Routledge.

Sherratt, A. (1995b). Alcohol and its alternatives: Symbol and substance in pre-industrial cultures. In J. Goodman, P. Lovejoy, & A. Sherratt (Eds.), *Consuming habits: Drugs in history and anthropology* (pp. 11–47). New York: Routledge.

Shimizu, S. (1985). Alucohl ranyo no shakaigakuteki shiten (in Japanese). [Alcohol Abuse from a Sociological Perspective]. *Japanese Journal of Social Psychiatry, 8*, 83–189.

Siegal, S. (1999). Drug anticipation and drug addiction. *Addiction, 94*, 1113–1124.

Simpura, J. (1985). Drinking: an ignored leisure activity. *Journal of Leisure Research, 17*, 200–211.

Single, E. (1993). Public drinking. In M. Galanter (Ed.), *Research developments in alcoholism* (Vol. 10). New York: Plenum.

Single, E., & Leino, V. (1998). The levels, patterns and consequences of drinking. In M. Grant & J. Litvak (Eds.), *Drinking patterns and their consequences*. Washington, DC: Taylor and Francis.

Steele, C. M., & Josephs, R. A. (1990, August). Alcohol myopia: its prized and dangerous effects. *American Psychologist*, 921–933.

Stockwell, T., Smail, P., Hodgson, R., & Canter, S. (1984). Alcohol dependence and phobic anxiety states. *British Journal of Psychiatry, 144*, 58–63.

Wada, K., Price, R., & Fukui, S. (1998). Reflecting adult drinking culture: Prevalence of alcohol use and drinking situations among Japanese junior high school students in Japan. *Journal of Alcohol Studies, 59*, 381–386.

Watson, C., Fleming, J., & Alexander, K. (1991). *A survey of drug use patterns in Northern Territory Aboriginal communities 1986–1987*. Darwin, Australia: Department of Health and Community Services.

Weil, A., & Rosen, W. (1993). *From chocolate to morphine*. Boston: Houghton Mifflin Co.

White, K. G., & Moesbergen, K. W. (1989). Alcohol and choice: the context for drinking. *New Zealand Journal of Psychology, 18*, 36–41.

Wiers, R. W., Hoogeveen, K. J., Sergeant, J. A., & Gunning, W. B. (1997). High and low-dose alcohol-related expectancies and differential associations with drinking in male and female adolescents and young adults. *Addiction, 92*, 871–888.

Wilks, J. (1985). University students' knowledge of alcohol and drink stereotypes. *Community Health Studies, 9*, 231–237.

Wilks, J., & Callan, V. J. (1984). Similarity of university students' and their parents' attitudes towards alcohol. *Journal of Studies on Alcohol, 45*, 326–333.

Wilks, J., Callan, V. J., & Austin, D. (1989). Parent, peer, and personal determinants of adolescent drinking. *British Journal of Addiction, 84*, 619–630.

Wilsnack, R. W., & Wilsnack, S. C. (1997). *Gender and alcohol: Individual and social perspectives*. New Jersey: Rutgers University, Rutgers Center of Alcohol Studies.

Wright, L. (1999). Young people and alcohol: What 11–24 year olds know, think and do. *Health Education Authority.*

Chapter 2

Acquiring the Competence to Drink Responsibly

Gerard M. Schippers, Marcel A. G. van Aken, Sylvia M. M. Lammers, and Laura de Fuentes Merillas

Alcohol drinking behavior, like many forms of acquired human activity, is learned behavior. A large majority of the world's population consume alcohol in a moderate, responsible manner. This behavior, in a wide variety of drinking practices, is acquired, mostly in early and later adolescence. From a psychological perspective, one regards drinking alcohol as learned behavior to be understood within a social and behavioral framework of socialization, development, social norms, and social sanctions. Learning to drink is merely one of the many behavioral patterns learned in the course of coming of age in Western societies. During adolescence a transition from the abstinent norms of childhood to the drinking norms of adulthood occurs. The acquisition of the competence to drink can more specifically be described as a developmental process whereby the individual "assimilates" role expectancies about the use of alcohol held by significant reference groups, and thereby adapts to the challenge offered by the continuous confrontation with alcohol and those who drink alcohol.

Learning to drink might have the connotation of learning to hold your liquor or learning to drink heavily or in a problematic way. These are not the meanings one wants to focus on in this chapter. Here one will devote oneself to the psychology of learning to drink responsibly: not just on the processing of information about alcohol, but on the acquisition of responsible alcohol drinking habits. This means that the factors and processes that lead youngsters into abuse and problematic drinking will not be referred to, although, because of the public health perspective, this aspect has been studied far more extensively. The reader will be referred to other publications for such considerations (e.g., Boyd, Howard, & Zucker, 1995; Jessor & Jessor, 1977; Kandel, 1980).

Alcohol drinking is predominantly social behavior, guided by social norms and occurring in a cultural context. Focus will be on the intraindividual mechanisms by which these influences are processed, not on the influences themselves. For a sociocultural perspective on the drinking of alcohol other sources will also be referred to (Heath, 1988, 1995, 2000).

The central theme in this chapter will be that drinking alcohol responsibly can be considered as a competence, an ability, acquired during the course of a person's development. Competence—or competencies—reflect a person's ability to solve problems, which might be related, for example, to development, new opportunities, or to new challenges such as drinking alcohol. Competence and competencies are strongly related to expectancies, which can be seen as their motivational bases. Expectancies can concern very general issues, such as a general feeling of self-efficacy, or a general sense of support, but can also concern more domain-specific issues, such as the expectancy to be able to handle alcohol, or the expectancy that alcohol can lead to certain outcomes: desired outcomes such as popularity and undesired outcomes such as feeling sick. The role of competencies and expectancies can be regarded from two different theoretical perspectives, that of social learning theory, with a focus on issues such as modeling and reinforcement and that of socialization theories, with a focus on issues such as parenting styles and relationships with parents or peers. In this chapter, an attempt will be made to combine both perspectives.

In Western countries most youngsters learn to drink alcohol between the ages of 12 and 18 years. In the U.S. 56% of the eighth graders have tried alcohol (National Institute on Alcohol Abuse and Alcoholism, 1997). In southern European countries children learn to drink somewhat earlier than in northern European countries. Around 25% of boys aged 11–12 years drink at least once a week in Italy and Greece, while this figure is far below 10% in most other countries. All over Europe, in the 13 to 15 year age group, 22% of boys and 13% of girls drink alcohol at least weekly (van Reek, Adriaanse, & Knibbe, 1994).This age does not represent the first experience with alcohol, however, since drinking alcohol is a common phenomenon in most Western families. Children form alcohol expectancies well before they actually start drinking alcohol. These expectancies are highly influential on later drinking behavior (Wiers, Hoogeveen, Sergeant, & Gunning, 1997).

The distribution of the amount of alcohol consumed over the life span is heavily skewed. A large majority of drinkers reach a peak in consumption habits in late adolescence or early adulthood, and subsequently adopt more moderate habits. Learning to drink responsibly is probably an oscillating process, in which periods of heavy drinking might alternate with periods of lower alcohol consumption. The "unlearning" of drinking patterns is also an interesting phenomenon in this light. Many adolescents "mature out" of heavy alcohol use once they have a stable position in society, start working steadily, leave college, and so on. Alcohol use characteristically increases up to the age of 25–29 years and generally decreases thereafter (Acuda & Alexander, 1998; Chen & Kandel, 1995; Temple & Fillmore, 1986). This young adult-limited effect has been shown in cross-sectional (Kandel, 1980) and longitudinal studies (Donovan, Jessor, & Jessor, 1983; Grant, Harford, & Grigson, 1988). On the other hand, as Gotham, Sher, and Wood (1997) mention, a proportion of young adults do not cut back on their alcohol consumption and continue a pattern of heavy drinking, or worse. As they demonstrated, both role transition variables, such as becoming involved in the workforce or having children, and individual differences, such as family history of alcoholism, personality traits, and positive alcohol expectancies, are factors in this self-limiting process. Overall, the large majority of heavy-drinking adolescents seems to find ways to adjust their alcohol consumption. Strangely enough, this impressive phenomenon has hardly been studied, but it will be seen later in this chapter that similar phenomena have been identified from studies on identity development.

FACTORS INFLUENCING YOUTH DRINKING

In their overview of theoretical conceptions of factors that influence youth to start drinking, Wagenaar and Perry (1995) present a schema with an integrated theory of drinking behavior. They first distinguish between factors on a macro/societal level and on a micro/individual level. In this model, drinking is directly affected by positive personal cognitions and perceptions regarding alcohol. When one expects alcohol to have a reinforcing effect, when one understands alcohol use in terms of its socially shared positive meanings, and when one perceives the expected rewards of acquiring alcohol and consuming alcohol to be high in relation to costs, one is likely to drink alcohol. In addition, however, exposure to drinking models is importantly affected by (a) public policy concerning media advertising and the depiction of alcohol use in media programming, and (b) market mechanisms that respond to and stimulate demand for alcohol. Public policy also directly affects formal social controls, as well as the legal, economic, and physical availability of alcohol, all of which in turn affect drinking directly, as well as through their influence on the meanings and perception of alcohol use.

Biological/pharmacological factors also play a role. Consuming alcohol may be intrinsically rewarding because of the psychopharmacological actions of alcohol on the body. The biological make-up of the person can be understood to influence the reinforcing effects of alcohol. The rewarding dimensions of alcohol use, however, are largely socially learned meanings rather than solely the outcome of the intrinsic biological processes resulting from the ingestion of alcohol (Akers, 1992; Wagenaar & Perry, 1995). These meanings direct the individual interpretation of the physiological effects of alcohol.

Biological / availability Reinforce

As Wagenaar and Perry go on to show, social roles, including those labeled as deviant or problematic, as well as other widespread social roles, in particular those that bring a person in regular contact with alcohol (e.g., the adolescent working in a venue selling alcohol) affect drinking directly by offering more opportunities to drink; they also affect drinking indirectly by their influence on alcohol-related cognitions and perceptions. In this conception, which relies heavily on principles from social learning theory, a link with socialization theories is established. General personality characteristics, such as self-esteem and locus of control, may be associated with drinking behavior. These personality characteristics are primarily the result of the accumulation of past and current socialization. In other words, they result from past and current experience in social interactions, which are in turn influenced by a variety of social and institutional structures. Although it is clear from this overview that many factors influence how an individual consumes alcohol, the process of socialization will be focused on here. In this process, acquiring the competence to drink responsibly is most explicit and the role of expectancies, which can be considered the operational link between competencies and actual behavior in differing environments, is most clearly delineated.

RESPONSIBLE DRINKING AS A DEVELOPMENTAL COMPETENCE

Competence and Developmental Tasks in Adolescence

Drinking alcohol responsibly can be considered as one of a person's competencies. As suggested above, competencies are those abilities that comprise a person's general capability to adapt to problems, and are the product of the person's solving of subsequent developmental tasks. Developmental tasks can be defined as thematically coherent problems which must be solved in order to adjust to new demands or to take advantage of new opportunities. Such tasks are unavoidable, and their solution typically produces the competence that is needed to cope with subsequent developmental tasks. Failure to solve a developmental task can put an adolescent at risk of failure in solving later tasks. Some developmental tasks are normative and occur for almost every person at the same point in the life course, such as the challenge of alcohol use in adolescence. Other developmental tasks may be non-normative, and occur only for some people and/or at variable points in the life course, such as a serious illness or a parental divorce.

This assumption explains the continuity of adaptation over the life course. Continuity in the development of competence results from the fact that the competencies achieved by handling developmental tasks build upon each other: the competence acquired in one developmental task is an important element in coping with a subsequent developmental task. Earlier competencies are prerequisites for later competencies. For example, competencies developed in the early parent-child relationship are important at the time the child develops peer relationships.

Aspects of the social environment, including parental support and socialization, are important for providing assistance in handling developmental tasks, i.e., for developing competence. Several theoretical frameworks for parental support or socialization are available, such as the seminal work of Baumrind (1991a, 1991b, 1991c) on parenting styles in terms of responsiveness and demandingness. In other theories these dimensions are reformulated or combined in dimensions such as warmth, emotional support, quality of instruction, involvement, monitoring or parental control, or parent-adolescent conflict.

Some theorists explain how parental support is inversely related to adolescent problem behavior (Mermelstein, Cohen, Lichtenstein, Kamarck, & Baer, 1986; Wills, 1990). A distinction can be made between emotional support and instrumental support. Emotional support, indexed by measures of closeness and confiding, strengthens the attachment between parent and child and develops the expectation that important other people are available when needed. Instrumental support consists of practical help in making decisions and solving problems (Wills, Mariani, & Filer, 1996). The way parental support influences the adolescent could be direct, in the context of supportive interactions, or indirect, as the child observes a parent interacting with others. Parental support seems to have a stress-buffering effect, so that the relationship between negative life events and adverse outcomes is reduced for adolescents with a higher level of emotional support from parents (Cohen & Wills, 1985; Greenberg, Siegel, & Leitch, 1983; Wills & Cleary, 1996; Wills, Vaccaro, & McNamara, 1992).

Other theories expand this framework, and describe how support from persons in the environment may consist of intentional support, to determine the importance of the developmental task and the desirability of the various outcomes; of behavioral support, to encourage the person to find and try out various solutions; of emotional support, to help the person deal with the emotions involved; and of cognitive support, to provide the information that is necessary to handle the task (van Lieshout, Cillessen, & Haselager, 1999).

Although recent theorizing on parenting styles and parenting practices suggests that research should go beyond Baumrind's dimensions to include cognitions and affect (see, e.g., Bugental & Goodnow, 1998; Darling & Steinberg, 1993), they have proven their usefulness and are still widely studied, particularly in connection with adolescents' psychosocial functioning, such as their responsible alcohol consumption. For this reason, the conceptualization of socialization in this chapter will rely heavily on her work. The basic idea behind all the above-mentioned theories is that socialization refers, at least in part, to support in handling developmental tasks, and in developing the competencies and expectancies related to them.

Identity Development as Central Developmental Task During Adolescence

During adolescence, three groups of developmental tasks can be distinguished:

1 personal tasks, having to do with gaining autonomy, coping;
2 relational tasks, having to do with the development of stable and/or intimate relationships;
3 socio-institutional tasks, having to do with school or work career.

The central developmental task during adolescence is the development of an identity. Identity formation can be viewed as a process of integrating personal changes, societal demands, and expectations for the future (see, e.g., Erikson, 1981). The broad developmental task of developing an identity can be regarded in terms of various subtasks, in domains such as relationships with parents, relationships with peers or an intimate partner, professional career, and societal opportunities or demands. Learning to drink too can be viewed as a subtask in identity development. This seems to be especially true for boys, because the drinking of alcohol has traditionally been more part of masculine than feminine roles (Lammers, 1991). Girls can often more easily choose to stay aloof from drinking. Boys, however, generally experience considerable pressure to use alcohol and have to learn to handle this in a responsible manner.

Marcia (1966) (see also Adams, 1985) formulated two dimensions that can be assumed to play an important role in identity formation: exploration and commitment. Exploration refers to the extent to which a person has explored the various options, beliefs, roles, activities, and so forth, within the specific domain, whereas commitment refers to the extent to which a person has made decisions regarding those options, beliefs, roles, and activities. Marcia combined these two dimensions to describe four identity statuses:

- identity achievement (a person has made commitments after a period of crisis and exploration);
- identity foreclosure (a person has made commitments without exploration);
- moratorium (the person has not made any commitments, and is in the middle of crisis and exploration);
- identity diffusion (a person has not made commitments, but is also not exploring).

Essential in the ideas of Marcia is that identity formation is not successfully completed unless there has been a period of exploration. Persons in the foreclosure status (where commitments have been made without exploration first) have been found to be most authoritarian and to have the highest need for social approval. These persons largely accept what authority figures or influential friends tell them to do. The status of foreclosure can therefore be considered to be a suboptimal outcome. Combining this with mechanisms from social learning theory would suggest that these persons are most susceptible to the influence of powerful models in real life or in the media.

Responsible Alcohol Drinking as a Competence

Responsible alcohol drinking can be seen as a form of competence. This competence is the result of handling the developmental task of using alcohol, i.e., handling the opportunities and demands that confrontation with people that drank and with the substance alcohol in the environment offer. The competence surrounding alcohol developed in the nondrinking ages affects the way the challenge of alcohol use is handled in the drinking age, just as social competence developed earlier will affect contacts with (deviant) peer groups during adolescence and problem-solving skills developed earlier will affect the handling of problems later. Correspondingly, the support (socialization) that has been relevant in handling developmental tasks up to adolescence will be important for handling developmental tasks when that period is reached. Adequate parental support will remain an important aspect of parental socialization and adequate peer relations will remain an important aspect of peer socialization during adolescence.

In Marcia's theory of identity development, exploration refers to trying out alternatives, for example, in terms of behaviors such as using alcohol. After a period of exploration, adolescents are assumed to commit themselves to one of those alternatives. The importance of a period of exploration before establishing commitments with respect to alcohol use is supported by studies of Baumrind (1991a, 1991b, 1991c) and Shedler and Block (1990), whose results suggest that adolescents who experiment with alcohol might even be somewhat better off than those who completely abstain. Also, Pape and Hammer (1996) found that, in males, both early and late beginners with alcohol may be at risk for psychological problems. In addition, Cook, Young, Taylor, and Bedford (1998) reported that persons who drink no alcohol at all are less well adjusted than persons who drink moderate amounts.

Only a few studies have directly addressed the relationships between Marcia's ego-identity status and drinking behavior. Basically, these studies seem to support the idea that a phase of exploration is necessary for developing responsible drinking behavior. Although Jones and Hartmann (1988) found that individuals in the "identity foreclosure" group reported lower frequencies of alcohol experiences than the other three status groups, both Jones, Hartmann, Grochowski, and Glider (1989) and Bishop, Macy-Lewis, Schnekloth, Puswella, and Struessel (1997) reported that identity foreclosure scores were associated with problematic alcohol use. The apparent inconsistency is explained by Bishop et al. (1997) from a developmental perspective. The subjects in the Jones and Hartmann (1988) study were younger than in the other two studies (early as compared to late adolescents). Foreclosed individuals may abstain from alcohol use in early adolescence, living up to the role that is expected from them by, for example, their parents. However, by late adolescence a certain amount of alcohol use may be expected and foreclosed individuals' lack of experimentation may now lead to a propensity to heavier use. This means that adolescence is a phase in which risk-taking behavior is not only quite common, but may also in the long run be beneficial. Towards the end of adolescence, this risk-taking behavior declines and a more stable identity (including, e.g., a way of dealing with alcohol) is achieved based on experiences during the exploration phase.

THE SOCIALIZATION OF THE COMPETENCE OF RESPONSIBLE ALCOHOL DRINKING

The Role of Parental Support and Modeling

Several studies have examined the relation between family socialization processes and responsible drinking behavior. In a meta-analysis of 30 studies, Foxcroft and Lowe (1991) found that low parental support and both extremely high and low parental control were dysfunctional for adequate socialization into normal drinking behavior. In a long series of studies, observing parents and their children longitudinally, Barnes, Farrell, and Banerjee (1994) demonstrated that high levels of parental support and monitoring, as well as positive parent-child communication, serve as key elements in the prevention of alcohol abuse and other deviant behaviors.

Partly overlapping models hypothesize about the way parental support is related to adolescent substance use (abuse). Stress-coping theory posits similar mechanisms as described above, in the sense that support will lead to more adaptive coping (e.g., problem-solving) and less maladaptive coping (e.g., coping through anger), and better competence in academic tasks, and therefore, indirectly, lead to less substance use (Newcomb, Maddahian, & Bentler, 1986). In the deviancy model developed by Jessor and Jessor (1977), a supportive relationship with parents is considered to contribute to the adoptation of conventional social values and the rejection of deviance-prone attitudes. In the affiliation model, high parental support is related to lesser affiliation with deviant peers, which can be seen as a risk factor for adolescent substance use. In testing these models, Wills and Cleary (1996) demonstrated that parental support operates by moderating both deviance-prone attitudes and peer affiliations. Behavioral coping skills and academic competence (or the lack of it) influence the risk of developing substance abuse. This risk is moderated, however, by the influence of parental support.

Since parental support clearly has such an important influence on a child's drinking behavior, one may wonder where the parent's own consumption patterns fit in as modeling behavior. It is often observed that parental alcohol consumption is associated with adolescent alcohol initiation (Kandel, Kessler, & Margulies, 1978), current use (Ary, Tildesley, Hops, & Andrews, 1993) and future use (Biddle, Bank, & Marlin, 1980). This influence can be direct, through behavioral modeling, or indirect, through the influence of the parents' attitudes and norms (Ary et al., 1993) or through family management practices (Dishion & Loeber, 1985). Peterson, Hawkins, Abbott, and Catalano (1995) studied the relative influence of these factors in the U.S. They interviewed 650 Black and White youngsters aged 12–15 years and their parents three times in 3 consecutive years in order to follow them longitudinally. Subjects came from public schools in Seattle, Washington. Their results were as follows. As expected, current alcohol use was strongly associated with proactive family management practices. Those parents who monitored their children's activities, communicated clear expectations for their children's behavior, and provided positive reinforcement for desired behaviors when their children were aged 12–13 years, found that their children were less likely to be consumers of alcohol at age 14–15. Good family management was, therefore, an important protective factor against early alcohol use. No ethnic differences were found. Most interestingly, the influence of parental drinking frequency on current alcohol use seems to be mediated by family management practices and parental alcohol norms. Although parental drinking frequency at ages 12–13 was associated with drinking habits of the adolescent children at ages 14–15, this frequency was no longer predictive when family management practices, parental norms, and children's exposure to their parents' drinking were taken into account. Parental drinking occurring in the context of good family management practices, parental norms unfavorable to adolescent alcohol use, and parents not involving their children in their own alcohol consumption seem to protect children from drinking irresponsibly (Peterson et al., 1995, p. 52).

One could conclude that the often-observed direct influence of parental drinking behaviors on their children's drinking is mediated by an overarching factor: the quality of their family management and the support they give to their children.

Socialization in Terms of Parenting Styles

In Baumrind's work on parenting styles (see, e.g., 1991a), identity formation during adolescence is described in terms of an integration of agency (the drive for independence and individuality) and communion (the need to be included and connected). In this process,

> "parents are caught on the horns of this dilemma: adolescents, in order to become . . . competent individuals, require both freedom to explore and experiment, and protection from experiences that are clearly dangerous" (p. 748).

She also describes how factor analyses of parenting behavior typically yield two dimensions, demandingness (or control) and responsiveness (or support, warmth). A fourfold classification based on these dimensions was made, leading to four prototypes of parenting styles: Authoritative (high on control and high on warmth), Authoritarian (high on control, low on warmth), Permissive (low on control, high on warmth) and rejecting-neglecting (low on control, low on warmth).

Authoritative parents want their children to be assertive and self-regulated as well as socially responsible and cooperative. They set standards for the child's conduct, but do so in a manner consistent with the child's needs and capabilities. Their children have been found to be more competent in several domains. Authoritarian parents are obedience- and status-oriented and expect their orders to be obeyed without any explanation. They tend not to encourage independent behavior and to restrict the child's autonomy. Boys from authoritarian homes tend to be relatively hostile and aggressive, whereas girls tend be relatively dependent and submissive. Permissive parents do not require responsible behavior, allow considerable self-regulation, and avoid confrontation. They tend to view themselves as resources which the child may or may not use instead of actively shaping their child's behavior. Their children are less self-assertive and less competent. Rejecting-neglecting parents do not structure and monitor, and are not supportive. They tend to be "parent-centered," and structure their home life primarily around their own needs and interests (Baumrind, 1991a). Although the dimensions have been refined somewhat for adolescents and although gender and culture differences have been found, these parental prototypes have proven to be useful for summarizing and examining relations between parenting styles or practices and adolescents' psychosocial development (Steinberg, 1996).

Several studies done by Gerald Adams and colleagues (Adams, 1985; Adams & Jones, 1983; Campbell, Adams, & Dobson, 1984) have shown that certain family variables are associated with individual differences in identity formation. Parental warmth and affection seem to differentiate between diffused adolescents, who are assumed to experience rejection and low levels of affection, and moratorium- and identity-achieved adolescents, who are assumed to come from homes that are affectionate and encouraging and that provide strong independence training. Parental control, on the other hand, seems to restrict successful individuation. Foreclosed adolescents seem to have affectionate but possibly emotionally enmeshed family lives.

In terms of Maccoby and Martin's (1983) combination of Baumrind's parenting styles, Shucksmith, Glendinning, and Hendry (1997) found that young people who viewed their parents as authoritarian, or as neglecting, were more likely to drink alcohol frequently, whereas those who viewed their parents as authoritative were less likely to do so. These results were found in older adolescents (15–16 years of age), but not in younger (13–14 years of age), suggesting that the impact of parenting practices becomes more evident once young people begin to drink more often.

Sprinthall and Collins (1995) describe mechanisms for how and why different family environments affect adolescent development. The first mechanism is that different parents provide different models for their children. Authoritative parents provide models of socially responsible and caring behavior, whereas authoritarian or permissive parents are not strong models for this kind of behavior. Authoritative parents may also provide more opportunities for practicing responsible behaviors, for example, by allowing the adolescent to make choices and then provide feedback on these choices. In such a way, adolescents may recognize the connection between their actions and the consequences of them, and to reflect on their own competence.

A second mechanism is that the different parenting styles reflect family atmospheres that vary in how well they support a healthy ego-identity. Grotevant and Cooper (1985) found that family atmospheres that tolerate differences between family members and also foster warm emotional ties between family members (characteristics that are comparable to an authoritative parenting style) are beneficial for the adolescents' ego development (see also Hauser, Powers, & Noam, 1991).

A third mechanism proposed by Sprinthall and Collins (1995) is that authoritative parenting may provide the adolescent with a general sense of confidence in a supportive family. Such a general sense of support may make it easier for an adolescent to explore various aspects of a developmental task at hand, and may also increase the likelihood that, if necessary, the adolescent will seek support from others outside the family.

Socialization by Peers

One of the first to present a theory for the development of responsible drinking among young people was Maddox (1962). He recognized the great influence of peers as determinants of adolescent drinking behavior. Maddox argued, however, against the notion that adolescents are compelled to drink because of irresistible peer pressure. In his view, teenage drinking primarily serves a function in status transition from adolescence into adulthood. Hendry, Glendinning, and Shucksmith (1996) described the age-related transition in casual and leisure activities characteristic of many adolescents. For example, "hanging about with friends" in the local neighborhood is at a peak at middle adolescence and falls away rapidly thereafter, while commercial leisure venues, such as cinemas, discos, clubs, and pubs, steadily increase in importance during the adolescent years. They present evidence that this transition is clearly linked with the amount of family support and control the adolescent has been given, but also with challenge to parental authority, peer acceptance, and perception of social competence and social integration. Age-related transitions are clearly complex phenomena where both macro societal factors and micro interpersonal factors have their influence.

The literature shows that, in general, contacts with peers in the form of friendships are beneficial for development, whereas contacts with deviant peers are not. Friendships, through their supportive function, can be expected to enhance competence and, thus, responsible drinking behaviors. Contacts with deviant peers, however, can be expected (and have been found) to be related to problematic drinking behaviors. Jessor and colleagues (Jessor, 1991; Jessor, Donovan, & Costa, 1996) found that adolescents who experienced nonsupportive family relationships were more likely to affiliate with peers who held nonconventional attitudes towards deviance. Scholte, van Lieshout, and van Aken (in press) found that adolescents who reported low parental support and at the same time high friend support showed more antisocial behavior, including higher levels of alcohol and drug use.

The drinking behavior of peers can have a direct influence on the drinking behavior of the adolescent. This is demonstrated in a series of studies observing adolescents in public drinking places in the Netherlands by van de Goor, Knibbe, and Drop (1990). They showed that boys, in particular, were influenced in their rate and quantity of drinking by their direct company; boys in large, all-male groups drank (far) faster and more than boys in mixed groups. The same was true when music was played loudly and/or when there was no other activity than conversation. The same authors found that in the same venues, evenings differed in the mean amount of drinking, showing higher drinking rates for all types of drinkers on "wet" drinking occasions. These findings support the adaptation hypothesis, suggesting that differences in amount of drinking by adolescents in these public drinking places is more the result of the adapting of the drinkers to each other than of the selection or choice of drinking companions.

Peer group influence is considered to be a major cause of initiation of drinking. It is assumed that youngsters are vulnerable in their attempts to join and remain in certain peer groups (Petraitis, Flay, & Miller, 1995). Numerous, mostly cross-sectional, studies have demonstrated the strong positive relationship between adolescents' alcohol use and that of their friends. These studies rely mostly on the assumption that similarities in behavior among friendships and partnerships must be attributed to peer and partner influences. However, homogeneity of behavior in friendships can also be interpreted as the outcome of a process of choosing persons with equal characteristics (Ennett & Bauman, 1994; Engels, 1999; Kandel et al., 1978). A process of selective attraction might be considered the basis of forming friendships and as such determine the similarity in drinking behavior. This is known as the selection hypothesis. In a longitudinal study in which 1,063 youngsters in the Netherlands were interviewed at ages 12, 14, and 16 years, Engels and Knibbe (1999) examined the relative influences of drinking behavior of two best friends and of parents on the youth's drinking habits. In the long run, the influence of parents on their children was small but consistent. Prior experiences with alcohol consumption were generally robust in predicting use a few years later. Youngsters were affected by exposure to "using" family members. The high cross-sectional associations, around .60, emphasized the importance of friendship with regard to drinking. This homogeneity, however, could hardly be explained by the influences of the subjects' two best friends. Engels (1999) concluded that it is selection that is largely responsible: "Instead of the hypothesized longitudinal impact of drinking friends, our findings suggest that adolescents themselves are for a greater part accountable for the homogeneity of behavior in friendships" (p. 77).

In accordance with such findings, Brook and Brook (1985) concluded that in order to prevent alcohol abuse, alcohol education programs should concentrate more on the preadolescent personality and should be directed not only at children, but also at their parents. By ameliorating the familial environment, focusing on the establishment of an affectionate and nonconflictual relationship in which the children identify with their parents, prevention programs can influence the development of personality and peer risk factors for alcohol abuse.

THE ROLE OF EXPECTANCIES IN THE SOCIALIZATION OF ALCOHOL DRINKING

Expectancy theory is a general theory of motivation going back to Tolman (1932), MacCorquodale and Meehl (1953), and Rotter (1954). The repeated perception of an association between an observed or actually performed behavior and certain outcomes leads to the storage of these associations in the memory in the form of expectancies of an "if-then" relation. These expectancies about if-then contingencies influence subsequent choices to initiate such behaviors. Expectancies with respect to alcohol are beliefs that alcohol will serve certain functions or will result in desirable or undesirable consequences for the individual. Many cross-sectional studies have shown the power of the concept of alcohol expectancies to predict drinking behavior significantly at all drinking levels (for reviews, see Goldman, Brown, Christiansen, & Smith, 1991; Leigh, 1989; Smith, Goldman, Greenbaum, & Christiansen, 1995; Stacy, Widaman, & Marlatt, 1990). Most prospective studies of the influence of alcohol expectancies on drinking behavior suggest that alcohol expectancies predict future drinking behavior in adolescents at a significant level: after 1 year (Christiansen, Smith, Roehling, & Goldman, 1989; Reese, Chassin, & Molina, 1994), 2 years (Aas, Leigh, Anderssen, & Jakobsen, 1998; Smith et al., 1995), 3 years (Sher, Wood, Wood, & Raskin, 1996), and 9 years (Stacy, Newcomb, & Bentler, 1991).

Alcohol Drinking and the Development of Alcohol Expectancies During Childhood and Adolescence

Although children seldom have direct experience of alcohol consumption, they learn about the effects of alcohol from a young age. Primary social sources of learning are observations of drinking behavior of parents, other adults, and adolescents, and assimilation of cultural stereotypes pictured by television and other media (Critchlow, 1986). The studies of Aas et al. (1998) and Smith et al. (1995) suggest that there is not a one-way influence of alcohol expectancies on drinking behavior but rather an interaction between these variables. In both studies a model that assumed that alcohol expectancies and alcohol consumption (measured three times over 2 years) influence each other reciprocally was tested. This interactive model fit the data significantly better than alternative models only incorporating paths from alcohol expectancies to alcohol consumption, or the other way around from alcohol consumption to alcohol expectancies. These studies analyzed only expectations with respect to social behavior, not the whole range of positive alcohol expectancies.

Oei and Baldwin (1994) formulated a theoretical explanation of the interplay between alcohol expectancies and the development of drinking habits. They made a distinction between an acquisition phase and a maintenance phase. Other principles of learning apply in each phase, and these are connected with a different role of alcohol expectancies. In the acquisition phase, controlled processing and instrumental learning are dominant. The individual chooses a behavioral response in a given situation on the basis of a conscious weighing of positive and negative consequences he or she has learned to expect of that behavior. The actually experienced consequences are fed back to inform future expectations. In this phase, alcohol expectancies are continuously reassessed and become more and more differentiated. After much practicing of the behavior, a qualitatively different process develops. Decisions to drink (or not to drink) take place faster and become more automatic in nature. The weighing of positive and negative consequences does not occur in every situation and is not as exhaustive as before. It is mainly the alcohol expectancies that are easily accessible in the memory that influence the behavioral choice. These are the alcohol expectancies that are proximal, probable, and personal. In this maintenance phase, eventually a behavioral sequence "once triggered runs to completion without conscious control and is subsequently difficult to interrupt or to alter" (Oei & Baldwin, 1994, p. 529). Instrumental learning has thus made way for a process of classical conditioning. Alcohol expectancies play a more modest role in the maintenance phase compared to the acquisition phase of drinking.

There are a number of empirical studies about the development of alcohol expectancies during childhood. The study of Aas et al. (1998) suggests that the period of initiation of drinking is a crucial one, in so far as a rapid development of alcohol expectancies in the positive direction takes place. Before initiation of drinking, negative alcohol expectancies are predominant, especially during the first grades in elementary school (Johnson & Johnson, 1995; Keefe 1994). With increasing age, alcohol expectancies become more differentiated and more positive (Gillmore et al., 1998; Miller, Smith, & Goldman, 1990), especially in boys (Kraus, Smith, & Ratner, 1994). Probably young children become acquainted with only the most salient effects of drinking, particularly with the negative cultural stereotypes of drunkenness. When children grow older they gain more and more experience with the effects of "normal" moderate drinking in parents, older siblings, and others. Together with cognitive ripening, this leads to more positive and differentiated alcohol expectancies. This trend continues throughout adolescence in drinkers and nondrinkers (Aas et al., 1998). However, with the first drinking experiences in adolescence a significant jump is made in the direction of more positive alcohol expectancies, at least with respect to social expectations. Alcohol expectancies and drinking experiences then increase simultaneously and in interaction with each other (Aas et al., 1998).

Psychotropic and Symbolic Alcohol Expectancies

Cox and Klinger (1988) distinguished between direct and indirect effects of drinking. A person has expectations about how drinking will modify his or her affect through the direct psychotropic effects of alcohol, i.e., the pharmacological action of alcohol on the brain or on mental processes. But there are also expectations about the indirect, nonchemical, or symbolic effects of alcohol, for example, approval of peers or feeling like an adult. These effects are not brought about by the pharmacological action of alcohol (or effects that are experienced as pharmacological), but by the social meanings of the behavior of drinking (Lammers, Schippers, & van der Staak, 1995). This elementary distinction in alcohol expectancies has not found its expression in the instruments that measure alcohol expectancies. Instruments such as the Alcohol Expectancy Questionnaire (AEQ), the most frequently used questionnaire in alcohol expectancies research, predominantly consist of items about expectations with respect to direct, psychotropic effects. As alcohol may symbolize conviviality and having fun, social acceptance, adulthood, toughness, and masculinity (Lammers, 1991), it is likely that expectations regarding these issues play a crucial role in the drinking motivation of adolescents. The fact that beliefs about "enhancement of social behavior" are the strongest predictor of drinking behavior in this age group (Christiansen et al., 1989) provides an indication of this. Enhancement of social behavior has partly been operationalized as expectations of effects that can be interpreted as symbolic—although the authors do not do this. For example, social acceptance and fun (Aas et al., 1998) are not so much psychotropic as they are symbolic effects of alcohol use. Lammers and Schippers (1999) constructed a questionnaire of symbolic alcohol expectancies (SAEQ) and compared this with the Dutch AEQ (Wiers et al., 1997). Factor analysis indicated three factors in the SAEQ: conviviality, positive expectancies of restrained drinking, and enhancement of identity. The SAEQ explained more variance in the drinking behavior of young adults—employed and college students—than the Dutch AEQ. The significance of symbolic expectancies for the development of drinking practices of adolescents and young adults needs to be clarified.

Alcohol Expectancies in Education and Intervention Strategies

Darkes and Goldman (1993) showed that an expectancy modification intervention, but not a traditional treatment, produced short-term reductions in drinking behavior in college students. With respect to alcohol expectancies, total AEQ scores did not decrease, but targeted social/sexual expectancies did. Kraus et al. (1994) used three videotaped interventions with schoolchildren in grades 2, 3, and 4. The first tape featured adult actors misbehaving at a party; the second, puppets with impaired cognitive and motor functioning; and, the third, facts about negative effects of drinking. Only the puppet video reduced the (positive) alcohol expectancies score, while the video with adult actors had the opposite effect. Thus, it seems that alcohol expectancies can be influenced, but that interventions can produce positive as well as negative effects. Recently, several authors (Gillmore et al., 1998; Wiers et al., 1997) have expressed doubts about the effectiveness of stimulating negative alcohol expectancies in the prevention of excessive drinking. In general, positive alcohol expectancies are more predictive of alcohol drinking behavior than negative ones. Also, as mentioned above, alcohol expectancies become more positive with increasing drinking experience. Hence, toning down positive expectancies, especially by pointing out the self-fulfilling effects of positive expectancies, may have more influence than stressing negative alcohol expectancies. Gillmore and colleagues argue that extremely negative educational messages regarding alcohol may backfire with older children. Because they widen the already existing gap with own drinking experiences, which are often very positive, they make negative alcohol expectancies appear even more exaggerated and unlikely to occur. It seems wiser in education, instruction, and prevention strategies to create a critical, but realistic, picture of negative and positive expectancies.

A possible important factor with influence on expectancies about alcohol are messages in the public media. Being confronted with them is part of the socialization process. Chapter 10 is referred to below for a further discussion of this topic. It is probably because of the different interests engaged in fields such as health prevention, alcohol industry, marketing, and policy that research on the effectiveness of public campaigns has produced conflicting reports. The magnitude of this influence is, therefore, far from fully understood, but does not seem to be dramatically large, in neither a positive or a negative way (Donohew, Lorch, & Palmgreen, 1998; Guild & Lowe, 1998).

CONCLUSIONS AND RECOMMENDATIONS

In this chapter, the concept of competence has been presented as the general ability in the development of young people to handle alcohol responsibly. Biological/genetic, general personality, and social factors influence drinking behavior. However, the development of the competence to drink responsibly can best be described as a learning process in which socialization and the acquisition of alcohol expectancies play a central role.

Competencies are the product of a person's mastery of developmental tasks. The competence of drinking alcohol responsibly can be seen as a part of the process of developing an identity, in which exploration and commitment are important dimensions. Exploring alcohol drinking behaviors, even by experimenting with occasions of heavy alcohol use, can be seen as part of the normal development when it ends in a commitment to adaptive drinking habits, which is the case for the large majority of adolescents. This is especially true for boys, because handling alcohol is a more demanding part of adapting a male as opposed to a female role.

The competence to drink responsibly is demonstrated in the individual's set of alcohol expectancies. In general, it may be hypothesized that responsible alcohol use will be characterized by more realistic alcohol expectancies. "Realistic" here means a balanced set of expectations, representing both the positive and negative consequences of alcohol in the short and the long run, and both the direct and the indirect consequences. Since such a realistic set of expectations can only be achieved by real life experiences, it may be hypothesized that adolescents who have experimented will more easily build a balanced view of alcohol. The findings that adolescents with a so-called foreclosure identity are more strongly related to problematic alcohol use gives some support to this idea.

In the process of acquiring a protective set of expectancies of this nature, both parents and peers are of central importance. It is the combination of risk factors that predicts less competence and the subsequent probability of developing problematic drinking habits. It has been amply demonstrated that both of these socialization agents are substantial influences in adolescence, and both should therefore be included in one's thinking about responsible alcohol use, and in attempts to develop programs to help adolescents to develop this competence. Parents should be characterized by involvement and support, eventually allowing some experimental forms of alcohol use. Involvement and support are manifested in the form of monitoring a child's behavior, maintaining open communication, and having the courage to set limits. Alcohol education should not focus primarily on the negative consequences, but should present a more balanced picture. Like sexuality, drinking alcohol should be a topic of discussion within an accepting and caring family context.

To summarize, the development of the competence to drink responsibly should be regarded in much the same way as the development of other kinds of competencies. It is also related to other developmental tasks. This means that in order to prevent alcohol abuse, alcohol education programs should concentrate not only on preadolescent children, but on their parents as well. By addressing the familial environment, focusing on the establishment of an affectionate and nonconflictual relationship in which the children identify with their parents, prevention programs can influence the development of responsible drinking habits. Given the continuity of the development of competence over the life course, prevention programs focusing on stimulating beneficial family environments should start early in life, thus promoting the development of a general competence in the adolescent to handle not only the consumption of alcohol, but also all the other challenges presented during this phase of the life course.

REFERENCES

Aas, H. N., Leigh, B. C., Anderssen, N., & Jakobsen, R. (1998). Two-year longitudinal study of alcohol expectancies and drinking among Norwegian adolescents. *Addiction, 93*, 373–384.

Acuda, W., & Alexander, B. (1998). Individual characteristics and drinking patterns. In M. Grant & J. Litvak (Eds.), *Drinking patterns and their consequences* (pp. 43–62). Washington, DC: Taylor & Francis.

Adams, G. R. (1985). Family correlates of female adolescents' ego-identity development. *Journal of Adolescence, 8*, 69–82.

Adams, G. R., & Jones, R. M. (1983). Female adolescents' identity development: Age comparison and perceived child-rearing experiences. *Developmental Psychology, 19*, 249–256.

Akers, R. L. (1992). *Drugs, alcohol, and society: Social structure, process, and policy*. Belmont, CA: Wadsworth.

Ary, D. V., Tildesley, E., Hops, H., & Andrews, J. A. (1993). The influence of parent, sibling, and peer modelling and attitudes on adolescent use of alcohol. *International Journal of the Addictions, 28*, 853–880.

Barnes, G. M., Farrell, M. P., & Banerjee, S. (1994). Family influences on alcohol abuse and other problem behaviors among Black and White adolescents in a general population sample. *Journal of Research on Adolescence, 4*, 183–201.

Baumrind, D. (1991a). Parenting styles and adolescent development. In R. Lerner, A. C. Petersen, & J. Brooks-Gunn (Eds.), *The encyclopedia on adolescence* (pp. 746–758). New York: Garland.

Baumrind, D. (1991b). The influence of parenting styles on adolescent competence and substance use. *Journal of Early Adolescence, 11*, 56–95.

Baumrind, D. (1991c). Effective parenting during the early adolescent transition. In P. E. Cowan & E. M. Hetherington (Eds.), *Advances in family research* (Vol. 2, pp. 111–163). Hillsdale, NJ: Erlbaum.

Biddle, B. J., Bank, B. J., & Marlin, M. M. (1980). Social determinants of adolescent drinking: What they think, what they do, and what I think and do. *Journal of Studies on Alcohol, 41*, 215–241.

Bishop, D. I., Macy-Lewis, J. A., Schnekloth, C. A., Puswella, S., & Struessel, G. L. (1997). Ego-identity status and reported alcohol consumption: A study of first-year college students. *Journal of Adolescence, 20*, 209–218.

Boyd, G. M., Howard, J., & Zucker, R. A. (1995). *Alcohol problems among adolescents: Current directions in prevention research*. Hillsdale, NJ: Erlbaum.

Brook, D. W., & Brook, J. S. (1985). Adolescent alcohol use. *Alcohol and Alcoholism, 20*, 259–262.

Bugental, D. B., & Goodnow, J. J. (1998). Socialization processes. In W. Damon (Series Ed.) & N. Eisenberg (Vol. Ed.), *Handbook of child psychology: Vol. 4. Social, emotional, and personality development* (5th ed., pp. 389–462). New York: Wiley.

Campbell, E., Adams, G. R., & Dobson, W. R. (1984). Familial correlates of identity formation in late adolescence: A study of the predictive utility of connectedness and individuality in family relations. *Journal of Youth and Adolescence, 13*, 509–525.

Chen, K., & Kandel, D. B. (1995). The natural history of drug use from adolescence to the mid-thirties in a general population sample. *American Journal of Public Health, 85*, 41–47.

Christiansen, B. A., Smith, G. T., Roehling, P. V., & Goldman, M. S. (1989). Using alcohol expectancies to predict adolescent drinking behavior after one year. *Journal of Consulting and Clinical Psychology, 57*, 93–99.

Cohen, S., & Wills, T. A. (1985). Stress, social support, and the buffering hypothesis. *Psychological Bulletin, 98*, 310–357.

Cook, M., Young, A., Taylor, D., & Bedford, A. P. (1998). Personality correlates of alcohol consumption. *Personality and Individual Differences, 24*, 641–647.

Cox, W. M., & Klinger, E. (1988). A motivational model of alcohol use. *Journal of Abnormal Psychology, 97*, 168–180.

Critchlow, B. (1986). The powers of John Barleycorn: Beliefs about the effects of alcohol on social behavior. *American Psychologist, 41*, 751–764.

Darkes, J., & Goldman, M. S. (1993). Expectancy challenge and drinking reduction: Experimental evidence for a mediational process. *Journal of Consulting and Clinical Psychology, 61*, 344–353.

Darling, N., & Steinberg, L. (1993). Parenting style as context. *Psychological Bulletin, 113*, 487–496.

Dishion, T. J., & Loeber, R. (1985). Adolescent marijuana and alcohol use: The role of parents and peers revisited. *American Journal of Drug and Alcohol Abuse, 11*, 11–25.

Donohew, L., Lorch, E. P., & Palmgreen, P. (1998). Applications of a theoretic model o
exposure to health interventions. *Human Communication Research, 24*, 454–468.

Donovan, J. E., Jessor, R., & Jessor, L. (1983). Problem drinking in adolescence and young
hood: A follow-up study. *Journal of Studies on Alcohol, 44*, 109–137.

Engels, R. C. M. E., & Knibbe, R. A. (1999). Influences of parental and best friends' smoking an drinking on adolescent use: A longitudinal study. *Journal of Applied Social Psychology, 29*, 337–361.

Ennett, S. T., & Bauman, K. E. (1994). The contribution of influence and selection to adolescent peer group homogeneity: The case of adolescent cigarette smoking. *Journal of Personality and Social Psychology, 67*, 653–663.

Erikson, E. H. (1981). *Youth: Change and challenge*. New York: Basic.

Foxcroft, D. R., & Lowe, G. (1991). Adolescent drinking behaviour and family socialization factors: A meta-analysis. *Journal of Adolescence, 14*, 255–273.

Gillmore, M. R., Wells, E. A., Simpson, E. E., Morrison, D. M., Hoppe, M. J., & Wilsdon, A. (1998). Children's beliefs about drinking. *American Journal of Drug and Alcohol Abuse, 24*, 131–151.

Goldman, M. S., Brown, S. A., Christiansen, B. A., & Smith, G. T. (1991). Alcoholism and memory: Broadening the scope of alcohol-expectancy research. *Psychological Bulletin, 110*, 137–146.

Gotham, H. J., Sher, K. J., & Wood, P. K. (1997). Predicting stability and change in frequency of intoxication from the college years to beyond: Individual-difference and role transition variables. *Journal of Abnormal Psychology, 106*, 619–629.

Grant, B. F., Harford, T. C., & Grigson, M. B. (1988). Stability of alcohol consumption among youth: A national longitudinal survey. *Journal of Studies on Alcohol, 49*, 253–260.

Greenberg, M. T., Siegel, J. M., & Leitch, C. J. (1983). The nature and importance of attachment relationships to parents and peers during adolescence. *Journal of Youth and Adolescence, 12*, 373–386.

Grotevant, H. D., & Cooper, C. R. (1985). Patterns of interaction in family relationships and the development of identity exploration in adolescence. *Child Development, 56*, 415–428.

Guild, T., & Lowe, G. (1998). Media messages and alcohol education: A school-based study. *Psychological Reports, 82*, 124–126.

Hauser, S. T., Powers, S. I., & Noam, G. G. (1991). *Adolescents and their families: Paths of ego development*. New York: Free Press.

Heath, D. B. (1988). Emerging anthropological theory and models of alcohol use and alcoholism. In C. D. Chaudron & D. A. Wilkinson (Eds.), *Theories of alcoholism*. Toronto, Canada: Alcohol Research Foundation.

Heath, D. B. (Ed.). (1995). *International handbook of alcohol and culture*. Westport, CT: Greenwood.

Heath, D. B. (2000). *Drinking occasions: Comparative perspectives on alcohol and culture*. Philadelphia, PA: Brunner/Mazel.

Hendry, L. B., Glendinning, A., & Shucksmith, J. (1996). Adolescent focal theories: Age-trends in developmental transitions. *Journal of Adolescence, 19*, 307–320.

Jessor, R. (1991). Risk behavior in adolescence: A psychosocial framework for understanding and action. *Journal of Adolescent Health, 12*, 597–605.

Jessor, R., & Jessor, S. (1977). *Problem behavior and psychosocial development: A longitudinal study of youth*. New York: Academic Press.

Jessor, R., Donovan, J. E., & Costa, F. (1996). Personality, perceived life chances, and adolescent behavior. In K. Hurrelmann & S. F. Hamilton (Eds.), *Social problems and social contexts in adolescence: Perspectives across boundaries* (pp. 219–233). New York: Aldine de Gruyter.

Johnson, H. L., & Johnson, P. B. (1995). Children's alcohol-related cognitions: Positive versus negative alcohol effects. *Journal of Alcohol and Drug Education, 40*, 1–12.

Jones, R. M., & Hartmann, B. R. (1988). Ego identity: Developmental differences and experimental substance use among adolescents. *Journal of Adolescence, 11*, 347–360.

Jones, R. M., Hartmann, B. R., Grochowski, C. O., & Glider, P. (1989). Ego identity and substance use: A comparison of adolescents in residential treatment with adolescents in school. *Personality and Individual Differences, 10*, 625–631.

...d drinking behavior among youth. In J. Coleman, A. Inkeles, & ... *review of sociology* (Vol. 6, pp. 235–285). Palo Alto, CA: Annual ...

... & Margulies, R. Z. (1978). Antecedents of adolescent initiation into ...elopmental analysis. *Journal of Youth and Adolescence, 7*, 13–40.

... normative social pressure and attitudes toward alcohol use: Changes ... *al of Studies on Alcohol, 55*, 46–54.

...ner, H. R. (1994). Modifying alcohol-related expectancies in grade- ... *f Studies on Alcohol, 55*, 535–542.

... roblem drinking women: Sex role conflict and gender identity. In G. M. Schippers, S. M. M. Lammers, & P. D. R. Schaap (Eds.), *Contributions to the psychology of addiction* (pp. 15–32). Amsterdam: Swets & Zeitlinger.

Lammers, S. M. M., & Schippers, G. M. (1999) *The symbolic alcohol expectancies questionnaire.* Nijmegen: The University of Nijmegen Research Group of Addictive Behaviors.

Lammers, S. M. M., Schippers, G. M., & van der Staak, C. P. F. (1995). Psychological functions of drinking in alcohol dependent women: An exploration based on a dimensional framework. *Addiction Research, 3*, 183–197.

Leigh, B. C. (1989). In search of the seven dwarves: Issues of measurement and meaning in alcohol expectancy research. *Psychological Bulletin, 105*, 361–373.

Maccoby, E. E., & Martin, J. A. (1983). Socialization in the context of the family: Parent-child interaction. In P. H. Mussen (Ed.), *Handbook of child psychology*, (Vol. 4, pp. 1–101). New York: Wiley.

MacCorquodale, K. M., & Meehl, P. E. (1953). Preliminary suggestions as to a formalization of expectancy theory. *Psychological Review, 60*, 55–63.

Maddox, G. (1962). Teenage drinking in the United States. In D. Pittman & C. Snyder (Eds.), *Society, culture and drinking patterns* (pp. 230–245). New York: Wiley and Sons.

Marcia, J. (1966). Development and validation of ego-identity status. *Journal of Personality and Social Psychology, 3*, 551–558.

Mermelstein, R., Cohen, S., Lichtenstein, E., Kamarck, T., & Baer, J. S. (1986). Social support and smoking cessation and maintenance. *Journal of Consulting and Clinical Psychology, 54*, 447–453.

Miller, P. M., Smith, G. T., & Goldman, M. S. (1990). Emergence of alcohol expectancies in childhood: A possible critical period. *Journal of Studies on Alcohol, 51*, 343–349.

National Institute on Alcohol Abuse and Alcoholism. (1997). *Ninth special report to the U. S. Congress on alcohol and health*. Rockville, MD: NIAAA.

Newcomb, M. D., Maddahian, E., & Bentler, P. M. (1986). Risk factors for drug use among adolescents: Concurrent and longitudinal analyses. *American Journal of Public Health, 76*, 525–531.

Oei, T. P. S., & Baldwin, A. R. (1994). Expectancy theory: A two-process model of alcohol use and abuse. *Journal of Studies on Alcohol, 55*, 525–534.

Pape, H., & Hammer, T. (1996). Sober adolescence: Predictor of psychosocial maladjustment in young adulthood? *Scandinavian Journal of Psychology, 37*, 362–377.

Peterson, P. L., Hawkins, D. J., Abbott, R. D., & Catalano, R. F. (1995). Disentangling the effects of parental drinking, family management, and parental alcohol norms on current drinking by black and white adolescents. In G. M. Boyd, J. Howard, & R. A. Zucker (Eds.), *Alcohol problems among adolescents: Current directions in prevention research* (pp. 33–57). Hillsdale, NJ: Erlbaum.

Petraitis, J., Flay, B. R., & Miller, T. Q. (1995). Reviewing theories of adolescent substance use: Organising pieces in the puzzle. *Psychological Bulletin, 117*, 67–86.

Reese, F. L., Chassin, L., & Molina, B. S. G. (1994). Alcohol expectancies in early adolescents: Predicting drinking behavior from alcohol expectancies and parental alcoholism. *Journal of Studies on Alcohol, 55*, 276–284.

Rotter, J. B. (1954). *Social learning and clinical psychology.* New York: Prentice–Hall

Scholte, R. H. J., van Lieshout, C. F. M., & van Aken, M. A. G. (in press). Relational support in adolescence: Factors, types, and adjustment. *Journal of Research in Adolescence.*

Shedler, J., & Block, J. (1990). Adolescent drug use and psychological health: A longitudinal inquiry. *American Psychologist, 45*, 612–630.

Sher, K. J., Wood, M. D., Wood, P. K., & Raskin, G. (1996). Alcohol outcome expectancies and alcohol use: A latent variable cross-lagged panel study. *Journal of Abnormal Psychology, 105*, 561–574.

Shucksmith, J., Glendinning, A., & Hendry, L. (1997). Adolescent drinking behavior and the role of family life: A Scottish perspective. *Journal of Adolescence, 20*, 85–101.

Smith, G. T., Goldman, M.S., Greenbaum, P. E., & Christiansen, B. A. (1995). Expectancy for social facilitation from drinking: The divergent paths of high-expectancy and low-expectancy adolescents. *Journal of Abnormal Psychology, 104*, 32–40.

Sprinthall, N. A., & Collins, W. A. (1995). *Adolescent psychology: A developmental view* (3rd ed.). New York: McGraw–Hill.

Stacy, A. W., Newcomb, M. D., & Bentler, P. M. (1991). Cognitive motivation and problem drug use: A nine-year longitudinal study. *Journal of Abnormal Psychology, 100*, 502–515.

Stacy, A. W., Widaman K. F., & Marlatt, G. A. (1990). Expectancy models of alcohol use. *Journal of Personality and Social Psychology, 58*, 918–928.

Steinberg, L. (1996). *Adolescence* (4th ed.). New York: McGraw–Hill.

Temple, M. T., & Fillmore, K. M. (1986). The variability of drinking patterns and problems among young men, age 16–31: A longitudinal study. *International Journal of the Addictions, 20*, 1595–1620.

Tolman, E. G. (1932). *Purposive behavior in animals and man*. New York: Appleton Century Crofts.

Van de Goor, L. A., Knibbe, R. A., & Drop, M. J. (1990). Adolescent drinking behaviour: An observational study of the influence of situational factors on adolescent drinking rates. *Journal of Studies on Alcohol, 51*, 548–555.

van Lieshout, C. F. M., Cillessen, A. H. N., & Haselager, G. J. T. (1999). Interpersonal support and individual development. In W. A. Collins & B. Laursen (Eds.), *Relationships as developmental contexts: The 29th Minnesota symposia on child psychology* (pp. 37–60). Hillsdale, NJ: Erlbaum.

van Reek, J., Adriaanse, H., & Knibbe, R. (1994). Alcohol consumption and correlates among children in the European Community. *International Journal of the Addictions, 29*, 15–21.

Wagenaar, A. C., & Perry, C. L. (1995). Community strategies for the reduction of youth drinking: Theory and application. In G. M. Boyd, J. Howard, & R. A. Zucker (Eds.), *Alcohol problems among adolescents: Current directions in prevention research* (pp. 225–224). Hillsdale, NJ: Erlbaum.

Wiers, R. W., Hoogeveen, K. J., Sergeant, J. A., & Gunning, B. W. (1997). High- and low-dose alcohol-related expectancies and the differential associations with drinking in male and female adolescents and young adults. *Addiction, July, 92*(7):871–888.

Wiers, R. W., Sergeant, J. A., & Gunning, W. B. (2000). The assessment of alcohol expectancies in school children: measurement or modification? *Addiction, 95*, 737–746.

Wills, T. A. (1990). Multiple networks and substance use. *Journal of Social and Clinical Psychology, 9*, 78–90.

Wills, T. A. , Mariani, J., & Filer, M. (1996). The role of family and peer relationships in adolescent substance use. In G. R. Pierce, B. R. Sarason, & I. G. Sarason (Eds.), *Handbook of social support and the family* (pp. 521–549). New York: Plenum.

Wills, T. A., & Cleary, S. D. (1996). How are social support effects mediated? A test with parental support and adolescent substance use. *Journal of Personality and Social Psychology, 71*, 937–952.

Wills, T. A., Vaccaro, D., & McNamara, G. (1992). The role of life events, family support, and competence in adolescent substance use: A test of vulnerability and protective factors. *American Journal of Community Psychology, 20*, 349–374.

Chapter 3

Family and Cultural Influences on Alcohol and Young People

Juan José Sanchez-Sosa and Flavio Poldrugo

All activities of the human individual start in the family and many of them remain within its realm for a long time. The family acts as the first niche and context for protecting the child and fostering all aspects of its maturation and development. Later the family acts as a launching pad for most initiatives, personal and social, of the child and the teenager. The family remains a cornerstone for a new couples' early life and, sometimes, for the new families of sons and daughters. Drinking, as a traditional custom, as part of daily eating routines, or as sign of dysfunctional relations, is also a human activity that starts within the family.

The very notion of family is not constant from culture to culture. In the context of this chapter, the term "family" will refer not only to traditionally defined structures such as the nuclear family (mother, father, offspring) and the extended family (nuclear plus grandparents, uncles/aunts, etc.), but to primary caregivers whoever they may be (Sroufe, Fox, & Pancake, 1983). Indeed, decades of research have shown that it is more the type and quality of human interaction in small groups rearing children than the specific genetic kinship that matters when it comes to human growth, development, and learning. It should remain clear, however, that heredity contributes key components of human functioning, specially those related to certain propensities.

Concerning learning to drink, the main difference between nuclear and extended families probably lies in the number and frequency of opportunities for children to acquire interactive skills. When both parents have to work (even at home), the presence of grandparents and other relatives or caregivers in the home is likely to effectively and successfully supplement child-rearing practices (Hernandez-Guzman & Lopez-Morales, 1999).

Systematic examination of the role of culture and the family in understanding how one learns about drinking involves consideration of several components of human life and social structure. Such components can be conceived of as interactive systems in the sense that they involve variables whose values affect each other's influence on human behavior, and learning to drink does not seem to be an exception. These systems can be rank ordered in terms of their inclusiveness or generality. Moving from a more general or macroscopic analysis to a more specific one, one could include, first, the larger social and cultural context; second, the small group system or family behavior and response; and third, the complex determinants of behavior within the individual (Ward & Faillace, 1970).

The present chapter is thus aimed at overviewing the two-way relationship between drinking and the family and takes a closer look at some specific ways in which certain psychological and social mechanisms seem to account for the acquisition of drinking patterns in the family. At every step the chapter seeks to base its analysis on research findings, both classic and recent, in such fields as psychology, public health, human development, and anthropology. The chapter, for example, draws on customs related to drinking in various parts of the world, and are based on either research conducted by the authors themselves or data collected expressly for inclusion in the chapter.

The chapter first looks at how alcohol consumption has become an inseparable component of culture expressed through family customs. Some key questions addressed include how socialization within the family helps to account for different ways of interacting with alcoholic beverages, and how social, emotional, and behavioral aspects of family life gradually shape both the styles and functions of drinking.

Next, the chapter looks at what happens when people drink. A behavior learned within the usually closed and relatively protected context of family and friends may quickly become an activity occurring in situations involving new people and different social rules as part of cultural discontinuities likely to occur anywhere in the world. As a natural continuation of this discussion the chapter goes on to examine how acculturation patterns can end up in either healthy or problem drinking as a function of parenting styles and family attitudes, values, and models.

The next section analyzes drinking in the family in greater depth—how seemingly informal or casual rules may well determine a good portion of how we drink, as well as how the dynamics of family interaction tend to either ameliorate a drinking problem or make it worse.

Finally, the chapter attempts to transform the main research findings discussed in the various sections into sets of recommendations on learning about drinking for educational institutions, primary health care providers, the media, and pertinent government agencies.

ALCOHOL, DRINKING, AND CULTURE

Drinking as an Expression of Traditional Values and Activities

Drinking is probably as ancient as civilization itself. Some anthropological hypotheses concerning early community life place the oldest accounts of drinking some type of alcohol beverage in periods starting as long as 10,000 years ago in the Near East and Meso-America (Heath, 1982). Although the actual craft of purposefully producing alcohol beverages seems to have developed only gradually over many years in the early history of community living, the bodily and psychological sensations produced by the ingestion of alcohol brews might well be as old as the first time a human became intoxicated. Perhaps as a result of both haphazard and deliberately sought contacts with alcohol, an everyday intimacy between drinking and daily living probably developed. For example, in the first encyclopedia (his *Historia Naturalis*), dating back to ancient Roman times, Pliny the Elder described both the positive attributes of wines as well as the harmful consequences of heavy consumption for the individual and society (Jellinek, 1976a; Poldrugo, 1993). Thus, increasing contact with alcohol and all its related experiences have ended up producing a sense of familiarity.

Families in many societies, primitive and contemporary, have engaged in celebrations whose natural or social histories include the use of alcohol. Traditional values thus become, at the same time, unwritten rules that socially govern family and individual behavior, and social characteristics likely to become objects of study for sociologists, anthropologists, and psychologists.

Drinking, Age and Sex

It is only natural to assume that the corresponding traditional family ways and activities will also come to determine such norms as how much, when, and who is expected to drink. These social and cultural boundaries usually relate more specifically to age and sex. While most societies, primitive or contemporary, set some type of formal norm, conventional limits for drinking relating to age and sex within specific communities are likely to act as more immediate regulating factors. Both sets of variables (i.e., age and sex) end up determining powerful learning opportunities. The first usually leads to such legal consequences as formal sanctions and arrests, which vary greatly among countries, not only in their formal definitions (Havard, 1992; Porter, Arif, & Curran, 1986) but also in implementation (Poldrugo & Patussi, 1996); the second leads to natural interpersonal sanctions such as acceptance or rejection (Block, 1983).

For example, in some small towns and rural areas of Latin American countries such as Mexico, old traditions became interwoven with more recent customs. One such tradition is a type of "organized" drinking during traditional festivities. In some communities a "godfather" is elected yearly and becomes the person responsible for seeing that access to alcoholic beverages is somehow guaranteed in the community for the following year. This is a very prestigious responsibility to hold. Drinking in these communities, however, is highly regulated. The rules do not apply equally to men and women or to different ages. Just as drinking and drunkenness are often tolerated in males and regarded as a sign of masculinity or autonomy, they are regarded as pernicious in females and children, or even in young teenage males. Sometimes, however, drinking becomes a regular component of initiating teenage males in the responsibilities of agricultural labor in the fields. Sharing small amounts of alcohol at the beginning and progressing toward larger amounts, the adolescent gradually acquires with increasing family status (surpassing that of his mother); this is also expected to serve as part of the initiation rites for becoming a man. This in turn will grant him further access to drinking, a privilege of grown-ups in its own right (Sanchez-Sosa, 1998b).

Attitudes Toward Drunkenness

In some cultural contexts drunkenness is relatively more tolerated (for instance, the North European countries), while in others (e.g., the South Mediterranean countries) drunkenness is not socially accepted (Poldrugo & Urizzi, 1992). Although social and cultural acceptance of underage drinking varies depending on the immediate context, nearly all cultures strongly disapprove of underage drunkenness, especially among women (Bahr, Marcos, & Maughan, 1995). However, some societies exert strong informal controls on drunkenness. In a study conducted in the U.S. and Italy, the frequency of intoxication among young subjects was found to be markedly lower in the latter country, where intoxication is strongly disapproved of (Cherpitel, Flaminio, & Poldrugo, 1993). Drunkenness is relatively more tolerated among elderly men because the community considers that they have fulfilled their obligations toward society (Gordon, 1989). In the appropriate social context, drunkenness is generally perceived as an opportunity for "time out" from daily or existential pressures, which serves the purpose of allowing people to reduce tension without a requirement of social propriety, in ways that would otherwise elicit criticism or rejection (Heath, 1982). Since both the social correctness of drunkenness and its explanations are usually sociocultural in nature, in the sense of dealing with attitudes and values, it has been suggested that the drunken component of alcohol use is an essentially learned affair (MacAndrew & Edgerton, 1969).

ALCOHOL, CULTURE AND THE FAMILY

Children's Socialization Process and the Family

Probably the most important factors that determine the way we learn most interactive patterns are the set of processes known as socialization. Learning about drinking is certainly no exception (Barnes, 1977; Levine & Kozak, 1979). Although definitions of socialization may vary depending on theoretical scope and methodologies, most conceptions are in accord in pointing out that adults in every culture face the same major tasks in rearing children. First, they must provide infants with the basic nurturing needed for development. Second, they must prepare children to function as adults in their particular social environment. In general, socialization involves passing on to children the rules, standards, and values of their culture (Sroufe, Cooper, & DeHart, 1996). Initially, socialization simply involves responding to the expectations that parents and others in charge express. During a second phase, which is especially important for learning about drinking, the child begins to internalize these standards, i.e., she or he will behave accordingly even when she or he is alone.

Two main mechanisms usually account for socialization as a general process. One implies that rules and values are somehow imposed upon an unwilling child by parents and other adults. The other proposes that children naturally take on those rules and values because, in the regular course of events, children want to comply with adults' requests and expectations (Sroufe et al., 1996). In any event, a good portion of the social, emotional, and instrumental skills that affect the way human beings establish and manage contact with alcohol beverages are very likely to stem from the way they were socialized. Socialization as a process starts in early childhood, but its components and basic mechanisms continue to affect the way we learn new socially adaptive skills all our lives. It probably includes both experiences and skills whose learning leaves little social room for options, as well as the incorporation of new standards which we voluntarily adopt to conform to new acculturation patterns.

Indeed, some well-documented contemporary models of adaptive functioning during the life span of human individuals propose that a good portion of the relative success by which human beings lead healthy, productive lives depends on the individual's effective interaction with the components of both successive and overlapping systems (Hernandez-Guzman, 1999; Kellam & Werthamer-Larsson, 1986). Thus, for example, the family system will dominate from birth and until the child enters the school system. This new system (peers, teachers, etc.) then starts to make key contributions in the sense that one learns new socially adaptive skills. Other systems will progressively appear on the scene, replacing for previous ones or overlapping with them, and each (or each new combination) demanding the acquisition of new social or interpersonal adaptive skills. Thus, when we get our first job, when we start living with a spouse, when we have our first child, and so on, we are actually interacting with the physical and social environments in such a way that each new system presents new demands. Indeed, losing our health, retiring and starting to lose our friends to sickness and old age represent more challenges, not fewer.

Each system transition or addition will present the human individual with challenges that may well involve demands that are difficult to meet, thereby generating stress and anxiety. It is the characteristics of such requirements and our own learned preparedness that will determine how successfully we cope with the demands posed by those new or overlapping systems. Sometimes we will not be able to cope fully with changing transitions even if they appear gradually. In principle, this can occur at any time during life's continuum: during very early transitions in childhood, all the way to the very last one. Hence, the importance of designing and implementing interventions designed to educate the family, schoolteachers, and others, on interactive or parenting strategies. Such interventions are very likely to be preventive in nature (Sanchez-Sosa, 1998a).

Although schools of thought in the area of human development and social learning differ in emphasis as to the processes leading to successful human functioning, many point to certain basic experiences and parenting styles during early childhood that tend to act as predictors for (or are associated with) later substance use. In general, positive parenting qualities include warmth, emotional responsiveness, sharing positive feelings with the child, and accepting his/her autonomy. Children reared by parents possessing these qualities tend to be socially competent with peers and cooperative with parents, especially if the internalization process mentioned above occurs on the basis of mutually positive affection (Kochanska, Aksan, & Koenig, 1995). Other more specific findings suggest that mutually hostile patterns of parental interaction are associated with aggression and related problems in children, while a pattern in which the father becomes angry and withdrawn is associated with such problems as anxiety (Katz & Gottman, 1993). In fact, parental hostility directed toward children has been associated with adolescent antisocial behavior, association with deviant peers, and alcohol use (Webster, Hunter, & Keats, 1994). Also, parental marital distress is directly related to adolescent drinking, as a possible strategy to cope with family stress, and perhaps through the disruption of parents' ability to function as effective agents of social control, leaving such control in the hands of peers (Simons, Whitbeck, Conger, & Melby, 1991; Vaz-Serra, Canavarro, & Ramalheira, 1998).

Another aspect of socialization involves personal effectiveness and self-management. Starting in middle childhood (ages 6 through 12 years) and consolidating in adolescence, children develop the belief that they can master and prevail in challenging circumstances, and that their successes come from resources within (Oettingen, Little, Lindenberger, & Baltes, 1994). This process is partially based on child-rearing patterns that promote the child's access to opportunities, providing approval for successes and support and understanding for failures. Middle childhood involves a period of social expansion. During this period children first form loyal friendships and peer relations based on mutual trust and support, so they understand the meaning of being part of a group with norms to which they adhere. Since children face these social and emotional tasks in the context of the family, parents' styles of discipline, attitudes toward sex roles, and marital conflict are likely to be very influential (Sroufe et al., 1996).

From middle childhood until adolescence there is a tendency to use others as a source of information in evaluating one's own behavior. This transition period usually involves gradually reducing parental influence and progressively taking peers into account as a basis for social comparisons leading to self-assessment

(Ruble, 1988; Collins & Repinski, 1994).This does not mean that parents' influence disappears, but it will tend to occur in the context of more complex and competing sources of social feedback. In addition, preferences for activities will progressively conform to traditional gender roles. This will also play an important role later on, when the adolescent has to cope with situations in which alcohol is available or actually offered to him/her. If such roles deviate from traditionally accepted gender roles, teenagers tend to criticize themselves (Bussey & Bandura, 1992) This, of course, assumes that the teenager's main socializing group is one where drinking is relatively customary. Again, it is highly likely that a good portion of both the personal style and its social consequences will be mediated by sex role socialization.

In general, sex role development for boys seems characterized more by socialization toward independent exploration and mastery of the external world, whereas girls are socialized more toward the interpersonal world, and independent exploration is often discouraged or closely monitored. Hence, by middle adolescence, boys may be less dependent than girls on family support for gender role identity issues and coping with stressful life events. For girls, low levels of family support may be perceived as inconsonant with their sex role and highly stressful (Block, 1983; Huston, 1983), which is a likely reason why girls seem to use alcohol for anxiety reduction more than boys (Pulkkinen & Pitkanen, 1994).

Cultural Continuities and Discontinuities Socialization and social learning always occur in a cultural context. It is possible that what we learned in a particular cultural context may not remain as useful or as socially adaptive if our own cultural context changes or if we must adapt to a different cultural system altogether. Thus, discontinuities within a culture or those reflecting a different one are very likely to require new learning, which might represent personal cost or social conflict.

Cultural discontinuities between the interpersonal contexts of the family and those present at school, work, or on the street also represent risk factors that may interfere with learning to drink moderately. Also, discontinuities between children's socialization in a family-dependent mode and demands for independence from adults can sometimes represent risk. In general, therefore, the discontinuity between the expectation of normal adult behavior and patterns of child-rearing lacking in adequate types of interaction and learning opportunities can act as predictors for maladaptive functioning (Bacon, Barry, & Child, 1965). Similar differences can be appreciated when we compare child-rearing philosophies, methods, beliefs, and values between home and care facilities in early child care (Honig, 1991).

For example, for adolescents from relatively affluent families, in large urban areas in Latin America, whether Buenos Aires, Mexico City, Lima, Santiago or Rio de Janeiro, and probably in the cities of many other countries, the "disco" is usually the mingling place of choice. In these settings, discos tend to appear, flourish, become the place where "the action is," and then gradually lose their appeal and eventually slip into oblivion, only to reappear in a few months newly and luxuriously remodeled, with a different highly attractive name, and become once more "the" place. Social behavior, drinking included, in these settings frequently represent formal or informal rules, usually tending toward ample tolerance, very different from those learned in the family. If adolescents lack the skills required to transfer interpersonal skills to this new setting, and the setting itself provides few opportunities to learn effective ways to interact, problem drinking may develop, specially if a priority of these types of settings is to make alcohol beverages very easily available in order to promote consumption (Sanchez-Sosa, 1998b).

In contrast, continuity between the cultural context in which we originally learn about drinking, and that requiring new general and useful social interaction for other purposes of human interaction (which may well involve the presence of alcohol) later in life, may help one to display overall adaptive behavior (Williams & Shams, 1998). Drinking and the drinking context can be integrative, conflict-reducing, and reinforcing of group identity and sense of belonging. Individuals, however, use alcohol and drinking contexts with either successful or unsuccessful results (Gordon, 1989). For example, it has been demonstrated that studying at a foreign university in a "wet" country resulted in Muslim students adopting the local drinking patterns, sometimes leading to more problematic drinking than among the locals (Poldrugo & Sferch, 1991). The less similar the conditions under which we learn to drink are to those in which we need to resist peer pressure, the lower the likelihood that we will succeed. Other discontinuities that may lead to unsuccessful outcomes are those where past and present traditions produce different social expectations about drinking. Again, discontinuities disrupt familiarity and hence adaptive (i.e., moderate) drinking behavior could require relearning.

Perhaps extreme cases of the deleterious effects of cultural discontinuity are exemplified in conditions such as those surrounding families that have to move to areas representing unfamiliar cultural contexts. This may involve relatively mild discontinuity, such as moving to a different region of one's own country, or having to move to a country that is radically unfamiliar in just about every respect. When one is suddenly in a place where unfamiliarity ranges all the way from the weather to nearly all aspects of culture (including language, religion, food, and so forth), social adaptation can be extremely stressful and, in some cases, traumatic (D'Avanzo, Frye, & Froman, 1994; Saenz & Sanchez-Sosa, 1996).

Acculturation Patterns Learning to adapt to other cultures or even to relatively fast transformations in our own requires not only establishing new interpersonal and instrumental skills but also achieving the appropriate cognitive and emotional changes. The cultural context for this readaptation in the case of alcohol consumption may be particularly complex. One reason, among several, for this complexity resides in the fact that the beliefs and behaviors that relate to alcohol are often unlike those that relate to other beverages. Sometimes adapting to new cultural demands may act as a two-edged sword in the sense that we need to adapt to both positive and negative demands. On the one hand, the more competent we become at dealing with new social and cultural demands, the higher the probability that we will function in productive and effective ways including personal and family well-being, in addition to having better opportunities for growth, economic or otherwise. On the other hand, we are also likely to learn values, beliefs, and behaviors that may well bring us closer to anxiety, conflict, personal attrition, addictions, hopelessness and, in general, mental health deterioration. This risk seems better documented in cases where individuals or families must migrate from relatively traditional societies and environments to highly industrialized ones, such as large urban areas that are especially likely to be experienced as impersonal or intolerant.

Once individuals or families start interacting with new social and cultural conditions, an acculturation process begins in which people develop patterns of behavior aimed at adopting the ways and customs of the host culture. This acquisition of other social customs, at the expense of losing those learned in a culture that may have emphasized, for example, family closeness and mutual support and affection as opposed to high competitiveness, can constitute a serious risk for alcohol misuse and other negative outcomes (O'Nell & Mitchell, 1996). Recent Chinese-, Korean-, Vietnamese-, or Mexican-American migrant families give greater importance to connectedness to the family, clan, and community than mainstream Americans (Spiegel, 1982). While some of these characterisics may arise partially as a general result of interactions within a society perceived as relatively impersonal, intolerant, or even xenophobic, most recent studies on the relation between acculturation and alcohol use focus on more specific aspects of everyday life.

Some studies have found that highly acculturated individuals are more likely to abuse alcohol and other substances (Balcazar, Peterson, & Cobas, 1996; Farabee, Walisch, & Maxwell, 1995; Vega, Gil, & Zimmerman, 1993). Others have included explorations of similar effects on other addictive and maladaptive behaviors, including mental health complaints (Beauvais, 1992; Santos, Bohon, & Sanchez-Sosa, 1998). Further studies have evaluated the role of lowered assertiveness and self-esteem as frequent components of the overall effects of acculturation (Goldberg & Botvin, 1993; Kahn & Fua, 1995). Still others link the negative effects to a more generalized acculturation stress response (Beauvais, 1992; Zimmerman & Sodowsky, 1993).

Acculturation processes vary with the time of observation. Studies have, for example, focused on acculturation and drinking in Italian families who had migrated to the U.S., examining age and sex as mediators of acculturational shifts (Blane, 1977; Williams & Straus, 1950). It was expected, from a traditional assimilation model, that drinking practices among Italian Americans would become more "Americanized" with succesive generations in the U.S. More particularly, it was expected that, over generations, drinking would become less prevalent and frequent, but peak experiences and heavy drinking would nevertheless increase, especially among young adults. It was also thought that the amount of absolute alcohol consumed would decrease, and emphasis on the traditional beverages—wine and cordials—shown in early generations would give way to an emphasis, in later generations, on the American beverages—beer and distilled spirits.

Decreases in daily drinking, frequency of drinking occasions, the general level of consumption, and the consumption of traditional beverages were indeed found. Additionally, an increase in amount consumed per drinking occasion, frequent heavy drinking and, among women, consumption of distilled spirits was confirmed. However, the predicted decrease in prevalence was not found and, in fact, prevalence increased somewhat among later-generation women. Beer consumption, rather than increasing, declined with generations, and consumption of distilled spirits by men neither decreased nor increased. Very interestingly, aspects of drinking behavior from both Italy and the U.S. were selected to form a third distinct drinking pattern. This drinking pattern differs from the patterns found in Italians today which are related to recent changes in the whole Italian culture. Italy is witnessing a drastic decrease in wine consumption at home and an increase in beer consumption by youth in public premises (Rossi, 1994).

The Family as the Main Resource Toward Healthy Drinking

In the context of both socialization and acculturation, there are natural psychological processes that play particularly important roles in social learning, and, hence, in healthy adaptation to changing conditions. One such process is modeling. Modeling has helped explain a wide array of human behaviors. As will be seen, modeling in the context of family interaction helps to clarify some key aspects of learning about drinking.

As early as the third decade of the 20th century, scientific opinion on the relation between family interaction and the development of human problems pointed to family life as both a key source and context for individual, interpersonal, or even social dysfunction. One such early account (Germane & Germane, 1929) describes some basic parental strategies aimed at "building the character of children." In addition to the enrichment of children's personality through cooperation between home and school, the authors make five interesting proposals. These were part of a program that would:

- take the laws of learning into consideration;
- reduce the use of coercion;
- institute a democracy in the home (with certain responsibilities for each family member);
- promote friendliness, companionship, and courtesy between children and adults; and
- foster reading of good books.

Another early report contains a study conducted with 288 children who presented different behavior problems ranging from organic nervous diseases to uncontrollable moodiness or having a disturbed social order (Klingmann, 1935). An interesting feature of these two early contributions is the specific suggestion that the imitation of faulty parental patterns of behavior was at least partially responsible for the children's problems, with the implicit idea that imitation (and hence modeling) can indeed act in either positive or negative ways.

Parental Attitudes and Behaviors Toward Food and Alcohol Within the area of substance abuse two early authors also linked family structure and function to both parental drinking and juvenile alcohol abuse (Channing, 1927; Gillin, 1933). As will be seen later, imitation and modeling are probably the most frequently cited mechanisms mediating parental influence on the development of youth's drinking patterns, although other factors also play key roles.

More recent attempts to look for family factors predicting the development of particular drinking patterns have included the analysis of variables ranging from inherited propensities and sociodemographic characteristics to relatively specific types of family interaction and child-rearing practices. The contribution of heredity to drinking behavior through the analysis of inherited characteristics or traits between parents and offspring is relatively extensively covered in the research literature and its review would fall beyond the scope of the present chapter. It is important to point out, however, that most such studies conclude that both heredity *and* family environment, in the form of interaction among the various family members since early childhood, help to form drinking patterns. Some relatively recent "fine-grain" studies involving cohorts of adoptive and biological adolescents point out that considerable portions of the total variance of drinking patterns can be attributed to family environmental variables shared by adolescents growing up in the same home (McGue, Sharma, & Benson, 1996). In any event, family environment is seen as an important mediator of genetic vulnerability regarding the development of drinking patterns (Bennett, Wolin, Reiss, & Teitelbaum, 1987).

Also, numerous studies have shown clear relations between socioeconomic and demographic variables of families and the development of drinking patterns (especially alcohol abuse). One reason why such contributions are not described in this chapter stems from the perspective of developmental research and the reasonable point cautioning against attributing causality to variables that could be described as "social address labels" such as social class or family structure. Such labels are more appropriately regarded as proxies for social processes that may covary with the category in question (Bronfenbrenner, 1986). It should remain clear, however, that such variables are highly valuable for other purposes such as analyzing general epidemiological trends or for institutional policymaking.

The Modeling Hypothesis Modeling is a factor that has received considerable attention as a key contributor to the establishment of alcohol consumption patterns. Since imitation is the core mechanism of modeling, the outcome of modeling as a type of interaction occurring in the family can, in principle, work on any behavior and in whatever direction, i.e., leading to low or high rates. Since most human learning develops on the basis of functional interactions among people living together rather than on the "formal" role of its member, by family will not only be referred to as those persons with biological kinship but also to the significant person or group of significant persons with whom the child who learns to drink primarily relates emotionally (Ablon, 1989).

The family members who are naturally most likely to serve as role models during childhood and early adolescence are the parents or other significant adults who perform the main child-rearing tasks. If these adults drink, the young person will learn to imitate part or most of the drinking patterns and associated behaviors, just as she or he will probably learn to associate particular emotions, expression, beliefs, interpersonal styles, and so on with particular drinking patterns. Thus, in principle, if role-model adults drink in moderation and behave in positive ways while doing so, most children would be expected to conform to the appropriate pattern by learning it along similar personal, family, and social dimensions (Casswell, Brasch, Gilmore, & Silva, 1985). This effect is especially likely to occur if there is a high-quality affective and interpersonal interaction between the learner and the model or models (Andrews, Hops, & Duncan, 1997). Correspondingly, young Australian males have been found to have attitudes towards drinking similar to those held by their fathers, and daughters tend to hold sets of attitudes similar to their mothers (Evans & Roche, 1998).

Numerous studies have documented the role of modeling in learning to drink. Since it is not likely that modeling alone can explain the acquisition of most drinking styles, and other interaction and learning factors also occur in the family context, most recent studies have tried to analyze the relative contribution of some such factors. It should be apparent that parental modeling does not exert its effects on learning to drink in an isolated fashion. Thus, some studies have explored modeling in interaction with other components of child-rearing. Such studies include, in addition to affection and family support, the establishment and enforcement of understandable and rational family rules about drinking. Being positive role models and maintaining clear family rules helps parents to teach children skills to strengthen their resistance to unhealthy alcohol use (Homonoff, Martin, Rimpas, & Henderson, 1994).

The case for modeling and social consequences as components of learning about alcohol has also been made in the context of relations with peers, especially during late childhood as well as adolescence. In general, most of the same factors or combinations of variables operating within the family also apply in the context of relations with peers, whether at school or work, in the community, or on the streets. One reason why adolescents drink is because they seem to derive benefits from the use or misuse of alcohol, such as increased self-confidence and adult status (Ziervogel, Ahmed, Flisher, & Robertson, 1997–1998), but a good portion of the peers' influence on the use of alcohol is actually modulated by the type and quality of previous family interaction. Sometimes the family, rather than peers, seems to be the strongest long-term influence on drinking patterns. Adolescents with drinking problems are likely to have more distant emotional ties to their families and poor coping abilities (Barnes, 1977). There also seem to be cross-time influences of an affectionate relationship with parents and prosocial peer affiliation, as well as with the type of self-esteem that derives from mastering some skill or ability (Spoth, Redmond, Hockaday, & Yoo, 1996). One effect of good affectionate parental and family relations is to make adolescents more sensible at peer selection (Frauenglass, Routh, Pantin, & Mason, 1997).

Sometimes peers' modeling and interaction can have a negative effect on learning responsible drinking patterns. Some peers may have a poor family and child-rearing history related to drinking, but otherwise appear "cool" and attractive as role models. Sometimes peers can promote alcohol abuse through group affiliation (via modeling), or by being outright manipulative and pushy (Swaim, Bates, & Chavez, 1997). Again, a solid family history can protect the child or adolescent from such negative peer influences in several ways. Family social support has been shown to reduce the influence of deviant peers on several problem behaviors, including alcohol abuse (Blanton & Gibbons, 1997). Child attachment to parents and association with peers having prosocial norms help to teach alcohol refusal skills, thereby becoming important protective factors (Frauenglass et al., 1997; Spoth, Yoo, Kahn, & Redmond, 1996). Also, adolescents whose parents have inculcated in them a commitment to high educational achievement, associated in turn with solid family bonds, tend to drink in smaller quantities and less frequently (Bahr et al., 1995).

Recent findings also suggest that resisting negative influences of peers can work through the effect of the emotional aplomb and assertiveness that go together with high self-esteem. Youths with consistently high or moderate but rising self-esteem show less susceptibility to peer pressure over time than youths with low or decreasing levels of self-esteem (Zimmerman, Copeland, Shope, & Dielman, 1997). It is also interesting to note that peer perception can be more influential in determining the effects of peer modeling or interpersonal influence than actual peer behavior. In fact, adolescents' perceptions of friends' alcohol use, perceptions of family use, and actual use of classmates have been shown to be better predictors of substance use than was friends' actual use, i.e., adolescents often overestimate alcohol use among peers (Iannotti & Bush, 1992). Thus, if a teenager believes that a friend she or he looks up to drinks heavily and seems to have a great time, it is likely that she or he may drink more, even if the "model" does not actually drink that much but perhaps brags a lot about it, or if others share the (exaggerated) view that the model drinks a lot and enjoys it. As in many other cases, it is more our cognitive interpretation of a fact than the actual features of the fact itself that is the moving mechanism that produces an attitude or a behavior change.

Another set of factors determining how we learn to drink in the family may be related to how well we learn to handle stress, pressure, and negative emotions in general. It appears that the contention that the primary function of alcoholic beverages in primitive societies was the reduction of anxiety (Horton, 1943) is becoming increasingly relevant in contemporary society (Hussong & Chassin, 1994). To the extent that stress seems to be an unavoidable component of modern life, and anxiety is a frequent human reaction to stress, it would be natural to expect that alcohol consumption and coping with stress are probably a two-way phenomenon. Recent research conducted on adults' motives for using alcohol consistently shows that reducing anxiety is a frequent reason to drink. This can occur because relating to our world makes us anxious, and drinking, it is assumed, helps to reduce the feeling, and/or because we see others dealing with life's tensions with alcohol's help (Baer, Garmezy, McLaughlin, Pokorny, & Wernick, 1987).

Few studies have specifically documented poor stress management or relatively high anxiety levels as leading to problem drinking among teenagers. Some recent studies with adolescents establish a coexistence of anxiety disorders with alcohol abuse. Such disorders may either lead to problem drinking, be the result of it, or result from the combination of other risk factors (Clark & Bukstein, 1998; Deas-Nesmith, Campbell, & Brady, 1998). In general, clinical observations suggest that anxiety and affective disorders contribute to the development of alcohol abuse in adolescents but, again, other factors may be producing both sets of problems (Clark & Neighbors, 1996). Interestingly, alcohol disorders in adolescents generally follow rather than precede the onset of other psychological problems (Rohde, Lewinsohn, & Seeley, 1996).

Children's Initiation to Regular Drinking As already discussed, the decision whether to drink and how much to drink is largely regulated through social norms and social control in various social settings, since alcohol drinking is to a large extent a social behavior that is learned and molded through social interaction with other people (Skog, 1987). However, while cultural norms that influence the drinking behavior of the defined alcoholic have been explored in the literature, the importance of sociocultural factors in shaping family behavior and interactions, and in shaping family attitudes toward drinking and the drinker, have been largely ignored (Ablon, 1989). This is paradoxical since the family is of great importance in exerting informal social control with regard to drinking. It is within the domain of the family that alcohol is introduced and enjoyed. The family thereby serves as the main resource for prevention and control of excessive drinking.

The family exerts a primary influence on children's early drinking through the child's initiation to drinking. This is a highly culture-specific process. The first taste of alcohol normally occurs with parents, although with little discussion or conscious modeling by them. When children are allowed to be present, or are actually encouraged to participate in family and social functions (which can be as simple as eating together or as complex as an elaborate ceremony), the feelings, ideas, behaviors, and sensations related to those situations become commonplace. Such familiarity is likely to produce a socially shared feeling that such occasions are comfortable and, eventually, desirable. This is true in very different countries; in South Africa, for example, African parents endorse their children's drinking on occasions when traditional home-brewed beer is served (Samuels, Schneider, & Everatt, 1998). As another example, early learning about wine, and its institutionalization in the home as part of the diet, are the main characteristics of Italian drinking (Jessor, Young, Young, & Tesi, 1970; Morgan, 1982; Poldrugo & Urizzi, 1992). In the "initiation phase," wine is introduced early (between 9 and 12 years of age), in the family context and in moderation (Jellinek, 1976b; Lolli et al., 1952). The "consolidation phase" follows (between 15 and 17 years of age); this is more related to peer behavior (Monarca et al., 1991). It is only later, when living outside the family for the first time, for example during compulsory military service for males, that continuous excessive drinking may be experienced (Poldrugo & Stratta, 1993). In France, it has been found that 10% of soldiers show alcohol-related problems because of their separation from the family and the monotony of military life (Osservatorio Permanente sui Giovani e l'Alcool, 1994).

The likely long-term outcome of turning experiences in the family into articulated habits probably involves a range of other variables acting in synergy at an individual level. Among such variables are habituation, social reinforcement, and the psychophysiological effects of alcohol itself, among many others. Thus, behaviors and attitudes of an intoxicated person that may initially be perceived by the child (and others) as exaggerated or even frightening (e.g., loud arguments or grotesque gesturing) may become, with repetition, an accepted or expected component of a custom or celebration or a person's mere presence. The mechanism that mediates this gradual loss of reactivity may well be the same one that regulates the decrease of alarm reactions in humans (Bradley, Lang, & Cuthbert, 1993; Vial, Fernandez, & Godoy, 1992). The combined sensation of interpersonal disinhibition typical of mild alcohol intoxication, socially expressed acceptance and affection, and fulfillment of some social duty or positive consequence also contribute to effective learning and maintenance of many behaviors and attitudes regarding the use of alcohol.

Drinking in the Family

Married people have been found to drink less (Celentano & MacQueen, 1984), less often to be heavy drinkers (Neve, Lemmens, & Drop, 1997) and to have fewer drinking problems (Horwitz & White, 1991). First, marriage contributes structure to everyday life. Marriage implies a mutual set of external social influences and pressure, of opportunities and constraints, which provide a common frame of reference including drinking contexts, and thereby different drinking patterns and social influences during drinking. Second, marriage acts as a normative mechanism. Being married implies social expectations and norms that do not necessarily refer to drinking, but to role obligations that can prevent heavy drinking.

Informal Control Among Family Members Normative control may be reinforced by the influence or control that spouses may exert on each other's drinking (Jarvinen, 1991; Room, Greenfield, & Weisner, 1991). However, studies have demonstrated that spouses tend to concur in regard to drinking behaviors. Hence, in married people, individual drinking behavior is in part structured at the level of the couple unit (Corbett, Mora, & Ames, 1991; Jacob & Bremer, 1986). This synchronization of alcohol drinking patterns is a result of different processes. A first process, occurring before the marital union, make the partners select each other according to their perceived characteristics, behaviors, attitudes and values, which include alcohol drinking. This is especially true for abstinence or heavy drinking (Jacob & Bremer, 1986). In studies conducted in alcoholics, it was found that females with an alcoholic father are more frequently married to an alcoholic husband (Sclare, 1970; Poldrugo & Fiore, 1988). The reciprocal influence in everyday life interaction, and the contextual cohesion of the couple unit, are the other processes coming into play.

How marriage regulates drinking behavior and which drinking behavior is regulated may be contingent upon the drinking culture. Different drinking cultures have different social norms and different ways and degrees of regulating drinking behavior through informal (as well as formal) social control. Empirical studies that shed light on such possible cultural differences are sparse. In a study of married couples living in Helsinki, Moscow, and Tallin, it was found that the spouses control over their partners drinking was less in the Finnish culture than in the Russian, although the Finnish couples drank more often together than did the Russian couples (Holmila, 1987; Holmila, Mustonen, & Rannik, 1990). In a study of alcoholic outpatients conducted in the U.S., it was reported that Black male alcoholics are more likely to drink with their spouses and to encourage them to drink than Puerto Rican alcoholics (Fernandez-Pol, Bluestone, Missouri, Morales, & Mizruchi, 1986).

An aspect of relevance to possible cultural differences is the impact of marriage on gender roles as they relate to drinking. These indeed may also be carriers of social norms regarding drinking in general, as well as deviant behavior. Social norms regarding drinking are gender-specific, and in most Western societies are more restrictive for women. The social control and social disapproval of women drinking have been said to serve two functions: to preserve the child-rearing role and to maintain social respectability (Waldron, 1988).

However, other confounding factors may act on role expectations. With regard to the effect of age, young couples are less likely to synchronize their drinking frequency than older ones, where drinking frequency is more likely to be structured outside the couple (Demers, Bisson, & Palluy, 1999).

There are indications that parenthood or the presence of young children results in less drinking and drunkenness (Cahalan & Room, 1974). The presence of children could therefore be at least partially responsible for the observed differences in drinking between married and unmarried people. Their influence is probably exerted through their contribution to the structure and regulation of everyday life (Bennett, Wolin, & Noonan, 1977; Wolin, Bennett, Noonan, & Teitelbaum, 1980). Let us be reminded that protective factors emerge from a family history of warmth, affection, support, and clear/consistent rules, and that this trend can start as early as in late childhood or early adolescence (Wills & Vaughan, 1989; Windle, 1992, 1995). Additional factors apparently acting as protectors include democratic styles at setting family rules (through rational discussion and agreement), educational/intellectual commitment and orientation, and some degree of religiousness (Heath, 1982; McGue et al., 1996). Again, different child-rearing practices mediated by diverse cultural patterns are likely to shape different ways of dealing with stress (King, Beals, Manson, & Trimble, 1992). Alcohol misuse is a possible outcome if our parental history does not provide us with either the emotional aplomb to resist negative feelings and pressures or the interpersonal and instrumental skills to deal with conflict (Hernandez-Guzman & Sanchez-Sosa, 1996; Johnson & Pandina, 1991).

Family Reaction to Heavy Drinking Another issue of concern is family reaction to heavy drinking. Heavy drinking produces continuous stress for others in the family and has different kinds of negative impacts on their health and ability to control their lives (Orford, 1984). The family members go through a process of adjustment to the crises of alcoholism over an extended period of time (Jackson, 1954). The concept of codependency has gained a prominant position in recent decades as one attempt to conceptualize the significant other's situation. However, the personality disorder assumption underlying the codependency concept has been extensively criticized (Hands & Dear, 1994). The spouses of alcoholics are now essentially viewed as normal people trying to cope with impaired partners (McCrady, Moreau, Paolino, & Longabaugh, 1982).

A recent study looking more closely into the actions and feelings of significant others (Holmila, 1997) showed that the more distant relatives, sisters and brothers, parents, and close friends typically adopted an attitude of resignation and trying to keep things looking normal. The spouses of the drinkers were the only ones who had a clear caregiving role in the family. The children of alcoholics, instead, attempted to minimize the harm by trying to keep out of the way of the parent drinker and managing their own lives. They also engaged in regulating and controlling the parent's drinking by making rules to govern it or by disposing of her or his drink. Having alcohol-abusing parents does not necessarily mean that the child will inevitably develop the same patterns, although it may be a risk factor for other psychological complaints because of the demands imposed by interacting with highly dysfunctional parents (Natera, Casco,

Herrejón, & Mora, 1993). Children of alcoholics, however, have higher probabilities of becoming alcoholics. In fact, between a quarter and a third of clinical alcoholics have been found to have an alcoholic parent (Cotton, 1979; Poldrugo & Fiore, 1988).

Parents who drink are less likely than nondrinking parents to monitor and articulate clear rules governing the behavior of their adolescent offspring (Peterson, Hawkins, Abbott, & Catalano, 1994). Alcoholic children have been found in families in which the rituals and the continuity of the family heritage over generations are substantially disrupted during the years in which the children grow up (Bennett et al., 1977; Wolin et al., 1980). The literature consistently shows that young people who frequently become drunk are often those with relational problems inside the family (especially alcohol misuse) (Osservatorio Permanente sui Giovani e l'Alcool, 1994; Poldrugo, 1988). Children of alcoholics are also genetically more vulnerable to alcohol, could have been hurt by alcohol during pregnancy, and are more frequently exposed to accidental overdose (Marchi, Messi, & Renier, 1991; Lamminpaa, 1995).

GENERAL RECOMMENDATIONS

For Educational Institutions

Since the influence of the family is essential in shaping childrens' attitudes towards alcohol drinking, greater attention should be paid to the educational role of the family from the early years on (Zucker, 1979). In general, children have positive attitudes toward alcohol drinking if no alcohol-related problems arise in their families (Casswell et al., 1985). As a consequence, family members could serve as a key resource in the promotion of healthy drinking in educational institutions, public or private. Updated curricula should probably include carefully chosen contents on alcohol norms and behaviors in the family, and not just describe the main consequences of excessive drinking. Innovative educational programs would include collaboration between teachers and parents (as well as other family members) on these issues, because reinforcing positive attitudes is the most appropriate target in addition to increasing knowledge. An appropriate level to begin to include these contents should probably be senior elementary school.

For Primary Health Care Providers

The family also acts as the primary group for alcohol-related problem prevention and intervention (Orford, 1994). As pointed out, the family exerts a cultural influence on drinking which should also become a crucial context in which the clinician designs and implements interventions with problem drinkers (Ablon, 1989; Holmila, 1992). Family members suffer psychological and economic distress (Holder & Hallan, 1986; Poldrugo, 1996) and require early intervention

(Baird, 1992). However, because of prevailing cultural attitudes and lack of competence, helping agencies in society tend to avoid intervention (Poldrugo, 1999). Unfortunately, the mainstream literature (Anglo-Saxon in origin) wrongly considers excessive alcohol use to be a private affair (Orford, 1994). Tackling alcohol problems, instead, needs to be culturally sensitive (Spiegel, 1982), and not every ethnic group feels comfortable with going into treatment (Kline, 1996) or with the emphasis on alcoholism as an individual's disease. Primary health care providers' efforts will prove unsuccessful if they omit to identify culture-specific attitudes, values, and expectancies; providing relevant information in a culturally sensitive manner to authoritative figures in the family (e.g., parents, or older brothers and sisters), who in turn would be asked to share the information with their children or younger siblings, can be, instead, a very effective preventive measure (Office for Substance Abuse Prevention, 1992).

Today, excessive alcohol consumption is wrongly considered to require professional and specialized therapy to the exclusion of other types of support. Primary health care providers often do not consider that health promotion is their responsibility, even though they may agree that most health systems are very likely to benefit from reducing the incidence of health problems related to alcohol abuse in their patients. Most health care providers could find ways to aim towards this goal, without much expense, with such simple strategies as using very brief alcohol problem screening questionnaires and without mentioning alcohol (Israel et al., 1996), or distributing low-cost, easy-to-understand leaflets in waiting rooms to patients and family members. In addition, if resources and conditions allow, physicians, health psychologists, nurses, social workers, and volunteers could incorporate comments and brief explanations on alcohol-related health problems into their regular contact with patients and family members (when appropriate). The formal addition of professional alcohol counseling is also a distinct possibility.

In cases of alcoholism, the role of the supporting network is essential for a positive treatment outcome (Favazza & Thompson, 1984), and primary health providers should enlist the powerful therapeutic alliance offered by family members. In some countries, e.g., in Italy, people still maintain strong ties and loyalty to the immediate and extended family, close friends, and perceived leaders of their social group (Rotunno & McGodrick, 1982). The active inclusion of families in the recovery process, following the initiation of community-based rehabilitative programs for the treatment of alcoholism, has proved to be the main ingredient leading to success (Fiore, Milievich, & Poldrugo, 1989; Aricò, Zannero, Galatola, Valenti, & Corrao, 1994).

For the Media

The media should contribute to the promotion of healthy drinking not only by abiding by norms with legal implications already in place, but by encouraging the adoption of additional self-designed ethical guidelines for the production and airing of alcohol-related messages, advertisements, etc. The alcohol industry and the media could attempt joint programs of mutual feedback on ways of turning research findings into effective advertising campaigns that promote healthy, moderate drinking by tapping into consumers' sensibility to the positive consequences of responsible alcohol consumption. It is especially important for the media to ensure that advertisements are presented so that it is practically impossible for any character portrayed to be interpreted as being younger than the local or national minimum legal age for drinking.

Some alcohol beverage companies are already doing a good job in inserting brief but easy-to-understand messages in advertisements directly suggesting to consumers that they drink in moderation. A fine example of intervention that could be promoted by the alcohol beverage industry was the experimental educational campaign launched in partnership with the European Commission (Osservatorio Permanente sui Giovani e l'Alcool, 1997). Preventive community action targeted French and Italian teenagers and included the distribution of documents, stickers, and posters and broadcasting of radio slogans. The result showed an increased awareness of the positive effects of moderate drinking and the role of parents in preventing excessive drinking. It is recommended that this practice be adopted by the whole industry.

For Government Agencies

The government departments responsible for education and health, and other appropriate institutions, should help to promote funding for research on the relatively specific conditions surrounding alcohol use and misuse in a country or region, with a special emphasis on the role of the family. This effort should also support the development of preventive interventions by experts and researchers so that universities and institutes also contribute to the overall program. Higher education and research institutions should also set up programs to provide feedback and help in the assessment of the effects of interventions and campaigns, including those that have family members as part of their focus.

REFERENCES

Ablon, J. (1989). Family research and alcoholism. In M. Galanter (Ed.), *Recent developments in alcoholism* (Vol. 7, pp. 383–395). New York: Plenum.

Andrews, J. A., Hops, H., & Duncan, S. C. (1997). Adolescent modeling of parent substance abuse: The moderating effect of the relationship with the parent. *Journal of Family Psychology, 11*, 259–270.

Aricò, S., Zannero, A., Galatola, G., Valenti, M., & Corrao, G. (1994). Family compliance to a treatment programme for alcoholics: A prospective study of prognostic factors. *Alcohol and Alcoholism, 29*, 679–685.

Bacon, M. K., Barry, H., & Child, I. L. (1965). A cross-cultural study of drinking. *Journal of Studies on Alcohol, 26* (Suppl. 3), 29–48.

Baer, P. E., Garmezy, L. B., McLaughlin, R. J., Pokorny, A. D., & Wernick, M. J. (1987). Stress, coping, family conflict, and adolescent alcohol use. *Journal of Behavioral Medicine, 10*, 449–466.

Bahr, S. J., Marcos, A. C., & Maughan, S. L. (1995). Family, educational and peer influences on the alcohol use of female and male adolescents. *Journal of Studies on Alcohol, 56*, 457–469.

Baird, M. (1992). Care of family members and other affected persons. In M. Fleming & K. Barry (Eds.), *Addictive disorders* (pp. 195–211). St. Louis, MO: Mosby-Yearbook.

Balcazar, H., Peterson, G., & Cobas, J. A. (1996). Acculturation and health-related risk behaviors among Mexican-American pregnant youth. *American Journal of Health Behavior, 20*, 425–433.

Barnes, G. M. (1977). The development of adolescent drinking behavior: An evaluative review of the impact of the socialization process within the family. *Adolescence, 12*, 571–591.

Beauvais, F. (1992). Characteristics of Indian youth and drug use. *American Indian and Alaska Native Mental Health Research, 5*, 51–67.

Bennett, L. A, Wolin S. J., & Noonan, D. L. (1977). Family identity and intergenerational recurrence of alcoholism. *Alcoholism. Journal on Alcoholism and Related Addictions, 13*, 100–108.

Bennett, L., Wolin, S., Reiss, D., & Teitelbaum, M. A. (1987). Couples at risk for transmission of alcoholism: Protective influences. *Family Process, 26*, 111–129.

Blane, H. T. (1977). Acculturation and drinking in an Italian-American community. *Journal of Studies on Alcohol, 38*, 1324–1346.

Blanton, H., & Gibbons, F. X. (1997). Role of family and peers in the development of prototypes associated with substance use. *Journal of Family Psychology, 11*, 271–288.

Block, J. H. (1983). Differential premises arising from differential socialization of the sexes: Some conjectures. *Child Development, 54*, 1335–1354.

Bradley, M. M., Lang, P. J., & Cuthbert, B. N. (1993). Emotion, novelty and the startle reflex: Habituation in humans. *Behavioral Neuroscience, 107*, 970–980.

Bronfenbrenner, U. (1986). Ecology of the family as a context for human development. *Developmental Psychology, 22*, 723–742.

Bussey, K., & Bandura, A. (1992). Self-regulatory mechanisms governing gender development. *Child Development, 63*, 1236–1250.

Cahalan, D., & Room, R. (1974). *Problem drinking among American men.* New Brunswick, NJ: Rutgers Center of Alcohol Studies.

Casswell, S., Brasch, P., Gilmore, L., & Silva, P. (1985). Children's attitudes to alcohol awareness of alcohol-related problems. *British Journal of Addictions, 80*, 191–194.

Celentano, D. D., & McQueen, D. V. (1984). Multiple substance abuse among women with alcohol-related problems. In S. Wilsnack & L. Beckman (Eds.), *Alcohol problems in women: Antecedents, consequences, and intervention* (pp. 97–116). New York: Guilford Press.

Channing, A. (1927). Alcoholism among parents of juvenile delinquents. *Social Service Review, 1*, 357–383.

Cherpitel, C., Flaminio, D., & Poldrugo, F. (1993). Alcohol and casualities in the Emergency Room: A US-Italy comparison of weekdays and weekend evenings. *Addiction Research, 3*, 223–238.

Clark, D. B., & Bukstein, O. G. (1998). Psychopathology in adolescent alcohol abuse and dependence. *Alcohol Health and Research World, 22*, 117–126.

Clark, D. B., & Neighbors, B. (1996). Adolescent substance abuse and internalizing disorders. *Child and Adolescent Psychiatric Clinics of North America, 5*, 45–57.

Collins, W. A., & Repinski, D. J. (1994). Relationships during adolescence: Continuity and change in interpersonal perspective. In R. Montemayor, G. R. Adams, & T. P. Gullotta (Eds.), *Personal relationships during adolescence* (pp. 7–36). Thousand Oaks, CA: Sage.

Corbett, K., Mora, J., & Ames, G. (1991). Drinking patterns and drinking-related problems of Mexican-American husbands and wives. *Journal of Studies on Alcohol, 52*, 215–223.

Cotton, N. (1979). The familial incidence of alcoholism. A review. *Journal of Studies on Alcohol, 40*, 89–116.

D'Avanzo, C. E., Frye, B., & Froman, R. (1994). Culture, stress and substance use in Cambodian refugee women. *Journal of Studies on Alcohol, 55*, 420–426.

Deas-Nesmith, D., Campbell, S., & Brady, K. T. (1998). Substance use disorders in an adolescent inpatient psychiatric population. *Journal of the National Medical Association, 90*, 233–238.

Demers, A., Bisson, J., & Palluy, J. (1999). Wives' convergence with their husbands' alcohol use: Social conditions as mediators. *Journal of Studies on Alcohol, 60*, 368–377.

Evans, K. R., & Roche, A. M. (1998). *Learning to drink.* Unpublished paper presented at a meeting of the Working Group on Learning about Drinking, International Center for Alcohol Policies, Washington, DC.

Farabee, D., Walisch, L., & Maxwell, J. C. (1995). Substance use among Texas Hispanics and non-Hispanics: Who's using, who's not, and why. *Hispanic Journal of Behavioral Sciences, 17*, 523–536.

Favazza, A. R., & Thompson, J. J. (1984). Social networks of alcoholics: Some early findings. *Alcoholism: Clinical and Experimental Research, 8*, 9–15.

Fernandez-Pol, B., Bluestone, H., Missouri, C., Morales, G., & Mizruchi, M. S. (1986). Drinking patterns of inner-city black Americans and Puerto Ricans. *Journal of Studies on Alcohol, 47*, 156–160.

Fiore, A., Milievich, C., & Poldrugo, F. (1989). Evaluation of an Italian program for the treatment of alcoholism. *Alcoholism: Journal on Alcoholism and Related Addictions, 25*, 57–61.

Frauenglass, S., Routh, D. K., Pantin, H. M., & Mason, C. A. (1997). Family support decreases influence on deviant peers on Hispanic adolescents' substance abuse. *Journal of Clinical Child Psychology, 26*, 15–23.

Germane, C. E., & Germane, E. G. (1929). *Character education.* Newark, NJ: Silver-Burdett.

Gillin, J. L. (1933). *Social pathology.* New York: Century.

Goldberg, C. J., & Botvin, G. J. (1993). Assertiveness in Hispanic adolescents: Relationship to alcohol use and abuse. *Psychological Reports, 73*, 227–238.

Gordon, A. J. (1989). Alcohol use in the perspective of cultural ecology. In M. Galanter (Ed.), *Recent developments in alcoholism* (Vol. 7, pp. 355–375). New York: Plenum Press.

Hands, M., & Dear, G. (1994). Co-dependency: A critical review. *Drug and Alcohol Review, 13*, 437–446.

Havard, J. D. (1992). Alcohol abuse and legislation in Europe. In *Alcohology in Europe* (pp. 1–12). Bologna: Editrice Compositori.

Heath, D. B. (1982). In other cultures they also drink. In E. Lisansky-Gomberg, H. Raskin-White, & J. A. Carpenter (Eds.), *Alcohol, science and society revisited* (pp. 63–79). Ann Arbor, MI: University of Michigan Press.

Hernandez-Guzman, L. (1999). *Toward psychological health: Socially competent children* (Hacia la salud psicologica: Niños socialmente competentes). Mexico City: National University of Mexico Press.

Hernandez-Guzman, L., & Lopez-Morales, E. G. (1999). Grandparents: An ignored resource in psychological assessment, diagnosis and intervention. *Mexican Journal of Psychology, 16*, 281–290.

Hernandez-Guzman, L., & Sanchez-Sosa, J. J. (1996). Parent-child interactions predict anxiety in Mexican adolescents. *Adolescence, 31*, 955–963.

Holder, H. D., & Hallan, J. B. (1986). Impact of alcoholism treatment on total health care costs: A six-year study. *Advances in Alcohol and Substance Abuse, 6*, 1–15.

Holmila, M. (1987). Young families and alcohol use in Finland and the Soviet Union. *Contemporary Drug Problems, 14*, 649–672.

Holmila, M. (1992). The family and alcohol: A review of the research literature. In A. Rolli & A. Cottino (Eds.), *The culture of alcohol: Sociology of daily drinking, between theory and intervention* (pp. 48–62). Milan: Franco Angeli.

Holmila, M. (1997). Family roles and being a problem drinker's intimate other. *European Addiction Research, 3*, 37–42.

Holmila, M., Mustonen, H., & Rannik, E. (1990). Alcohol use and its control in Finnish and Soviet marriages. *British Journal of Addiction, 85*, 509–520.

Homonoff, E., Martin, J., Rimpas, D., & Henderson, M. (1994). It takes a village to raise a kid: A model of training for prevention of youth abuse of alcohol and other drugs. *Child and Adolescence Social Work Journal, 11*, 53–61.

Honig, A. S. (1991). Varieties of research in early care. *Early Child Development and Care, 68*, 1–7.

Horton, D. J. (1943). The functions of alcohol in primitive societies: A cross-cultural study. *Journal of Studies on Alcohol, 4*, 199–220.

Horwitz, A. V., & White, H. R. (1991). Becoming married, depression, and alcohol problems among young adults. *Journal of Health and Social Behavior, 32*, 221–237.

Hussong, A. M., & Chassin, L. (1994). The stress-negative affect model of adolescent alcohol use: Disaggregating negative affect. *Journal of Studies on Alcohol, 55*, 707–718.

Huston, A. C. (1983). Sex typing. In P. H. Mussen & E. M. Hetherington (Eds.), *Handbook of child psychology: Vol. 4, Socialization, personality and social behavior* (4th ed., pp. 387–457). New York: Wiley.

Iannotti, R. I., & Bush, P. J. (1992). Perceived vs actual friends' use of alcohol, cigarettes, marijuana, and cocaine: Which has the most influence? *Journal of Youth and Adolescence, 21*, 375–389.

Israel, I., Hollander, O., Sanchez-Craig, M., Booker, S., Miller, V., Gingrich, R., & Rankin, J. G. (1996). Screening for problem drinking and counseling by the primary care physician-nurse team. *Alcoholism: Clinical and Experimental Research, 20*, 1443–1450.

Jackson, J. K. (1954). The adjustment of the family to the crisis of alcoholism. *Journal of Studies on Alcohol, 15*, 562–586.

Jacob, T., & Bremer, D. A. (1986). Assortive mating among men and women alcoholics. *Journal of Studies on Alcohol, 47*, 219–222.

Jarvinen, M. (1991). Controlled controllers: Women, men, and alcohol. *Contemporary Drug Problems, 18*, 389–406.

Jellinek, E. M. (1976a). Drinkers and alcoholics in ancient Rome. *Journal of Studies on Alcohol, 37*, 1718–1741.

Jellinek, E. M. (1976b). Italy. In R. E. Popham (Ed.), *Jellinek working papers on drinking patterns and alcohol problems* (Monograph No. 804). Toronto, Canada: Addiction Research Foundation.

Jessor, R., Young, H. B., Young, E. H., & Tesi, G. (1970). Perceived opportunity, alienation, and drinking behavior among Italian and American youth. *Journal of Personality and Social Psychiatry, 8*, 215–222.

Johnson, V., & Pandina, R. J. (1991). Effects of the family environment on adolescent substance use, delinquency and coping styles. *American Journal of Drug and Alcohol Abuse, 17*, 71–88.

Kahn, M. W., & Fua, C. (1995). Children of South Sea Island immigrants to Australia: Factors associated with adjustment problems. *International Journal of Social Psychiatry, 41*, 55–73.

Katz, L., & Gottman, J. (1993). Patterns of marital conflict predict children's internalizing and externalizing behaviors. *Developmental Psychology, 29*, 940–950.

Kellam, S. G., & Werthamer-Larsson, L. (1986). Developmental epidemiology: A basis for prevention. In M. Kessler & S. E. Goldston (Eds.), *A decade of progress in primary prevention.* Hanover, NH: University Press of New England.

King, J., Beals, J., Manson, S. M., & Trimble, J. E. (1992). A structural equation model of factors related to substance use among American Indian adolescents. *Drugs and Society, 6*, 253–268.

Kline, A. (1996). Pathways into drug user treatment: The influence of gender and racial/ethnic identity. *Substance Use and Abuse, 31*, 323–342.

Klingmann, T. (1935). Our children's children. *Medical Record (NY), 141*, 171–173.

Kochanska, G., Aksan, N., & Koenig, A. (1995). Mother child mutually positive effect, the quality of child compliance to requests and prohibitions, and maternal control as correlates of early internalization. *Child Development, 66*, 236–254.

Lamminpaa, A. (1995). Alcohol intoxication in childhood and adolescence. *Alcohol & Alcoholism, 30*, 5–12.

Levine, E. M., & Kozak, C. (1979). Drug and alcohol use, delinquency, and vandalism among upper middle class pre- and post-adolescents. *Journal of Youth and Adolescence, 8*, 91–101.

Lolli, G., Serianni, E., Banissoni, F., Golder, G., Mariani, A., McCarthy, R. G., & Toner, M. (1952). The use of wine and other alcoholic beverages by a group of Italians and Americans of Italian extraction. *Journal of Studies on Alcohol, 13*, 27–48.

MacAndrew, C., & Edgerton, R. B. (1969). *Drunken comportment: A social explanation.* Chicago: Aldine.

Marchi, A. G., Messi, G., & Renier, S. (1991). Changing patterns of children acute intoxication in Trieste in the years 1979–90. *Alcohol & Alcoholism, 26*, 252.

McCrady, B. S., Moreau, J., Paolino, T. J., & Longabaugh, R. (1982). Joint hospitalization and couples therapy for alcoholism: A four year follow-up. *Journal of Studies on Alcohol, 43*, 1244–1250.

McGue, M., Sharma, A., & Benson, P. (1996). Parent and siblings influences on adolescent alcohol use and misuse: Evidence from a U.S. adoption cohort. *Journal of Studies on Alcohol, 57*, 8–18.

Monarca, S., Donato, F., Modolo, M. A., Brunelli, L., Spiazzi, R., Pasquale, L., & Nardi, G. (1991). Drinking habits among high school students in Perugia, Italy, in 1981 and 1988: Time trends and correlates. *International Journal of the Addictions, 26*, 1101–1122.

Morgan, P. (1982). Notes on the Italian alcohol experience. *The Drinking and Drug Practices Surveyor, 13*, 115–117.

Natera, G., Casco, M., Herrejón, E., & Mora, J. (1993). Interaction among Mexican couples with a different pattern of alcohol intake and their relation with a family history of alcoholism (Interaccion entre parejas con diferente patron de consumo de consumo de alcohol y su relacion con antecedentes familiares de consume en Mexico). *Salud Mental, 16*(2), 33–43.

Neve, R. J. M., Lemmens, P. H., & Drop, M. J. (1997). Gender differences in alcohol use and alcohol problems: Mediation by social roles and gender-role attitudes. *Substance Use and Misuse, 32*, 1439–1459.

Oettingen, G., Little, T., Lindenberger, U., & Baltes, P. (1994). Causality agency and control belief in East versus West Berlin children: A natural experiment on the role of context. *Journal of Personality and Social Psychology, 66*, 579–595.

Office for Substance Abuse Prevention. (1992). *Cultural competence for evaluators. A guide for alcohol and other drug abuse prevention practitioners working with ethnic/racial communities.* Rockville, MD: U.S. Department of Health and Human Services.

O'Nell, T. D., & Mitchell, C. M. (1996). Alcohol use among American Indian adolescents: The role of culture in pathological drinking. *Social Science and Medicine, 42*, 565–578.

Orford, J. (1984). The prevention and management of alcohol problems in family settings: A review carried out in English-speaking countries. *Alcohol & Alcoholism, 19*, 109–122.

Orford, J. (1994). Empowering family and friends: A new approach to secondary prevention of addiction. *Drug and Alcohol Review, 13*, 417–430.

Osservatorio Permanente sui Giovani e l'Alcool. (1994). *Young people and alcohol in Europe: A tool for monitoring consumption and institutional action policies.* Rome: Edizioni OTET.

Osservatorio Permanente sui Giovani e l'Alcool. (1997). *Young people between school and work. A community action.* Rome: Edizioni Logica.

Peterson, P. L., Hawkins, J. D., Abbott, R. D., & Catalano, R. F. (1994). Disentangling the effects of parental drinking, family management and parental alcohol norms on current drinking by black and white adolescents. *Journal of Research on Adolescence, 4*, 203–227.

Poldrugo, F. (1988). Atteggiamento degli studenti nei confronti degli alcolici e degli alcolisti in Friuli-Venezia Giulia. In S. D. Ferrara & L. Gallimberti (Eds.), *La dipendenza alcolica* (Alcohol dependence) (pp. 307–314). Padua, Italy: Edizioni Turato.

Poldrugo, F. (1993). Alcohol use and abuse: An Eurohistorical perspective. *Alcoholism: Journal on Alcoholism and Related Addictions, 29* (Suppl. 1), 3–9.

Poldrugo, F. (1996). Alcohol misuse: What is the price for the society and who is paying for it. *Alcoologie, 18*, 120–122.

Poldrugo, F. (1999). Recognition and treatment of alcohol-related problems in primary healthcare. *Alcoscope: International Review of Alcoholism Management, 2*, 12–15.

Poldrugo, F., & Fiore, A. (1988). Family, gender and treatment outcome of alcoholism. In *Proceedings of an International Congress on Alcohol, Other Drugs and the Family* (p. 43). Sydney, Australia.

Poldrugo, F., & Patussi, V. (1996). Alcoholism and alcohol-related problems in Italy: An overview on recent developments in societal responses and treatment systems. *Journal of Addictive Diseases, 15*, 59–65.

Poldrugo, F., & Sferch, D. (1991). Attitudini e consumi di alcool in studenti di varie nazionalità (Attitudes and alcohol consumption among students of various nationalities). In *Proceedings of the 7th Congress of the Italian Society of Alcohology, Nov. 23–25* (pp. 627–630). Rome, Italy: Mediserve.

Poldrugo, F., & Stratta, P. (1993). Alcoholism among young people in Italy: An attempt to analyse the phenomenon. *Alcoholism: Journal on Alcoholism and Related Addictions, 9*, 73–79.

Poldrugo, F., & Urizzi, R. (1992). The Italian paradox: Treatment initiatives and falling alcohol consumption. In H. Klingemann, J. P. Takala, & G. Hunt (Eds.), *Cure, care or control: Alcoholism treatment in sixteen countries* (pp. 191–204). Albany, NY: State University of New York Press.

Porter, L., Arif, A. E., & Curran, W. J. (1986). *The law and the treatment of drug- and alcohol-dependent persons: A comparative study of existing legislation.* Geneva, Switzerland: World Health Organization.

Pulkkinen, L., & Pitkanen, T. (1994). A prospective study of the precursors to problem drinking in young adulthood. *Journal of Studies on Alcohol, 55*, 578–587.

Rohde, P., Lewinsohn, P. M., & Seeley, J. R. (1996). Psychiatric comorbidity with problematic alcohol use in high school students. *Journal of the American Academy of Child and Adolescent Psychiatry, 35*, 101–109.

Room, R., Greenfield, T. K., & Weisner, C. (1991). "People who might have liked you to drink less": Changing responses to drinking by U.S. family members and friends, 1979–1990. *Contemporary Drug Problems, 18*, 573–595.

Rossi, D. (1994). Youth and alcohol in Italy. *Alcologia, 6*, 165–169.

Rotunno, M., & McGodrick, M. (1982). Italian families. In M. McGodrick, J. K. Pearce, & J. Giordano (Eds.), *Ethnicity and family therapy* (pp. 340–363). New York: Guilford Press.

Ruble, D. (1988). Sex role development. In M. Bornstein & M. Lamb (Eds.), *Developmental psychology: An advanced textbook* (2nd ed., pp. 411–460). Hillsdale, NJ: Erlbaum.

Saenz, I., & Sanchez-Sosa, J. J. (1996). Development and identity of Guatemalan refugee children in Mexico: Conditions and options for support interventions. *Refuge, 15*, 34–41.

Samuels, T., Schneider, M., & Everatt, D. (1998). *Learning to drink: A report on how some youth in Southern Africa learn to drink.* Unpublished paper presented at a meeting of the Working Group on Learning about Drinking, International Center for Alcohol Policies, Washington, DC.

Sanchez-Sosa, J. J. (1998a). From primary prevention to supporting dignified dying: The role of the research-intervention interface in health psychology. In G. Rodriguez & M. Rojas (Eds.), *Health psychology in Latin America* (pp. 35–44). Mexico City, Mexico: M. A. Porrua.

Sanchez-Sosa, J. J. (1998b). *Culture and drinking patterns among Latin American adolescents: An exploratory study*. Unpublished paper presented at a meeting of the Working Group on Learning about Drinking, International Center for Alcohol Policies, Washington, DC.

Santos, S. J., Bohon, L. M., & Sanchez-Sosa, J. J. (1998). Childhood family relationships, marital and work conflict, and mental health distress in Mexican immigrants. *Journal of Community Psychology, 26*, 491–508.

Sclare, A. B. (1970). The female alcoholic. *British Journal of Addiction, 65*, 99–107.

Skog, O. J. (1987). The collectivity of drinking cultures. A theory of the distribution of alcohol consumption. *British Journal of Addiction, 82*, 83–99.

Simons, R. L., Whitbeck, L. B., Conger, R. D., & Melby, J. N. (1991). The effect of social skills, values, peers, and depression on adolescent substance abuse. *Journal of Early Adolescence, 11*(4), 466–481.

Spiegel, J. (1982). An ecological model of ethnic families. In M. McGodrick, J. K. Pearce, & J. Giordano (Eds.), *Ethnicity and family therapy* (pp. 31–51). New York: Guilford Press.

Spoth, R., Redmond, C., Hockaday, C., & Yoo, S. (1996). Protective factors and young adolescent tendency to abstain from alcohol use: A model using two waves of intervention study data. *American Journal of Community Psychology, 24*, 749–770.

Spoth, R., Yoo, S., Kahn, J., & Redmond, C. (1996). A model of the effects of protective parent and peer factors on young adolescent alcohol refusal skills. *Journal of Primary Prevention, 16*, 373–394.

Sroufe, L. A., Cooper, R. G., & DeHart, G. B. (1996). *Child development: Its nature and course*. New York: McGraw–Hill.

Sroufe, A., Fox, N., & Pancake, V. (1983). Attachment and dependency in developmental perspective. *Child Development, 54*, 1615–1627.

Swaim, R. C., Bates, S. C., & Chavez, E. L. (1997). Structural equation model of substance use among Mexican-American and White non-Hispanic school dropouts. *Journal of Adolescent Health, 23*, 128–138.

Vaz-Serra, A., Canavarro, M. C., & Ramalheira, C. (1998). The importance of family context in alcoholism. *Alcohol & Alcoholism, 33*, 37–41.

Vega, W. A., Gil, A. G., & Zimmerman, R. S. (1993). Patterns of drug use among Cuban-American, African-American and white non-Hispanic boys. *American Journal of Public Health, 83*, 257–259.

Vial, J., Fernandez, M. C., & Godoy, J. (1992). The cardiac defense response in humans: Effects of stimulus modality and gender differences. *Journal of Psychophysiology, 6*, 140–154.

Waldron, I. (1988). Gender and health-related behavior. In D. S. Gochman (Ed.), *Health behavior. Emerging research perspectives* (pp. 193–208). New York: Plenum Press.

Ward, R. F., & Faillace, G. A. (1970). The alcoholic and his helpers. *Journal of Studies on Alcohol, 31*, 684–691.

Webster, R. A., Hunter, M., & Keats, J. A. (1994). Peer and parental influences on adolescents' substance use: A path analysis. *International Journal of the Addictions, 29*, 647–657.

Williams, R., & Shams, M. (1998). Generational continuity and change in British Asian health and health behaviour. *Journal of Epidemiology and Community Health, 52*, 558–563.

Williams, P. H., & Straus, R. (1950). Drinking patterns of Italians in New Haven: Utilization of the personal diary as a research technique. *Journal of Studies on Alcohol, 11*, 51–91, 250–308, 452–483, 586–629.

Wills, T. A., & Vaughan, R. (1989). Social support and substance use in early adolescence. *Journal of Behavioral Medicine, 12*, 321–339.

Windle, M. (1992). A longitudinal study of stress buffering for adolescent problem behaviors. *Developmental Psychology, 28*, 522–530.

Windle, M. (1995). An alcohol involvement typology for adolescents: Convergent validity and longitudinal stability. *Journal of Studies on Alcohol, 57*, 627–637.

Wolin, S. J., Bennett, L. A., Noonan, D. L., & Teitelbaum, M. A. (1980). Disrupted family rituals: A factor in the intergenerational transmission of alcoholism. *Journal of Studies on Alcohol, 41*, 199–214.

Ziervogel, C. F., Ahmed, N., Flisher, A. J., & Robertson, B. A. (1997–1998). Alcohol misuse in South African male adolescents: A qualitative investigation. *International Quarterly of Community Health Education, 17*, 25–41.

Zimmerman, M. A., Copeland, L. A., Shope, J. T., & Dielman, T. E. (1997). A longitudinal study of self-esteem: Implications for adolescent development. *Journal of Youth and Adolescence, 26*, 117–141.

Zimmerman, J. E., & Sodowsky, G. R. (1993). Influences of acculturation on Mexican-American drinking practices: Implications for counseling. *Journal of Multicultural Counseling and Development, 21*, 22–35.

Zucker, R. A. (1979). Developmental aspects of drinking through the young adult years. In H. T. Blane & M. E. Chafetz (Eds.), *Youth, alcohol and social policy* (pp. 91–146). New York: Plenum Press.

Chapter 4

Alcohol Influences: The Role of Family and Peers

Gail Gleason Milgram

Alcohol is a socially accepted legal commodity that is widely used throughout the world. Drinking alcohol is a custom of almost every society (Bacon, 1962), and alcohol itself is valued as a food, medicine, promoter of fellowship, and a part of ritual functions (Lemert, 1991). However, public attitudes toward its use are often confused, paradoxical, and predominantly focused on excessive use and related problems (Zinberg & Bean, 1981). One reason proposed by Bacon (1962) for the focus on problems is that modern society has eliminated alcohol's value as a food and medicine, which were important reasons for its use in primitive society. The lack of significant reasons to consume alcohol and the inability of societies to define standards of acceptable/appropriate consumption and to differentiate this from unacceptable/inappropriate use have resulted in many dilemmas.

Feelings and attitudes toward alcohol are even more complicated when young people are considered. Most societies are protective of their young and have a significant commitment to ensuring that they are appropriately raised. During the period of dependency on the family, the child undergoes a process of intense socialization (Cooper, 1989). Drinking customs are also learned through socialization. Every culture has rules that govern who can or cannot drink, when alcohol may or may not be consumed, how much or how little may be consumed, where consumption may or may not take place, and so forth. The cultural context in which alcohol use occurs and the adult social behavior associated with it sets the stage for children to learn about drinking. Children learn what to expect from alcohol, and these expectancies are further reinforced by society, thus playing a role in drinking patterns and behaviors that develop in adulthood. Perceiving adult roles to include alcohol consumption contributes to the development of young persons' identification of themselves as adults and as consumers of alcohol (Maddox & McCall, 1964). Young people may be said to act like society's children (Males, 1990). As Maddox (1962) stated, "The teenager, then, does not invent the idea of drinking; he learns it" (p. 234).

The role of family and peers in an individual's introduction to alcohol is the focus of this chapter. The family and peers are significant factors in the initiation to alcohol, attitudes toward it, and its continued use. Other factors (for example, mass media, television, advertising, or music) may also influence use; they are addressed elsewhere in this volume.

INFLUENCES OF THE FAMILY

> A child's first exposure to and experiences with alcohol are likely to be in the context of the family (Barnes, 1990, p. 137).

The family is the basic unit of society and the primary source of socialization of children (Barnes & Windle, 1987). The family that consumes alcohol provides specific examples of when, why, and how alcohol is consumed. Children are exposed to the occasions and settings in which members of their immediate family, as well as their extended family and friends, consume alcohol. Not only do they learn from these examples when people drink, but they also learn what types and quantity of beverage are determined by the occasion. While children observe drinking in both the family and in broader social life, it is the parents who are a key source of information. Most children ask their parents questions about alcohol (Huetteman, Sarvela, & Benson, 1992). Moreover, they are strongly influenced by their parents' views. When young people are surveyed to determine who has the most influence on their initial decision to drink, parents are ranked first (Akers, 1985).

Families also operate as one of the principal conduits for the transfer of cultural values about alcohol and drinking. Drinking is part of a culturally defined pattern of behavior. Indeed, cultures can be defined by their patterns of drinking and attitudes toward alcohol (Heath, 1990). Klein (1991) stresses the importance of understanding the influence of culture on drinking behaviors and attitudes. Cultural factors may declare when a particular type of beverage is consumed (e.g., a beer after outdoor work) or with what kinds of food (e.g., wine with spaghetti). It is within the family setting that an individual is first, and most powerfully, exposed to cultural notions pertaining to alcohol. Acquisition of these cultural values occurs at a very early age.

Almost all (95%) of Scottish and English children aged 5 to 10 years old were able to identify at least one alcoholic beverage by smell (Fossey, 1993a). By the age of 8, most of the children in Fossey's (1993b) study in the United Kingdom had an operational schema for alcohol which included stereotypical beliefs and negative attitudes. Casswell, Gilmore, Silva, and Brasch (1988) interviewed 9-year-olds in New Zealand and found that even by that early age children have clear concepts about alcohol and most are able to describe some effects of drinking. Understanding the processes by which alcohol is introduced to young people is important, as is the manner in which an individual first comes into contact with alcohol.

Other factors may also influence adolescent drinking behaviors. Drinking in the extended family, which includes aunts, uncles, and cousins, and the community in which the family interacts also influences what is learned about what, when, and how alcohol is to be consumed. Though not the focus of this chapter, the impact on children of alcoholism in the family should be noted. Children who have an alcoholic parent are more likely to report stressors in childhood (Sher, Gershuny, Peterson, & Raskin, 1997). Research has demonstrated a correlation between a family history of alcoholism and alcohol use disorders in adults. This may be related to the stressors themselves (e.g., physical abuse), modeling, disruption in family rituals, genetics, or a combination of these and other variables.

The Role of Parents

In addition to being an important source of information about alcohol for young children, parents are often the individuals who introduce their children to alcohol. This may occur as part of a family ritual or religious celebration (Milgram, 1990), or as part of regular day-to-day events. For instance, alcohol is an integral part of family life in France, and the family plays an important role in the introduction of alcohol to the children (Weill & LeBourhis, 1994). In Italy almost all drinking is done in connection with food (Lolli, 1969), and consumption of wine by young people during meals is not considered in any way a remarkable or special event. In some rural areas in Mexico, the custom of giving children local alcoholic drinks persists, while in other areas children are often allowed to taste their parents' drinks (Rey, 1995). Similarly, in Cameroon it is not uncommon for traditional drinks to be given to children under 15 years of age (Yguel, 1990).

In the present context, there are two pivotal aspects of the relationship of parents to youthful drinking: imitation and social reinforcement (Kandel, 1983). Young people are more likely to drink if their parents drink (imitation) and will exhibit behaviors approved of by the parents (social reinforcement). Parents serve as very powerful role models for drinking (Barnes, 1990). Abrams and Niaura (1987) stress the importance of modeling and note that the drinking rate (i.e., light versus heavy) of the role model significantly influences the subject's drinking rate. Similarly, parents who drink frequently are more likely to have adolescents who drink and drink frequently (Smart & Fejer, 1974). However, Hawkins and Fraser (1987) point out that modeling has differential importance at different developmental phases. As with many other aspects of life, at early ages parental modeling has a direct and more potent effect, and at later ages an indirect effect.

Parents may also influence adolescent drinking by expressing their attitudes towards alcohol (Thompson & Wilsnack, 1987). It is less likely for teenagers to have tried or be currently using alcohol if their parents do not accept adolescent drinking (Hawkins, Lishner, Catalano, & Howard, 1986). In studying two groups of adolescents—those who used substances and those who abstained—and their parents, Coombs and Paulson (1988) found that adolescents were more likely to remain substance-free if their parents and siblings were not drinkers.

An informal method of understanding the location of alcohol in a young person's life is illustrated in the text box. Questions were developed to draw

A Useful Values Clarification Exercise

To determine the location of alcohol in a person's life try the following simple but revealing group exercise. It will help to highlight details regarding age of initial consumption, drinking confederates, place of drinking, and beverages consumed.

To proceed, form a small group and invite your group to participate in a simple name tag exercise. Ask the members of the group to put their first name in the middle of a label and then to identify themselves under their name as a "drinker" or a "nondrinker." This first step usually evokes questions such as: How much do you have to drink to be defined as a drinker? Does the beverage make a difference? If you only drink on special occasions, are you a drinker? The questions may demonstrate individuals' discomfort in calling themselves drinkers.

Note that for many people the term "drinker" is not neutral and may connote that a person has an alcohol problem. The inability to hear the word "drinker" as simply meaning one who consumes alcohol highlights the ambivalence surrounding alcohol use in many societies. Interestingly, after questions are answered and explanations given in this exercise, the majority of the group in most cultural settings will probably identify themselves as drinkers.

The next item inquires about how old you were when you had your first drink. It often raises questions such as: Is it considered "having a drink" if you were with your parents? Does a drink as part of a religious ceremony count? Do you mean a whole drink? Once it has been clarified that the only question being asked is how old you were when you first remember consuming alcohol, most individuals indicate an age between 6 and 13–14 years. A few members of the group may nominate an age over 14 years and an even smaller number of the group identify themselves as never having had a drink.

(*continued*)

A Useful Values Clarification Exercise (*Continued*)

The next question is: Who were you with when you had your first drink? For the most part, those who indicated an early introduction to alcohol (i.e., ages 6 to 13–14 years) state that they were with their parents. Those who indicated a later age of introduction (i.e., 14 and above) say that they were with their peers. Responses to the question "where were you when you had your first drink?" correspond with the previous information, whereby early introduction to alcohol with parents usually occurs at home or a location directly connected to the family (e.g., grandparents' home, a wedding). Conversely, later introduction to alcohol with peers often takes place in a location not connected to the family; it may be in a car, friend's home, parking lot, etc.

out details on drinking behavior; the exercise can be expanded to include other questions (e.g., type of beverage, event, and quantity consumed). The importance of the family and peers in the introduction of young people to alcohol is clearly identified by this simple exercise. The outcome tends to reflect the following points:

- Parents were usually the introducers of alcohol for those who had their first drink at relatively young ages.

  Foxcroft and Lowe (1991) found that many young people are introduced to alcohol by their parents at relatively early ages in the United Kingdom. Similarly, in South Africa, alcohol is initially consumed under the supervision of parents (Samuels, Schneider, & Everatt, 1998).
- Most individuals have consumed alcohol at some point during the previous year.

  U.S. Statistics for the United States in Alcohol and Health: Ninth Special Report to the U. S. Congress (National Institute on Alcohol Abuse and Alcoholism, 1997) indicated that approximately two-thirds of the population over the age of 14 years are drinkers.
- The majority of individuals had their first drink at an early age.

  Blane and Hewitt's (1977) review of research on alcohol and youth between 1960 and 1975 found that "[in] the United States, the first exposure to alcohol often occurs before the age of twelve" (p. V–1). More recently, Botvin and Wills (1985) described initial experimentation and the development of patterns of alcohol use as usually occurring during preadolescence and adolescence.
- Early initiation to alcohol usually took place at home or a location at which the family was present.

  In the U.S., most young people are introduced to alcohol by their parents in the home setting (Milgram, 1990).

Peers are the introducers of alcohol for those who indicate a later age for their first drink. The location of peer introduction to alcohol is external to the individual's home, for example, at a friend's home, in a park, and so on.

Reasons for Drinking

Though most parents drink to be social or to relax, others drink to cope with problems or to escape. However, the same individual can drink for different reasons at different times (Milgram, 1990). While parents have certain reasons for drinking, they may not be the same reasons that young people identify for their own consumption. It is important to consider both age and gender when considering young people's attitudes toward alcohol (Wilks, 1991). A poll reported by Borton (1991) asked students in grades 4 through 6 (i.e., approximately 9 to 12 years old) why young people might drink beer, wine, or distilled spirits. Most responded "to fit in" (39%); the next most common response was "to feel older" (26%), followed by "to have a good time" (17%), "to not feel bad" (9%), and "other" (7%). Younger adolescents have also been found to be less likely than older adolescents to agree with the social benefits of drinking (e.g., relaxing, socializing) (Wilks, 1991).

Though parental modeling and attitudes are important, other factors may also contribute to the adolescent's consumption of alcohol: family structure, motivations to drink, the parent-child relationship, and the age and gender of the child. Brody and Forehand (1993), for example, found that family processes, including the parent-child relationship, discipline, and problem-solving strategies are important variables in adolescents' substance use, as is peer affiliation.

The parent-child relationship is critical to many developmental tasks and much of the learning that a child experiences. Various studies have indicated that a strong relationship with one's parents is positively correlated with lower levels of substance use (Rhodes, Gingiss, & Smith, 1994; Selnow, 1987). The importance of parental support and monitoring has also been reported (Barnes & Farrell, 1992). Parental involvement through accepting, monitoring, and enforcing is related to parents' effectiveness at preventing alcohol use and impaired driving (Beck & Lockhart, 1992). On the other hand, the combination of a low level of parental caring and a high level of protection is associated with adolescent drug use (Clausen, 1996). Correspondingly, a more democratic parenting style has been found to be associated with less adolescent drug use (Jurich, Polson, Jurich, & Bates, 1985).

Family and Religion

Parents' religious beliefs and behaviors also play an important role (Coombs & Paulson, 1988; Mullen, Williams, & Hunt, 1996). Perkins (1987) found that the religious traditions of parents and their degree of religiosity determine their children's traditions and commitments, which ultimately may influence the child's drinking. College students with no religious affiliation have reported significantly higher levels of drinking, getting drunk, and celebratory drinking than students who identified their religious affiliation as either Catholic or Protestant (Patock-Peckham, Hutchinson, Cheong, & Nagoshi, 1998).

Religion has been found to provide some protection from drug use by adolescents (Amey, Alrecht, & Miller, 1996). It has also been considered an agent of social change, especially when few other social influences are present (Hadaway, Elifson, & Petersen, 1984). Though Perkins (1985) found no difference with regard to the alcohol and drug use of college students with no religious background or only a nominal Christian background, he found that increasing levels of religiosity appeared to moderate alcohol use among Christians and Jews.

Engs, Hanson, Gliksman, and Smythe (1990) concluded from their study of United States and Canadian students that religious norms have a greater influence on drinking behaviors in cohesive religious groups, whereas cultural norms are more influential among less cohesive groups. Cochran's (1993) survey of 3,065 male adolescents in grades 7 through 12 in three Midwestern states found that the effects of religiosity varied across faith groups. The effects were strongest where official doctrine proscribes use, and muted where doctrine does not deal with use. The survey also showed that the effects of religiosity varied by beverage type for beer and spirits, which are generally restricted to recreational use, and are strongest for wine, which is consumed for functional and ceremonial reasons as well as recreational purposes (Cochran, 1993). The influence of religion on drinking patterns is discussed more fully in Chapter 5.

In addition to religious affiliation, ethnic background also appears to significantly mediate alcohol use, even within a given cultural setting. Poulin (1991), for example, found significant ethnic differences in the alcohol consumption among youth and young adults in Chester, Pennsylvania, U.S. Black youth and young adults had lower consumption rates than their White peers. Similarly, Catalano et al. (1992) compared urban fifth grade students from three groups (i.e., Black, White, and Asian Americans) and found differences in rates of initiation of alcohol use. Initiation rates were found to be highest among Whites, followed by Blacks, and were lowest among Asian Americans. Although there may be a multitude of reasons for these ethnic variations they are, nonetheless, important to note.

Social Class and Economic Status as a Mediator of Drinking

While there is some evidence to support the view that economic hardship in the family is a principal contributor to youth substance use, including drinking alcohol, this is not consistently supported by the research (Fawzy, Coombs, Simon, & Bowman-Terrell, 1987; Lawrence & Maxwell, 1962). Both lower-class and upper-class youth have been found to be the most frequently involved in substance use and delinquent activities, while middle-class youth consistently ranked last in one study (Lorch, 1990). Rather than considering family social class as the key variable, Lorch (1990) proposes that the discrepancy between aspirations and perceived accomplishment may be the key. Other factors, such as parenting style, the child's expectations for the future, and family dynamics, may also be contributing variables to adolescent drinking.

Education is an indicator of the employment and socioeconomic status of the individual and family unit, but it does not appear to have a linear relationship with the prevalence of alcohol use by young adults in the U.S. Johnston and colleagues (1998) found little difference in the use of alcohol by young adults who attend college and those who do not. With respect to differential effects of maternal versus paternal parental employment level, Hillman and Sawilowsky (1991) found no significant difference in consumption levels of early adolescents in relation to maternal employment. However, Fawzy et al. (1987) found a positive correlation between fathers who were professionals and abstaining adolescents, and greater levels of alcohol consumption where fathers were managers and foremen.

parents status

Gender Differences in Motivations to Drink

There has been minimal research into the differential influences on boys and girls and drinking behaviors, and comparatively little done to interpret the gender differences that have been observed. However, this is an area of growing interest that has received greater attention in recent years (Barnes, Farrell, & Dinlcheff, 1997). Wilks (1992) studied adolescents from Central Queensland, Australia, and found that young males and females share common views: They think that drinking will be fun and something new. Among older teenagers (aged between 16 and 19 years) from Humberside in the United Kingdom, males were found to be more likely to drink for reasons of self-confidence and enhancement than females (Foxcroft & Lowe, 1993).

The Role of Siblings

Siblings are another major influence on youth alcohol consumption. It seems apparent that the long-term sibling relationship would have an impact on adolescent drinking and attitudes toward use. It is also possible that the sibling may be the source of alcohol. Brook, Whiteman, Gordon, and Brook (1990) studied male college students and their oldest brothers and found that modeling by the sibling had a greater association with younger brothers' alcohol consumption than did modeling by parents. They also found that sibling models of use had the same degree of influence as did peer models. Younger brothers were least likely to drink if both older brothers and peers did not drink (Brook et al., 1990). Needle et al. (1986) also examined the relationship between older siblings' attitudes and drinking behaviors and the drinking behaviors of younger siblings;

they found that older siblings constitute an important and influential reference group that influence the drinking behaviors of younger siblings. Gfroerer (1987), using data from the U.S. National Survey on Drug Abuse, studied adolescents who were living in the same household as older family members and found a strong relationship between teenage alcohol use and alcohol use of older family members. Adolescent drinking was also found to be significantly influenced by sibling modeling in a study of families with two or more children (Ary, Tidesley, Hops, & Andrews, 1993); however, siblings were found to be somewhat less influential than peers. McGue, Sharma, and Benson (1996) used an adoption study design to examine the relationship between adolescent alcohol use and parental drinking behavior, sibling drinking behavior, and the extent to which these associations were correlated with genetic or shared environmental influences. They found that adolescent alcohol use was substantially related to the drinking behavior of siblings. Though older siblings seem to be more important role models for adolescents than the parents, it should be noted that the older siblings were influenced themselves by parental modeling as they grew up. It seems clear from the studies that older siblings are a significant influence on adolescent substance use and nonuse and that they are a separate and important group to study.

YOUTH DRINKING AND THE PEER GROUP

Adolescent Drinking

It has long been held that by studying the age of introduction, who is present and, therefore, sanctioning the activity, and the purpose surrounding consuming the first drink, much can be learned about the values associated with drinking (Ullman, 1962). Alcohol is introduced at early ages in many parts of the world. Segal (1987) indicates that Russian children begin drinking at a young age. In New Zealand, the following ages of first consumption of alcohol have been identified: from 1 to 5 years of age, 8%; 6 to 10 years, 67%; 11 to 12 years, 16%; and 13 years or older, 9% (Fergusson, Lynskey, & Horwood, 1994). Drinking often begins between 12 and 15 years of age in China (Newman & Ming, 1998). The introduction to alcohol in Poland happens between the ages of 11 and 15 (Zagonski, 1986). In Spain, the initiation of alcohol consumption was found to occur at 13–14 years of age and beer was identified as the first drink consumed in a study conducted by Torres and Sanchez (1985). In the U.S., most young people are introduced to alcohol between the ages of 11 and 13 (Milgram, 1990).

Youthful drinking initially takes place at home or at social occasions with parents and then moves to locations outside the home with peers. In Nigeria, drinking now takes place in pubs and hotels with increasing frequency (Odejide, Ohaeri, Adelekan, & Ikuesan, 1989). Locations of adolescent drinking in Australia are home (53%), a friend's house (27%), and cars, parks, and other locations outside the home such as hotels and discos (Saunders & Baily, 1993).

Internationally, the percentage of young people who identify themselves as drinkers is relatively high. In Cameroon, approximately 60% of individuals over 15 years of age indicate that they regularly drink alcohol and the percentage rises to 70% on feast days (Yguel, 1990). Since young Australians are exposed to drinking as a normative behavior early in their lives (Wilks, 1987), it is not surprising that 93% of adolescents under the age of 18 have consumed alcohol (Mak & Kinsella, 1996). Approximately 75% of the population 15 years of age and older consumes alcohol in Canada; however, drinking patterns vary across the regions of the country (Kellner, 1997). In a 1991–1992 study of students in grades 6–12 in western Canada, Hindmarsh, Porter-Serviss, and Opheim (1994) identified the following rates of consumption: beer, 64.9%; wine coolers, 68.1%; and liquor, 58.1%. In China, approximately 70% of adolescents drink (Newman & Ming, 1998) and beer is the most commonly consumed beverage, followed by wine and then liquor. However, it must be noted that significant gender differences exist in drinking, as in most areas of life in China.

Gilvarry, McCarthy, and McArdle (1995) studied students aged 11–16 years in eight schools in Newcastle-upon-Tyne, England, and found that 75% had consumed alcohol and 20% of those drank on a regular basis. An age-related increase in use was also found; 50% of the 11-year-olds and 89% of the 16-year-olds reported consumption. Boys were found to be more likely than girls to drink on a regular basis (Gilvarry et al., 1995). Irish post-primary students in the greater Dublin area were studied by Grube, Morgan, and Seff (1989). Although 47% of the students had consumed alcohol within the month prior to the survey, the prevalence of drinking was considerably higher (i.e., 62%) for students aged 17 years or older. A study of Italian young people in southern Italy by Salvagnini (1985) showed that 77% had consumed alcohol.

Ahlström (1991) found that 45% of Finnish 14-year-olds, 85% of the 16-year-olds, and 94% of the 18-year-olds admitted to drinking alcohol; considerable gender differences were found in drinking frequency, boys drinking more frequently than girls. Johnston et al.'s (1998) national survey of school students in the U.S. found that 54% of eighth graders had consumed alcohol, 72% of tenth graders, 82% of twelfth graders, and 87% of college students.

Reasons for Drinking

As discussed earlier in this chapter, when young people are introduced to alcohol by their parents, they begin drinking for the same reasons that underlie the parents' consumption, e.g., as an accompaniment to a meal. However, as they get older and drink with their friends, other reasons for drinking emerge. For example, Mexican adolescents share attitudes towards alcohol prevalent in their country and consider having a drink as a way of experiencing pleasure and showing friendship (Rey, 1995). A study of the influences on the drinking of 15-year-old New Zealanders by Connolly, Casswell, Stewart, and Silva (1992) found that greater independence from the parents and family was associated with reports of larger quantities of alcohol consumed. In the Congo, young people participate in contemporary alcohol use as part of group activities, which make adolescents feel as if they belong to a special group (Moukolo, 1990).

Russian adolescents indicate that they consume alcohol to interact socially with a group (Klimova, 1993). Young people in South Africa cite boredom and peer pressure as reasons for their increase in alcohol consumption (Samuels et al., 1998). Thorlindsson and Vilhjalmsson (1991) conducted a national survey of Icelandic adolescents aged 15 and 16 who were in the ninth grade in 1989 and found that in addition to peer interaction and support, psychological distress, such as anxiety, was positively related to alcohol use.

Heavy Drinking

Adolescent heavy drinking has been highlighted by some researchers. Johnston et al. (1998) found that in the U.S. 15% of eighth graders, 25% of tenth graders, 31% of twelfth graders, and 40% of college students reported drinking five or more drinks in a row at least once during the prior 2 weeks. In a study of young people aged 11–12 and 14–16 years in Northern Ireland and Scotland, the Northern Irish teenagers were less likely than those from Scotland to have consumed alcohol. However, the findings showed that Northern Irish young drinkers were more likely than their Scottish counterparts to be heavy drinkers, and more likely to drink with their peers in uncontrolled settings (Loretto, 1994).

Among young people who acknowledged drinking at least once in Brazil, Pechansky and Barros (1995) found that 31% reported that they had experienced some type of problem (e.g., waking up late, fighting, missing class, missing work, being involved in an accident) related to consumption. Weill and LeBourhis' (1994) study of adolescent French males found that those who were dissatisfied with life, unconstrained, and pessimistic in 1985 were the heaviest drinkers some 5 years later in 1990.

A significant group of adolescent drinkers in Australia drink to get drunk (Homel & Flaherty, 1986). Intoxication from strong alcohol beverages was found to be more frequent among Russian children than children in several Western cultures (Segal, 1987). Monarca and Modolo (1985) surveyed high school students in 10 Italian towns and found that 29% of males and 14% of females in the final year of high school had experienced drunkenness during the previous 12 months. Of the young people in southern Italy studied by Salvagnini (1985), 7% indicated that they had been drunk once or more every month. In Rossi's (1994) study, also of Italian young people, 12% reported that they had drunk a bit too much more than once in the previous 3 months, while 2% said that they had been drunk more than once in the previous 3 months.

Peer Group Influence

Family and peers are important because they are the most significant people in a child's life and a principal vehicle through which culture is introduced (Maddox & McCall, 1964). As children get older, they become more independent of their parents and their involvement with peers increases (Bahr, Marcos, & Maughan, 1995). Peer group influence also increases with age (Andrews, 1991).

Youth drinking is often seen either as a family activity or a peer activity. In reality, it may very well be both; young people who have their first drink at home with their family may also drink with their peers, and those who have their first drink with their peers may also consume alcohol with their family.

Adolescence is a time during which changes occur in almost all facets of an individual's life. It is often characterized as a period of upheaval and disturbance (Mayer, 1986). It is during this period of transition that there is a gradual shift in influence from parents to peers (Duncan, Tildesley, Duncan, & Hops, 1995). It appears that peer influences follow family influences on adolescent drinking behavior (Barnes & Farrell, 1992). As shown in Figure 1, modeling of parents and peers exerts influence at different points in time and for different reasons. Kandel and Andrews' (1987) explanation of the process of initiation is that in the early stage of initiation to alcohol, modeling by parents occurs as the child is aware of the parents' drinking. During the transition from childhood to adolescence, the peer group then strongly influences behavior. Peer modeling is ongoing and based largely on friends' behaviors.

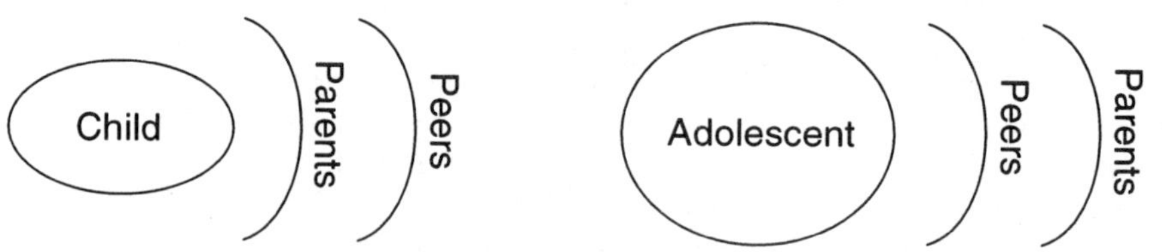

Figure 1 The shifting influence of family and peers on youth drinking.

Not only does peer drinking serve as a model for alcohol use, but it may also make alcohol accessible to the young person (Zucker, 1979). White, Bates, and Johnson (1991) note that peer activities also "provide the context in which drinking most often occurs" (p. 186). Most Australian teenagers, for example, state that their friends drink; drinking also increases as they get older (Wilks, 1987). In Brazil, as in many other countries, as young people get older they drink outside the home with their peers at night (Pechansky & Barros, 1995). Drinking situations may also serve to provide the opportunity for social interactions (Oostveen, Knibbe, & DeVries, 1996). During adolescence, the peer context for learning and reinforcing behaviors is important as it functions as the adolescent socialization framework (Barnes & Windle, 1987). It is normal and natural for a young person to want to belong to a group; participating in group activities is also part of the growth and development process.

Perception of friends' drinking, whether accurate or not, exerts a strong influence on the peer. Iannotti, Bush, and Weinfurt (1996) found that the influence of perceived use by friends increased by age from preadolescence to adolescence. In New Zealand, friends' approval of the amount consumed was found to be more important to adolescents than parental approval (Connolly et al., 1992). However, Clark (1991) points out that the individual reciprocally influences the "nodes of influence," that is, it is a two-way process and adolescents are not simply passive recipients to be acted upon, but also instigate and initiate.

The term "peer pressure" is widely used when discussing adolescent drinking. This term often has negative connotations. It implies that adolescents themselves are passive recipients of pressure. Lowe, Foxcroft, and Sibley (1993) suggest that rather than being coerced into drinking by the peer group, the young person wants to drink as part of social behavior and the opportunity to do so is provided by the peer group. This raises the controversial issue of whether adolescent drinking is the result of peer pressure or peer preference. Young people who wish to engage in drinking may select friends who accept (Smart, 1980), encourage (Gilvarry, 1996), and support (Coggans & McKellar, 1994) drinking. Thompson (1989) suggests that drinking in groups serves a social function for adolescents and helps to ease psychological distress.

DISCUSSION

Family

The significance of the family's influence on alcohol consumption by children is often overlooked or underestimated. It is important to stress the potency of the socialization process and the pivotal role that parents and family play in this process. Parents and siblings are the principal and most influential role models regarding when, where, how much, and to what extent alcohol is consumed.

It is important for parents and family members to be aware that their behavior in regard to the use of alcohol will be one of the strongest predictors of their child's later drinking patterns. All actions, both covert and overt, and all attitudes displayed will be registered by the younger members of the family. The extent to which they are then internalized and acted upon later in life will be mitigated by numerous other factors. But it is essential not to gloss over the extent to which parents and family can play a significant role in relation to the development of positive low-risk behaviors in regard to the consumption of alcohol.

It is also important to appreciate that children's alcohol expectancies develop during the early years while they are learning how alcohol is used in the family. Parents need to consider the reasons (e.g., curiosity, a party) why teenagers might choose to drink with their peers. Moreover, it would be helpful for parents to attempt to accurately assess how much and how often their children's friends might drink. It is not uncommon for parents to underestimate the level of drinking by close friends of their children and also to underestimate the frequency with which their children's friends become intoxicated (McDuffie & Bernt, 1993). This may be because parents are unwilling to believe that their children's friends—and, by implication, their own children—drink and that such drinking might be excessive on occasion.

This point is further illustrated by the work of Deffenbaugh, Hutchinson, and Blankschen (1993), who studied young people in grades 4–12 and their parents. They concluded that parents were not aware of the percentage of students in their child's grade who drank alcohol. In another study, parents of high school students in a suburban community were asked what adolescent health issues were important (Fisher, 1992). Most parents responded that substance use warranted national attention, many felt that local attention was also required, fewer considered the issue to need attention by their children's friends, and only some felt that this was an important issue for their own children. A realistic appraisal of the world of adolescent drinking is required so that parents can hold open and frank discussions with their children about situations with which they may have to cope. Communication between parents and their children is essential in order to prevent and/or solve problems, as are intervention strategies, rule-setting, and clear guidelines for behavior.

Communication with other parents is also helpful, as it helps parents to realize that others are in the same position. Parent groups can discuss the adolescent drinking situation in the community and identify practical ways that they can minimize drinking and eliminate risks, e.g., safe transport arrangements, supervision of adolescent events, and alternative entertainment options. They can also assess the recreational outlets available in their community and act as advocates for the adolescents if more activities are needed.

For parents to be able to provide information to their children, communicate with their children and other parents, and actively support school and community alcohol education, they need relevant knowledge and skills. The fact that parents may not have received alcohol information or participated in discussions about drinking when they were adolescents is often overlooked. Society expects adults, especially parents, to be able to handle such issues and problems. To do so effectively and comfortably, parents need to receive education, support, and guidance in these matters.

School

Heath (1995) considers education a key to changing norms and attitudes. The term "education" is offered here in its broadest sense and is not to be construed as meaning a one-shot program on alcohol. One of the challenges for the school system is the establishment of a philosophical base for alcohol education programs; this is pivotal in that other aspects of school-based programs revolve around the base. That is, a school system can select a no-use philosophy, a responsible decision-making philosophy, or some other approach. The no-use position may support zero tolerance to alcohol prior to the age of 21 and present alcohol as a legitimate substance for those over 21. In this position, teachers must be trained and a curriculum introduced to implement the program. It is also clear that the program's goal would be abstinence in order to accord with the philosophy.

It is important to note, however, that alcohol education programs grounded in the no-use philosophy seem to be ineffective in eliminating adolescent drinking. If approximately 90% of high school seniors indicate that they have consumed alcohol at some point in their life, the goal of abstinence is not achievable and educational programs designed to achieve this goal would not succeed. Saunders and Baily (1993) point out that programs that have attempted to stop young people from drinking are antagonistic to adolescents' behavior. If, however, the philosophy selected by the school is responsible decision-making or minimization of risk, the educational goal would be the reduction of high-risk consumption and/or the reduction in problems related to alcohol. From this perspective, the number of young people who have ever consumed alcohol is not relevant. The key issue is the program's impact on behavior. Such goals are often difficult for schools and communities to accept because they imply recognition and acceptance that some students consume alcohol at home and drink with friends. A successful educational outcome might be that a student no longer drinks to intoxication but may still consume alcohol.

Just as the goal needs to be related to the philosophical position, so too must the curriculum. The curriculum presents information and understanding in a context and can be used to influence young people's decisions (Tudor, 1986). It is critical that the curriculum be connected to the agreed upon philosophy. If the curriculum is not in accord with the philosophy and the goal, the messages are mixed. For example, exercises in a responsible decision-making curriculum might ask peers to discuss what to do if someone brings a bottle to a party, to role-play how to refuse a drink, or to present options for getting home if the driver of the car has been drinking. All of these examples realistically deal with the fact that alcohol is available and may be present in the activity described. Teachers need to be trained in the content and exercises that are suggested, as they need to be comfortable with the exercises so that they will consider using them. If teachers are not trained in the use of experiential exercises to discuss alcohol, they will have difficulty in facilitating a group discussion on what adolescents consider key elements for a party and other such issues.

It is not intended here to suggest that alcohol education be offered only at the secondary school level—it needs to be a comprehensive program that spans all grade levels. Grimes and Swisher (1989) argue the need for a comprehensive program that covers "information, self-esteem, peer acceptance, coping, alternatives, adult models, and fair policies" (p. 13). Children between the ages of 8 and 11 years in the United Kingdom were found by Lloyd (1996) to consider alcohol education information relevant to their experiences and a good platform for teacher-assisted learning. At higher grades, other issues can be brought into the discussion. For example, what does a 12-, 13-, or 14-year-old babysitter do when the person who is supposed to drive him or her home is intoxicated? Though older adolescents may also have to consider the babysitting scenario, they could also need to discuss what to do if they have consumed alcohol at a party and need to get the car home. Parents have a role to play in these scenarios as they may wish to offer options (e.g., leave the car and ride with a friend, stay overnight at the friend's home). "Building a bridge to identify where parents and peer groups overlap is a role of the school" (Milgram, 1996, p. 362). Scheier, Botvin, and Baker's (1997) study of 8th–10th-grade students in the U.S., concluded that prevention strategies should reinforce developmentally appropriate skills and also enhance personal competence.

Schools also need to take into consideration students who are having difficulty related to their own personal use of alcohol or the drinking of a significant person in the student's life. A student assistance program in the school can identify and provide assistance to students whose behaviors are interfering with learning (Milgram, 1998). Since teachers are part of society, it is more than likely that a number of them are also experiencing problems related to their drinking or the alcohol use of a loved one. Employee assistance programs, relatively common phenomena in the corporate world, need to be established by school systems for their staff.

It is important for schools to allow all programs the time needed to achieve their full impact. All too often a program is introduced into a school for a year and then is removed because the results fail to meet expectations.

Community

The community is composed of civic groups, businesses, governmental agencies, places of worship, law enforcement agencies, and so on. All of these significant groups require information on adolescent alcohol use, activities where alcohol may be a factor, and potential problems related to drinking. The community needs to clarify the existing situation and to sponsor awareness programs and recreational activities for young people. Community support is also essential for the alcohol education programs in schools. Wertz and Bigley (1985) suggest that the community create a task force to focus the energies of individuals and groups in the community and to make recommendations on needed services. The task force would be made up of representatives from the various groups in the community, which would provide a communication network.

CONCLUSION

Adolescent drinking is relatively common throughout the world, despite a variety of controls and rules. Most young people indicate that they have little difficulty in obtaining alcohol, even if they are under the minimum age of purchase. Drinking is largely viewed by them as a social activity. Parents, siblings, peers, and other members of the community influence an adolescent's attitudes and behaviors related to alcohol. However, it is also clear that the level of influence exerted depends on the individual's stage of life. That is, the family exerts a major impact on a young child, whereas this influence is diminished as the child enters adolescence. Peers play a significant role in the life of the young person during the developmental stage of adolescence.

Though parents are often the introducers of alcohol to their children, the issue of youthful drinking produces anxiety and concern among adults. Parents often do not appreciate that giving their child a small glass of a beverage containing alcohol is drinking. Not only is their significant role in their child's alcohol consumption overlooked, but the peer group is seen as being the force behind youthful drinking.

Interventions to reduce youthful drinking must take into consideration the reality of the youthful experience and focus on when, where, and with whom drinking is taking place. A first step would be to educate parents to help them understand their role in their child's drinking and also the need to discuss alcohol with their child. Dealing with the adolescent's peer group is equally important, as they need to understand the effects that alcohol has on the body and the risks that an individual may be exposed to through drinking. Helping young people to identify ways to minimize risk is essential.

The school has been designated as the provider of alcohol education in many countries. However, the school and the community are often unclear about their approach. Goals, curriculum, and teacher training need to be based on the same philosophical position. School-based alcohol education needs to be comprehensive and integrated into the curriculum in all grades.

Education, and indeed learning about drinking, should be seen as a lifelong process. Heath (1992) has urged that "entire communities be considered the target rather than just children and adolescents" (p. 141). Involving a broad cross-section of the community will provide needed support for efforts designed to minimize problems related to alcohol. It is also important to recognize the role of corporations throughout the world; a company's policy, information in newsletters, and educational sessions conducted by the company's employee assistance program can educate the employees once adulthood is reached.

Adolescent drinking is a complex phenomenon, requiring a variety of policies and programs. A partnership between the sources of influence on adolescents is essential, so that the many issues and concerns can be faced in a positive and constructive manner.

REFERENCES

Abrams, D. B., & Niaura, R. S. (1987). Social learning theory. In H. T. Blane & K. E. Leonard (Eds.), *Psychological theories of drinking and alcoholism* (pp. 131–178). New York: Guilford Press.

Ahlström, S. (1991). Social control of teenage drinking in Finland. *Contemporary Drug Problems, 18*, 433–451.

Akers, R. L. (1985). *Deviant behavior: A social learning approach.* Belmont, CA: Wadsworth.

American Psychiatric Association. (1994). *Diagnostic and statistical manual of mental disorders* (4th ed.). Washington, DC: American Psychiatric Association.

Amey, C. H., Alrecht, S. L., & Miller, M. K. (1996). Racial differences in adolescent drug use: The impact of religion. *Substance Use and Misuse, 31*, 1311–1332.

Andrews, F. K. (1991). A 1990s view of research on youthful alcohol use: Building from the work of Selden D. Bacon. In P. M. Roman (Ed.), *Alcohol: The development of sociological perspectives on use and abuse* (pp. 175–186). New Brunswick, NJ: Rutgers Center of Alcohol Studies.

Ary, D. V., Tidesley, E., Hops, H., & Andrews, J. (1993). The influence of parent, sibling, and peer modeling and attitudes on adolescent use of alcohol. *International Journal of the Addictions, 28*, 853–880.

Bacon, S. (1962). Alcohol and complex society. In D. J. Pittman & C. R. Snyder (Eds.), *Society, culture, and drinking patterns* (pp. 78-93). Carbondale, IL: Southern Illinois University Press.

Bahr, S. J., Marcos, A. C., & Maughan, S. L. (1995). Family, educational and peer influences on the alcohol use of female and male adolescents. *Journal of Studies on Alcohol, 56*, 457–469.

Barnes, G. M. (1990). Impact of the family on adolescent drinking patterns. In R. L. Collins, K. E. Leonard, & J. S. Searles (Eds.), *Alcohol and the family: Research and clinical perspectives* (pp. 137–161). New York: Guilford Press.

Barnes, G. M., & Farrell, M. P. (1992). Parental support and control as predictors of adolescent drinking, delinquency, and related problem behaviors. *Journal of Marriage and the Family, 54*, 763–776.

Barnes, G. M., Farrell, M. P., & Dintcheff, B. A. (1997). Family socialization effects on alcohol abuse and related problem behaviors among females and male adolescents. In R. W. Wilsnack & S. C. Wilsnack (Eds.), *Gender and alcohol: Individual perspectives* (pp. 156–175). New Brunswick, NJ: Rutgers Center of Alcohol Studies.

Barnes, G. M., & Windle, M. (1987). Family factors in adolescent alcohol and drug abuse. *Pediatrician: Drug and Alcohol Abuse in Children and Adolescence, 14*, 13–18.

Beck, K. H., & Lockhart, S. J. (1992). A model of parental involvement in adolescent drinking and driving. *Journal of Youth and Adolescence, 21*, 35–51.

Blane, H. T., & Hewitt, L. E. (1977). *Alcohol and youth: An analysis of the literature, 1960–75*. Rockville, MD: National Institute on Alcohol Abuse and Alcoholism.

Borton, T. (1991). The Weekly Reader National Survey on Drugs and Alcohol. *Weekly Reader.* Middletown, CT: Freid Publications.

Botvin, G. J., & Wills, T. A. (1985). Personal and social skills training: Cognitive-behavioral approaches to substance abuse prevention. In C. S. Bell & R. Battjes (Eds.), *Prevention research: Deterring drug abuse among children and adolescents* (pp. 8–49). (National Institute on Drug Abuse Monograph No. 63). Washington, DC: Government Printing Office.

Brody, G. H., & Forehand, R. (1993). Prospective associations among family forms, family processes, and adolescents' alcohol and drug use. *Behaviour Research and Therapy, 31*, 587–593.

Brook, J. S., Whiteman, M., Gordon, A. S., & Brook, D. W. (1990). The role of older brothers in younger brothers' drug use viewed in the context of parent and peer influences. *Journal of Genetic Psychology, 15*, 59–75.

Casswell, S., Gilmore, L. L., Silva, P., & Brasch, P. (1988). What children know about alcohol and how they know it. *British Journal of Addiction*, 83, 223–227.

Catalano, R. F., Morrison, D. M., Wells, E. A., Gillmore, M. R., Iritani, B., & Hawkins, J. D. (1992). Ethnic differences in family factors related to early drug initiation. *Journal of Studies on Alcohol, 53*, 208–217.

Clark, J. (1991). Learning to drink and learning how to behave when drunk. *Drug Education Journal of Australia, 55*, 215–222.

Clausen, S. E. (1996). Parenting styles and adolescent drug use behaviours. *Childhood, 3*, 403–414.

Cochran, J. K. (1993). The variable effects of religiosity and denomination on adolescent self-reported alcohol use by beverage type. *Journal of Drug Issues, 23*, 479–491.

Coggans, N., & McKellar, S. (1994). Drug use amonst peers: Peer pressure or peer preference? *Drugs: Education, Prevention and Policy, 1*, 15–26.

Connolly, G. M., Casswell, S., Stewart, J., & Silva, P. A. (1992). Drinking context and other influences on the drinking of 15-year-old New Zealanders. *British Journal of Addiction, 87*, 1029–1036.

Coombs, R. H., & Paulson, M. J. (1988). Contrasting family patterns of adolescent drug users and nonusers. *Journal of Chemical Dependency Treatment, 1*, 59–72.

Cooper, A. M. (1989). How different societies learn to drink: Well and badly. In D. Anderson (Ed.), *Drinking to your health: The allegations and the evidence* (pp. 206–220). London: Social Affairs Unit.

Deffenbaugh, K. B., Hutchinson, R. L., & Blankschen, M. P. (1993). Substance use among youth (grades 4–12) in rural Indiana: Students' reported use vs. parents' perceptions of students' use. *Journal of Alcohol and Drug Education, 39*, 19–33.

Duncan, T. E., Tildesley, E., Duncan, S. C., & Hops, H. (1995). The consistency of family and peer influences on the development of substance use in adolescence. *Addiction, 90*, 1647–1660.

Engs, R. C., Hanson, D. J., Gliksman, L., & Smythe, C. (1990). Influence of religion and culture on drinking behaviors: A test of hypotheses between Canada and the USA. *British Journal of Addiction, 85*, 1475–1482.

Fawzy, F. I., Coombs, R. H., Simon, J. M., & Bowman-Terrell, M. (1987). Family composition, socioeconomic status, and adolescent substance use. *Addictive Behaviors, 12*, 79–83.

Fergusson, D. M., Lynskey, M. T., & Horwood, J. (1994). Childhood exposure to alcohol and adolescent drinking patterns. *Addiction, 89*, 1007–1016.

Fisher, M. (1992). Parents' views of adolescent health issues. *Pediatrics, 90*, 335–341.

Fossey, E. (1993a). Identification of alcohol by smell among young children: An objective measure of early learning in the home. *Drug and Alcohol Dependence, 34*, 29–35.

Fossey, E. (1993b). Young children and alcohol: A theory of attitude development. *Alcohol and Alcoholism, 28*, 485–498.

Foxcroft, D. R., & Lowe, G. (1991). Adolescent drinking behavior and family socialization factors: A meta-analysis. *Journal of Adolescence, 14*, 255–273.

Foxcroft, D. R., & Lowe, G. (1993). Self-attributions for alcohol use in older teenagers. *Addiction Research, 1*, 1–9.

Gfroerer, J. (1987). Correlation between drug use by teenagers and drug use by older family members. *American Journal of Drug and Alcohol Abuse, 13*, 95–108.

Gilvarry, E. (1996). Use of alcohol and drugs among young people: Influences and responses. *Current Opinion in Psychiatry, 9*, 268–272.

Gilvarry, E., McCarthy, S., & McArdle, P. (1995). Substance use among schoolchildren in the north of England. *Drug and Alcohol Dependence, 37*, 255–259.

Grimes, J. D., & Swisher, J. D. (1989). Educational factors influencing adolescent decision making regarding use of alcohol and drugs. *Journal of Alcohol and Drug Education, 35*, 1–15.

Grube, J. W., Morgan, M., & Seff, M. (1989). Drinking beliefs and behaviors among Irish adolescents. *International Journal of the Addictions, 24*, 101–112.

Hadaway, C. K., Elifson, K. W., & Petersen, D. M. (1984). Religious involvement and drug use among urban adolescents. *Journal for the Scientific Study of Religion, 23*, 109–128.

Hawkins, J. D., & Fraser, M. W. (1987). The social network of drug abusers before and after treatment. In S. Einstein (Ed.), *Drug and alcohol use: Issues and factors* (pp. 73–91). New York: Plenum Press.

Hawkins, J. D., Lishner, D. M., Catalano, R. F., & Howard, M. O. (1986). Childhood predictors of adolescent substance abuse: Toward an empirically grounded theory. *Journal of Children in Contemporary Society, 8*, 11–48.

Heath, D. B. (1990). Anthropological and sociocultural perspectives on alcohol as a reinforcer. In W. M. Cox (Ed.), *Why people drink: Parameters of alcohol as a reinforcer* (pp. 263–290). New York: Gardner Press.

Heath, D. B. (1992). Prohibition or liberalization of alcohol and drugs? A sociocultural perspective. In M. Galanter (Ed.), *Alcohol and cocaine: Similarities and differences* (Recent developments in alcoholism, Vol. 10, pp. 129–145). New York: Plenum Press.

Heath, D. B. (1995). Some generalizations about alcohol and culture. In D. B. Heath (Ed.), *International handbook on alcohol and culture* (pp. 348–361). Westport, CT: Greenwood Press.

Hillman, S. B., & Sawilowsky, S. S. (1991). Maternal employment and early adolescent substance use. *Adolescence 26*, 829–837.

Hindmarsh, K. W., Porter-Serviss, S., & Opheim, E. E. (1994). Alcohol and drug use by students from Western Canada in grades 6 through 12 (1992): Have there been any changes over the past five years? *International Journal of the Addictions, 29*, 829–835.

Homel, P., & Flaherty, B. (1986). Alcohol use by Australian secondary school students. *Journal of Drug Issues, 16*, 199–207.

Huetteman, J. D., Sarvela, P. D., & Benson, R. (1992). Knowledge and attitudes toward alcohol and tobacco use among elementary school children. *Journal of Alcohol and Drug Education, 38*, 61–72.

Iannotti, R. J., Bush, P. J., & Weinfurt, K. P. (1996). Perception of friends' use of alcohol, cigarettes, and marijuana among urban schoolchildren: A longitudinal analysis. *Addictive Behaviors, 21*, 615–632.

Johnston, L. D., O'Malley, P., & Bachman, J. G. (1998). *National survey results on drug use from monitoring the future study, 1975–1997*. Washington, DC: Government Printing Office.

Jurich, A. P., Polson, C. J., Jurich, J. A., & Bates, R. A. (1985). Family factors in the lives of drug users and abusers. *Adolescence, 20*, 143–159.

Kandel, D. B. (1983). Socialization and adolescent drinking. In O. Jeanneret (Ed.), *Alcohol and youth* (Child Health and Development, Vol. 2, pp. 66–75). New York: Karger.

Kandel, D. B., & Andrews, K. (1987). Processes of adolescent socialization by parents and peers. *International Journal of the Addictions, 22*, 319–342.

Kellner, F. (1997). Alcohol. In P. MacNeil & I. Webster (Eds.), *Canada's alcohol and other drugs survey 1994: A discussion of the findings*. Ottawa, Canada: Minister of Public Works and Government Services Canada.

Klein, H. (1991). Cultural determinants of alcohol use in the United States. In D. J. Pittman & H. R. White (Eds.), *Society, culture, and drinking patterns reexamined* (pp. 114–134). New Brunswick, NJ: Rutgers Center of Alcohol Studies.

Klimova, S. (1993). Young people's alcohol habits: What good does prohibition do? *Russian Education and Society, 35*, 5–18.

Lawrence, J. J., & Maxwell, M. A. (1962). Drinking and socio-economic status. In D. J. Pittman & C. R. Snyder (Eds.), *Society, culture, and drinking patterns* (pp. 141–145). Carbondale, IL: Southern Illinois University Press.

Lemert, E. M. (1991). Alcohol, values, and social context. In D. J. Pittman & C. R. Snyder (Eds.), *Society, culture, and drinking patterns reexamined*. New Brunswick, NJ: Rutgers Center of Alcohol Studies.

Lloyd, J. (1996). Alcohol and young people: A case for supporting education about alcohol in primary and secondary schools. *Educational Review, 48*, 153–161.

Lolli, G. (1969). *Tuned in or turned off*. New York: Lion Press.

Lorch, B. (1990). Social class and its relationship to youth substance use and other delinquent behaviors. *Social Work Research Abstracts, 26*, 25–31.

Loretto, W. A. (1994). Youthful drinking in Northern Ireland and Scotland: Preliminary results from a comparative study. *Drugs: Education, Prevention and Policy, 1*, 143–152.

Lowe, G., Foxcroft, D. R., & Sibley, D. (1993). *Adolescent drinking and family life*. Chur, Switzerland: Harwood.

Maddox, G. L. (1962). Teenage drinking in the United States. In D. J. Pittman & C. R. Snyder (Eds.), *Society, culture, and drinking patterns* (pp. 230–245). Carbondale, IL: Southern Illinois University Press.

Maddox, G. L., & McCall, B. C. (1964). *Drinking among teenagers*. New Brunswick, NJ: Rutgers Center of Alcohol Studies.

Mak, A. A., & Kinsella, C. (1996). Adolescent drinking, conduct problems, and parental bonding. *Australian Journal of Psychology, 48*, 15–20.

Males, M. (1990). Youth behavior: Subcultural effect or mirror of adult behavior? *Journal of School Health, 60*, 505–508.

Mayer, J. E. (1986). Adolescent alcohol misuse: A family systems perspective. In C. M. Felsted (Ed.), *Youth and alcohol abuse: Readings and resources*. Phoenix, AZ: Oryx Press.

McDuffie, T. E., & Bernt, F. M. (1993). Contrasts between the perceptions of parents and their adolescent children regarding alcohol use and prevention. *Journal of Alcohol and Drug Education, 39*, 92–106.

McGue, M., Sharma, A., & Benson, P. (1996). Parent and sibling influences on adolescent alcohol use and misuse: Evidence from a U.S. adoption cohort. *Journal of Studies on Alcohol, 57*, 8–18.

Milgram, G. (with Editors of Consumer Reports Books). (1990). *The facts about drinking: Coping with alcohol use, abuse, and alcoholism.* Mount Vernon, NY: Consumers Union.

Milgram, G.G. (1996). Responsible decision making regarding alcohol: A re-emerging prevention/education strategy for the 1990s. *Journal of Drug Education, 26*, 357–365.

Milgram, G. G. (1998). An analysis of student assistance programs: Connecticut, New Jersey, and New York. *Journal of Drug Education, 28*, 107–116.

Monarca, S., Modolo, M. A. (1985). Alcohol, tobacco and psychoactive medicine consumption among high school students of 10 Italian towns. In International Council on Alcohol and Addictions (Ed.), *Proceedings of the 31st International Institute on the Prevention and Treatment of Alcoholism* (pp. 282–292). Lausanne, Switzerland: International Council on Alcohol and Addictions.

Moukolo, A. (1990). Alcohol and its main functions in the Congo. In J. Maula, M. Lindblad, & C. Tigerstedt (Eds.), *Alcohol in developing countries* (pp. 127–133). Helsinki, Finland: Nordic Council for Alcohol and Drug Research.

Mullen, K., Williams, R., & Hunt, K. (1996). Irish descent, religion, and alcohol and tobacco use. *Addiction, 91*, 243–254.

National Institute on Alcohol Abuse and Alcoholism. (1997). *Alcohol and health: Ninth special report to the U.S. Congress* (National Institute of Health Publication No. 97-4017). Washington, DC: Department of Health and Human Services.

Needle, R., McCubbin, H., Wilson, M., Reineck, R., Lazar, A., & Mederer, H. (1986). Interpersonal influences in adolescent drug use: The role of older siblings, parents, and peers. *International Journal of the Addictions, 21*, 739–766.

Newman, I. M., & Ming, Q. (1998, January). *Learning to drink in China.* Unpublished paper presented at a meeting of the Working Group on Learning about Drinking, International Center for Alcohol Policies, Washington, DC.

Odejide, A. O., Ohaeri, J. U., Adelekan, M. F., & Ikuesan, B. A. (1989). Alcohol use among Nigerian youth: The need for drug education and alcohol policy. In National Directorate for the Prevention of Alcohol and Drug Problems (Ed.), *35th International Congress on Alcoholism and Drug Dependence: Vol. 3* (Proceedings, pp. 441–450). Oslo, Norway: National Directorate for the Prevention of Alcohol and Drug Problems.

Oostveen, T., Knibbe, R., & DeVries, H. (1996). Social influences on young adults' alcohol consumption: Norms, modeling, pressure, socializing, and conformity. *Addictive Behaviors, 21*, 187–197.

Patock-Peckham, J. A., Hutchinson, G. T., Cheong, J., & Nagoshi, C. T. (1998). Effect of religion and religiosity on alcohol use in a college student sample. *Drug and Alcohol Dependence, 49*, 81–88.

Pechansky, F., & Barros, F. C. (1995). Problems related to alcohol consumption by adolescents living in the city of Porto Alegre, Brazil. *Journal of Drug Issues, 25*, 735–750.

Perkins, H. W. (1985). Religious traditions, parents, and peers as determinants of alcohol and drug use among college students. *Review of Religious Research, 27*, 15–31.

Perkins, H. W. (1987). Parental religion and alcohol use problems as intergenerational predictors of problem drinking among youth. *Journal for the Scientific Study of Religion, 26*, 340–357.

Poulin, J. E. (1991). Racial differences in the use of drugs and alcohol among low income youth and young adults. *Journal of Sociology and Social Welfare, 18*, 159–166.

Rey, G. N. (1995). Mexico. In D. B. Heath (Ed.), *International handbook on alcohol and culture* (pp. 179–189). Westport, CT: Greenwood Press.

Rhodes, J. E., Gingiss, P. L., & Smith, P. B. (1994). Risk and protective factors for alcohol use among pregnant African-American, Hispanic, and White adolescents: The influence of peers, sexual partners, family members, and mentors. *Addictive Behaviors, 19*, 555–564.

Rossi, D. (1994). Youth and alcohol in Italy. *Alcologia, 6*, 165–169.

Salvagnini, M. (1985). The drinking habits of a student population in Southern Italy. In International Council on Alcohol and Addictions (Ed.), *31st International Institute on the Prevention and Treatment of Alcoholism* (*Proceedings*, p. 263). Lausanne, Switzerland: International Council on Alcohol and Addictions.

Samuels, T., Schneider, M., & Everatt, D. (1998, January). *Learning to drink: A report on how some youth in Southern Africa learn to drink*. Unpublished paper presented to the Working Group on Learning about Drinking, International Center for Alcohol Policies, Washington, DC.

Saunders, B., & Baily, S. (1993). Alcohol and young people: Minimizing the harm. *Drug and Alcohol Review, 12*, 81–90.

Scheier. L. M., Botvin, G. J., & Baker, E. (1997). Risk and protective factors as predictors of adolescent alcohol involvement and transitions in alcohol use: A prospective analysis. *Journal of Studies on Alcohol, 58*, 652–667.

Segal, B. M. (1987). *Russian drinking: Use and abuse of alcohol in pre-Revolutionary Russia*. New Brunswick, NJ: Rutgers Center of Alcohol Studies.

Selnow, G. W. (1987). Parent-child relationships and single and two parent families: Implications for substance usage. *Journal of Drug Education, 17*, 315–326.

Sher, K. J., Gershuny, B. S., Peterson, L., & Raskin, G. (1997). The role of childhood stressors in the intergenerational transmission of alcohol use disorders. *Journal of Studies on Alcohol, 58*, 414–427.

Smart, R. G. (1980). *The new drinkers: Teenage use and abuse of alcohol*. Toronto, Canada: Addiction Research Foundation of Ontario.

Smart, R. G., & Fejer, D. (1974). *Drug education: Current issues, future directions* (Program Report Series No. 3). Toronto, Canada: Addiction Research Foundation of Ontario.

Thompson, K. M. (1989). Effects of early alcohol use on adolescents' relations with peers and self-esteem: Patterns over time. *Adolescence, 24*, 837–849.

Thompson, K. M., & Wilsnack, R. W. (1987). Parental influence on adolescent drinking: Modeling, attitudes, or conflict? *Youth & Society, 19*, 22–43.

Thorlindsson, T., & Vilhjalmsson, R. (1991). Factors related to cigarette smoking and alcohol use among adolescents. *Adolescence, 26*, 399–418.

Torres, M. A., & Sanchez, J. H. (1985). A comparative study of the characteristics of the consumption of alcohol between the province and the city of Valencia (Spain) among secondary school students. In International Council on Alcohol and Addictions (Ed.), *Proceedings of the 31st International Institute on the Prevention and Treatment of Alcoholism* (pp. 304–321). Lausanne, Switzerland: International Council on Alcohol and Addictions.

Tudor, R. (1986). The school: Influences and approaches. *Australian Drug and Alcohol Review, 5*, 233–237.

Ullman, A. D. (1962). First drinking experience as related to age and sex. In D. J. Pittman & C. R. Snyder (Eds.), *Society, culture, and drinking patterns* (pp. 259–266). Carbondale, IL: Southern Illinois University Press.

Weill, J., & LeBourhis, B. (1994). Factors predictive of alcohol consumption in a representative sample of French male teenagers: A five-year prospective study. *Drug and Alcohol Dependence, 35*, 45–50.

Wertz, D. C., & Bigley, T. C. (1985). Mobilizing a community to challenge adolescent substance abuse: An educator's perspective. *Journal of Alcohol and Drug Education, 31*, 1–6.

White, H. R., Bates, M., & Johnson, V. (1991). Learning to drink: Familial, peer, and media influences. In D. J. Pittman & H. R. White (Eds.), *Society, culture, and drinking patterns reexamined* (pp. 177–196). New Brunswick, NJ: Rutgers Center of Alcohol Studies.

Wilks, J. (1987). Drinking among teenagers in Australia: Research findings, problems and prospects. *Australian Drug and Alcohol Review, 6*, 207–226.

Wilks, J. (1991). Adolescent attitudes toward alcohol. *Drug Education Journal of Australia, 5*, 239–244.

Wilks, J. (1992). Adolescent views on risky and illegal alcohol use. *Drug and Alcohol Review, 11*, 137–143.

Yguel, J. (with Luciani, S., Duflo, B., M'Bamezoui, C., Froment, A., Bard, D., & Gentilini, M.). (1990). Consumption of alcohol drinks in three different parts of Cameroon. In J. Maula, M. Lindblad, & C. Tigerstedt (Eds.), *Alcohol in developing countries* (pp. 113–126). Helsinski, Finland: Nordic Council for Alcohol and Drug Research.

Zagonski, A. (1986, June). Drinking of alcohol by the Polish youth. In International Center for Alcohol and Alcoholism (Ed.), *32nd International Institute on the Prevention and Treatment of Alcoholism* (Abstracts/Resumes). Budapest, Hungary: International Center for Alcohol and Alcoholism.

Zinberg, N. E., & Bean, M. H. (1981). Introduction: Alcohol use, alcoholism, and the problems of treatment. In M. H. Bean & N. E. Zinberg (Eds.), *Dynamic approaches to the understanding and treatment of alcoholism* (pp. 1–35). New York: Free Press.

Zucker, R. A. (1979). Developmental aspects of drinking from birth through the young adult years. In H. T. Blane & M. E. Chafetz (Eds.), *Youth, alcohol and social policy* (pp. 91–146). New York: Plenum Press.

Chapter 5

Religious Influences on Drinking: Illustrations From Select Groups

Shoshana Weiss

"Drink is a great sin and makes you forget Allah"
"Drink is the weapon of Satan"
(Moslem proverbs)

"Wine brings joy to the human heart"
"Man comes from dust and ends in dust, and in between, let's have a drink"
(Jewish proverbs)

The *Oxford English Dictionary* defines "learning" as the "action of *learn*," and defines "learn" as "to get knowledge of a subject being studied, to become skilled in a particular activity and to be told or hear information."

The formal and informal psychosocial mechanisms by which people learn to drink or not to drink encompass a wide range of components, such as religious affiliation, ethnic customs, parental supervision, peer influence, personal experiences, observations of behaviors of others, media impact, legal intervention, and school-based education programs. Thus, people learn about drinking by modeling, reinforcement, and instruction (Stumphauzer, 1983).

Although alcohol has been used in most societies throughout the world, there is no universal use, meaning, or function for alcohol. Patterns of belief and behavior with respect to alcoholic drinks vary enormously from one society to another (Heath, 1982), and the existence of these differences in drinking practices is well documented (Greeley, McCready, & Theisen, 1980; Heath, 1995).

Alcohol is seen in different societies in different ways—as a depressant medicine, hard drug, teratogenic agent, religious symbol, social symbol, appetizer, food, solvent, chemical that changes mood, anesthetic compound, disinfectant, and economic product. People throughout the world use it for different purposes, in different ways, and with different consequences. These differences in the perception of alcohol and in drinking practices may at least partly stem from different religious frameworks. Such differences are expressed in attitudes toward alcohol, the extent and location of use, and the tolerance of intoxication. In societies in which adults widely consume alcohol, children appear to gain strong impressions about its use from an early age, while in societies in which drinking is not widespread children learn about drinking in their late teens.

Social context is a prime regulator of alcohol use, and religious precepts may play a major role in determining constraints on its use in society. In the field of studies on alcohol there is an extensive literature that attempts to associate differences in religious norms across various populations with the prevalence of alcohol-related harm among these populations (Frankel & Whitehead, 1981; Heath, 1980; Mäkelä, 1975; White, 1982).

Religious denominations have been shown to affect the drinking behavior of their members. Although a comprehensive interplay of multiple influences is probably entailed in the processes involved in learning about drinking, consideration of religious explanatory factors may contribute to one's understanding. Religion is one social characteristic that has been found to be associated with drinking (Hawks & Bahr, 1992) and to be a powerful force in molding societies. Religious commandments and edicts impact upon a person's drinking, and can determine who has access to alcohol as well as how, when, where, and in what circumstances people are expected or allowed to drink alcoholic beverages. Religious orientation shapes beliefs and norms governing the use of alcohol and has an influence on various elements such as gender roles, folklore, ethnic habits, nutrition, and social control (Gilbert & Collins, 1997; Heath, 1995).

This chapter examines sociological and epidemiological studies on religion and drinking in relation to the way one learns about drinking in different social, cultural, and religious settings. Particular reference is made to two religions, Judaism and Islam, and also to some Christian denominations. The chapter is presented in two main sections. The first focuses on prescriptive religious groups. Judaism is depicted as an illustrative case of the application of clear and precise prescriptive guidelines in regard to alcohol. This is followed by examples from other prescriptive and nonproscriptive religions. The second main section addresses religions where alcohol consumption is clearly proscribed, with case illustrations from Mormons, Methodists, and Moslems. Finally, the chapter draws together the findings and speculates on the role and impact of different religious affiliations.

PRESCRIPTIVE RELIGIOUS GROUPS

The Jews

Early research suggests that societies that have a ritual orientation toward alcohol consumption have lower rates of alcohol-related problems (Bales, 1946; Frankel & Whitehead, 1981; Glad, 1947; Shuval & Krasilowsky, 1963; Snyder, 1958; White, 1982). It further suggests that the prevalence of alcohol-related harm and intoxication are low in societies characterized by drinking practices that are an integral part of life, i.e., attitudes toward drinking are consistent and unambiguous, prescriptions advocate moderate, nondisruptive drinking, and proscriptions exist against excessive consumption.

Jews, and especially religious Jews, are the most commonly cited example of a group that has this constellation of ritual orientation toward the consumption of alcohol. The consumption of alcohol is an integral part of rituals on the Sabbath and on many feast days celebrated throughout the year. It has been argued that moderate drinking is modeled for the young and maintained by social custom (Bales 1946; Peele, 1984). Children are gradually introduced to alcohol in the family setting, and they thereby become "literate" about alcohol. Drinking is not presented as a rite of passage into adulthood and is not associated with masculinity or social power. Children observe adults drinking, and it is the adults who control the amounts drunk and who model proper behavior when drinking. Strong disapproval is expressed when an individual violates the standards set. Sobriety is stressed as a religious obligation and abstinence is acceptable.

The early socialization of Jewish children to the ritual, ceremonial and familial use of alcohol beverages provides a comprehensive orientation to the when, where, and how of drinking. Further, such a comprehensive and structured introduction is thought to foster moderate consumption. It is believed that the association of drinking with ritual occasions also helps to protect Jews from intoxication and harm. Jewish norms about drinking are explicit. Intoxication is seen as an abomination, a perversion, or a profanity. Jews learn to drink in moderation through acquiring knowledge of the unequivocal prescriptions and proscriptions about alcohol consumption and about what constitutes appropriate drinking behavior. They manage to combine a high level of acceptability of drinking in respect of specific and frequently occurring occasions with clear proscriptions against intoxication. Moreover, Jews also hold a stereotype of the drunken Gentile and the sober Jew. Thus, through the ceremonial use of alcohol Jews learn how to drink in a controlled manner. And it is through reference to outsiders and a broader pattern of religious ideas that Jews also learn how *not* to drink.

All Jews (Orthodox, Conservative, or Reform) have in common the association of drinking small amounts of alcohol during religious observances. Such religious observances are participated in from childhood, and thus from an early age they help to build a stable, consistent attitude toward drinking. This is a convivial type of drinking, and sharp sanctions exist within the religion against excessive alcohol consumption. The only exception to this is one holiday, Purim, when intoxication is allowed.

Throughout the anthropological and sociological literatures, much is made of the fact that a high proportion of Jews in the Diaspora drink and that, inspite of having a high frequency of drinking occasions, they have a relatively low prevalence of alcohol-related harm and low rates of alcoholism. However, it has been argued that as Jews begin to assimilate more into foreign societies, they become increasingly acculturated and adopt patterns and beliefs of the mainstream population. Moreover, as they decrease observance of Orthodox rituals and become more secular, or as their religious affiliation moves from Orthodox to Conservative or to Reform, their alcohol-related problems and intoxication levels increase because of less strict religious orders.

So far, most studies in the Diaspora have shown that Jews do exhibit drinking problems and alcoholism, but they have fewer problems than other religious groups. Moreover, there is good evidence to suggest that although Orthodoxy has declined, the traditional disapproval of intoxication probably continues (Bainwol & Gressard, 1985; Cahalan, 1982; Frankel & Whitehead, 1981; Glad, 1947; Glassner & Berg, 1980; Glatt, 1970; Gressard & Bainwol, 1988; Keller, 1970; Knupfer & Room, 1967; Monteiro & Schuckit, 1989; Olitzky, 1992; Perkins, 1987; Schuckit, 1990; Snyder, Palgi, Eldar, & Elian, 1982; Wilkinson, 1970; Zimberg, 1977).

Jews still use alcohol as part of their rituals and in order to distinguish certain events. Alcohol is still a symbol that gives an event importance, whether the occasion is secular or religious. And children are still exposed to the religious and ritual symbolism of drinking in their formative years in the home and family, which sets a good example and incorporates drinking into the course of everyday life. Children are served alcohol but they avoid getting drunk when they perceive that the adults around them do not get drunk. Religious standards are verbalized again and again during the young person's upbringing, and a consensus is established on when, where, and how to drink.

Thus, beginning at an early age, children are gradually introduced to alcohol, in small amounts, on special occasions, within a strong, well-integrated family group. It is a "natural" process and not a conscious, detailed decision-making process. Most of the children do not even consider these situations to be "drinking occasions," since the consumption of alcohol is but a small part of another event and not the primary focus of the activity. Drinking accompanies rather than dominates or controls. No moral importance is attached to drinking or not drinking. It is neither a virtue nor a sin. It is an ordinary thing.

The children are not taught to use alcohol in order to overcome unpleasant mood states, discomfort, fears, or depression. Nor are they taught to consume alcohol in order to maintain a positive self-concept, sleep well, or show manhood and virility. Alcohol consumption is regarded as serving convivial social functions, not psychoactive ones. This focus on alcohol presumably has a deep and lasting influence on children's attitudes and behavioral intentions toward alcohol. What has been learned in this way might later determine their preference for special drinking contexts and the kind of experience associated with them. However, it cannot be assumed that every Jewish person conforms to this learning process or prescribed religious norms. Thus, being Jewish is not in itself a protection against alcoholism or alcohol problems. Moreover, it may lead to underdiagnosis of those who have become alcoholics.

The results of most studies conducted over the past three to four decades among Jews support the view that prescriptive rules about drinking are effective in creating a protective barrier against alcohol-related problems when Jews are compared to other religious groups. While it is difficult to garner definitive evidence to prove that religious prescriptions and their implementation are the sole explanatory factors, religious conviction nonetheless serves as a strong predictor of the low levels of alcohol-related problems among Jews both in the Diaspora and in Israel.

Although there is a lack of methodologically sound research that might prove that religion is the ultimate factor, it is likely that a range of complex factors interact to produce decreased levels of alcohol-related problems among Jews. There remains, however, consistent and compelling evidence to support the positive impact of particular religious orientations to alcohol.

There are substantial epidemiological data that support this view. For instance, Israel consistently ranks lowest, among nations for which statistics are available, on alcohol consumption and alcohol-related problems (Harkin, Anderson, & Goos, 1997; Kandel & Sudit, 1982). In comparison with Western and Eastern European countries, North America, and Australia, the figures for alcoholism and problem drinking in Israel are low, despite the fact that there has been an increasing trend of alcohol-related problems and alcoholism in Israel over the past two decades (Weiss, 1988, 1993, 1995). In addition, a 1994 study (Harel, Keny, & Rahav, 1998) revealed that compared to 23 European countries and Canada, Israel ranked lowest in regard to youth drunkenness (last place among youngsters aged 15 years, 22nd place among adolescents aged 13 years).

However, there is some increased concern about changing levels and patterns of consumption among Israeli Jews. A part of the increase in alcohol use among adults in Israel (Rahav, Teichman, Gil, Rosenblum, & Bar-Hamburger, 1998) has been attributed to the waves of immigration from the former Soviet Union, where the prevalence of alcoholism is estimated to be very high (Weiss, 1994). Some of the newcomers are not Jewish, and most of the Jewish people were separated from the Jewish tradition in the former Soviet Union. Thus, they brought with them patterns of excessive drinking, despite the argument that Russian Jews drink less than Gentile Russians (Manilowitz, 1992). What Israeli Jews consider heavy drinking is the norm for many Russian people. They have not learned to drink moderately in the "Jewish way," which manages to combine a high level of acceptability of drinking in specific occasions with proscriptions against intoxication. Indeed, a study conducted in 1995 among 18 to 40-year-old long-

Table 1 Past year drunkenness and consumption of distilled spirits among 18 to 40-year-olds in Israel by father's country of origin (%).

	Israel	Asia & Africa	W. Europe & America	E. Europe (old)	E. Europe (newcomers)
Drank distilled spirits	15.4	15.3	24.1	23.3	31.3
Got drunk	10.4	5.7	13.7	14.2	18.5

Source: Rahav & Teichman (1998).

term residents and newcomers in a nationwide sample of households (Rahav & Teichman, 1998) showed that newcomers from the former Soviet Union got drunk in the past year more than the long-term residents, and drank more distilled spirits (see Table 1). Other data indicate that among younger Israeli people aged 12–18 years the proportion reporting "ever getting drunk" is substantially higher for newcomers than long-term residents (Harel, Keny, & Rahav, 1998).

There is also interest and concern about the changing drinking patterns of Jewish youth. Table 2 shows that the proportion of Israeli Jewish adolescents in the north of Israel ($N = 1{,}458$) who engage in nonritual drinking with friends increases through grades 9 to 12 (15 to 18-year old), while the proportion drinking with their family decreases (Weiss & Moore, 1994). These data also show that drinking at home decreases through grades 9 to 12 and drinking in pubs increases, and that Jewish adolescents hardly ever drink alone (3.5% of male drinkers, 1.7% of female drinkers). Increasingly, they drink with same-age or older friends and they drink primarily for pleasure or because the drink is tasty. However, only 3.3% of drinkers acknowledged drinking because of peer pressure. In the U.S., friends appear to have a significant influence on alcohol use, and adolescents cite peers as their primary source of access to alcohol (Lorion, Bussell, & Goldberg, 1991).

Table 2 Companion of drinkers and preferred places of drinking among Jewish adolescents, by school grade (%).

	Grade level			
	9	10	11	12
Companion(s)				
Family	47.6	33.4	22.1	21.5
Friend(s)	33.3	49.8	64.0	64.3
Location				
Home	51.1	35.6	23.9	20.4
Pub	13.9	20.0	43.9	45.8

Source: Weiss & Moore (1994).

Part of the increase in alcohol-problems reported in Israel in the last decades may also be attributed to the consumption of beer among adults and youth, which is not a typically traditional Israeli-Jewish alcohol drink, as are wines or distilled spirits. Thus, consumption of beer may be influenced by foreign elements and other sources such as the media and advertisements. Until 1998, beer was the most popular alcohol drink among youth when consumed in nonritual drinking settings such as in pubs, or at parties, etc. (Rahav et al., 1998; Weiss & Moore, 1994). In 1998, wine became the most popular beverage among youth. Beer consumption is also the main concern of those who deal with alcohol abuse prevention. There are more advertisements for beer in newspapers, magazines, and on television in comparison with the more traditional Jewish alcohol beverages—wines and distilled spirits. This may reflect the fact that drinking wines and distilled spirits are more integral to learning about drinking within the religious framework, whereas beer drinking is encouraged by other nonreligious, foreign orientations.

The Jewish schools in Israel provide alcohol education programs that emphasize Jewish values and norms concerning alcohol consumption (Moore & Weiss, 1985). Thus, the main objective is not to achieve "dryness," but rather to strengthen those who choose to abstain and to strengthen patterns of "correct drinking," among those who choose to drink, i.e., controlled and moderate nonritual drinking, to recommend nondrinking before driving and during pregnancy, to emphasize the deep-seated opposition to drunkenness as a constituent element of Jewish identity, and to present intoxication as an non-Jewish vice (Weiss, 1988; Yanai & Weiss, 1994). A study carried out among 1,346 religious and secular Jewish students in 1993 in the northern region of Israel (Weiss & Moore, 1995b) showed that parents are an important source of alcohol information for both religious and secular Jewish youth. School is an important source for secular students, but does not appear to hold the significance for those more religious. Students also gain information from other sources, particularly the media.

The Jews, as a case illustration of particular way of learning about drinking, appear therefore to offer support for the long-held view that clear, consistent, and comprehensive rules, which are both proscriptive and prescriptive, are associated with relatively low rates of alcohol-related harm.

Other Prescriptive and Non-Proscriptive Religious Groups

As far as other religious denominations are concerned, there are various Christian denominations, such as Catholics, Presbyterians, or Episcopalians, which hold prescriptive views with regard to alcohol. There are also some denominations, such as Baptists or Seventh-Day Adventists, which are classified as proscriptive; they do not use alcohol in their religious ceremonies and they prohibit alcohol use by members. However, actual behavior does not always directly reflect these religious beliefs.

Various studies have shown that religious Christian groups permitting alcohol use may be associated with higher rates of consumption in general but lower rates of binge drinking than groups with a proscriptive orientation (Amoatengy & Bahr, 1986; Bock, Cochran, & Leeghley, 1987; Lorch & Hughes, 1988). For example, a recent American study (Kutter & McDermott, 1997) confirmed that among people who have ever used alcohol, there is a positive relationship between proscription and binge drinking. Table 3 presents the incidence of binge drinking by religious proscription among 238 adolescents (13 to 18 years old) of various Protestant affiliations, who reported ever having used alcohol. Those affiliated with proscriptive religious groups reported the highest rates of binge drinking. Though abstaining from alcohol was reported more frequently by members of proscriptive religious groups than by members of other groups, the incidence of binge drinking among adolescents was two to three times higher in the proscriptive group.

Religions that focus on abstinence often do not provide information about alcohol or guidelines to assist in the control of consumption, if one should choose to drink. Forbidding drinking and conveying negative attitudes toward alcohol may prevent some members from experimenting with alcohol, but when members violate that prohibition by using alcohol, they have no guidelines by which to control their behavior and are at increased risk of heavy use (Bock et al., 1987; Kutter & McDermott, 1997). For the majority of people, providing information about alcohol and guidelines to help them control their own use appears to be more effective than condemning alcohol consumption, if the goal is to prevent binge drinking (Lorch & Hughes, 1988; Kutter & McDermott, 1997). An alternative explanation is that a proscriptive orientation may encourage rebellion among youth and thereby foster heavy drinking behaviors (Amoatengy & Bahr, 1986).

Although various Christian religions are prescriptive, some have higher rates of heavy drinking, intoxication, and alcohol problems in comparison to Judaism (Monteiro & Schuckit, 1989; Perkins 1987; Weiss, in press). Table 4 provides data comparing rates of heavy drinking, problems, and alcoholism among male

Table 3 Alcohol use, binge drinking and religious affiliation among Protestant adolescents (%).

	Drinking patterns		
Religious affiliation	Ever used	Ever binged	Binged 5+ times
Nonproscriptive ($N = 80$)			
Unitarian, Episcopal, Presbyterian	90.0	38.9	6.9
Moderate ($N = 71$)			
Lutheran, Methodist	85.9	44.3	11.5
Proscriptive ($N = 84$)			
Baptist	65.5	49.1	21.8

Source: Kutter & McDermott (1997).

Table 4 Alcohol consumption variables among male Jewish and Christian* students at a U.S. university (%).

	Jews ($N = 110$)	Christians ($N = 594$)
≥2 alcohol problems	13	22
Alcoholism-any relative	3	10
≥6 drinks on single occasion†	36	47

*The Christian group included proscriptive and prescriptive religions.
†A drink is defined as one 12 oz. (355 ml) can of beer, one 4 oz. (ca. 118 ml) glass of wine, or 1.5 oz. (ca. 45 ml) of 80° proof distilled spirits.
Source: Monteiro & Schuckit (1989).

Jewish and Christian students at a university in the U.S., and alcoholism within their families. The proportion of individuals falling into any of these three problem categories was found to be consistently higher among those from Christian religions.

While some studies have found differences in alcohol consumption and alcohol problems such as heavy drinking between Protestants and Roman Catholics (Partanen, 1990; Perkins, 1987), other studies have not revealed such differences (Cronin, 1995). Comparisons between Christian groups have not always shown consistent results. For instance, a recent study (Peckham-Patock, Hutchinson, Cheong, & Nagoshi, 1998) of 263 American college students who consumed alcohol found that students with no religious affiliation reported higher levels of intoxication than those with either Catholic or Protestant religious affiliations.

Higher alcohol consumption among Roman Catholics than among Protestants has been reported in the Netherlands (Schippers, 1998) and the U.S. (Engs, Diebold, & Hanson, 1996). Studies of drinking habits in various Christian countries, such as France, Ireland, Italy, Mexico, and the United Kingdom and even within the same religious groups in the U.S. and Canada (Engs, Hanson, Gliksman, & Smythe, 1990) suggest that wider environmental influences have a strong effect on alcohol use patterns that go beyond the influence of a Christian religious affiliation.

It is obvious that there are conflicting findings from various studies. The prevalence of alcohol problems and the processes involved in learning about drinking appear less clear within the framework of Christianity. Religion has less impact in contexts where intoxication and binge drinking are socially acceptable and tolerated, and especially among people who are less involved in church activities (Heath, 1995; Schippers, 1998). Thus, in various prescriptive Christian societies other factors may ultimately dominate in the processes entailed in learning about drinking.

ABSTINENCE-TEACHING RELIGIOUS GROUPS

Let us now turn to religious groups where total abstinence is taught. It has been suggested that if a society is characterized predominantly by religious proscriptive rules about alcohol use, deviation from those rules may be associated with higher rates of problems because of the absence of prescriptive rules about how to behave if one does drink (Bales, 1946; Mizruchi & Perrucci, 1962, 1970; Skolnick, 1958; Snyder, 1958; Straus & Bacon, 1953). Thus, where proscriptive beliefs dominate and prescriptive beliefs are absent, the prevalence of alcohol-related harm among drinkers may be high because of the absence of guidelines concerning appropriate drinking behavior or because of the sole emphasis on the negative consequences of alcohol consumption.

Early studies of Mormons and Methodists—two religious groups in which the use of alcohol is proscribed—reported a relatively high probability of alcohol problems (mainly high frequency of intoxication) among Mormons (Snyder, 1958; Straus & Bacon, 1953) and Methodists (Skolnick, 1958) who drink. These early studies found that, when members of an abstinence-teaching group drink, they tend to do so more heavily than their peers in groups that do not teach abstinence, and, furthermore, that a relatively large proportion of these individuals may develop problems. However, when abstainers and drinkers are considered together, Mormons in the U.S. overall have a low proportion of problem drinkers, and alcoholism among Mormons is relatively uncommon (Hawks, 1990; Hawks & Bahr, 1992; Mäkelä, 1975; Snyder, 1958).

Although recent studies among Mormons have not always confirmed more heavy drinking among Mormon drinkers (Hawks & Bahr, 1992), earlier work found that people with no religious experience concerning moderate drinking, no specific directives about drinking, and no practice in learning how to stop were more likely to have alcohol-related health and social problems (Mizruchi & Perrucci, 1962, 1970; Wilkinson, 1970). In these conditions, those who drank learned to do so at an older age and outside their home or their community (Hawks & Bahr, 1992). This type of learning experience in relation to alcohol has been postulated in the earlier studies as contributing to the development of alcohol problems. In contexts where any drinking at all is viewed as a break with the group's beliefs, it has been argued that extremes in behavior and problems are more likely to occur. It was reasoned that where alcohol is considered a "forbidden fruit," it becomes all the more tempting.

Among groups such as Moslems, where "drinking runs contrary to the Islamic innermost religious beliefs" (Heath, 1995) and who espouse complete abstinence (Baasher, 1981), it is often assumed that the prevalence of drinking and of alcohol-related harm will be low. However, this appears not always to be the case. There is some evidence that Moslems do drink alcoholic beverages (Weiss & Moore, 1992; Abu-Sa'ad, 1996) and that the prevalence of daily drinking among Moslems in Israel, for example, is relatively high compared to other groups (Teichman, Rahav, & Barnea, 1994). There is also concern that Moslems who drink alcohol may be more likely to incur problems than drinkers whose religion views alcohol less negatively.

While there are many descriptions in the literature of Moslems as an example of an abstinent society with a total prohibition on consumption of alcohol

Table 5 Alcohol consumption among Arab ($N = 581$) and Jewish ($N = 2,374$) male adults in Israel in past week (%).

	Frequency of consumption			
Beverage type	**None**	**1–2**	**Almost daily**	**Daily**
Beer				
Arabs	51.4	25.3	15.2	8.2
Jews	51.3	37.9	8.1	2.7
Distilled spirits				
Arabs	71.1	19.7	5.7	3.5
Jews	84.0	14.4	1.1	0.5
Wine				
Arabs	76.7	16.6	4.7	1.9
Jews	72.1	26.6	0.9	0.5

Source: Teichman, Rahav, & Barnea (1994).

beverages, there is only limited literature comparing Moslems to other religious groups within the same society. Some systematic studies have been conducted among Moslems and Druze[1] in Israel (e.g., Weiss, Sawa, Abdeen, & Yanai, 1999) and among Moslems in Egypt (e.g., Soueif & Darweesh, 1986; Soueif & Hannourah, 1987; Soueif & Youssuf, 1990; Soueif & Yunis, 1988). But fewer studies have been conducted in the many other countries with Moslem populations (e.g., Dass, 1981; Dogan, 1982; Drower, 1956; Garretsen & van de Goor, 1995; Ifabumuyi, 1982; Jernigan, 1997; Midgley, 1971; Samarasinghe, 1990; Touhami & Bouktib, 1990; United Nations, 1993). In many countries with a Moslem minority population no data are available.

A nationwide study of Jewish and Arab (mainly Moslem) adult males aged 18–40 years was conducted in Israel in 1989. The sample comprised 581 non-Jewish and 2,374 Jewish males (Teichman et al., 1994). Tables 5 and 6 present alcohol consumption during the past week and month. Daily and almost daily drinking were more prevalent among Arab adults across all beverage types, most notably for the consumption of beer and distilled spirits. Reports of non-consumption in the previous week were similar for each beverage type and religious denomination, with the exception that more Jews reported a lower consumption of spirits. The most commonly consumed beverage among both Jews and Arabs was beer, followed by distilled spirits for Arabs, and then wine for both groups.

It appears from the data presented in Tables 5 and 6 that daily and almost-daily alcohol consumption in the Israeli Moslem male population is not uncommon and that this level of consumption is higher than that of the Jewish population.

[1]The Druze broke away from Islam in the 10th century.

Table 6 Alcohol consumption among Arab ($N = 581$) and Jewish ($N = 2{,}374$) male adults in Israel in past month (%).

	Frequency of consumption				
Beverage type	**None**	**1–2**	**3–9**	**10–24**	**≥25**
Beer					
Arabs	40.9	14.0	14.6	17.2	13.3
Jews	33.8	21.3	24.1	13.6	7.1
Distilled spirits					
Arabs	53.6	16.1	14.3	10.1	6.2
Jews	64.8	19.2	10.6	3.4	2.0
Wine					
Arabs	62.0	14.6	11.6	6.7	5.1
Jews	49.6	26.0	17.0	4.7	2.7

Source: Teichman, Rahav, & Barnea (1994).

Findings from a 1996 study of 16- to 18-year-old Druze, Moslem, Jewish, and Christian male adolescents in the north of Israel are shown in Tables 7 and 8 (Weiss, 1997). The study revealed similar levels of consumption across the four religious groups and slightly higher percentages of heavy drinking among Moslems and Druze in comparison to Jews. Christians and Jews were more predominant among the moderate consumers, i.e., those drinking 1–2 drinks per occasion. Overall, among drinkers in each of these four religious groups, Jews and Christians tended to be slightly lighter drinkers, and Druze and Moslems tended to be slightly heavier drinkers.

When patterns of heavy drinking according to respondents' religious denomination were examined, Christian youth were the group most likely to report drinking 3–4 drinks either daily or every 2–3 days. Druze youth, followed

Table 7 Percentages of young male drinkers consuming specific amounts of alcohol on a drinking occasion, by religion.*

No. of drinks†	Druze ($N = 68$)	Moslems ($N = 246$)	Jews ($N = 266$)	Christians ($N = 84$)
1–2	60.29	60.16	68.80	65.47
3–4	25.00	26.82	20.30	22.61
5 or more	14.70	13.00	10.90	11.90

*Percentages may not add to 100 because of rounding errors.

†A drink is defined as one 330 ml can of beer, one 100 ml half-glass of wine, or one 40 ml small glass of distilled spirits.

Source: S. Weiss (1997).

Table 8 Percentages of heavy drinking among young males in northern Israel, by religion.

Drinking patterns	Druze ($N = 68$)	Moslems ($N = 246$)	Jews ($N = 266$)	Christians ($N = 84$)
Drinking daily/every 2–3 days				
3–4 drinks in a row	4.41	2.03	1.50	7.14
5 or more drinks in a row	2.94	4.06	2.25	2.38
Drinking once per week				
5 or more drinks in a row	7.35	4.87	2.63	5.95

Source: S. Weiss (1997).

by Christians, were the groups with the highest percentages reporting that they drank five or more drinks per session on a weekly basis (see Table 8). Overall, Jewish youth were the most moderate drinkers, in terms of both quantity and frequency of consumption.

Furthermore, a proportion of Moslem and Druze adolescents in an earlier study reported that their fathers drank (Weiss & Moore, 1991). In that study, 17% of Moslem males and 30% of Druze males reported drinking by their fathers. It can be assumed that this modeling by fathers may contribute to increased drinking among adolescents. Indeed, a 1997 study of 799 Arab adolescents (340 Moslems, 108 Druze, 351 Christians) in Haifa and in three smaller villages in the north of Israel well known for high rates of alcoholism among adults (Weiss, 1999) revealed that drinking rates were about 10% higher among Moslems and Druze than reported in previous studies (Weiss, 1997; Weiss & Moore, 1995a). Studies conducted among Moslems and Druze in Israel indicate a significant prevalence of intoxication and heavy drinking (Weiss et al., 1999). Such patterns are found largely among males, as Moslem and Druze females in many Arab communities in Israel are subject to tight controls in many areas of life, including drinking alcohol, and the majority of females, in accordance with religious rules, do not drink.

Questions therefore arise as to why these patterns might be emerging. Are these changes due to the weakening of religiosity and the general trend toward secularization, so that such religious rules now have less effect on actual behavior? One may also wonder what impact the surrounding alcohol-consuming environment, Western norms, and drinking patterns, or foreign influences in general have had on the consumption of alcohol among non-observant people. For example, a small study conducted in Italy (Poldrugo & Sferch, 1989) revealed that after being in Italy more than 5 years, a larger proportion of foreign Moslem students from Algeria, Iran, Iraq, and Syria reported higher levels of drunkenness compared to foreign Orthodox Christian students. This finding suggests that exposure to different cultural norms influences drinking patterns, and that those who are less familiar with those norms are more vulnerable to excess and negative consequences from this drinking.

Does drinking at all by nonpracticing members of abstinence-teaching religious groups make it more likely that one will drift into daily and eventual heavy drinking (Teichman, Rahav, & Barnea, 1994)? Some have suggested that in the absence of clear religious guidelines, ambivalence, confusion, and guilt can easily be associated with drinking. The individual is seen to be caught between prohibition and drinking, without standards to follow, and drink in an inappropriate or damaging manner. Can people's religious orientation have negative effects in promoting alcohol problems among drinkers rather than preventing such problems among those who choose to drink? Some might speculate that the lack of training in how to handle alcohol beverages may contribute to excessive levels of consumption and higher rates of problems.

How do Moslems—or young people from other proscriptive religious groups—learn about drinking? There are no positive norms that regulate alcohol consumption among children. Nobody tells them what, when, or how to drink, because their religious prohibition against any use of alcohol makes it a nonissue. Children are dependent on their parents to discuss drinking, but the parents have no guidelines of their own to share with the children. In such a situation, when the traditional pattern is broken, youngsters experiment with alcohol on their own, and they often start drinking at a later stage. Alcohol education mostly takes place among peers. Moslem youth, for example, obtain their alcohol from friends or purchase it themselves. They drink at home, perhaps for privacy, or at restaurants, perhaps in order to drink "while eating" (Weiss & Moore, 1995). In the latter circumstances, parents may have little or no influence. Adolescent experimentation with alcohol using a trial-and-error approach may lead to many problems. Alcohol beverages are not seen as something that requires special reference and learning. They consume them in large quantities (Weiss, 1997), perhaps imitating what they see on television, in the movies, or in advertisements, and they are open to influences of "wet" patterns. But no educational programs are available in Arab schools in Israel (Weiss et al., 1999), and no other preventive mechanisms are presented to this sector of the community.

SUMMARY

This chapter aimed to examine the relationship between religion and drinking through some select case illustrations. Data were presented to highlight aspects of the patterns of consumption and their consequences of a number of religious groups, including those with either prescriptive or proscriptive attitudes to drinking. The chapter also explored possible explanations as to the contribution of various religious orientations to the way people learn about drinking.

Contrary to expectation, the prevalence of daily use and the amounts of alcohol consumed on a drinking occasion among some abstinence-teaching religious groups were reported to be higher than in prescriptive religious groups. Even where overall consumption levels and patterns are lower in such groups, when drinking does occur there is a tendency to a greater propensity for excess and more problems. In contrast, prescriptive religious groups that have a ritualized orientation toward alcohol drinking, moderate drinking practices that are an integral part of the religious group life, and gradual introduction of children to alcohol in the family setting are characterized by a low prevalence of intoxication and harm.

The chapter referred in some detail to Judaism and Islam, but also in brief to a number of Christian denominations. It introduced a number of epidemiological studies that were conducted in the last decades of the 20th century and were related to the process of learning about drinking within different religious frameworks. It showed that learning processes in nonproscriptive religious groups appear to be more effective in preventing daily use and consumption of large quantities of alcohol among those who choose to use alcohol. The situation in Islam and Judaism appeared to be more clear-cut than in various Christian groups. Further investigation of the observed relationships with more religiously diverse samples is therefore recommended, especially among the Christian groups, but also within religions such as Buddhism and Hinduism. Overall, there is a lack of studies in the literature concerning those religions that can contribute knowledge to the issue of learning about drinking.

REFERENCES

Abu-Sa'ad, A. (1996). Drug abuse survey among Bedouin adolescents in the Negev (in Hebrew). Beer-Sheba, Israel: Ben-Gurion University.

Amoatengy, A. Y., & Bahr, S. J. (1986). Religion, family and adolescent drug use. *Sociological Perspectives, 29*, 53–76.

Baasher, T. (1981). The use of drugs in the Islamic world. *British Journal of Addiction, 76*, 235–238.

Bainwol, S., & Gressard, C. F. (1985). The incidence of Jewish alcoholism: A review of the literature. *Journal of Drug Education, 15*, 217–224.

Bales, R. F. (1946). Cultural differences in rates of alcoholism. *Quarterly Journal of Studies on Alcohol, 6*, 480–499.

Bock, E. W., Cochran, J. C., & Leeghley, L. (1987). Moral messages: The relative influence of denomination on the religiosity-alcohol relationship. *Sociological Quarterly, 28*, 89–105.

Cahalan, D. (1982). Epidemiology: Alcoholism in American society. In E. L. Gomberg, H. R. White, & J. A. Carpenter (Eds.), *Alcoholism, science and society revisited* (pp. 96–118). New Brunswick, NJ: Rutgers Center of Alcohol Studies.

Cronin, C. (1995). Religiosity, religious affiliation and alcohol and drug use among American college students living in Germany. *International Journal of the Addictions, 30*, 231–238.

Dass, D. (1981). Alcoholic psychosis and alcoholism in a Malaysian population. *British Journal of Addiction, 76*, 191–194.

Dogan, Y. B. (1982). Turkey: Drinking behavior in a changing society. *British Journal of Addiction, 77*, 209–210.

Drower, E. S. (1956). *Water into wine: A study of ritual idiom in the Middle East*. London: Murray.

Engs, R. C., Diebold, B. A., & Hanson, D. J. (1996). The drinking patterns and problems of a national sample of college students 1994. *Journal of Alcohol and Drug Education, 41*, 13–33.

Engs, R. C., Hanson, D. J., Gliksman, L., & Smythe, C. (1990). Influence of religion and culture on drinking behaviours: A test of hypotheses between Canada and the USA. *British Journal of Addiction, 85*, 1475–1482.

Frankel, B. G., & Whitehead, P. C. (1981). *Drinking and damage: Theoretical advances and implications for prevention* (Monograph No. 14). New Brunswick, NJ: Rutgers Center of Alcohol Studies.

Garretsen, H. F. L., & van de Goor, I. (1995). Alcohol and culture in The Netherlands. In D. B. Heath (Ed.), *International handbook on alcohol and culture* (pp. 190–200). Westport, CT: Greenwood Press.

Gilbert, M. J., & Collins, R. L. (1997). Ethnic variation in women's and men's drinking. In R. W. Wilsnack & S. C. Wilsnack (Eds.), *Gender and alcohol: Individual and social perspectives* (pp. 357–378). New Brunswick, NJ: Rutgers Center of Alcohol Studies.

Glad, D. D. (1947). Attitudes and experiences of American-Jewish and American-Irish male youth as related to differences in adult rates of inebriety. *Quarterly Journal of Studies on Alcohol, 8*, 406–472.

Glassner, B., & Berg, B. (1980). How Jews avoid alcohol problems. *American Sociological Review, 45*, 647–664.

Glatt, M. M. (1970). Alcoholism and drug dependence amongst Jews. *British Journal of Addiction, 64*, 297–306.

Greeley, A. M., McCready, W. C., & Theisen, G. (1980). *Ethnic drinking subcultures*. New York, NY: Bergin.

Gressard, C. F., & Bainwol, S. (1988). Jewish drinking practices: Implications for prevention. *Journal of Alcohol and Drug Education, 33*, 67–75.

Harel, I., Keny, D., & Rahav, G. (1998). Youth in Israel: Social welfare health and risk behaviors in an international perspective. In I. Harel, D. Keny, & G. Rahav (Eds.), *Alcohol drinking* (in Hebrew, pp. 147–167). Jerusalem: Brookdail Institute.

Harkin, A. M., Anderson, P., & Goos, C. (1997). *Smoking, drinking and drug taking in the European Region*. Copenhagen, Denmark: WHO Regional Office for Europe.

Hawks, R. D. (1990). Alcohol use among LDS and other groups teaching abstinence. In R. R. Watson (Ed.), *Drug and alcohol abuse prevention* (pp. 133–149). Clifton, NJ: Humana Press.

Hawks, R. D., & Bahr, S. H. (1992). Religion and drug use. *Journal of Drug Education, 22*, 1–8.

Heath, D. B. (1980). A critical review of the sociocultural model of alcohol use. In C. T. Harford, D. A. Parker, & L. Light (Eds.), *Normative approaches to the prevention of alcohol abuse and alcoholism* (Research Monograph No. 3, pp. 1–18). Bethesda, MD: National Institute for Alcohol Abuse and Alcoholism.

Heath, D. B. (1982). In other cultures they also drink. In E. L. Gomberg, H. R. White, & J. A. Carpenter (Eds.), *Alcohol, science and society revisited* (pp. 63–79). New Brunswick, NJ: Rutgers Center of Alcohol Studies.

Heath, D. B. (Ed.). (1995). *International handbook on alcohol and culture*. Westport, CT: Greenwood Press.

Ifabumuyi, O. I. (1982). Alcoholism: A missed diagnosis. In O. E. Erinosho & N. W. Bell (Eds.), *Mental health in Africa* (pp. 115–121). Ibadan, Nigeria: University of Ibadan Press.

Jernigan, D. H. (1997). *Thirsting for markets: The global impact of corporate alcohol*. San Rafael, CA: Marin Institute for the Prevention of Alcohol and Other Drug Problems.

Kandel, B., & Sudit, M. (1982). Drinking practices among urban adults in Israel. *Journal of Studies on Alcohol, 43*, 1–16.

Keller, M. (1970). The great Jewish drink mystery. *British Journal of Addiction, 64*, 287–296.

Knupfer, G., & Room, R. (1967). Drinking patterns and attitudes of Irish, Jewish and White Protestant American men. *Quarterly Journal of Studies on Alcohol, 28*, 676–699.

Kutter, C., & McDermott, D. S. (1997). The role of the church in adolescent drug education. *Journal of Drug Education, 27*, 293–305.

Lorion, R. P., Bussell, D., & Goldberg, R. (1991). Identification of youth at high risk for alcohol or other drug problems. In E. N. Goplerud (Ed.), *Preventing adolescent drug use: From theory to practice* (OSAP Prevention Monograph No. 8, pp. 53–89). Rockville, MD: Office for Substance Abuse Prevention.

Lorch, B. R., & Hughes, R. H. (1988). Church, youth, alcohol and drug education programs and youth substance use. *Journal of Alcohol and Drug Education, 33*, 14–26.

Mäkelä, K. (1975). Consumption level and cultural drinking patterns as determinants of alcohol problems. *Journal of Drug Education, 5*, 344–357.

Manilowitz, B. (1992). Drinking and alcoholism. In Y. Mirski (Ed.), *Pictures from life in the former Soviet Union* (in Hebrew, pp. 21–26). Jerusalem: Association for the Development of Workers in the Social Services in Israel.

Midgley, J. (1971). Drinking and attitudes toward drinking in a Muslim community. *Quarterly Journal of Studies on Alcohol, 32*, 148–158.

Mizruchi, E. H., & Perrucci, R. (1962). Norm qualities and differential effects of deviant behavior: An exploratory analysis. *American Sociological Review, 27*, 391–399.

Mizruchi, E. H., & Perrucci, R. (1970). Prescription, proscription and permissiveness: Aspects of norms and deviant drinking behavior. In G. L. Maddox (Ed.), *The domestical drug: Drinking among collegians* (pp. 234–253). New Haven, CT: College & University Press.

Monteiro, M. G., & Schuckit, M. A. (1989). Alcohol, drug and mental health problems among Jewish and Christian men at a university. *American Journal of Drug and Alcohol Abuse, 15*, 403–412.

Moore, M., & Weiss, S. A. (1985). Alcohol and drunkenness: A newly developed curricular unit as a model for drug-education, science-oriented curricular programs. *Journal of Drug Education, 15*, 263–271.

Olitzky, K. M. (1992, July/August). Exposing the myth: The Jewish client in recovery. *The Counselor*, 17–19.

Partanen, J. (1990). Abstinence in Africa. In J. Maula, M. Lindblad, & C. Tigerstedt (Eds.), *Alcohol in developing countries* (pp. 70–85). Helsinki, Finland: Nordic Council for Alcohol and Drug Research.

Peckham-Patock, J. A., Hutchinson, G. T., Cheong, J., & Nagoshi, C. T. (1998). Effects of religion and religiosity on alcohol use in a college student sample. *Drug and Alcohol Dependence, 49*, 81–88.

Peele, S. (1984). The cultural context of psychological approaches to alcoholism. *American Psychologist, 39*, 1337–1351.

Perkins, W. H. (1987). Parental religion and alcohol use problems as intergenerational predictors of problem drinking among college youth. *Journal of the Scientific Study of Religion, 26*, 340–357.

Poldrugo, F., & Sferch, D. (1989, November 23–25). *Attitudini a consumi di alcool in studenti universitari di varie nazionalità* (Attitudes towards alcohol consumption among university students of various nationalities). Paper presented at VII Congresso Nazionale, Rome, Italy.

Rahav, G., & Teichman, M. (1998, June 1–5). *Drinking and acculturation of immigrants from the former Soviet Union*. Paper presented at the 24th Annual Alcohol Epidemiology Symposium of the Kettil Bruun Society for Social and Epidemiological Research on Alcohol, Florence, Italy.

Rahav, G., Teichman, M., Gil, R., Rosenblum, Y., & Bar-Hamburger, R. (1998). *The use of psychoactive substances among Israeli citizens 1998: Epidemiological study 4* (in Hebrew). Jerusalem: Anti-Drugs Authority.

Samarasinghe, D. S. (1990). The Buddhist, Hindu and Islamic influence on alcohol. In J. Maula, M. Lindblad, & C. Tigerstedt (Eds.), *Alcohol in developing countries: Proceedings from a Meeting in Oslo, Norway, August 7–9, 1988* (pp. 231–233). Helsinki, Finland: Nordic Council for Alcohol and Drug Research.

Schippers, G. (1998, January). *Learning to drink in Europe*. Unpublished paper presented at a meeting of the Working Group on Learning about Drinking, International Center for Alcohol Polices, Washington, DC.

Schuckit, M. A. (1990, October). Are alcoholism rates really lower among Jews? *Drug Abuse & Alcoholism Newsletter*, 19.

Shuval, R., & Krasilowsky, D. (1963). A study of hospitalized male alcoholics. *Israel Annals of Psychiatry and Related Disciplines, 1*, 277–292.

Skolnick, J. H. (1958). Religious affiliation and drinking behavior. *Quarterly Journal of Studies on Alcohol, 19*, 452–470.

Snyder, C. R. (1958). *Alcohol and the Jews: A cultural study of drinking and sobriety* (Monograph No. 1). New Brunswick, NJ: Rutgers Center of Alcohol Studies.

Snyder, C. R., Palgi, P., Eldar, P., & Elian, B. (1982). Alcoholism among the Jews in Israel: A pilot study. *Journal of Studies on Alcohol, 43*, 623–654.

Soueif, M. I., & Darweesh, Z. A. (1986). The extent of drug use among Egyptian male university students. *Drug and Alcohol Dependence, 18*, 389–403.

Soueif, M. I., & Hannourah, M. A. (1987). The use of psychoactive substances by female Egyptian university students. *Drug and Alcohol Dependence, 19*, 233–247.

Soueif, M. I., & Youssuf, G. S. (1990). Use of psychoactive substances among male secondary school pupils in Egypt: A study on a nationwide representative sample. *Drug and Alcohol Dependence, 26*, 63–79.

Soueif, M. I., & Yunis, F. A. (1988). The use of psychoactive substances among Egyptian workers. *Drug and Alcohol Dependence, 21*, 217–229.

Straus, R., & Bacon, S. D. (1953). *Drinking in college*. New Haven, CT: Yale University Press.

Stumphauzer, J. S. (1983). Learning not to drink: Adolescents and abstinence. *Journal of Drug Education, 13*, 39–48.

Teichman, M., Rahav, G., & Barnea, Z. (1994). Alcohol consumption among non-Jewish men in Israel. *Alcologia, 6*, 201–206.

Touhami, M., & Bouktib, M. (1990). A study on attitudes among Moroccan medical students toward the use of alcohol: Preliminary results. In J. Mauls, M. Lindblad, & C. Tigerstedt (Eds.), *Alcohol in developing countries* (pp. 162–167). Helsinki, Finland: Nordic Council for Alcohol and Drug Research.

United Nations. (1993). *Impact of drug abuse among youth in the Economic and Social Commission for Western Asia region (ESCWA): Approaches to social reintegration* (Publication No. E/ESCWA/SD/1993/3). New York: United Nations.

Weiss, S. (1988). Primary prevention of excessive drinking and the Jewish culture: Preventive efforts in Israel 1984–1985. *Journal of Primary Prevention, 8*, 218–225.

Weiss, S. (1993). Non-ritual alcohol use among Israeli Jews. *Jewish Journal of Sociology, 53*, 49–55.

Weiss, S. (1994). Prevention of alcoholism in Israel among adult immigrants from the former Soviet Union and Ethiopia. *Addiction, 89*, 351–352.

Weiss, S. (1995). From a medical-psychiatric-individual problem to a public health social problem: The development over time of the Israeli governmental alcohol treatment system. *Addiction Research, 3*, 49–56.

Weiss, S. (1997). Urgent need for prevention of alcohol drinking among Arab youth in 1996 (in Hebrew). *Harefuah, 132*, 229–231.

Weiss, S. (1999). Attitudes of Israeli Jewish and Arab high school students toward alcohol control measures. *Journal of Drug Education, 29*, 41–52.

Weiss, S., & Moore, M. (1991). Alcohol drinking habits of Israeli Jewish, Moslem and Druze adolescents in the north of Israel in 1990. *Israel Journal of Psychiatry and Related Sciences, 28*, 20–28.

Weiss, S., & Moore, M. (1992). Perception of alcoholism among Jewish, Moslem, and Christian teachers in Israel. *Journal of Drug Education, 22*, 253–260.

Weiss, S., & Moore, M. (1994). Why, where and with whom do Israeli teenagers drink? To whom do they turn for help with alcohol problems? *Alcohol and Alcoholism, 29*, 465–471.

Weiss, S., & Moore, M. (1995a). How do Israeli adolescents of four religions obtain alcoholic beverages and where? *Journal of Child and Adolescent Substance Abuse, 4*, 79–87.

Weiss, S., & Moore, M. (1995b). Sources of alcohol and drug information among Israeli urban adolescents. *Journal of Drug Education, 25*, 211–222.

Weiss, S., Sawa, G. H., Abdeen, Z., & Yanai, J. (1999). Substance abuse studies and prevention efforts among Arabs in the 1990's in Israel, Jordan and the Palestinian Authority: A literature review. *Addiction, 94*, 177–198.

White, H. R. (1982). Sociological theories of the etiology of alcoholism. In E. L. Gomberg, H. R. White, & J. A. Carpenter (Eds.), *Alcohol, science and society revisited* (pp. 205–232). New Brunswick, NJ: Rutgers Center of Alcohol Studies.

Wilkinson, R. (1970). *The prevention of drinking problems: Alcohol control and cultural influences.* New York: Oxford University Press.

Yanai, J., & Weiss, S. (1994). Drug abuse primary prevention research and programs among Jewish youth in Israel: A review. *Drugs: Education, Prevention and Policy, 1*, 49–58.

Zimberg, S. (1977). Sociopsychiatric perspectives on Jewish alcohol abuse: Implications for prevention of alcoholism. *American Journal of Drug and Alcohol Abuse, 4*, 571–579.

Chapter 6

Learning By Experiment

Martin Plant

You must learn by doing the thing;
For though you think you know it,
You have no certainty until you try.
Sophocles (490–406 BC)

Alcohol consumption by young people frequently attracts a mixture of attention, concern, and censure. Popular mass media comment often laments the adverse consequences of youthful drinking. It is claimed in some instances that the young are inexperienced and therefore vulnerable to pitfalls which their elders, it is supposed, know how to avoid. In other instances, it is implied that some young drinkers are simply feckless, willful, malevolent, and antisocial. In fact, most young people drink—if they do so—in moderation, and without serious harm most of the time. In addition, in spite of the highly publicized excesses of some, the majority of teenagers and young adults mature into people most of whom generally drink in moderation and who do not experience, or inflict upon others, serious harm due to their drinking. Somewhere between childhood and adulthood, the majority of people in most cultures learn to drink. Like the successful acquisition of any behavior, their learning involves a process of experimentation, trial, and error. That process is the main focus of this chapter.

FIRST IMPRESSIONS: CHILDHOOD AND ALCOHOL

The passage from childhood to adulthood involves a host of complex biological, psychological, and social factors. Broadly, the process of learning to live and interact with other people is termed "socialization." This involves the individual absorbing information to facilitate life within his or her current social milieu. Socialization is a continuing, lifelong process. The processes of learning about alcohol and learning how to use it are one aspect of socialization, of becoming a fully functional member of one's own social group.

Most people obtain their first impressions of alcohol from their parents, relatives, other adults, and people with whom they are in contact. These include casual acquaintances, strangers, and people viewed in other ways, such as through television and cinema. Such people are likely to serve as possible role models and exemplars of drinking behavior, and they may provide either "good" or "bad" examples of how to drink.

Children's perceptions of drinking appear to develop at a very early age and strongly influenced by their view of adults' consumption of alcohol. Jahoda and Cramond (1972), in a study of Scottish children aged between 5 and 10 years, concluded that even among the very young there was an emerging concept (including sight and smell) of alcoholic beverages as a distinct entity. Moreover, these authors reported that young people often had a negative and disapproving view of alcohol consumption, especially by women. A replication of this study many years later among children in England and Scotland concluded that the findings were still largely the same (Fossey, 1994). These studies were striking in that so little appeared to have changed over more than 20 years. During that time, alcohol consumption in Britain had risen considerably and drinking was a normal activity for most of the adults in the areas in which the children studied lived. The children involved in the investigations had typically absorbed some profound, and often highly prejudiced, views about drinking by adults. These views were evident among children living in a society in which most adults, including most of their own parents, did drink and alcohol beverages had long been a normal part of social life (Bennet, Jarvis, Rowlands, Singleton, & Haseldon, 1996; M. L. Plant, 1997).

Different societies have varied drinking behaviors, and the expectations surrounding drinking are culturally diverse. These variations include the levels of acceptability of alcohol consumption at specific occasions and for particular groups of people, such as women, children, students, young people, and the elderly. Each subgroup in every society has its own norms, values, and expectations, which are often very complex. Many societies have strict norms or laws related to drinking. In some countries, alcohol consumption is illegal or is considered deviant. In most countries, however, neither is the case, and the consumption of beverage alcohol is not only legal and widespread, but is strongly supported by history, tradition, and popular sentiment. In such societies, most people consume alcohol, if only on special or particular occasions. Some, but not all, countries have laws that are largely designed to curb driving while under the influence of alcohol by limiting youthful access to alcohol beverages. In several countries, such as the U.S. and Canada, the minimum legal age for consumption or purchase is set very high, while in others it is either nonexistent or is set much lower (Osservatorio Permanente sui Giovani E L'Alcool, 1994). The U.S. is one of the most restrictive jurisdictions, defining the minimum legal drinking age as 21 years (Hingson, Berson, & Dowley, 1997), while in the United Kingdom it is legal for an individual to drink (though not in licensed premises) at the age of 5. Such variations reflect religious and other deeply held values. They also serve to define the extent to which youthful drinking may itself be regarded as deviant or problematic.

WHY DO YOUNG PEOPLE DRINK?

In many cultures being an adult involves a number of behaviors, one of which is the periodic social consumption of beverage alcohol. What is important in the current context is the transition phases that a young person passes through to become a mature, sensible drinker, and the role that risk-taking, limit-testing, and experimentation plays in the developmental process.

While young children may often have a negative view of alcohol, this is in marked contrast to teenagers and young adults. A classic study involving teenagers in Scotland (Davies & Stacey, 1972) noted that drinking was viewed as a hallmark of adult status and leisure time behavior. Subsequent studies have reiterated this conclusion. Moreover, the initiation of young people into drinking is frequently ascribed to "peer pressure" and curiosity (Plant & Plant, 1992; Plant, Peck, & Samuel, 1985). The etiology (causation) of drinking is complex; even so, continued drinking is often attributed to enjoyment of the taste of alcohol, combined with a host of social, cultural, economic, and psychological factors (Fazey, 1977; Peck, 1982). People commonly drink because they derive pleasure and refreshment from the effects of alcohol and because it suits the company they are in, specifically their main "reference group."

One study of English school students aged 14–16 years (Plant, Bagnall, Foster, & Sales, 1990) examined their reasons for drinking. The main reasons cited were curiosity about alcohol, a liking for the taste of alcoholic beverages, and the fact that drinking was believed to make parties more enjoyable. Some young women also believed that alcohol consumption would make their sexual experiences more pleasurable (Traeen & Kvalem, 1996). Davies and Stacey (1972) found that teenagers who did not drink were regarded by their peers as being less "sociable" or "tough" than those who did drink.

DRINKING PATTERNS AMONG YOUNG PEOPLE

Drinking habits vary markedly between different societies, and the drinking patterns of the young reflect these disparities. The drinking pattern of specific groups of drinkers is a key variable in determining the likely consequences of alcohol consumption:

> Until recently, epidemiological research on the relationship between alcohol consumption and the consequences of drinking has focused largely on the level of consumption. Relatively little attention has been given to temporal rhythms of drinking,

> the number and characteristics of heavy drinking occasions, the settings where drinking takes place, the activities associated with drinking, the characteristics of drinking confederates, and the types of beverage consumed. These aspects of drinking behavior have important influences on the incidence of both positive and negative drinking consequences. Indeed, preliminary evidence indicates that drinking patterns have an impact on drinking problems as great as, or even greater than, level of drinking (Single & Leino, 1998, p. 21).

Thus, national drinking patterns clearly have an impact on the types of drinking experiences reported by the young. Youth in Denmark or the United Kingdom, for example, are far more likely to report drinking heavily than are those in countries with much higher general levels of per capita alcohol consumption, such as France and Italy.

Studies, mainly from industrialized societies, show that alcohol consumption by preadolescent children is very limited or unusual. Even so, in some societies, parents and other adults may allow young children to taste alcoholic beverages in small quantities as part of the accepted process of learning to drink (Heath, 1995; Pittman & Raskin White, 1991). Regular drinking is increasingly commonplace during the teenage years. Drinking, for most, is a secondary part of social activities. It is both facilitated and constrained by spending power, leisure opportunities, and social norms.

Although most young people who drink generally do so in moderate and harm-free ways, it is clear that some teenagers, often a large minority, sometimes drink heavily and consume much more than would normally be considered advisable. Teenage boys tend to drink more than girls. Even so, a number of studies have shown that a proportion of either gender often drinks heavily. The international comparative study by Hibell et al. (1997) showed that intoxication had been experienced by 3–38% of girls and 7–46% of boys by the age of 13 years. The proportions of 15- and 16-year-olds who had reportedly been intoxicated 20 times or more in their lifetime ranged from 0% to 30% among the girls and from 3% to 36% amongst the boys. Sometimes, small children imbibe dangerous quantities of alcohol while they are not under adult supervision and protection. This has led to a number of serious, even fatal consequences (Plant & Plant, 1992).

Drinking behavior is highly situation-specific, and an individual may drink in quite different ways in different situations. For example, a teenager may only sip a single drink when with parents or adult relatives, but drink heavily and to intoxication while at a party, on a date, before watching a soccer match, or while with friends or workmates. An individual may drink heavily as a student, but drastically reduce her or his consumption upon graduating and securing employment in a setting that does not foster such behavior. The workplace may either encourage or inhibit a person from drinking heavily (Baillie, 1996; Hore & Plant, 1981; M. A. Plant, 1979). Surveys of teenagers indicate that, while many of those who are younger often report drinking at home with their parents, older individuals are more likely to drink outside the home, in licensed premises, and in other places with their friends rather than with adult relatives (May, 1992; Plant & Plant, 1992). The place in which drinking takes place may have an important influence on the pattern of drinking and the behaviors that accompany it.

Expectancies about drinking have a substantial impact on the formation and maintenance of youthful drinking habits (for further discussion of expectancies also see Chapters 2 and 8). A recent comparative study of 15–16 year olds in 26 European countries (Hibell et al., 1997) revealed major differences in the patterns of positive and negative consequences expected by teenagers in the countries surveyed. In some countries, such as Croatia, Ireland, Portugal, Malta, Slovenia, Poland, Lithuania, and Slovakia, teenagers reported expecting more negative than positive consequences from drinking. In other countries, such as Cyprus, Denmark, Sweden, the Ukraine, Finland, and the United Kingdom, the reverse was true. Moreover, Finnish and British teenagers reported expecting only positive consequences from their drinking. These variations in expectancies serve to underline the heterogeneous *meanings* of drinking for young people in different countries. (It should be pointed out that the pattern of responses just described does not relate in any simple or obvious way to actual drinking habits.)

In all societies in which alcohol is imbibed, it appears that males are more likely than females to drink. Males who drink also generally consume larger amounts than female drinkers (Hibell et al., 1997; M. L. Plant, 1997). In many countries, there persists stronger disapproval towards alcohol consumption by women than by men, even though many women do drink (M. L. Plant, 1997).

Studies from many countries confirm that young females generally drink much less than their male counterparts (Wilsnack & Wilsnack, 1995). In some countries, such as Nigeria, South Africa, and the United Kingdom, females have been drinking more in recent years and there is some evidence to suggest that the traditional gap in alcohol consumption of the sexes may have narrowed (Ikuesan, 1994; M. L. Plant, 1997; Rocha-Silva, de Miranda, & Erasmus, 1996). Fillmore (1987) has suggested that men are likely to be more alcohol-involved for a longer part of their lives than women. The heavier drinking of young males, she suggests, persists longer into adulthood than is the case with females.

It is a feature of some youthful drinking cultures that competitive heavy drinking is encouraged and that failure to engage in such competitions may be regarded as a token of cowardice. Accordingly, young women and men are sometimes pressured into drinking more than they would choose otherwise or than they would usually. It has been suggested that such peer pressure may be especially strong in all-male settings or within male-only occupational groups (M. A. Plant, 1979). However, the growing economic power of women in many societies has meant that females have become increasingly subject to similar occupational pressures.

Heavy drinking is also mainly a feature of the young and single. Some people may maintain this type of pattern into later life, but most reduce their drinking markedly once they have increased work and family commitments. As a person passes through various life stages, beliefs of which behaviors are appropriate (or inappropriate) change over time. In the context of beverage alcohol, it has been noted that people typically have not just a static pattern of consumption. Instead, they have "drinking careers" (Fillmore, 1988; M. A. Plant, 1979).

EXPERIMENTATION WITH DRINKING

Young people often engage in a variety of risky or potentially hazardous activities. Some of these activities, such as sports (e.g., skiing, mountaineering, white water canoeing, sky diving, caving) or activities such as driving motor bicycles or other vehicles, may be held in great social esteem or at least accepted as legitimate, appropriate, and desirable for young people to engage in. Other activities, however, such as drinking alcohol, often arouse far more concern or disapproval. It is frequently viewed as being at least potentially unhealthy, dangerous, or an immoral activity (Plant & Plant, 1992). Research evidence suggests that risk-taking and experimentation are essential for a young person to develop into a healthy, mature, and well-balanced adult. The challenge is to ensure that, if young people engage in such activities, they do so with the maximum degree of protection that society can make available to them.

A Period of Exploration

Many commentators have emphasized that youth is a period of exploration, of trying new experiences, and of testing one's personal limits. It is also often a period of rebellion against adults, and against anything perceived as representing authority or orthodox wisdom. The behavior of the young sometimes appears to adults to be perverse and misguided. This can be particularly true in regard to alcohol, where young people's behavior at times suggests either a lack of risk awareness or a blatant disregard for potential harms. Moreover, many teenagers and young adults appear to regard themselves as being immune to harm. In short, some young people simply do not take the concept of personal jeopardy very seriously. This world view of one's personal immunity can be further compounded if one is intoxicated, which makes the individual a poorer judge of risk than when sober. Not only can judgement (in terms of situational assessment) be impaired if a person is intoxicated, but problem-solving skills, hand-eye coordination, and visual-spatial skills are also compromised, further amplifying any potential risk. The adverse effects of drinking while driving serves as a good example of this phenomenon. It is largely through personal and vicarious learning that young people adjust their perception of risk and their own immunity to harm.

A useful perspective on this perceived invulnerability has been provided by Elkind (1967, 1984, 1985), who has termed it the "personal fable." The personal fable refers to the belief held by many people that they can do things safely and that dangers really only apply to other people. The fact that there is danger attached to some activities may be acknowledged, but discounted on the basis of personal skill, ability, or some other factor, such as a belief that one is being sufficiently careful.

Elkind stresses that this "fable," or false belief, may have positive as well as negative consequences. Positive outcomes may include encouraging young people to strive to attain difficult goals. The negative result of the personal fable may be to foster an unrealistic and potentially dangerous indifference to danger. Because of this fable, or myth of personal immunity, people may engage in activities which from an objective point of view really are hazardous, while accepting or convincing themselves that the risks are negligible or nonexistent.

Partly as a consequence of young persons' experimental and, at times, risk-taking behavior with alcohol, its use by "the young" (children, adolescents, teenagers, or other young adults) has periodically been the cause of much concern in many countries. This is often reflected in reports where the young have frequently been demonized by the mass media (Baillie, 1996; Cohen, 1972; May, 1992). The fact that young people have a distinctive culture with its own values, fashions, and patterns of behaviors has been evident since the 1960's (Dorn, 1983; Goode, 1972; Musgrove, 1964; Neville, 1971; M. A. Plant, 1975; Young, 1971). The emergence of a "youth culture" in industrialized societies and, increasingly, in the developing world has attracted a vast amount of comment, much of it concerned with youthful activities such as the consumption of alcohol and the use of other, often illicit forms of psychoactive drugs (Plant, 1987; Plant & Plant, 1992).

For many young people, early experiences with alcohol are pleasant (Rocha-Silva et al., 1996). For others, however, learning to handle alcohol is unpleasant, involving an initial dislike of the taste of alcohol beverages or experiencing more tangible problems. As part of the process of learning to drink, with its unfamiliarity and experimentation, many teenagers sometimes drink heavily and report experiencing fairly minor adverse consequences, such as the discomfort of hangovers and nausea. Some young people incapacitate themselves so much that they provoke criticism from others or even miss days at school, college, or work (Plant et al., 1985; Plant & Plant, 1992). A minority experiences more serious consequences, such as accidents, injuries, and involvement in public disorder.

Part of the process of learning to drink is to discover the effects of drinking certain amounts in specific situations. This is often a process of trial and error, which may be influenced by a wish to compete with or outdo one's peers. Sometimes it may involve unpleasant, even serious consequences.

IS THE EXPERIMENTAL DRINKING OF YOUTH "A PROBLEM?"

Most young people generally drink in only moderate amounts and do not suffer serious consequences from their drinking. Nevertheless, some young people drink heavily and are at risk of experiencing and inflicting adverse consequences upon others. In some countries, they constitute a large number of people who are clearly a high-risk group in terms of potential adverse consequences. In particular, acute alcohol poisoning, accidents, and injuries are among some of the major concerns, together with public disorder and alcohol-impaired driving accidents (Giesbrecht et al., 1989). Heavy drinking by young men and women is also clearly associated with disorderly behavior. The latter, though, is also influenced by many other factors (Collins, 1982).

Drinking is often associated with sexual activity. It is a commonplace accompaniment of dating, and some drinking locales have clear sexual associations and identities. Even so, available evidence does not suggest that drinking of itself leads people to engage in greater levels of sexual risk-taking than they otherwise might do. The meaning of drinking may be quite different for males and females in relation to sexuality. The popular view certainly assumes that alcohol may be a disinhibitor and therefore may increase an individual's inclination to engage in sexual activity. For males, this belief may portray alcohol as an aid to seduction. Conversely, for women, drinking may carry with it a more threatening implication of loss of control, of victimization, and of unwanted pregnancy (M. L. Plant, 1997). What does emerge from available information is that some people are clearly more risk-oriented than others. Such risk-taking individuals are more likely to drink heavily, smoke, use illicit drugs, engage in unprotected sex with greater numbers of partners, and drive in a dangerous manner (Plant & Plant, 1992).

Young people who drink heavily constitute a serious problem, both for medical services and often also for the police. The personal accounts of people with drinking problems reveal a huge range of unique and individual factors. Many simply developed patterns of harmful drinking for social reasons, conforming to the norms of heavy-drinking peers. Others have experienced major personal tragedies, been depressed, or been under stress. Some attribute their heavy drinking to some form of illness or disability (M. L. Plant, 1997). As noted by several commentators, drinking problems may well be purely temporary. Many of those who experience such problems while young will move out of them as they grow older. Conversely, some of those who drink in moderation while young may develop problems later in life (Cameron, 1995). Sometimes an upsurge of heavy and problematic drinking may reflect profound and far-reaching social changes and dislocations (see also Chapter 2). The dramatic sociopolitical transformations in Eastern Europe have been accompanied by escalating levels of alcohol consumption and a rapid rise in rates of alcohol-related problems (Iontchev, 1998; Varvasovsky, 1996; Vroublevsky & Harwin, 1998).

Available evidence shows that the problems experienced by most young people because of their drinking are attributable to periodic heavy intake rather than to chronic or daily heavy alcohol consumption (May, 1992; Plant & Plant, 1992). Heavy drinking by young people is associated with relatively few cases of alcohol dependence ("alcoholism") or mortality from liver disease, stroke, or cancer (Giesbrecht et al., 1989; M. A. Plant, 1989; Plant & Plant, 1992). The latter typically involve middle-aged and older people.

EXPERIMENT IN CONTEXT

Alcohol consumption patterns vary markedly between young people in different social groups. For example, there is evidence that teenagers who are raised in single-parent homes drink more than those who are not (Miller, 1997; Plant et al., 1985), which is probably a reflection of numerous psychological, social, and economic factors. Miller and Plant (1999) have also concluded that teenagers who had been truant from school or who rated their school performance as being poor were more likely than others to be heavy drinkers and to come from single-parent backgrounds. This study also showed that parental control was a more important factor in truancy than alcohol consumption itself.

These findings serve to emphasize that family background does exert powerful pressures upon young people and does influence youthful drinking, but that this relationship is a complex one. Parents act as powerful role models, for either good or ill (Plant, Orford, & Grant, 1989). Parental heavy drinking, for example, does appear to be a risk factor in relation to heavy drinking among the parents' children and provides an excellent example of the vicarious, yet potent learning experiences to which young people can be exposed.

To further illustrate the importance of "context," recent surveys have shown that teenagers in the Western Isles of Scotland were far more likely to report heavy drinking (or abstinence) than those in other parts of the United Kingdom (Anderson & Plant, 1996; Goddard, 1997a, 1997b). This is consistent with other evidence that some areas are characterized by a polarization between drinking heavily and abstaining. Iceland, Ireland, the Faroe Islands, and the "Bible Belt" of the U.S. are further examples of this phenomenon (Hibell et al., 1997; Hilton, 1987). Young people raised in such areas are likely to receive inconsistent and confusing messages from adults in relation to alcohol. Moreover, some of these messages are incompatible with their personal observations and the views of their friends.

There is little doubt that such polarization both reflects and promotes heavy drinking. Young people raised in homes in which alcohol consumption is proscribed will not experience the socialization that might help them to drink in moderation, should they choose to drink later in life. Conversely, those raised by heavy-drinking parents have very poor role models to influence their own drinking. Some young people will respond to this by also adopting patterns of heavy and inappropriate drinking, while others may react against their early experiences by not drinking at all.

There is persuasive evidence to show that teenagers and others are likely to drink differently in specific settings and in particular circumstances. First, older teenagers are less likely to drink at home and are more likely to drink in other places and in the company of people of their own age. Survey evidence suggests that older teenagers drink more than younger teenagers and that people also tend to drink more outside the home with friends than when at home with their parents or other adult relatives. Moreover, it appears that teenagers who drink heavily are especially likely to report drinking out-of-doors, or in other locales beyond the constraints of their family home. For example, heavier-drinking teenage males have been shown to be more likely to have been drinking with girlfriends or with a mixed group of friends (Anderson, Plant, & Plant, 1998; Plant, Bagnall, & Foster, 1990; Plant & Plant, 1992). Further information about the effects of the drinking situation has been provided by a study of young people in the Netherlands. This showed that adolescent drinking patterns varied greatly between different situations. The author concluded that "when drinking in a family context occurs, the influence of peer-pressure in the drinking group will be absent. The number of heavy drinkers among family members and pressure from parents or siblings to drink will, however, be of importance" (van de Goor, 1990, p. 116). Researchers from South Africa have reported that drinking among Black youths often occurs in uncontrolled settings, where there is strong pressure to drink. "Taverns/shabeens, bottle-stores, and clubs/discothèques are particularly popular drinking places among male drinkers, and the homes of friends among female drinkers" (Rocha-Silva et al., 1996, pp. ii–iv).

A further insight into the importance of social context of drinking behaviors and their possible consequences has been provided by Graham and Homel (1997). These authors have concluded that the ambience, design, layout, décor, theme, size, and organization of bar rooms, together with the availability of activities such as pool, the type of music being played, and the demeanor and training of bar staff, influence both patterns of drinking and levels of intoxication. There is clearly ample scope for "social engineering" and experimentation here. Moreover, Saltz (1997) has described a number of strategies to curb trouble in and around bars. These include the operation of a "responsible beverage service."

WHO ARE THE RISK-TAKERS?

As noted previously, risk-taking is extremely widespread and, indeed, a normal phenomenon among youth. Its pattern and the particular behaviors with which it is associated, however, vary considerably among different subgroups of the population as well as between social, cultural, ethnic, and national groups. Drinking is one part of a constellation of leisure-time/pleasure-seeking behaviors which may comprise a risk-taking repertoire.

Just as leisure-time/pleasure-seeking behaviors are mediated by personal and social factors that influence the degree of involvement and the patterns of activity, young people who drink heavily or who experience the most serious problems as a result of their drinking may be distinctive in a number of ways. "Problem behavior theory" as described by Jessor and Jessor (1977) and by Jessor, Donovan, and Costa (1991) suggests that people raised in deprived circumstances or whose parents engaged in high-risk behavior such as heavy drinking have an increased prospect of engaging in high-risk forms of behavior themselves. In this view, risk-taking is part of a structure of behaviors that reflect the "social ecology of adolescent life, an ecology that provides socially organized opportunities to learn risk behaviors together and normative expectations that they be performed together" (Jessor et al., 1991, p. 9).

Wolff (1970) also notes a connection between problem behavior and a number of social factors. In his study, *Children Under Stress*, Wolff concluded that patterns of problems, such as delinquency and unprotected sex, are not only the result of unstable family life or social deprivation, but in some cases are transmitted from generation to generation. Children living in socially disadvantaged circumstances are thus likely to be "at risk" in more than one way.

Some people, however, simply take more risks than others, and drinking may be a part of this range of options (M. A. Plant, 1990; Plant & Plant, 1992; World Health Organization, 1994). Youth involved in certain types of sporting activities, for instance, may be more prone to risk-taking behavior. A study by Young (1990) found an association between sensation-seeking and self-reported criminal behavior among student athletes, but not among other students. Student athletes were also more likely to report interest in such risky activities as climbing, parachute jumping, drinking, "partying," gambling, and sex. A more recent study from England has concluded that adolescent drinking occupied "a low threshold position" in the range of psychoactive substance use amongst those aged 11–16 years (Sutherland & Willner, 1998). A similar point had been made much earlier by Goode (1972).

Some people drink heavily in response to serious, stressful life events. Several surveys of young people have shown that while most young people enjoy drinking and report doing so for positive reasons, a minority report drinking because they are bored, need to calm nerves or to relax, lack confidence, are under some form of pressure, or have been depressed. Teenagers who drink heavily are more likely to attribute their drinking to such factors than are those who drink lesser amounts (Anderson et al., 1998; Miller & Plant, 1999). Moreover, heavier-drinking teenagers appear to be highly socially active and to be more likely than others to attribute their drinking to curiosity about the effects of alcohol, and to the belief that drinking is good for them and that it facilitates social interaction, such as enjoyment at a party, ability to talk to members of the opposite sex, and other perceived benefits. Heavier-drinking teenagers also simply mix more with others who drink. They are also more likely to drink illegally in licensed premises and to go to clubs and discos. One ominous finding is that male teenagers who drink more heavily are more likely than others to support the belief that it is safe to drive after drinking. It should, however, be noted that in several countries alcohol involvement in vehicle accidents and road fatalities has declined. The young are generally better than older people in refraining from driving while under the influence of alcohol (Plant, Bagnall, & Foster, 1990; Stewart & Sweedler, 1997).

THE IMPLICATIONS OF YOUTHFUL DRINKING

There is frequently a profound cultural ambiguity about alcohol. On the one hand, its consumption is often an important adjunct of conviviality and leisure, or is part of key rituals to mark important *rites de passage*. On the other hand, there is in many societies deep-rooted (and often fully justified) concern about the adverse effects associated with heavy or inappropriate consumption of alcohol, particularly by people viewed as being either vulnerable or "at risk" (Heath, 1995; Pittman & Raskin White, 1991); this especially includes the young.

It is clear that most people, even if they do drink heavily when young, appear to "mature" into adults whose alcohol consumption is largely unremarkable (Baer, Marlatt, & McMahon, 1993; Bagnall, 1991; Fillmore, 1988; Plant & Plant, 1992). Even among those who may periodically experience serious harm from their drinking, it is not unusual for spontaneous remissions to occur. Moreover, many of those who, perhaps later in life, drink in a damaging manner alternate between periods of heavy and lighter drinking (Cameron, 1995). One of the main fears often expressed, albeit implicitly, is that alcohol consumption by the young will unleash otherwise repressed inclinations and behaviors such as violence or sexual activity. Central to this assumption is the concept of *disinhibition*. The latter is the belief that alcohol consumption will release the individual from the constraints of morality or prudence which operate while the person is sober (Room & Collins, 1983).

While heavy drinking is associated with a variety of adverse consequences, the effects of beverage alcohol depend upon an interaction between the drinker, the context of drinking, and the chemistry of ethyl alcohol. Neither violence nor sexual inappropriateness necessarily result from drinking (Cavan, 1966; Collins, 1982; Plant & Plant, 1992; World Health Organization, 1994).

CONCLUSIONS AND DISCUSSION

Drinking, like other activities, involves a process of learning and evolves throughout the life course as one aspect of an individual's socialization into the host society or subgroups with which she or he interacts. *Drinking careers* typically involve the development of perceptions and images of drinking, experimentation, and the refinement of drinking habits, subject to personal experiences. Perceptions frequently—indeed, normally—change over time and in different contexts. Most people in most societies drink and do so mainly in moderation and without serious harm (Plant & Cameron, 2000; Single, Robson, Xie, & Rehm, 1996).

Indeed, it has been shown that, at least for the middle-aged, moderate alcohol consumption is protective in relation to certain health effects such as heart disease and ischaemic (but not haemorrhagic) stroke (M. A. Plant, 1997; Single et al., 1996). Among the young, however, the impact of alcohol consumption on mortality is negative, since some young men and women die in alcohol-related accidents (Single et al., 1996). Many young people drink heavily at times. Even so, it should be emphasized that in many societies, most young people tend not to be heavy drinkers. Surveys typically show that most youthful drinking is moderate and that even the adverse consequences sometimes evident are not often serious, nor do they appear to be a prelude to long-term heavy drinking or to the onset of alcohol dependence.

Experimentation with alcohol is a normal and inevitable part of the process of learning about alcohol. It is natural that young people wish to experiment with a range of experiences and to engage in behaviors some of which entail a degree of risk. Learning to drink involves putting into practice behaviors that have usually been observed among adults, friends, and significant others. Less positive views about alcohol held during childhood are commonly superseded by the view that drinking is both pleasant, worthwhile, and desirable. In some societies, drinking to intoxication is widespread and traditional, while in others there is great ambivalence about alcohol consumption—the young people receiving mixed and confusing messages. An important aspect of youthful drinking practices is the view of many young people that they are invulnerable to possible harm. This is certainly an important element in explaining why some people do things that are "obviously" dangerous.

The power and pervasiveness of the personal fable, described by Elkind (1967, 1984, 1985), has been noted above. Young people, like their elders, enjoy the effects of alcohol. Moreover, the young also enjoy taking risks, which sometimes include indulging in heavy, potentially hazardous drinking. Experimentation is necessary and is an indispensable part of learning to drink in a manner that is both personally rewarding and enjoyable as well as being socially acceptable.

It should, however, be acknowledged that there is not a single, monolithic norm for drinking. Drinking norms vary markedly both between societies and within societies. Young people, physically mature, generally vigorous, healthy and sometimes highly motivated to push their experiences to the limit, often have quite different definitions of "normal" drinking from their elders. Whether driven by testosterone or a rebellious and assertive group ethos, some young people do, on occasion, take their drinking to extremes. The consequences of such extreme and atypical behavior may be serious: public disorder, accidents, illnesses, injury, and premature deaths (Giesbrecht et al., 1989; Single et al., 1996). Most are not.

The main objective from the perspective of public health, order, and policy should be to minimize the harm sometimes associated with youthful drinking. It is true that in many countries the heaviest drinkers are the young and single. Even so, while some control policies might well be particularly relevant to the young, it is doubtful that many have relevance only for the young. There may be exceptions to this, such as special laws related to young and inexperienced drivers (Stewart & Sweedler, 1997). The major single cause of adverse consequences among younger drinkers is periodic heavy consumption, sometimes referred to as "binge" drinking. In may ways, this is particularly hazardous and is associated with most of the ills attributed to youthful drinking. Binge drinking should therefore be a matter for particular concern (Marlatt & Baer, 1997).

The precise policies to curb harmful patterns of drinking have to be adapted to suit specific legal, political, and social circumstances. It is suggested that the best practical and most humane approach to the control of alcohol-related problems is *harm minimization*. This has been discussed in detail elsewhere (Plant, Single, & Stockwell, 1997). Harm minimization sets out to reduce the adverse consequence of drinking, but without necessarily reducing the drinking itself. This approach has been referred to as making the world safer from drinkers as well as making it safer for drinkers. In fact, many harm minimization strategies are likely to involve discouraging both heavy drinking and intoxication. The main objective of these approaches is to discourage patterns of drinking that are especially likely to lead to harm.

The range of options is now quite extensive. They include a number of measures designed to construct or tighten controls on the places in which drinking occurs in order to curb key problems or potential problems, e.g., intoxication, aggression, accidents, driving under the influence of alcohol. Education and health promotion have a role to play in this respect. Even so, there is little evidence to suggest that education alone has been effective in reducing levels of heavy or harmful drinking among young people. Accordingly, education, though important, especially (but not exclusively) for the young, should be seen as part of a much broader approach, often as an adjunct to harm minimization measures of the type noted above. The value and role of alcohol education, as well as its limitations, are discussed in detail in Chapters 4, 9, and 11.

Alcohol problems are not insoluble, either at an individual level or at the societal level. Effective action to curb such problems requires the recognition that something constitutes a real problem and the formation of appropriate responses. Such responses often involve the cooperation of coalitions of concerned people. To be of much value, harm minimization strategies need to be assessed. Successful approaches also need to be sustained, and this requires both commitment and adequate resources.

RECOMMENDATIONS/IMPLICATIONS

It is clear that some young people do consume alcohol heavily or in a manner that causes problems for themselves or others. In view of this, steps should be taken to minimize the harm associated with youthful drinking.

Health promotion has an obvious role to play. It is important that the young should be provided with accurate information about alcohol and its positive and negative effects. In addition, the young should be encouraged to discuss their own drinking and its consequences. It is emphasized, however, that evidence does not suggest that health promotion by itself has led to falls in rates of heavy or inappropriate drinking by young people. Parents should ideally be actively involved in health promotion. They too are likely to require accurate information about alcohol in order to be able to advise and support their children most effectively. Parents and agencies such as schools and colleges should encourage young people to discuss their own drinking and any related problems in confidence. It is emphasized that the best example a parent can provide is by avoiding heavy or inappropriate drinking. Parents who drink should set an example of responsible alcohol use. There is obvious value in teaching young people to drink in moderation in the controlled and safe setting of the family home.

Harm minimization policies should be devised and implemented that have particular relevance to young people. Harm minimization may simply be defined as "avoiding problems when you drink." Such policies involve making the drinking environment safer and more controlled. The reduction of alcohol consumption may not be involved in some of these policies (such as the use of safer drinking glasses in bars). Even so, most initiatives do involve people drinking less and, in particular, avoiding intoxication (Plant et al., 1997). Some policies that have particular relevance to young people include the rigorous enforcement of laws related to (a) serving underage individuals with alcohol, (b) alcohol-impaired driving, and (c) the prohibition of the sale of alcohol to intoxicated persons.

REFERENCES

Anderson, K., & Plant, M. A. (1996). Abstaining and carousing: Substance use among adolescents in the Western Isles of Scotland. *Drug and Alcohol Dependence, 41*, 189–196.

Anderson, K., Plant, M. A., & Plant, M. L. (1998). Associations between drinking, smoking and illicit drug use among adolescents in the Western Isles of Scotland: Implications for harm minimisation. *Journal of Substance Misuse, 3*, 13–20.

Baer, J. S., Marlatt, G. A., & McMahon, R. J. (1993). *Addictive behaviours across the lifespan: Prevention, treatment and policy*. London: Sage.

Bagnall, G. (1991). Alcohol and drug use in a Scottish cohort: Ten years on. *British Journal of Addiction, 86*, 895–904.

Baillie, R. (1996). Determining the effects of media portrayals of alcohol: Going beyond short term influence. *Alcohol and Alcoholism, 33*, 235–242.

Bennet, N., Jarvis, L., Rowlands, O., Singleton, N., & Haseldon, L. (1996). *Living in Britain: Results from the 1994 General Household Survey*. London: Her Majesty's Stationery Office.

Cameron, D. (1995). *Liberating solutions to alcohol problems: Treating problem drinkers without saying 'No.'* Northvale, NJ: Jason Aronson.

Cavan, S. (1996). *Liquor license: An ethnography of bar behavior*. Chicago, IL: Aldine.

Cohen, S. (1972). *Folk devils and moral panics*. London: MacGibbon & Kee.

Collins, J. J., Jr. (1982). *Drinking and crime*. London: Tavistock.

Davies, J. B., & Stacey, B. (1972). *Teenagers and alcohol: A developmental study in Glasgow*. London: Her Majesty's Stationery Office.

Dorn, N. (1983). *Alcohol, youth and the state*. London: Croom Helm.

Elkind, D. (1967). Egocentrism in adolescence. *Child Development, 30*, 1025–1034.

Elkind, D. (1984). Teenage thinking: Implications for health care. *Pediatric Nursing, 10*, 383–385.

Elkind, D. (1985). Cognitive development and adolescent disabilities. *Journal of Adolescent Health Care, 6*, 84–89.

Fazey, C. (1977). *The aetiology of psychoactive substance use*. Paris: UNESCO Press.

Fillmore, K. (1987). Women's drinking across the life course as compared to men's. *British Journal of Addiction, 82*, 801–811.

Fillmore, K. (1988). *Alcohol use across the life course: A critical review of seventy years of international longitudinal research.* Toronto, Canada: Addiction Research Foundation.

Fossey, E. (1994). Growing up with alcohol. London: Tavistock/Routledge.

Giesbrecht, N., Gonzalez, R., Grant, M., Österberg, E., Room, R., Rootman, I., & Towle, L. (Eds.). (1989). *Drinking and casualties: Accidents, poisonings and violence in an international perspective*. London: Tavistock/Routledge.

Goddard, E. (1997a). *Young teenagers and alcohol in 1996: England* (Vol. 1). London: Office for National Statistics.

Goddard, E. (1997b). *Young teenagers and alcohol in 1996: Scotland* (Vol. 2). London: Office for National Statistics.

Goode, E. (1972). *Drugs in American society*. New York: Knopf.

Graham, K., & Homel, R. (1997). Creating safer bars. In M. A. Plant, E. Single, & T. Stockwell (Eds.), *Alcohol: Minimising the harm. What works?* (pp. 171–192). London: Free Association Books.

Heath, D. B. (Ed.). (1995). *International handbook on alcohol and culture*. Westport, CT: Greenwood Press.

Hibell, B., Andersson, B., Bjarnason, T., Kokkevi, A., Morgan, M., & Narusk, A. (1997). *The 1995 ESPAD report: Alcohol and other drug use among students in 26 European countries*. Stockholm: Swedish Council for Information on Alcohol and Other Drugs.

Hilton, M. (1987). Drinking patterns and drinking problems in 1984: Results from a general population survey. *Alcoholism: Clinical and Experimental Research, 11*, 167–175.

Hingson, R., Berson, J., & Dowley, K. (1997). Interventions to reduce college student drinking and related health and social problems. In M. A. Plant, E. Single, & T. Stockwell (Eds.), *Alcohol: Minimising the harm. What works?* (pp. 143–170). London: Free Association Books.

Hore, B. D., & Plant, M. A. (Eds.). (1981). *Alcohol problems in employment*. London: Croom Helm.

Ikuesan, B. A. (1994). Drinking problems and the position of women in Nigeria. *Addiction, 89*, 941–944.

Iontchev, A. (1998). Central and Eastern Europe. In M. Grant (Ed.), *Alcohol and emerging markets: Patterns, problems, and responses* (pp. 177–202). Philadelphia, PA: Brunner/Mazel.

Jahoda, G., & Cramond, J. (1972). *Children and alcohol: A developmental study in Glasgow*. London: Her Majesty's Stationery Office.

Jessor, R., & Jessor, S. (1977). *Problem behavior and psychosocial development: A longitudinal study of youth*. New York: Academic Press.

Jessor, R., Donovan, J. E., & Costa, F. M. (1991). *Beyond adolescence*. Cambridge, England: Cambridge University Press.

Marlatt, A., & Baer, J. S. (1997). Harm reduction and alcohol abuse: A brief intervention for college-student binge drinking. In P. G. Erickson, D. Riley, Y. W. Cheung, & P. A. O'Hare (Eds.), *Harm reduction: A new direction for drug policies and programs* (pp. 245–264). Toronto, Canada: University of Toronto Press.

May, C. (1992). A burning issue? Adolescent alcohol use in Britain 1970–1991. *Alcohol and Alcoholism, 27*, 109–115.

Miller, P. (1997). Family structure, personality, drinking, smoking and illicit drug use among 15 and 16 year olds in the United Kingdom. *Drug and Alcohol Dependence, 45*, 121–129.

Miller, P., & Plant, M. (1999). Truancy, perceived school performance, family structure, lifestyle, alcohol, cigarettes, and other drugs: A study of UK teenagers. *Alcohol and Alcoholism, 34*, 886–893.

Musgrove, F. (1964). *Youth and social order*. London: Routledge & Kegan Paul.

Neville, R. (1971). *Playpower*. London: Paladin.

Osservatorio Permanente sui Giovani E L'Alcool. (1994). *Young people and alcohol in Europe: A tool for monitoring consumption and institutional action policies*. Rome: Edizioni OTET.

Peck, D. F. (1982). Problem drinking: Some determining factors. In M. A. Plant (Ed.), *Drinking and problem drinking* (pp. 65–83). London: Junction Books.

Pittman, D., & Raskin White, H. (Eds.). (1991). *Society, culture and drinking patterns re-examined.* New Brunswick, NJ: Rutgers Center of Alcohol Studies.

Plant, M. A. (1975). *Drugtakers in an English town.* London: Tavistock.

Plant, M. A. (1979). *Drinking careers: Occupations, drinking habits and drinking problems.* London: Tavistock.

Plant, M. A. (1987). *Drugs in perspective.* London: Hodder and Stroughton.

Plant, M. A. (Ed.). (1989). *Alcohol-related problems in high-risk groups: Report on a WHO study* (EURO Reports and Studies No. 109). Copenhagen, Denmark: WHO Regional Office for Europe.

Plant, M. A. (Ed.). (1990). *AIDS, drugs and prostitution.* London: Tavistock/Routledge.

Plant, M. A. (1997). Alcohol, drugs and social milieu. In G. Scambler & A. Scambler (Eds.), *Rethinking prostitution* (pp. 164–179). London: Tavistock/Routledge.

Plant, M. A., Bagnall, G., & Foster, J. (1990). Teenage heavy drinkers: Alcohol-related knowledge, beliefs, experiences, motivation and the social context of drinking. *Alcohol and Alcoholism, 25*, 691–698.

Plant, M. A., Bagnall, G., Foster, J., & Sales, J. (1990). Young people and drinking: Results of an English national survey. *Alcohol and Alcoholism, 25*, 685–690.

Plant, M. A. & Cameron, D. (Eds.) (2000). *The alcohol report.* London: Free Association Books.

Plant, M. A., Orford, J., & Grant, M. (1989). The effects on children of parents' heavy drinking: An international review. *Public Health Reports, 104*, 433–442.

Plant, M. A., Peck, D. F., & Samuel, E. (1985). *Alcohol, drugs and school leavers.* London: Tavistock.

Plant, M. A., & Plant, M. L. (1992). *Risk-takers: Alcohol, drugs, sex and youth.* London: Tavistock/Routledge.

Plant, M. A., Single, E., & Stockwell, T. (Eds.) (1997). *Alcohol: Minimising the harm. What works?* London: Free Association Books.

Plant, M. L. (1997). *Women and alcohol: Contemporary and historical perspectives.* London: Free Association Books.

Rocha-Silva, L., de Miranda, S., & Erasmus, R. (1996). *Alcohol, tobacco and other drug use among black youth.* Pretoria, South Africa: Human Sciences Research Council.

Room, R., & Collins, G. (Eds.). (1983). *Alcohol and disinhibition: Nature and meaning of the link* (NIAAA Research Monograph No. 12). Washington, DC: U.S. Department of Health and Human Services.

Saltz, R. F. (1997). Prevention where alcohol is sold and consumed: Server intervention and responsible beverage service. In M. A. Plant, E. Single, & T. Stockwell (Eds.), *Alcohol: Minimising the harm. What works?* (pp. 72–84). London: Free Association Books.

Single, E., & Leino, V. E. (1998). The levels, patterns, and consequences of drinking. In M. Grant & J. Litvak (Eds.), *Drinking patterns and their consequences* (pp. 7–24). Washington, DC: Taylor & Francis.

Single, E., Robson, L., Xie, X., & Rehm, J. (1996). *The cost of substance abuse in Canada.* Toronto, Canada: Canadian Centre on Substance Abuse.

Stewart, K., & Sweedler, B. M. (1997). Driving under the influence of alcohol. In M. A. Plant, E. Single, & T. Stockwell (Eds.), *Alcohol: Minimising the harm. What works?* (pp. 126–142). London: Free Association Books.

Sutherland, I., & Willner, P. (1998). Patterns of alcohol, cigarette and illicit drug use in English adolescents. *Addiction, 93*, 1199–1208.

Traeen, B., & Kvalem, I. (1996). Sex under the influence of alcohol amongst Norwegian adolescents. *Addiction, 91*, 995–1006.

van de Goor, I. (1990). *Situational aspects of adolescent drinking behaviour.* Maastricht: University of Limburg.

Varvasovsky, Z. (1996, April). *Alcohol policy and prevention in Hungary*. Paper presented at 41st Scottish Alcohol Problems Research Symposium, Pitlochry, Scotland.

Vroublevsky, A., & Harwin, J. (1998). Russia. In M. Grant (Ed.), *Alcohol and emerging markets: Patterns, problems, and responses* (pp. 203–222). Philadelphia, PA: Brunner/Mazel.

Wilsnack, S. C., & Wilsnack, R. (1995). Drinking and problem drinking in US women. In M. Galanter (Ed.), *Recent developments in alcoholism: Women and alcoholism* (Vol. 12, pp. 29–60). New York: Plenum.

Wolff, S. (1970). *Children under stress*. London: Allen Lane.

World Health Organization. (1994). *Alcohol and HIV/AIDS*. Copenhagen, Denmark: WHO Regional Office for Europe.

Young, J. (1971). *The drugtakers*. London: Paladin.

Young, T. (1990). Sensation seeking and self-reported criminality among student-athletes. *Perceptual and Motor Skills, 70*, 959–962.

Chapter 7

Past Influences, Current Issues, Future Research Directions

Ruth Clifford Engs

Over the last few decades alcohol consumption patterns have been changing in many cultures.[1] For instance, Italian youth are consuming more beer and spirits and Scandinavians are consuming more wine. Traditional drinking patterns are becoming less defined as the world increasingly becomes a "global village." Risky youthful drinking, in particular, has led to concern about potential emerging problems among young people in many countries. However, the traditional norms within a culture still have a powerful influence upon the way a nation perceives alcohol and drinking and also the research supported by its official bodies. For instance, most alcohol and drinking research is undertaken in Northern European cultures or their former colonies. In these cultures, studies, conferences, and professional journals focus heavily on negative aspects of drinking such as alcoholism, alcohol abuse, drunk driving, youthful drinking, and health problems associated with risky drinking. Few studies, however, have investigated how young people learn to drink in a sensible way, how alcohol enhances a meal, or factors that encourage moderate drinking practices within a

[1]Changes in the second half of the 20th century are recorded in Hupkens, Knibbe, and Drop (1992) and in various statistical yearbooks published by the Food and Agriculture Organization of the United Nations (FAO) (1984, 1991). A few publications discuss drinking patterns and attitudes towards alcohol in cultures outside Western Europe and its former colonies, including Bonavia (1980), Chafetz (1964), Hanson (1996), and Heok (1990). See also the many works by Heath, and especially his *International Handbook on Alcohol and Culture* (1995), where numerous authors discuss patterns in specific cultures.

culture. Other cultures of the world have different opinions, practices, and norms concerning drinking. Asian cultures differ from African cultures, which in turn differ from some Middle Eastern Islamic cultures with norms of complete abstinence. Although it would be of interest to compare youth in many cultures, owing to space limitations this chapter will focus on Western European cultures and their youth.

The chapter highlights the deep entrenchment of cultural differences that have their origins in antiquity. Without an understanding of these differences, there is a tendency to restrict research to limited topics or to repeat or implement, policies that have little effect in reducing problematic alcohol consumption. The chapter will briefly touch upon the origins of Western culture's drinking norms and the association of the past with present attitudes and behaviors in regard to drinking, including religious differences, health reform, and temperance cycles, and transmission of cultural values through the family and other vehicles. In doing so, it identifies emerging directions for research, especially involving youth issues.

ORIGINS OF DRINKING NORMS, CULTURAL CLASHES, AND TEMPERANCE CYCLES

Attitudes and Beverage Preference: Patterns from Ancient Barbarians and Romans

Is the drinking cup half empty or half full? Differences in learning about drinking, and even research, depend upon how a society perceives this cup. Western European cultures and their former colonies in North America, Australasia, and South Africa span the range. The most restrictive attitudes are found in the "Barbarian," "Northern," or "Nordic" cultures such as Denmark, Finland, Sweden, Norway, and Iceland in the northern region of Europe. These cultures tend to be preoccupied with "alcohol problems" and are ambivalent about drinking. The cup is half empty, and they often struggle to pour the rest out. These drinking cultures primarily drink grain-based beverages (ale, beer, spirits), often without food. They have a low per capita consumption, are predominately Protestant, do not have viticulture, and were not under the influence of the Roman expansion and urbanization process in antiquity. Episodic "feast drinking" to intoxication is common among males and drunkenness in specific situations is acceptable. Many of these Northern cultures tend to have periodic temperance movements where strict legislation to regulate alcohol consumption is implemented in an effort to eliminate perceived drinking problems.[2]

[2]A number of works have discussed the different attitudes and practices concerning drinking within Western cultures, possible origins of these attitudes and practices, the association of these norms with religion, and the continuation of patterns among colonies spawned by the European cultures. (See Austin (1985), Engs (1995; 1999; 2000), Heath (1984; 2000), Levine (1983), Wiseman (1997), and most of the chapters in Pittman and Snyder (1962). See also the special issue of *Addiction Research* (1995; 2 (3)) edited by Engs, Heath, and Room.)

In contrast, "Romanized," "Southern European," or "Mediterranean" cultures and their descendants in South America and other areas of the world do not have as great concerns about alcohol consumption. They merrily fill the drinking cup to enhance the quality of their meal and the pleasure of good company. Wine is considered part of the diet, and has been since antiquity. They frown upon drunkenness, and see few problems related to drinking even though their per capita consumption of alcohol, and liver cirrhosis rates, are among the highest in the world. They have few alcohol control policies, tend to be Roman Catholic cultures, have a climate that supports viticulture, and for generations had all been Roman provinces. These cultures include southern France, Spain, Portugal, Italy, and Greece.[3]

"Blended cultures" found in midcentral Western Europe, and their former colonies in North America, Australasia, and South Africa, consume both wine and grain-based beverages, both with and without meals, and tend to frown on drunkenness. Northern-blended drinking cultures are found in the United Kingdom and its former colonies. Like Nordic cultures, they have concerns about drinking. Continental-blended cultures have more Mediterranean attitudes. In Western Europe, most blended cultures were Roman provinces in antiquity. During the disruption of the early Middle Ages, they retained the Roman urban customs of daily wine drinking and viticulture but also incorporated the grain-based drinking preferences of the Germanic invaders and settlers into their cultures. Dominant religious beliefs include both Protestantism and Roman Catholicism. Continental-blended cultures include much of Austria and Germany, the Netherlands, Belgium, central and northern France, and Switzerland.[4]

Eastern European drinking cultures, including Poland and Russia, have tended since antiquity to consume grain-based beverages. Spirits, in particular, after the introduction of distillation, became popular as they did in many Nordic cultures. These Eastern European cultures were not Roman provinces, did not have viticulture, and are either Roman Catholic or Eastern Orthodox countries. They have episodic feast drinking patterns and the aim of drinking is usually to get drunk. These cultures have had some brief but unsuccessful experimentation with rationing to cut down consumption (Levine, 1992; Tyrrell, 1979; Wald, Moskalewicz, & Morawski, 1990).

Several works focus upon the more Northern drinking cultures, including Bales (1962), Blane (1977), Blocker (1989), Gusfield (1986), and Rorabaugh (1979). Ahlström-Laakso (1976), Eriksen (1990), and Mäkelä (1986) focus on the Nordic region. Levine (1984, 1992), in particular, discusses the exclusivity of temperance cycles and alcohol control policies to English or Nordic-speaking Protestant countries.

[3]See previous footnote and Davies (1984). For discussion of Italian patterns, see, in particular, Lolli, Serianni, and Golder (1958) and Cottino (1995).

[4]Although Scotland is included with the rest of the United Kingdom, it has different drinking patterns from England and Wales. In antiquity, Scotland was not Romanized and did not have viticulture as found in southern England. In more recent times there were profound political struggles between Roman Catholicism and Protestantism in Scotland that may have had an influence on drinking patterns. The Republic of Ireland, in the same geographic region, was not Romanized, did not have viticulture, is Roman Catholic, and retains more Northern patterns (Engs, 1995, 1999).

The Protestant Temperance Connection

During the Reformation, Protestantism took root in the Northern cultures. Levine (1992) notes that "in Western societies, only Nordic and English-speaking cultures developed large, ongoing, extremely popular temperance movements in the nineteenth century and the first third or so of the twentieth century" (p. 17). He also observes that temperance—antialcohol—cultures have been, and still are, "Protestant" societies. Today, rigid alcohol control policies, and, in particular, policies to control youthful drinking, are primarily found in these Northern Protestant cultures and their former colonies. Protestants within these cultures, also tend to consume less alcohol compared to Roman Catholics. Heavier drinking has also been found among Irish Roman Catholic adults living in Western Scotland, and Roman Catholic youth in Australia, Canada, Scotland, and the U.S. (Engs, 1980; Engs, Diebold, & Hanson, 1996; Engs, Hanson, Glicksman, & Smythe, 1990; Engs & Mullen, 1999; Mullen, Williams, & Hunt, 1996).

Protestantism is not merely a set of theological beliefs. It is a social psychology system with a focus on self-restraint and self-regulation. Drunkenness and episodic drinking patterns leading to mayhem, vomiting, and brutality are perceived as "out of control" behaviors. By extension, temperance movements, and, in particular, abstinence movements, which reached their greatest influence in the U.S., were the middle-class Protestant establishment's effort to force self-restraint upon groups that were perceived as being out of control, and to impose control on certain segments of the society.[5] In many Western countries today, with either traditional Northern, blended, or Southern European attitudes, the drunken "barbarian" behavior is primarily found among youth consuming spirits or even beer, and not the traditional alcoholic beverages consumed with meals and within a family context (Donato et al., 1995: Engs, 1999, 2000; Geertz 1973; Levine, 1983, 1992).

Wide-scale temperance movements and antialcohol sentiments have not been, and generally are not, found in Southern European Catholic countries, although this benign attitude towards alcohol may be beginning to change in regard to young people in, for example, Italy (Donato et al., 1995). In the largely

[5] Anglo-American Protestant revivalists were particularly interested in temperance and spawned wide-scale temperance and/or prohibition movements. Missionaries from these revivalist religious groups successfully evangelized several countries, such as Sweden, which in turn developed a large temperance movement early in the twentieth century. Australia and some Northern European countries have had temperance movements, but not to the extent found in the U.S. and the United Kingdom. Iceland and Finland also developed temperance movements and instituted some prohibition efforts during this era. There was also some temperance interest among Protestants in Denmark, the Netherlands, Switzerland, and Germany (Ásmundsson, 1995; Levine, 1992). However, it did not develop into a national movement which Eriksen (1990) argues was likely to have been due, particularly in Denmark, to pietistic Lutheranism. Engs (1999, 2000) discusses the hostility of American Protestants towards Irish Catholic immigrants and the use of prohibition measures as a method of control over this group.

spirits-drinking Eastern Orthodox countries, such as Russia and Poland, sporadic antidrink campaigns have been launched but have only been short-lived (Wald et al., 1990). A similar history of sporadic, short-lived anti-alcohol campaigns has also been found in Ireland (Levine, 1992; Tyrrell, 1979).

Protestant "Awakenings," "Clean Living" Cycles, and the Control of Youthful Drunks

Beginning in the sixteenth century, immigrants to the Americas, Australasia, and other colonies took their drinking cultures with them. Successive waves of immigrants from different regions of Europe set the stage for cultural clashes in regard to attitudes and behaviors concerning alcohol consumption, especially in North America.[6] One factor influencing temperance cycles and concerns about drunkenness, particularly in the U.S., is thought to be a clash of values between the dominant Protestant Anglo-Saxon blended drinking culture and Roman Catholic groups with different drinking norms. Temperance cycles have generally emerged with Protestant religious "awakenings" (Billington, 1974; Engs, 1999, 2000; Fogel, 1995; McLoughlin, 1978; Wilson, 1980).

Youthful Irish immigrants exhibited drunken behaviors resulting in urban riots and perceived health and social problems in the 1840s. A reason for the passage of prohibition laws in 13 eastern states in the U.S. and two Canadian provinces during the 1850s was to control these "dangerous" lower class Catholic "infidels" who were increasingly becoming involved in the liquor business (Billington, 1974; Blocker, 1989; Engs, 2000; Gienapp, 1987; Rosenberg, 1987; Tyrrell, 1979).

A factor in the American Prohibition experiment of the 1920s, was to gain control over heavy-drinking Eastern Europeans who habituated "saloons" and daily wine-drinking Italians who were wresting political control from "old-stock" Protestants. Other factors having an impact on the late nineteenth and early twentieth century movements included rapid industrialization, which called for sober laborers, and a reaction to unprecedented per capita consumption precipitated by rapid socioeconomic changes and stress in the early and late nineteenth century (Blocker, 1989; Engs, 2000; Pittman & Snyder, 1962; Timberlake, 1963).[7]

[6]Brewing and distilling came with the British and Northern European immigrants into North America, Australasia, and South Africa. Viticulture followed the Spanish conquerors, monks, and colonists as they migrated to Peru, Bolivia, Colombia, and Chile. See, in particular, the following authors for further information concerning the dispersion of drinking cultures to the colonies: Gusfield (1963), Heath (1990), Timberlake (1963), Wiseman (1997).

[7]For details of theories that discuss the etiology of temperance movements, Protestant "awakenings," control of immigrant and youthful behavior, need for sober workers, and the elimination of perceived problems such as saloons, see, in particular: Billington (1974), Blocker (1989), Engs (1992, 1999, 2000), Fogel (1995), Gusfield (1963), Hofstadter (1968), Musto (1996), Rorabaugh (1979), and Rumbarger (1989).

Temperance movements come in cycles of approximately 80 years in the U.S.[8] Because these movements are cyclical and have different phases, the phase of the cycle will determine what research programs will be allowed, particularly for youth. For example, because of current laws and attitudes, it would be impossible in the U.S. today to conduct a study with teenagers that examined the effect of beer, wine, and spirit-tasting classes in the public schools on drinking patterns. In the U.S., temperance cycles are part of a generalized "clean living movement" where "opposition towards alcohol, tobacco, drugs, sexual-related behaviors, and advocacy for exercise, pure water, vegetarian diets, and the prevention and elimination of other health, social, and environmental problems are common" (Engs, 1997, p. 223).

Each cycle has different phases within the overall ebb and flow of the movement. Each phase lasts about a generation. The phases in a cycle, for alcohol in particular, include: *moral suasion, coercion, backlash*, and *complacency* (Engs, 2000). In the first phase public efforts are deployed to eliminate perceived problems through moral suasion (education) campaigns. When the problem is not immediately eradicated, alcohol is then seen as *the* problem, and the substance becomes "demonized" (considered evil). Abstinence and prohibition measures are instituted as public policy. The backlash phase begins when a large part of the population, in particular youth, ignores the restrictive policies and continues to consume alcohol illegally in underground situations that precipitate negative alcohol-related behaviors. Because the laws are not working, they begin to be officially ignored, changed, or repealed. This then leads to a complacency stage. As problems begin to arise again, the cycle begins again (Blocker, 1989; Engs, 1997: Musto, 1996). A key to learning about drinking, and to research concerning youthful drinking, particularly in the U.S., is the awareness that temperance movements are cyclical. During the latter phases of the cycle, which the U.S. may now be entering, creative research on learning about drinking may be more easy to accomplish.

Emerging Research Questions I

- Does religiosity have an effect on youthful drinking patterns?
- What role can religion play in promoting sensible drinking among youth?
- In countries that have large immigrant populations, what are the drinking patterns of immigrant youth compared to native-born youth?

[8]For more information on temperance cycles, see Blocker (1989), Engs (2000), Heath (1989), Musto (1996), Pittman (1980), Room (1987, 1989), and Wagner (1987). Although Blocker has identified five movements, most other authors have collapsed these into three broad movements over the past 200 years with a cycle of about 80 years in the U.S. These three movements have tended to emerge shortly before peaks in per capita consumption of alcohol, which were in 1830, 1910, and 1980 (Rorabaugh, 1979).

- Why do Roman Catholic youth in Protestant cultures tend to consume more alcohol than Protestant youth in those cultures?
- What are the drinking patterns of Protestant youth in Catholic cultures?

ACQUISITION OF DRINKING NORMS AND YOUTHFUL DRINKING PATTERNS

Transmission of Family Drinking Values

Societies' drinking norms are transmitted through the family, as outlined in more detail in other chapters and particularly by Sanchez-Sosa and Poldrugo (see Chapter 3). Drinking in Southern and in many blended and Northern drinking cultures first takes place in the home. In Italy, the classic Southern culture, "families are still the central socialization agency all the way through from urban areas to the countryside, and the first contact with alcoholic beverages can take place between ages 5 and 14" (Forni, 1997, p. 66).

Likewise, in Northern-Blended cultures, the majority of young people are introduced to alcohol within the family. However, most drinking tends to occur with peers. In the United Kingdom youth first begin to taste alcohol between the ages of 10–12 (Bagnall, 1991). Although the legal drinking age there is 18 years, it is "widely flouted" and there appears to be a general social and cultural acceptance of adolescent alcohol use. Teenage drinking is viewed as a "normative developmental transition" (Foxcroft, Lowe, & May, 1994, p. 64). In the U.S., the legal purchase age is 21. However, 50% of youth have tried alcohol by the age of 14 (Johnson, 1993). One study showed that 65% of adolescents indicated that their first use took place in the context of a family gathering (LaBouvie, Bates, & Pandina, 1997). In Australia, 43% of 13-year-olds and 93% of 18-year-olds reported that they had used alcohol. Younger students tended to drink at home. However, there was peer pressure to drink among younger students outside the home (Wilks, 1992a, 1992b).

Peer influence on drinking outside the home leads to two types of drinking patterns among youth in some cultures. In Italy, although traditional patterns of moderate wine drinking with meals are found among youth, peer-influenced behaviors are more likely to lead to drunkenness. Donato et al. (1995) suggest that two

> distinct drinking patterns [are] found among Italian adolescents: on the one hand, the daily drinking of moderate wine with meals, together with parents, which [is] more common among males than females, as in other 'Latin' countries; and on the other hand, the occasional intake of alcoholic beverages in excess, especially beer and spirits, out of the family but together with peers (p. 59).

Forni (1997) also found these two patterns in another study of Italian youth. These and other researchers have concluded that peer-related drinking is likely to be due to the adolescent development phase of striving for independence apart from their parents, a symbol of adulthood, and a rite of passage. In addition, most young people mature out of heavier uses of alcohol (LaBouvie et al., 1997; Wilks, 1992b).

Current Youthful Drinking Patterns Outside the Home

In many Western cultures today the drunken Northern, "barbarian," or "binge" drinking behavior is primarily found among youth consuming spirits or beer with peers outside family settings. Drinking within the family is still associated with more moderate consumption. For example, in a sample of over 9,000 Italian youth, Donato et al. (1995) found that the "frequency of beer drinking and especially the quantity of spirits consumed showed the strongest association with frequency of drunkenness" (p. 63). In this study, twice as many males in grade 13 who consumed five or more drinks of spirits per month reported being intoxicated at least two times or more during the previous year compared to those who were daily wine drinkers.

On the whole, adolescents from Northern and Northern-blended cultures are more likely to report becoming drunk than those in Southern drinking cultures. For example, in the United Kingdom young adults aged between 16 and 24 consume the highest amount of alcohol. After 24 years of age there is a decline in alcohol use. A higher percentage of men (38%) exceeded their "sensible limit" than women (18%); sensible or safe consumption is defined as 21 units or drinks for men and 14 units or drinks for women per week.[9] In Scotland, alcohol is the most commonly used recreational substance, 93% of men and 84% of women consuming alcohol at least occasionally. Scottish men were found to consumed 16.9 drinks per week compared to 4.6 for women (Thomas, Goddard, Hickman, & Hunter, 1993). A difference in drinking patterns between Scottish and English/Welsh adolescents has been repeatedly found. A greater tendency for Scottish teenagers to drink to intoxication is thought to reflect cultural differences surrounding the use of alcohol (Marsh, Dobbs, & White, 1986). In the Northern Scandinavian cultures young adults are considerably more permissive of both drinking and intoxication than are older respondents (Mäkelä, 1986).

A 1993/1994 World Health Organization study (Gabhainn & François, 2000) of youth in Europe and North America found that students in Northern and Northern-blended cultures were more likely to report perceived drunkenness on two or more occasions by the age of 15. This included 31% of youth in the U.S., 40% in Sweden, and 42% in Austria. A high percentage of students in Northern Ireland, England, Scotland, and Wales also reported this behavior. This was in contrast to France, Greece, Portugal, and Switzerland. It appears

[9]See, for example, Engs & Aldo-Benson (1995), Garg, Wagener, & Mandans (1993), and Thomas et al. (1993) for information on safe drinking limits in terms of health.

that even among youth, the ancient patterns of more moderation are still found in the Southern drinking cultures.

Beer appears to be the most popular beverage for youth in most Western cultures, followed by spirits and wine. However, French students report higher frequencies of wine consumption. In Wales, Denmark, England, and Greece, over 40% of 15-year-old boys consumed beer on a weekly basis (Gabhainn & François, 2000). Beer has consistently been found to be the most popular beverage in numerous studies of university students in North America, Europe, and Australia.

Drinking patterns among university students show a wide variation. However, on the whole, the majority of students consume within the limit for sensible drinking in the Northern-blended drinking cultures. For example, a study comparing 1,687 U.S. American to 4,911 Canadian students attending universities in states and provinces surrounding the Great Lakes found that U.S. students consumed more drinks per week (14.2) than did their Canadian counterparts (12.3). However, both groups were within sensible limits (Engs et al., 1990).

In the United Kingdom most studies show moderate drinking among university students. A study of 13 medical schools in England, Scotland, and Wales found that 86% of students consumed alcohol on a regular basis. Of these 82% were within the recommended limit for sensible drinking (Howse & Ghodse, 1997). Another study of helping-profession students showed, however, that about 50% of university students consumed over the recommended amount. Men consumed 26.7 drinks per week compared to 17.3 for women (Engs & Teijlingen, 1997).

Two reports by Engs (1980, 1982) of 1,691 helping-profession university students in Australia showed that males consumed a mean of about two drinks per day, whereas females consumed less than a drink per day. Among all students, 26.3% drank at least once a week. Most students (67.6%) appeared to be "light to moderate drinkers" (less than 40 g of alcohol, or four drinks per day). A later Australian study suggested that 37% of 18-year-old (legal age to drink) males and 18% of females had consumed six or more drinks per week. About 77% of males and 56% of females aged 18 had consumed alcohol during the proceeding week (Wilks, 1992b).

Drinking among Polish university students, in the Eastern European drinking culture, showed dramatic differences when compared with students from the U.S. In a study of 1,408 Polish and 3,375 American university students, significantly more drinks per week were consumed by Polish male (24.9) and female (15.2) students compared to U.S. male (15.0) and female (7.6) university students. U.S. and Polish students both consumed about 7.4 beers per week. However, significantly more wine was consumed by Polish (8.7 drinks) compared to U.S. (0.8 drinks) students. The authors concluded that the unexpectedly high consumption of wine, a nontraditional Polish drink, may have been due to the students' attempts to reinforce upper class and elite values of university students in Poland (Engs, Slawinska, & Hanson, 1991).

SOCIETAL PERCEPTIONS OF DRINKING: IS CURRENT THINKING CONTRIBUTING TO PROBLEMS RATHER THAN SOLUTIONS?

Most of the research concerning drinking reflects the Northern culture's focus on "serious problems of youthful drinking." Indeed, most studies on alcohol problems among adolescents have been carried out in Northern Europe or the U.S. (Clark & Hilton, 1991). Does the negative focus on drinking problems, and, in particular, youthful problems, exacerbate problematic drinking patterns?

Are Media Perceptions of Dramatic Increases in Alcohol Use Correct?

Over the course of the last 20 years, and, in particular, during the last decade of the 20th century, the news media have focused on reports of increased "binge" drinking among college students, particularly in the U.S. In Great Britain, there is also concern about problematic drinking among youth. In Italy, drunkenness at discos is on the rise. Could news items about wild youth consuming more beer and spirits have led to misconceptions about actual alcohol consumption levels and patterns among youth? When the research literature is examined, the results suggest that most college and university students do not as a rule routinely drink to intoxication, and that there has been a decrease in alcohol consumption overall since the 1980s in most cultures.

From 60% to 80% of college and university students in the U.S. are light to moderate drinkers (Engs et al., 1996; Wechsler, Dowdall, Davenport, & Castillo, 1995). It should be borne in mind that studies are generally presented in the negative, i.e., from 20% to 40% are heavy or "binge" drinkers in this instance. In the U.S., among 12,000 university students across the nation, 61% of males and 81% of females were found to consume alcohol within the limits for sensible drinking or moderate drinking (Engs et al., 1996). A recent study found that among students from the same universities there had be no change in the percentage of heavy or "binge" drinkers over a 12-year period, which remained at about 20% in each of the five time periods sampled (Engs & Hanson, 1999). The misrepresentation by the media in terms of drinking patterns raises some questions for research concerning the effect of focusing on negative patterns as opposed to more moderate drinking behaviors.

Emerging Research Questions II

- Does the focus on negative aspects of alcohol use among college students increase negative behaviors?
- If the media were to focus on positive drinking situations and the characteristics of young adults who drink in nonproblematic ways would more positive drinking patterns be exhibited?

Do Negative Expectations Increase Problems?

Drinking attitudes are related to expectations. There is much historical and cross-cultural evidence suggesting that people not only learn how to drink, but they also learn through the process of socialization how drinking will affect them (Heath, 1998; MacAndrew & Edgerton, 1969). Heath (1998) contends that "those who expect [drink] to make them feel sexy become amorous; those who view it as disinhibiting are demonstrative" (p. 115).

In Southern European cultures, such as Italy, Spain, and much of France, and blended cultures such as Austria, the United Kingdom, and the Bavarian region of Germany, individuals who consume wine with meals are not expected to become intoxicated, get into fights, and exhibit other problematic behaviors. Wine is treated as a food. On the other hand, young Italians who consume spirits and beer tend to exhibit more Northern episodic patterns (Cottino, 1995; Donato et al., 1995). Perhaps expectations of drunkenness, based upon media reports of youthful behaviors in North America, the United Kingdom, or Scandinavian cultures when consuming spirits or beer, encourage a similar expectation of drinking to intoxication when Southern European young people consume these beverages.

In the early 1990s some researchers and the media began to use the term "binge drinking" for heavier bouts of drinking. This term has emotional connotations and conjures up an image of the rapid consumption of alcohol for the exclusive purpose of getting drunk. As discussed previously, some young people in all cultures do engage in this type of behavior. However, since "binge drinking" is often defined as five or more drinks in any one sitting, not all young people, or even adults, who drink this amount may be consuming in a rapid manner or even become intoxicated. It is not unknown for adults in many countries to consume this amount during the course of an extended dinner; five drinks consumed over 5 or 6 hours would result in a near-0 blood alcohol level at the end of the evening. Most research reports from before the 1990s define five or more drinks as "heavy" or "riskier" drinking—terms that are neutral in emotional content.

Could the focus on negative drinking behaviors and the use of an emotionally laden term, rather than a more neutral word, to describe youthful drinking actually have increased problematic drinking behavior among youth? Recent research suggests a relationship between the perception of drinking and other behaviors, and the individual's own behavior. Students consistently overestimated both the amount of alcohol other students routinely consumed and the proportion of their fellow students who were heavy drinkers (Evans, Gilpin, Farkas, Shenassa, & Pierce, 1995; Perkins & Berkowitz, 1986).

The hypothesis that a change in expectations and perception could change behavior was recently tested by Haines and Spear (1996) at one university. They found that "a media campaign designed to change student perception of the amount of binge drinking showed an 18.5% drop in the number of students who perceived binge drinking as the norm (from 69.7% to 51.2%) and a corresponding reduction in self-reported binge drinking of 8.8% (from 43.0% to 34.2%)" (Haines & Spear, 1996, p. 134). The program informed students of the actual percentage though skits, fliers, and other activities. Traditional education programs had little effect.

Emerging Research Questions III

- Do emotionally laden words such as "binge" precipitate high-risk drinking behaviors among youth as they perceive this to be the norm? Would more neutral words such as "heavy" or "unsafe" be less likely to do this?
- If university students were allowed to drink in supervised environments, such as campus pubs and restaurants, with the expectation of exhibiting responsible behaviors and immediate sanctions for irresponsible behavior, what would be the effect on their drinking behaviors?

Reactance and Control of Consumption Theories: Do Restrictive Alcohol Control Policies Create a Backlash?

Current alcohol public policy efforts in the U.S. are predominantly geared toward curbing drunk driving and illegal drinking. To date, these public policies have included severe penalties against drunk driving, lowering of legal blood alcohol concentration (BAC) to designate impaired driving in many states, a 21-year-old lower age limit for alcohol purchase laws, government-sponsored abstinence education in schools and colleges, and warning labels on alcohol beverages. These alcohol policy measures have had only a temporary effect on some of the social problems they were attempting to eliminate. It is possible that they may also have increased other problems.

Among university students an increase in social, personal, and health problems related to drinking began to occur after the mandatory 21-year-old purchase law was implemented in the U.S. in 1987. Yet, as previously discussed, the data show no increase in frequency or quantity of drinking—or even heavy "binge" drinking (five or more drinks per occasion)—among university students since 1980, when per capita consumption reached a peak. In addition, fatal motor vehicle crashes began to decline before implementation of the 21-year-old purchase policy on a national level (Engs & Hanson, 1989, 1994, 1999). Could the increase in some behaviors related to drinking, while per capita consumption was decreasing, be explained by reactance theory and the lack of support for the "control of consumption" theory?

Reactance Theory Reactance theory suggests that telling persons not to do something often produces the opposite reaction. People value their sense of freedom and autonomy and like to perceive themselves as being in control.

According to the theory suggests that whenever people believe that their freedom either has been or will be unjustly threatened, they enter into a reactance motivational state and act to regain control by not complying. Coercion, in particular, leads to the arousal of reactance, which in turn tends to reduce compliance (Barnes & Welte, 1983; Brehem, 1972).

Since 1987, several reports have suggested that reactance may be occurring in drinkers under the age of 21 in the U.S. (Allen, Sprenkel, & Vitale, 1994; Engs & Hanson, 1989). A study by Engs and Hanson (1989) to test this theory in over 3,000 university college students found that, after the national 21-year-old purchase age policy had been implemented, a significantly lower percentage of legal age students consumed over five drinks per sitting per week (15.4%) compared to those who were under 21 years of age (24.1%). A more recent survey with more than 12,000 students from across the nation still showed that a lower percentage (18.6%) of legal age students consumed five drinks or more compared to students under 21 (22.1%) (Engs et al., 1996). In contrast, the results of two previous surveys, at the same universities, had found few significant differences in problems related to drinking before the drinking laws changed. After the change in the law, younger students began to drink in underground situations away from adult monitoring (Engs & Hanson, 1986, 1988).

As noted above, U.S. university students consumed a greater amount of alcohol and exhibited more problems related to drinking than Canadian students. The major difference between the two countries was that the legal purchase age in Ontario was 19 years while in the states contingent to the Great Lakes it was 21. It is hypothesized that the higher consumption levels and problems might be the result of reactance (Engs et al., 1990).

Some could argue that decreased drinking among legal age students was due to maturation. However, in some countries where it is legal for young adolescents to consume alcohol it is the older students who consume the most and exhibit more drinking-related problems. For example, in Scotland, where it is legal to drink at age 18, a study in over 3,000 university students found that the mean amount of alcohol consumed by both males and females increased as they grew older. The 19- to 24-year-old drinkers consumed the largest amount of alcohol. After age 24, consumption decreased (Engs & Teijlingen, 1997).

Reduction- (or Control-) of-Consumption Theory Beyond reactance theory, increases in negative behaviors related to drinking also suggest that the "reduction-of-consumption model" may be ineffective, and even counterproductive. This model suggests that regulating and limiting the supply of alcohol determines the extent to which it will be consumed; if less is consumed, fewer drinking-related problems will result. Therefore, measures such as higher taxes, raising the age of consumption, decreasing advertisements, limiting the number of sales outlets and hours of purchase, and placing warning messages on alcoholic beverages should decrease drinking and alcohol problems (Schmidt, 1985; Single, 1988). However, it appears from recent research that public policies, such as the minimum age 21 purchase law to control consumption among youthful drinkers, may have actually produced a backlash in the form of some negative behaviors related to drinking among youth.

In the U.S., a recent study tested the control-of-consumption theory. A sample of students from the same universities were sampled five times over a 12-year period (Engs & Hanson, 1999). The results showed a significant increase in the percentage of abstainers and a significant decrease in the mean number of drinks per week consumed since 1980. There was a significant decrease in variables related to drinking and driving. However, a significant increase in many problems related to drinking after, but not before, 1987 was found. It was concluded that the reduction-of-consumption hypothesis was supported only by the drinking and driving variables. This decrease in drinking and driving fatalities is often used to back current control-of-consumption polices and has been discussed in numerous reports. However, support for this argument does not take into account the increased health, school, legal, and social problems related to alcohol consumption among youth that has occurred since the implementation of the 21-year minimum age purchase policy. Reactance motivation and the potential ineffectiveness of the control-of-consumption model in countering many negative behaviors related to alcohol consumption need to be further explored.

Emerging Research Questions IV

- Does the control-of-consumption model lead to reactance motivation and backlash behaviors?
- In the U.S., would reducing the legal purchase and drinking age in controlled situations such as restaurants and taverns promote positive drinking?

School-Based Abstinence Education and Zero Tolerance Public Policy: Part of the Problem or Part of the Solution?

School-based alcohol education programs in the U.S. reflect the ingrained Northern drinking culture's ambivalence and negative attitudes towards alcohol. In 1989, the Federal Government's Office for Substance Abuse Prevention (OSAP) mandated abstinence as the only message to be taught in public schools (OSAP, 1989). Safe, responsible, sensible, or "low-risk" drinking could not be presented by schools or teachers who received funding from this program. Other programs had goals of decreasing harm, but rarely promoting positive drinking behaviors for those consuming alcohol even if a high proportion of "underage" youth were consuming alcohol illegally (Engs, 1981, 1991; Haines & Spear, 1996; Hanson, 1996).

Public policies on "zero" tolerance and negative messages regarding drinking have resulted in otherwise law-abiding young people acquiring police records. In general, zero tolerance may cause increased ambivalence about alcohol. More positive educational approaches have also primarily focused on messages designed to prevent alcohol consumption and reduce harm. Few have discussed sensible ways of consuming different alcoholic beverages, taught how to use alcohol as a adjunct to a party rather than its focus, or suggested what beverage tastes best with different foods. However, even school-based programs that have been more positive in their approaches have met with only marginal successes in promoting more responsible drinking behaviors (Fors, 1990; Hanson, 1996; Milgram, 1996).

Drinking among youth in many cultures is considered a recreational activity. As in other recreational activities, such as bicycle racing, football, sky-diving, or mountaineering, there are various steps that can be taken to reduce risk and increase safety. Examination of drinking-related risks, as a factor in this recreational pastime, can put drinking in a different light in terms of education, prevention, and research. In general, the greater amount of alcohol consumed, the greater the risk. However, other factors such as the age of the drinker need to be kept in mind in designing prevention strategies or research concerning learning about drinking (Roche & Evans, 1998).

A sample research proposal for U.S. colleges and universities

It is time to try and test new ideas. Some Colorado university administrators and politicians have discussed the possibility of selling licenses to drink a low-alcohol beer, in certain establishments, to students under 21 years of age. This is an innovative idea that could easily be implemented and studied on the college campus today.

Although the state might lose federal highway funding if this type of program were carried out under present law, the deficit could be eliminated through the license fee. (Ideally, instead of a state being punished for an innovative experiment by taking away highway funding, it should be rewarded for attempting to promote more positive behaviors.)

SUMMARY

The range of attitudes and behaviors concerning drinking in the Western world have deep roots in ancient cultures. Cultural attitudes and beliefs are also influenced by religion and social reform and temperance cycles. There have been some changes in drinking preferences and practices among Western youth. However, deep cultural differences still remain between Northern and Southern European cultures and their attitudes towards alcohol. Values concerning drinking are transmitted by the family. However, a culture's perception of drinking, expectations in regard to alcohol consumption, reactance motivation, and even restrictive control-of-consumption policies may be associated with more problematic drinking among youth. Creative and imaginative research on learning about drinking in a positive manner as presented in this chapter needs to be conducted.

REFERENCES

Ahlström-Laakso, S. (1976). European drinking habits: A review of research and some suggestions for conceptual integration of findings. In *Cross-cultural approaches to the study of alcohol* (p. 119–132). Paris: Mouton.

Allen, D. N., Sprenkel, D. G., & Vitale, P. A. (1994). Reactance theory and alcohol consumption laws: Further confirmation among collegiate alcohol consumers. *Journal of Studies on Alcohol, 55*, 34–40.

Ásmundsson, G. (1995). Iceland. In D. B. Heath (Ed.), *International handbook on alcohol and culture* (pp. 117–127). Westport, CT: Greenwood Press.

Austin, G. A. (with the staff of the Southern California Research Institute). (1985). *Alcohol in Western society from antiquity to 1800: A chronological history*. Santa Barbara, CA: ABC-Clio Information Services.

Bagnall, G. (1991). Alcohol education for 13 year olds: Does it work? Results from a controlled evaluation. *British Journal of Addiction, 86*, 895–904.

Bales, R. F. (1962). Attitudes toward drinking in the Irish culture. In D. J. Pittman & C. R. Snyder (Eds.), *Society, culture, and drinking patterns* (pp. 157–187). New York: Wiley.

Barnes, G., & Welte, J. (1983). Predictors of alcohol among college students in New York. *Journal of American College Health, 4*, 150–157.

Billington, R. A. (1974). *The origins of nativism in the United States: 1800–1844*. New York: Arno Press.

Blane, H. (1977). Acculturation and drinking in an Italian American community. *Journal of Studies on Alcohol, 38*, 1324–1346.

Blocker, J. S. (1989). *American temperance movements: Cycles of reform*. Boston: Twayne.

Bonavia, D. (1980). *The Chinese*. New York: Lippincott & Crowell.

Brehem, J. (1972). *Response to psychological reactance: A theory of freedom and control*. Morrisville, NJ.: General Learning Press.

Chafetz, M. (1964). Consumption of alcohol in the Far and Middle East. *New England Journal of Medicine, 217*, 297–301.

Clark, W. B., & Hilton, M. E. (1991). *Alcohol in America: Drinking practices and problems*. Albany, NY: State University of New York Press.

Cottino, A. (1995). Italy. In D. B. Heath (Ed.), *International handbook on alcohol and culture* (pp. 156–167). Westport, CT: Greenwood Press.

Davies, P. (1984). *Alcohol-related problems in the European Community*. Oxford: Oxford Rehabilitation Research Unit.

Donato, F., Monarca, S., Chiesa, R., Feretti, D, Modolo, M. A., & Nardi, G. (1995). Patterns and covariates of alcohol drinking among high school students in 10 towns in Italy: A cross-sectional study. *Drug and Alcohol Dependence, 37*, 59–69.

Engs, R. C. (1980). The drug-use patterns of helping-profession students in Brisbane, Australia. *Drug and Alcohol Dependence, 6*, 231–246.

Engs, R. C. (1982). Drinking patterns and attitudes toward alcoholism of Australian human-service students. *Journal of Studies on Alcohol, 43*, 517–531.

Engs, R. C. (1991). Resurgence of a new "clean living" movement in the United States. *Journal of School Health, 61*, 155–158.

Engs, R. C. (1992, June). *American cycles of prohibition: Do they have roots in the ancient past?* Paper presented at the Kettil Bruun Society Alcohol Epidemiology Conference, Toronto, Canada.

Engs, R. C. (1995). Do traditional western European drinking practices have origins in antiquity? *Addiction Research, 2*, 227–239.

Engs, R. C. (1997). Cycles of social reform: Is the current anti-alcohol movement cresting? *Journal of Studies on Alcohol, 58*, 223–224.

Engs, R. C. (1999). Protestants and Catholics: Drunken barbarians and mellow Romans? Available: http://www.indiana.edu/ engs/articles/cathprot.htm

Engs, R. C. (2000). *Clean living movements: American cycles of health reform.* Westport, CT: Praeger.

Engs, R.C., & Aldo-Benson, M. (1995). The association of alcohol consumption with self-reported illness in university students. *Psychological Reports, 76*, 727–736.

Engs, R. C., Diebold, B. A., & Hanson, D. J. (1996). The drinking patterns and problems of a national sample of college students, 1994. *Journal of Alcohol and Drug Education, 41*, 13–33.

Engs, R. C., & Hanson, D. J. (1986). Age-specific alcohol prohibition and college students' drinking problems. *Psychological Reports, 59*, 979–984.

Engs, R. C., & Hanson, D. J. (1988). University students' drinking patterns and problems: Examining the effects of raising the purchase age. *Public Health Reports, 1*, 65–83.

Engs, R. C., & Hanson, D. J. (1989). Reactance theory: A test with collegiate drinking. *Psychological Reports, 64*, 1083–1086.

Engs, R. C., & Hanson, D. J. (1994). Boozing and brawling on campus: A national study of violent problems associated with drinking over the past decade. *Journal of Criminal Justice, 22*, 171–180.

Engs, R. C., & Hanson, D. J. (1999). Reduction of consumption theory: A test using the drinking patterns and problems of collegians in the United States, 1983–1994. *College Student Journal, 33*, 333–345.

Engs, R. C., Hanson, D. J., Glicksman, L., & Smythe, C. (1990). Influence of religion and culture on drinking behaviours: A test of hypotheses between Canada and the USA. *British Journal of Addiction, 85*, 1475–1482.

Engs, R. C., Heath, D. B., & Room, R. (Ed.). (1995). *Addiction Research, 2*, 227–239.

Engs, R. C., & Mullen, K. (1999). The effect of religion and religiosity on drug use among a selected sample of post secondary students in Scotland. *Addiction Research, 7*, 149–170.

Engs, R. C., Slawinska, J., & Hanson, D. J. (1991). Drinking patterns of American and Polish university students: Cross-national study. *Drug and Alcohol Dependence, 27*, 167–175.

Engs, R. C., & Teijlingen, E. (1997). Correlates of alcohol, tobacco and marijuana use among Scottish post secondary helping-profession students. *Journal of Studies on Alcohol, 58*, 435–444.

Eriksen, S. (1990). Drunken Danes and sober Swedes? Religious revivalism and the temperance movements as keys to Danish and Swedish folk cultures. In B. Stråth (Ed.), *Language and construction of class identities. The struggle for discursive power in social organization: Scandinavia and Germany after 1800.* Gothenburg: Department of History, Gothenburg University.

Evans, N., Gilpin, E., Farkas, A. J., Shenassa, E., & Pierce, J. P. (1995). Adolescents' perceptions of their peers. *American Journal of Public Health, 85*, 1064–1069.

Fogel, R. W. (1995). The fourth great awakening and the political realignment of the 1990s. *Brigham Young University Studies, 35*, 31–43.

Food and Agriculture Organization of the United Nations. (1984). *Food Balance Sheets: 1979–81 Average.* Rome: Food and Agriculture Organization of the UN.

Food and Agriculture Organization of the United Nations. (1991). *Food Balance Sheets: 1984–86 Average.* Rome: Food and Agriculture Organization of the UN.

Forni, E. (1997). Alcohol and youth. *Alcologia, 9*, 65–68.

Fors, S. (1990). School-based alcohol and drug education programs can be effective. In R. C. Engs (Ed.), *Controversies in the addiction field.* Dubuque, IO: Kendall-Hunt.

Foxcroft, D. R., Lowe, G., & May, C. (1994). Adolescent alcohol use and family influences: Attributive statements by teenage drinkers. *Drug Education, Prevention and Policy, 1*, 63–69.

Gabhainn, S. N., & François, Y. (2000). *Substance use: Health and health behaviour among young people.* Copenhagen: WHO Regional Office for Europe.

Garg, R., Wagener, D. K., & Mandans, J. H. (1993). Alcohol consumption and risk of ischemic heart disease in women. *Archives of Internal Medicine, 153*, 1211–1216.

Geertz, C. (1973). *The interpretation of cultures.* New York: Basic Books.

Gienapp, W. E. (1987). *The origins of the Republican Party, 1852–1856.* New York: Oxford University Press.

Gusfield, J. R. (1986). *Symbolic crusade: Status politics and the American temperance movement* (2nd ed.). Urbana: University of Illinois Press.

Haines, M. S., & Spear, S. F. (1996). Changing the perception of the norm: A strategy to decrease binge drinking among college students. *Journal of American College Health, 45*, 134–140.

Hanson, D. J. (1996). *Alcohol education: What we must do*. Westport, CT: Praeger.

Heath, D. B. (1984). *Historical and cultural factors affecting alcohol availability and consumption in Latin America* (Research Papers in Anthropology). Providence, RI: Brown University.

Heath, D. B. (1989). The new temperance movement: Through the looking glass. *Drugs and Society, 3*, 143–168.

Heath, D. B. (1990). Cultural factors in the choice of drugs. In: M. Galanter (Ed.). *Recent developments in alcoholism, Vol. 8*. New York: Plenum Press.

Heath, D. B. (Ed.). (1995). *International handbook on alcohol and culture*. Westport, CT: Greenwood Press.

Heath, D. B. (1998). Cultural variations among drinking patterns. In M. Grant & J. Litvak (Eds.), *Drinking patterns and their consequences* (pp. 103–125). Washington, DC: Taylor & Francis.

Heath, D. B. (2000). *Drinking occasions: Comparative perspectives on alcohol and culture*. Philadelphia: Brunner Mazel.

Heok, K. E. (1990). Drinking habits of elderly Chinese. *British Journal of Addiction, 85*, 571–573.

Hofstadter, R. (1968). *The age of reform: From Bryan to FDR*. New York: Knoff.

Howse, K., & Ghodse, A. H. (1997). Hazardous drinking and its correlates among medical students. *Addiction Research, 4*, 355–366.

Hupkens, C. L. H., Knibbe, R. A., & Drop, M. J. (1992). *Alcohol consumption in the European Community: Uniformity and diversity in national drinking patterns*. Paper presented at the Kettil Bruun Society Alcohol Epidemiology Conference, Toronto, Canada.

Johnson, L. (1993). *National survey results on drug use from the Monitoring the Future Study, 1975–1992*. Rockville, MD: Department of Health and Human Services.

LaBouvie, E. W., Bates, M. E., & Pandina, R. J. (1997). Age of first use: Its reliability and predictive utility. *Journal of Studies on Alcohol, 58*, 538–643.

Levine, H. G. (1983). The good creature of God and the demon rum: Colonial and 19th century American ideas about alcohol, accidents and crime. In R. Room & G. Collins (Eds.), *Alcohol and disinhibition* (Research Monograph No. 12). Washington, DC: National Institute on Alcohol Abuse and Alcoholism.

Levine, H. G. (1984). The alcohol problem in America: From temperance to alcoholism. *British Journal of Addiction, 79*, 109–119.

Levine, H. G. (1992). Temperance cultures: Concern about alcohol problems in Nordic and English-speaking cultures. In M. Lader, G. Edwards, & D. C. Drummond (Eds.), *The nature of alcohol and drug related problems*. Oxford, England: Oxford University Press.

Lolli, G., Serianni, E., & Golder, G. M. (1958). *Alcohol in Italian culture: Food and wine in relation to sobriety among Italians and Italian Americans*. Glencoe, IL: Free Press.

MacAndrew, C., & Edgerton, R. B. (1969). *Drunken comportment: A social explanation*. Chicago: Aldine Publishing.

Mäkelä, K. (1986). Attitudes towards drinking and drunkenness in four Scandinavian countries. *Annals of the New York Academy of Sciences, 472*, 21–32.

Marsh, A., Dobbs, J., & White, A. (1986). *Adolescent drinking*. London: Her Majesty's Stationery Office.

McLoughlin, W. G. (1978). *Revivals, awakenings, and reform: An essay on religion and social change in America, 1607–1977*. Chicago: University of Chicago Press.

Milgram, G. G. (1996). Responsible decision making regarding alcohol: A re-emerging prevention/education strategy for the 1990s. *Journal of Drug Education, 26*, 357–365.

Mullen, K., Williams, R., & Hunt, K. (1996). Irish descent, religion, and alcohol and tobacco use. *Addiction, 91*, 243–254.

Musto, D. (1996). Alcohol in American history. *Scientific American, 274*, 78–83.

Office for Substance Abuse Prevention. (1989). *Policy review guidelines: Message and material review process*. Rockville, MD: Office for Substance Abuse Prevention.

Perkins, H. W., & Berkowitz, A. D. (1986). Perceiving the community norms of alcohol use among students: Some research implications for campus alcohol education programming. *International Journal of the Addictions, 21*, 961–976.

Pittman, D. (1980). *Primary prevention of alcohol abuse and alcoholism: An evaluation of the control of consumption policy*. St. Louis, MO: Social Science Institute, Washington University.

Pittman, D. J., & Snyder, C. R. (Eds.). (1962). *Society, culture, and drinking patterns*. Carbondale, IL: Southern Illinois University Press.

Roche, A. M., & Evans, K. R. (1998). The implications of drinking patterns for primary prevention, education, and screening. In M. Grant & J. Litvak (Eds.), *Drinking patterns and their consequences* (pp. 243–265). Washington, DC: Taylor & Francis.

Room, R. (1987). *Social dimensions of alcohol dependence*. Berkeley, CA: Alcohol Research Group, Medical Research Institute of San Francisco.

Room, R. (1989). Cultural changes in drinking and trends in alcohol problem indicators: Recent U.S. experience. *Alcologia, 1*, 83–89.

Rorabaugh, W. J. (1979). *The alcoholic republic: An American tradition*. New York: Oxford University Press.

Rosenberg, C. E. (1987). *The cholera years: The United States in 1832, 1849, and 1866*. Chicago: University of Chicago Press.

Rumbarger, J. J. (1989). *Profits, power and Prohibition: Alcohol reform and the industrialization of America 1800–1830*. Albany, NY: State University of New York Press.

Schmidt, W. (1985). Regulating the supply of alcoholic beverages: A new concept for an old ideology? In J. P. von Wartburg, P. Magnenat, R. Muller, & S. Wyss (Eds.), *Currents in alcohol research and the prevention of alcohol problems: Proceedings of an International Symposium held in Lausanne, Switzerland, November 7–9, 1983* (pp. 107–118). Bern, Switzerland: Huber.

Single, E. W. (1988). The availability theory of alcohol-related problems. In C. D. Chaudron & W. D. Adrian (Eds.), *Theories on alcoholism* (pp. 325–351). Toronto, Canada: Addiction Research Foundation.

Thomas, M., Goddard, E., Hickman, M., & Hunter, P. (1993). *General Household Survey*. London: Her Majesty's Stationery Office.

Timberlake, J. H. (1963). *Prohibition and the progressive movement, 1900–1920*. Cambridge, MA: Harvard University Press.

Tyrell, I. R. (1979). *Sobering up: From temperance to prohibition in antebellum America, 1800–1860*. Westport, CT: Greenwood Press.

Wagner, D. (1987). The new temperance movement and social control at the workplace. *Contemporary Drug Problems, 14*, 539–545.

Wald, I., Moskalewicz, J., & Morawski, J. (1990, June). *Development of market economy and system of alcohol control in Poland*. Paper presented at the 35th International Institute on the Prevention and Treatment of Alcoholism, Berlin, Germany.

Wechsler, H., Dowdall, G. W., Davenport, A., & Castillo, S. (1995). Correlates of college student binge drinking. *American Journal of Public Health, 85*, 921–926.

Wilks, J. (1992a). Adolescent views on risky and illegal alcohol use. *Drug and Alcohol Review, 11*, 137–143.

Wilks, J. (1992b). Drinking habits of central Queensland adolescents: Local research for local needs. *Drug and Alcohol Review, 11*, 187–191.

Wilson, J. Q. (1980). Reagan and the Republican revival. *Commentary, 70*, 25–32.

Wiseman, J. (1997). In vito veritas. *Archaeology, Sept./Oct.*, 12–14.

Chapter 8

Multiple Influences on Adolescents

Ian Newman

There are a number of conundrums surrounding how young people learn about drinking and learn how to drink. When studying how young people learn about drinking, one must consider the many and varied factors in an adolescent's world that subtly, indirectly, and directly influence attitudes and practices that shape alcohol-related behavior. Factors that influence learning about drinking may be as subtle as a reference to alcohol in the lyrics of a song or as direct and obvious as the information on an alcohol-specific Internet website. Influences as diverse as price, advertising and availability, local norms regarding consumption, religion, and the death of a friend in an automobile crash could all affect a young person's attitudes and practices in regard to alcohol.

Such factors may work independently of each other or, more likely, work together as a complex matrix, each factor influencing the others. Because young people are all different, their responses to even similar factor matrices are likely to be different as well. But as groups of young people share common cultures within varied societies, there are patterns of responses that are similar among particular groups of young people and different from others.

Influences may also be through intermediaries, as when an alcohol-related event generates significant news media coverage that in turn stimulates discussion within a community. Not only are there multiple influences at any single point in time, but the influences occur in combinations that are constantly shifting and rearranging over time. It is this mix of sociocultural and psychological variables that confounds the simple, single-influence programs often proposed for reducing the consequences of inappropriate alcohol use.

The effects of combinations of influences are, however, not as well documented or understood as the effects of single-variable influences such as parental attitudes toward alcohol, alcohol education, or the pricing and availability of alcohol. The effects of combined influences are, therefore, subject to more discussion and debate. Individual influences have been discussed in detail elsewhere in this book. This chapter now invites the reader to step back from considering only single-variable influences—keeping in mind their significance—to contemplate how a matrix of these influences may interact to explain how adolescents learn about drinking and why adolescents apparently exposed to similar influences behave differently. By necessity, the coverage of such a topic here is limited and is not intended to diminish the complexity of the issue, which is fully acknowledged.

It is challenging from a purely academic perspective to try to understand how young people learn about drinking, but it is also challenging from a practical perspective. How young people learn about drinking informs the behavioral outcome, i.e., their behavior in a drinking context, which can also include not drinking.

Any attempt to explore the interaction of many influences suggests the need for an organizing framework. At the risk of being oversimplistic, a modified version of Green and Kreuter's (1999) PRECEDE/PROCEED public health planning model will be used here for this purpose. PRECEDE/PROCEED is an outcome-based planning model that begins with the analysis of a community and the identification of its important developmental objectives. An epidemiological analysis of community health data identifies health problems that affect the community. Then follows an analysis of the environmental and behavioral factors that contribute to and shape health problems. Next comes the identification of factors that predispose to, enable, and reinforce changes in behaviors and in the environment.

Used in its classic form, this step-by-step analysis *precedes* any program initiatives. Program initiatives flow from the analysis and *proceed* in the opposite direction to effect change (Figure 1). In that context, only the PROCEED part of the model is used. Here we are going to apply the model not to a community but to individuals. In this way, we can consider what predisposes a young person to use or not to use alcohol in a particular way and what enables and reinforces this use or nonuse.

Based on the PRECEDE/PROCEED model, this chapter organizes the process of learning about drinking according to three types of factors: factors that *predispose* the learner to alcohol use or nonuse, factors that *enable* alcohol use or nonuse, and factors that *reinforce* use or nonuse of alcohol. Influences in these three areas shape both individual behavior and the environment. How *behavior*, in turn, both changes and is changed by the *environment* is considered in the second level in this analysis. The third level represents what happens to a person as a consequence of the first two levels. At each step, this model allows for the interaction of multiple behavioral and environmental variables. As

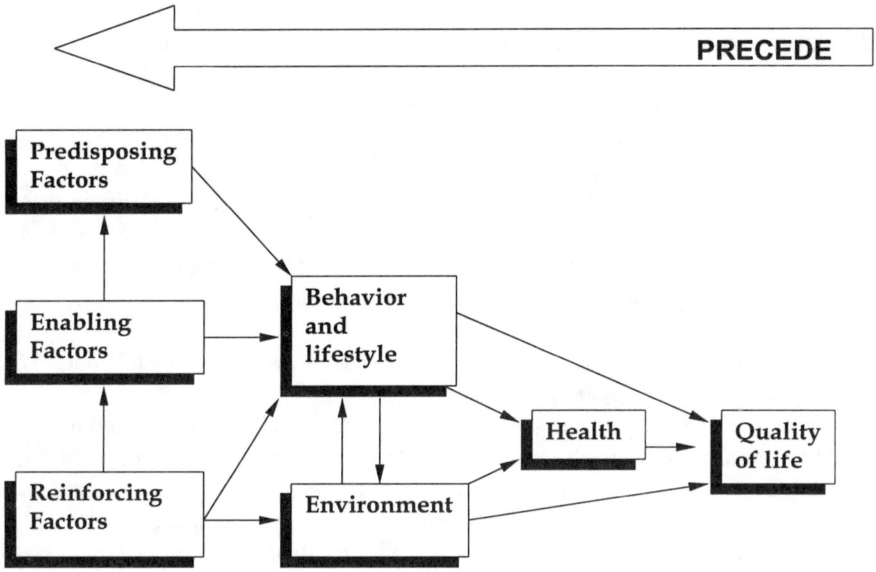

Figure 1 Partial PRECEDE/PROCEED health promotion planning model. *Source:* Modified from Green, L. W., & Kreuter, M. W. (1999).

with any model, attempts to organize many variables can be helpful, but they can also exclude otherwise important issues. The objective here is to encourage consideration of learning about drinking as a multivariable process.

Before one begins to explore how a sample of these multiple variables intersect in the learning process, it is useful to acknowledge that learning about drinking is a developmental and life-long process which takes place within a person who is herself or himself continuously developing. That is, the process is ongoing and the subject dynamic, not static. Also underlying this developmental process is the important fact that all individuals are unique.

LEARNING ABOUT DRINKING AS A DEVELOPMENTAL PROCESS

Individual behaviors are the result of multiple influences (Lerner, 1993, 1995a, 1995b, 1998). These multiple influences, diffuse and indirect as some of them are, have to be considered in a multivariate context. Lerner and Castellino (1998) have noted that adolescent behavior needs to be seen as a systematic developmental process that becomes both increasingly complex and increasingly organized as the individual matures. This developmental progression occurs in the context of multiple factors that influence development and are themselves influenced by the developing adolescent. This interaction is illustrated in the behavior-environment link in Figure 1.

For example, the family network influences the developing adolescent as the developing adolescent also influences the family. The family in turn is influenced by work, community, marriage, school, the larger society and its cultures, and the physical environment in which all of these interactions occur. And, in differing ways, the individual and her or his family influence each of these systems over time and in a developmental fashion.

In some adolescents, learning about drinking progresses to learning to drink. It is significant that, at first, the new behavior—drinking, in this case—is tentative. Few people become regular drinkers overnight. The constantly rearranging combinations of influences during the time a young person is learning about drinking contributes to this tentativeness. The young person must—more or less consciously—sort through all these influences and determine which ones will actually shape her or his behavior.

In reality, the insights and relationships identified in both single- and multiple-variable research may still be limited in their significance. Lerner and Castellino (1998) suggest that in the future one can expect to see much more attention paid to natural experiments in which policies and programs are implemented and examined in terms of their effects on individuals and varied social systems (environment) and how the individuals and these social systems affect the implementation of these policies and programs.

As highlighted in other chapters, learning about drinking is part of a universal process of socialization. Socialization is the process by which an individual learns to function as a member of a society. This learning process is, in a small way, the result of formal and structured experiences and, in a large way, the result of informal, unstructured experiences. Formal learning experiences are organized experiences of school and other social organizations such as family, religious groups, and youth clubs. Informal learning experiences result from watching, listening, reading about others' behaviors, noticing how the environment is organized, and observing one's own reactions to different experiences. Some have called these informal learning experiences the result of a "hidden curriculum." The concept of a hidden curriculum acknowledges that informal influences present a scope and sequence of learning experiences and have as much, if not more, potential to shape behavior as the institutional curriculum.

Predisposing Influences

Green and Kreuter's (1999) model suggests that one of the first results of learning is predisposition—predisposition to behave in a particular way. Creating a predisposition regarding alcohol involves establishing and expanding a knowledge base, and developing attitudes, beliefs, and values. The most structured way of forming predispositions is through the formal education process.

Education Education campaigns and programs are regarded by many as an effective form of adolescent alcohol abuse prevention. However, only under certain conditions do formal education programs generate evidence that they may affect alcohol consumption. Educational messages about alcohol use and the need for moderation are scattered throughout the environment, where they are constantly competing with opposing messages. As outlined by Hanson (see Chapter 9), a major problem for educational campaigns is that they are often underfunded, unclear in focus, poorly implemented, deficient in sound theoretical or pedagogical foundation, and lacking in evaluation. Frequently, alcohol education is, or is seen as, countering prevailing practice and values in a community. It is difficult to teach young people that drinking alcohol can be dangerous when it appears to the very same youth that so many people drink and get a lot of pleasure from drinking without apparent harm. Prevailing practices and values have a stronger influence on young people than most formal educational initiatives. This is in part because prevailing practices and values reflect common perception rather than try—as alcohol education seeks to do—to change common perceptions about alcohol (Montonen, 1997).

Kline and Canter (1994) suggest that effective educational programs must be intensive and of sufficient duration, with clearly defined goals and specific skills training components. Perry and Kelder (1992) argue that prevention programs are most effective when they (a) target behavior that has received increasing societal disapproval, (b) include multiple years of behavioral health education, and (c) are community-wide, involving mass media and school-based peer-led components. Perry and Kelder further suggest that educational programs will be even more effective if they ensure that students:

- learn to identify short-term consequences of use;
- explore reasons why adolescents use substances;
- discover that substance use is not a normative behavior for adolescents;
- learn how meanings attached to use are established in our society through the media and peer and adult role models;
- learn and practice skills to resist these influences and become competent in the use of these skills in a variety of social situations;
- learn about problems associated with drugs and their effects on their community and their friends; and
- make a public commitment or set a goal of abstaining from substance use.

Educational effectiveness may be influenced by a range of other variables, such as the location of alcohol education within the overall school curriculum. For example, Regis, Bish, and Balding (1994) note that education that took place in the personal social education curriculum (PSE) was more effective than alcohol education in the science curriculum. Newman, Anderson, and Farrell (1992) show data that indicate that alcohol education that aims to teach specific resistance skills is more effective when taught in English classes than when taught in social studies classes. At the 1-year follow-up, students in the 9th grade in the U.S. who were taught alcohol education curriculum by English teachers were less likely to ride with a driver who had been drinking than were those taught by social studies teachers. The investigators speculate that the increased effectiveness resulted from the fact that English teachers were better at organizing and leading role-playing activities and at teaching communication, debate, and argument skills—all essential components of English language skills and essential for effectively resisting pressure to use alcohol.

Bandura (1977) has identified the development of self-efficacy as an important element in managing behavior. Self-efficacy, i.e., the general sense of one's ability to do something well, coupled with the value placed on the behavioral outcome, enhance the likelihood that the behavior will be achieved. Young people's personal belief that they can indeed resist pressure to use alcohol when they choose, and a belief that there is value in doing so, appear to be important factors in the likelihood that they will resist pressures to drink. Rissel and colleagues (1996) developed this concept as one of empowerment, i.e., "a feeling of greater control over one's own life that an individual experiences following active membership in groups or organizations." According to this view, if students are taught to increase their levels of empowerment, they will be better prepared to resist the pressure to use alcohol.

Still another element that appears important in effective alcohol education is that of youth-teaching-youth. An evaluation of the Gloucester Prevention Network (GPN) in South Carolina (Shaw, Rosati, Salzaman, Coles, & McGreary, 1997) concluded that changes in consumption that occurred in the senior classes were possibly because of the peer programs in place where older students were responsible for teaching alcohol education materials to younger students. Shaw et al. (1997) suggested that the seniors may have related to the materials better and developed a personal investment in changing the behaviors and attitudes of younger students, thus changing their own behaviors and attitudes in the process.

Perry and Kelder (1992) reported several similar studies that found peer-led programs to be more effective in reducing the onset and use of alcohol than the same programs taught by teachers or adults. Because so much of the alcohol education materials available has been developed in the U.S., the World Health Organization (WHO) initiated a program in 1985 to explore how well these programs translated to other countries and other cultures. Four countries (Australia, Chile, Norway, and Swaziland) representing four continents, four languages, and four different culture groups were involved in the study. Two of the countries were developing economically and two were "developed" countries (Perry et al., 1989). The study population included students in grade 9 (i.e., approximately 14–15 years of age) in five 50-minute classes, four held at weekly intervals, with a booster session held 1 month after the fourth class. The external validity of peer teaching seemed to be supported by evidence from the four countries. Students in peer-led programs reported fewer drinkers, gained more knowledge, developed better attitudes, and reported fewer of their friends drinking at the end of the program than did teacher-led programs.

To date, the impact of alcohol education programs has typically been studied in terms of one dependent variable, lower-risk use of alcohol. Little attention has been given to how education reinforces existing values and attitudes, how it helps young people to incorporate alcohol use or nonuse into their future adult lifestyles, the social values associated with alcohol—or alcohol abuse—or understanding a wide range of other ways alcohol affects a community. In other words, formal education as a predisposing factor includes variables such as knowledge, attitudes, beliefs, and values, each variable interacting with the others and each variable being potentially significant in its own right.

Alcohol education programs highlight the scope to influence behavior via formal education. Learning about normative standards, in contrast, often occurs as the result of informal education. In fact, part of formal education aims to help young people to attend to the lessons of their *informal* education, i.e., to correctly interpret normative standards or expectations. One case in point is the tendency of young people to overestimate certain occurrences in their environment, which, in turn, leads to the misinterpretation of normative standards. The significance of this has been recognized in the U.S., where college students overestimate the percentage of their peers who drink, how often they drink, and how much they drink. This leads to the generalized adolescent conclusion that "everybody's doing it," creating significant personal pressure to follow suit.

Expectancies No matter what country or what culture young people are from, they start from a very early age to form both conscious and unconscious answers to the question, "What happens if you drink alcohol?" A person forms expectancies about alcohol and these have important effects on future behaviors. Two types of expectancies develop: (1) an expectancy about the relationship between a specific stimulus (drinking alcohol) and outcomes, and (2) an expectancy about the individual's own response to the stimulus. Thus an individual may develop a set of outcome expectancies without actually participating in a certain behavior. In the psychological literature, the term *expectancy* typically refers to intervening cognitive variables that characterize a systematic relationship between actions and outcomes. Often, the word expectancy is used interchangeably with *attitude, belief*, and *attribute*.

In a recent review of the expectancy literature, Hittner (1997) drew a number of conclusions from the various reports on adolescent expectancies:

1. Alcohol expectancies about drinking predict adolescent drinking both cross-sectionally and longitudinally.
2. Expectancies and drinking reciprocally influence each other during adolescence. That is to say, greater expectancy endorsement leads to higher subsequent drinking levels, and high drinking levels lead to greater subsequent expectancy endorsement.
3. Expectancies account for significant variance in drinking styles above and beyond background demographics.

4 University students' expectancies predict future drinking indirectly via intended future drinking.
5 Expectancies predict nonproblem and problem drinking, alcohol abuse status, and post-treatment relapses.

Expectancies are not unidimensional. They are unique to each individual. They represent subtle and not-so-subtle influences that shape and are shaped by the learning process, the drinking process, and the feedback loop associated with both.

Direct Messages Health warnings on alcohol containers are utilized as a means to increase knowledge about consequences and ways of using alcohol and provide another example of a predisposing influence. The content of these warning labels ranges from the very general, such as Colombia's "Excessive alcohol is damaging to your health," to the specific, such as "Operating machinery or driving after consumption of alcohol is not advisable" (Zimbabwe), and "Excessive consumption of alcohol may cause liver cirrhosis or liver cancer. Women who drink while they are pregnant increase the risk of congenital abnormalities" (Republic of Korea).

The U.S. National Institute for Alcohol Abuse and Alcoholism (NIAAA) reported in 1995 that public support for warning labels was high and that awareness of the labels' messages and meanings had increased substantially over time (MacKinnon, 1995). Awareness of the risks described on the label, however, was high before the labels were introduced (Hilton, 1993).

Despite moderate message penetration there is little evidence to suggest warning labels alone have an impact on behavior, according to expert witnesses to the Canadian House of Commons Standing Committee on Health in 1996 (International Center for Alcohol Policies, 1997, p. 4). If alcohol warning labels have any effect on how young people learn about drinking, it is probably to provide one more message to reinforce awareness of some of the potential dangers associated with alcohol.

Enabling Factors

Predisposition alone is not the sole factor to effect behavior change. A further element can be thought of as enabling factors. Enabling factors can either make something possible or, conversely, make something impossible or at least difficult. In other words, enabling factors can facilitate or obstruct change. Enabling or facilitating factors typically result from the way a group or community is organized, or from the skills a person possesses.

Normative standards, for example, can predispose an individual to a particular behavior. Normative standards can also block an action, as when they are codified in a society's laws and regulations.

Normative Standards Normative standards are expressed informally through cultural constructs such as those that delineate gender roles and unacceptable behaviors—those things that "are just not done." Typically, codification of prohibitions follows the breakdown of earlier, informal prohibitions. Either as informal expressions of expectations or as formal laws and regulations, normative standards shape the way young people behave in relation to alcohol. In combination with predisposing factors, enabling factors directly shape behavior and define, via the environment, behavioral possibilities (Figure 1). For example, a young person predisposed to behave in a certain way may be constrained by a law and by how difficult it is to behave in this way in her or his community.

Law Normative standards expressed as laws and regulations are significant because they link certain behavioral standards to penalties when the standards are not met or are contravened. Laws regulate alcohol use in at least seven ways. In different societies, laws regulate the manufacture and sale of alcohol, who can purchase it, who can consume it, where it can be consumed, specific activities that are restricted for someone who has consumed it (such as operating automobiles, boats, or airplanes), its price (e.g., through taxation), and the information contained on warning labels on alcohol containers. Some countries regulate all these variables; others regulate almost none. For example, Denmark, Poland, Turkey, and Indonesia regulate the age of purchase but not consumption, except when consumption is prohibited in combination with another activity such as driving an automobile (International Center for Alcohol Policies, 1998).

Laws are expressions of social expectations. As such, they also serve society as an educational device—a characteristic of law that is often overlooked. Going beyond symbolism, laws usually include penalties for those who do not learn the implicit lessons.

Sometimes the law, as a teacher of societal standards, produces unexpected outcomes. Some people interpret social expectations, even laws, as a challenge to their sense of freedom. This often occurs when there are conflicting social values. A law prohibiting alcohol use before age 21, for example, clearly suggests that the respective society regards alcohol use as an adult activity. A young person might take this as a cue to use alcohol to appear grown up—apparently meeting one expectation while violating another.

Another way in which law, the exemplar of societal standards, teaches unexpected lessons comes from the inconsistency between legal standards for different behaviors. As O'Malley and Wagenaar (1991) point out in terms of the U.S.:

> It may seem unfair to many observers to allow 18–20 year olds to marry, have children, own cars, homes and firearms, and to be financially and socially independent and yet to be legally prohibited from drinking a glass of wine in a restaurant, or even a glass of champagne at their own wedding (p. 490).

Such inconsistencies can foster disobedience of the laws and disrespect for the social expectations such laws embody.

Laws are examples of influences that enable or constrain behavior. Minimum drinking age laws are one such example. Of 54 countries surveyed by the International Center for Alcohol Policies (1998), 48 countries specify a minimum purchasing age (see Chapter 11, Table 1). Portugal and China have no minimum age for purchasing alcohol, while the U.S., the Ukraine, and Russia allow the purchase of alcohol only by people aged 21 years and older.

Laws also serve as predisposing factors because they are educational statements—either literally or figuratively. The degree to which a law is enforced also carries meaning. Judicious enforcement gives credence to the social expectation embodied in the law. Inconsistent or occasional enforcement of a law conveys a different message. In addition to discrediting the standard implicit in the law and, thereby, encouraging disobedience, inconsistent enforcement of laws suggests that society's normative standards are actually different from those expressed in its laws, or that society lacks consensus. Indeed, such a lack of consensus is often reflected in the international scene, as seen in the varying legal minimum drinking ages mentioned previously.

The social message contained in laws restricting access to drinking establishments on the basis of who can purchase and who can consume is often ambiguous. Moreover, the alcohol merchant is made the law enforcer by being required to check for proof of age and then potentially to refuse a sale. In choosing between profit and the chance of getting caught for the illegal sale, a merchant may decide that the penalty is so small as to take the risk to sell illegally. Similarly, the chances of being caught illegally consuming alcohol, for a minor, are relatively low and, therefore, may be judged worth the risk compared to the social and peer group benefits.

The very same laws designed to reduce access affect the setting for alcohol use for those who choose to violate the laws and may, thereby, unintentionally increase the risks. For example, access laws in some countries induce young people who choose to violate the law to drink in places where they are least likely to be observed and, therefore, most lacking in adult supervision. Despite criticisms and potential weaknesses in strategies to reduce access, there is a growing belief among public health and social policy practitioners that enabling or "disenabling" influences such as "the law of the land" can be effective in reducing undesired alcohol-related consequences (Wagenaar & Perry, 1994).

"Approved" Exceptions Socially approved exceptions to the law greatly influence what young people learn about drinking. In South Africa, for example, despite laws regulating access, Black children reported first alcohol use between the ages of 7 and 8 years. Unlike their African or Indian peers, Black children's first drinking experience was usually under the supervision of an adult relative and involved tasting the adult's drink. The typical first drinking experience among African and Indian young people came from sampling alcohol left around by adults at social functions, especially at festival times. African girls began alcohol consumption much later than boys (Samuels, Schneider, & Everatt, 1998).

Sanchez-Sosa (1998) has described the "culturized" acceptance of underage drinking in Latin America. Despite legal prohibitions, boys are often given small amounts of alcohol by adults. This custom provides a young boy with an increasing masculine status as he approaches manhood at the same time as the mother's control is declining. In the same way, the prohibition against underage drinking is often temporarily lifted for celebrations and festivals. As long as the small concessions are not taken advantage of or do not lead to adverse outcomes, they are tolerated by the family and the community.

Practical approved exceptions to the law involve entertainment and recreation. As young people get older, the possibility of leaving the family for "places of action," like discos, even for short periods of time, provide new opportunities to have access to alcohol. Part of the attraction of these places is the fact that, despite protestations to the contrary, they frequently have lax alcohol access policies and practices.

In most countries, it appears that acceptance of underage drinking is more likely to apply to males than to females. There is a widespread acceptability of male alcohol use, usually coupled with an understanding that men who can consume considerable amounts of alcohol without obvious side-effects have special stature. Such men are considered "real men." Allowing young boys to begin preparing for this expectation is accepted as an important part of learning about drinking and learning to drink despite the law. Developing prowess in alcohol use is also often linked to other male-oriented competitive activities such as competition in sport or the military. On these occasions, not only is tolerance for underage drinking acceptable but so too is drunkenness. Such practices are well described in the rugby and other sport-related literature of Australia and New Zealand (Evans and Roche, 1998; Room, 1988; Sargent, 1979).

There are also ambiguities and approved exceptions with regard to religious laws. Despite the prohibitions against alcohol use in the teachings of Islam and Buddhism, exceptions are often made, especially among the wealthier and/or more Westernized groups. Regional differences also exist. While there is a long tradition of appreciation of alcohol among the Muslims of Spain, predominantly Muslim countries like Saudi Arabia have long-standing public prohibitions which are now being replicated in other countries such as Malaysia. Buddhism has a prohibition against alcohol use as one of its basic tenets, yet drinking is not uncommon among practicing Buddhists, and alcohol is used as a special offering. Different sects within Judaism view alcohol as either forbidden or favored. The alcohol use practices of Hindus and Confucians are shaped by their religious beliefs and modified by country. Among Christian sects, rules for alcohol use range from prohibitionist (found in central Europe and North America) to the nonproscriptive attitude of the Latin American Roman Catholics (Madrigal, 1989).

Perhaps the most significant challenge for young people in learning about drinking is understanding some of these apparent inconsistencies in both civil and religious teachings. Failure to understand and appropriately reconcile these inconsistencies may increase risk for problematic alcohol use. There is some evidence that young people who grow up in families that are exceptionally strong in their antialcohol beliefs may be at greater risk for alcohol abuse than those who grow up in more tolerant households where the ambiguities associated with alcohol use are more open and accepted.

For most people, laws and norms are intangible, symbolic influences. Only a few are actually caught breaking the laws. Most are influenced by their perception of risk.

Price Alcohol availability is controlled by price. Society can affect the price of manufactured alcohol by taxation. From a policy perspective, tax on alcohol represents a powerful tool for raising revenue and discouraging or encouraging consumption (Bachman, Lloyd & O'Malley, 1981; Bursick & Webb, 1982; Murray, Richards, Luepker, & Johnson, 1987).

Because the sale of alcohol is such a significant tax revenue source for many countries, attempts to use tax as a means to control consumption are often resisted. For example, San Miguel, the Philippines' largest brewery, contributes 6.8% of the national treasury's tax receipts (Luce, 1996). When tax increases led to a reduction in consumption, the result was not only a direct loss in tax revenue, but also a loss in jobs, further reducing tax revenues. Between 1990 and 1991, when the Philippines' value added tax was increased from 37% to 50%, sales dropped by 15%, illustrating the power of tax policy as a method to reduce access ("Opposition," 1993).

Regulating access through tax policy has the greatest effect on those with the least discretionary income—the poor and the young. Price can have a direct influence on learning about drinking either by delaying first use or by limiting consumption. However, in societies with significant home brew practices, price may be a less effective mediator of access. Also, higher prices may increase risks for those who choose cheaper forms of alcohol. Very inexpensive alcohol is more likely to be produced in unregulated settings, increasing the chances of contaminants being introduced during production.

Learning about drinking is shaped by how easy or how difficult a society makes it for young people to gain access to and use alcohol. Drinking alcohol can also be considered a skill; drinking too much or too quickly can have adverse outcomes. A slow, careful, and closely maintained introduction to drinking is likely to reduce acute problems. Therefore, societies that make access to alcohol difficult delay or limit opportunities to learn how to drink. On the one hand, the logic behind delayed access seems to be the assumption that drinking skills are better acquired when one is older. On the other hand, it can be argued that learning such skills over time and under adult supervision is a safer way to proceed. Either way, skill-building along with access to alcohol and the social milieu are all examples of what Green and Kreuter call enabling factors—factors that contribute to a particular behavior (1999).

Reinforcing Influences

In the paradigm presented by Green and Kreuter, the reinforcing factors are usually the factors least explored. This is partly because reinforcement typically comes from people other than the person of interest, i.e., the adolescent. Reinforcement is also implicit in predisposing and enabling factors. Predisposing knowledge, attitudes, and values are often reinforced by other people. Similarly, factors that enable a behavior implicitly reinforce it. For example, easy access to alcohol reinforces its continued consumption. Evidence of a tendency to overlook reinforcing factors is seen in education's tendency, at least in health-related issues, to focus on "curing the ill" rather than supporting and encouraging the "well." Similarly, society fixates on the problematic aspects of a health issue, e.g., on binge drinking, to the exclusion of understanding low-risk, responsible, and legal alcohol use better.

Family and Peer Influences Family and peer influences could be viewed as strongly predisposing factors, but they are also examples of reinforcing influences.

Lerner (1993) has pointed out that any behavior has to be seen in the larger context of family, community, peers, neighborhood, workplace, and school. Family and peer influences are discussed in detail elsewhere in this volume, but it is important to acknowledge their role in the reinforcement of many other influences. The family has the longest term, and perhaps the most pervasive, influence on the majority of young people and it is the peer group which often competes with this influence. Research in this area indicates that parental and sibling substance use increases the likelihood of adolescent use (McDermott, 1984); that inconsistent parental discipline and low parental aspirations for children predict early and more frequent use of alcohol and other substances (Kandel & Andrews, 1987); and that family conflicts, marital discord, and low family bonding are associated with delinquency and increased alcohol and drug use (Brook, Brook, Gordon, Whiteman, & Cohen, 1990).

In an analysis of data from approximately 90,000 students in 80 U.S. schools, Blum & Rinehart (undated) conclude that alcohol use among young people is related to parental and family connectedness. Connectedness is not necessarily related to the presence or absence of parents in the house, but to a sense of caring and satisfaction with parental relationships and to a feeling of being wanted and paid attention to by the other family members—even if one or both parents were not present.

Many family characteristics appear to be related to alcohol use and learning about drinking, but only recently have attempts been made to untangle these influences. In one example of this process, Peterson, Hawkins, Abbott, and Catalano (1994) examine parental alcohol consumption, family management practices, and parents' stated positions on alcohol and alcohol use by their young people. Parental drinking frequency when the study population is aged 12–13 years is predictive of young people's drinking when they are 14–15 years old, but this relationship is mediated by family management styles and stated positions against young peoples' use of alcohol. Significant ethnic differences exist. Parents of African-American youth drink less often, hold stronger views against drinking, are more likely to judge alcohol as harmful, and are less likely to involve their children in family alcohol use than European-Americans.

Separate from a family's characteristics and the way its members handle alcohol is the set of influences generated by the way they view, discuss, and react to alcohol use. For instance, concealing or making excuses for an intoxicated person's actions in order to avoid embarrassment of the drinker may send a message to young people that inappropriate alcohol use can be excused and ignored—or that "I was drinking" is an acceptable excuse for otherwise bad behavior.

Although peer influence, or peer pressure, is often understood in terms of direct pressure by one or more persons on another to gain compliance with their wishes, it can also be much more subtle. Peer pressure reflects personal understandings of what others expect a person to do or to be like. Peer pressure, in other words, exists in the mind of an individual as a set of expectations developed from the totality of life experiences but shaped by an individual's social aspirations. Rather than being direct pressure from the outside, "peer pressure" in this sense may be a strong inward desire to be liked or to be part of a group, a desire which is outwardly expressed by certain behavior or appearances. Such peer pressure is not unique to adolescents. It shapes everybody's behaviors to some degree.

The important point about reinforcement is that it largely results from the behavior of others. Therefore, understanding behaviors of other people is an important part of describing how young people learn about drinking: when to drink, when not to drink, and whether to drink at all. Similarly, encouraging appropriate behavior from other people, especially significant others, who may not be the main target of alcohol education efforts, is as important a strategy as teaching young people who are the main targets of most alcohol education programs.

Media The media, like so many influences, play both a predisposing role and, to the extent that they teach skills, an enabling role (see also Chapter 10). Yet their significant role as a reinforcing factor is often overlooked.

Media, and advertising in particular, are encroaching on formal education through sponsorship for school events, book covers, school bus signs, and cafeteria tray liners (McNeal, 1992). The worldwide web increasingly involves students in a world of multiple advertisements and largely unregulated information. The future promises even more media exposure.

The diversity of media has to be juxtaposed with the diversity of adolescents. Not all media appeal equally to all adolescents. Different adolescents have very distinct characteristics. Brown and Witherspoon (1998) have suggested that an adolescent's media "diet" can be presented as a triangle. At the base, they describe a "common teen culture" consisting of the most popular TV programs, music, movies, music videos, and magazines. At this level, these activities are likely to appeal to the widest range of young people. Above this on the triangle is a more selective array of media representing more individualized preferences. These consist of personally selected music—tapes, CDs, and radio—as well as personally selected television—music videos, soap operas, talk shows, sports, and movies. Selections at this level are made by some young people, but not likely by the majority as at the "common teen culture" level. Still more selective, and on the next level of the triangle, are magazines, comics, books, video games, the Internet, and movies on video. This level of selection accommodates an even greater level of individual preference. At the apex of the triangle are highly specialized, individualistic activities like web pages, chatrooms, and diaries, which, in combination, tend to vary from individual to individual.

As individuality increases, so does the degree of interactivity. At the common culture level—the base of the triangle—exposure is mostly passive. It is, in fact, the bulk of the media noise in the environment. At the top of the triangle, however, the personalized nature of the media demands interactivity. The participant must interact fully to meet her or his goal or need. Brown and Witherspoon have illustrated this array of input as a teen's "media diet" (Figure 2).

Within this media diet are various opportunities for learning about drinking. Drinking can be referenced in the words of songs, articles in magazines, scenes in television and movies, topics of talk programs, advertisements, chatroom discussions, and Internet bulletin boards.

Alcohol is reported to appear in more than 70% of U.S. prime time television shows (Brown & McDonald, 1995) and 41% of all television programs (Mathios, Avery, Bisogni, & Shanahan, 1998). Beer and wine are among the most advertised products on TV and radio and are a major source of revenue for magazines and some newspapers (Novelli, 1990).

The media typically depict situations involving alcohol in a positive manner (Atkin, Hocking, & Block, 1984). The individuals involved tend to be young, attractive, well-to-do, and male more often than female (Mathios et al., 1998). Alcohol use is usually portrayed as a natural, pleasant part of everyday life with few negative consequences (Connolly, Casswell, Zhang, & Silva, 1994), suggesting that alcohol is a "constant part of everyday life" (Atkin, 1990).

In addition to modern media are the "older" media of literature and poetry. Their subtle influences should be added to the media mix in which young people learn about drinking. Classical and popular literature frequently describes alcohol use. Most societies have beloved authors and poets who are renowned as much for their alcohol use as for their art, perhaps lending credence to the idea that alcohol use is essential for creativity and art.

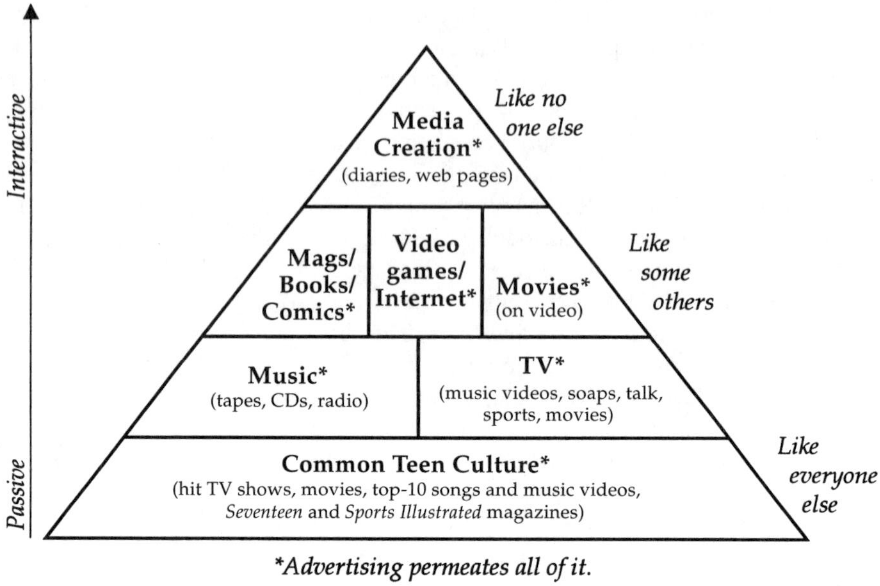

Figure 2 A teen's media diet: A guide to daily media choices. *Source:* Brown, J. D., & Witherspoon, E. M. (1998).

Humor, in its many forms, should also be included in the discussion of media. Joke-sharing has become a new e-mail phenomenon. Greeting cards represent another form of humor transmission that often refers to alcohol. There is a natural connection between humor and the pleasure motive for using alcohol. However, for a young person who is sorting through multiple influences involved in the process of learning about drinking, joking about what would otherwise be treated as a serious problem (drunkenness) is one more contradictory message. This fact is often overlooked as an issue by most adults.

Experts disagree on the actual effects of media on young people. Strickland (1982, 1983), for example, argues that advertising has no affect on adolescent drinking, although drinkers are more likely to have a positive attitude toward drinking after watching television advertisements. Conversely, Atkin (1993) argues that media exposure does influence adolescent attitudes toward drinking and may affect the initiation of drinking.

Grube, Wallack, and Madden (1991) report that young people who were more aware of alcohol advertising had greater knowledge of product slogans and brands and had more positive beliefs about drinking than young people exposed to less advertising. They further note that these effects were maintained even when differences in parental and peer attitudes and drinking behaviors were controlled for. Grube and colleagues argue, therefore, that alcohol advertising does appear to support a predisposition to alcohol use. Similarly, Kelley and Edwards (1998) suggest that image advertising is associated with intentions to use alcohol, especially among younger adolescents.

In a review of studies exploring the effects of the frequent portrayals of alcohol in entertainment television, Brown and McDonald (1995) find that the results of the review were inconsistent and suggest that the inconsistency may have resulted from the differing characteristics of adolescent viewers. For example, boys may be exposed to more advertising of alcohol because they tend to watch more sports programs.

Steele and Brown (1995) propose a media practice model to help to describe mass media's apparent inconsistent effects on young people. They suggest that, as adolescents develop and seek their unique identities, they may see the media as "a tool kit for possible ways of being." Teens possess a set of experiences and motives that affect the way they use media. These experiences and motives affect their choice of media to use and the extent to which they will become involved and interact with them. Teens evaluate the media in terms of their present interests and motives and seek out information accordingly. Younger teens' interests will differ from older teens', as will males' interests from females'. These differences will dictate different patterns of media use.

To an increasing degree, media programs—be they music, magazine stories, or movies—are developed for specific audiences. Advertising is based on careful marketing studies and on message and image-testing and involves close attention to message design.

Often overlooked in discussions about the mass media is the additional media visibility generated by discussions about who are the intended target audiences. Disagreement about who a particular advertising campaign is directed at can itself become the focus of mass media attention. Media advocacy, a new field in public health, specifically attempts to generate media visibility around issues its supporters think are important, and the media—especially advertising—have been one such issue. The objective of media advocacy is to expose deceptive or misleading statements or to raise enough visibility to expose all sides of a particular issue. Schools have recognized the mass media as a significant influence on the behavior of young people, and they are increasingly teaching skills in media analysis and consumerism.

There is little doubt that the media diet available to young people can influence their knowledge, attitudes, and practices. The unanswered questions are who is influenced, to what degree, and how society should respond.

ORGANIZING INFLUENCES

One means of thinking about the relationships between the many variables that shape the process of learning about drinking and the outcomes of that process, i.e., whether and how one does or does not drink, is represented by Figure 3.

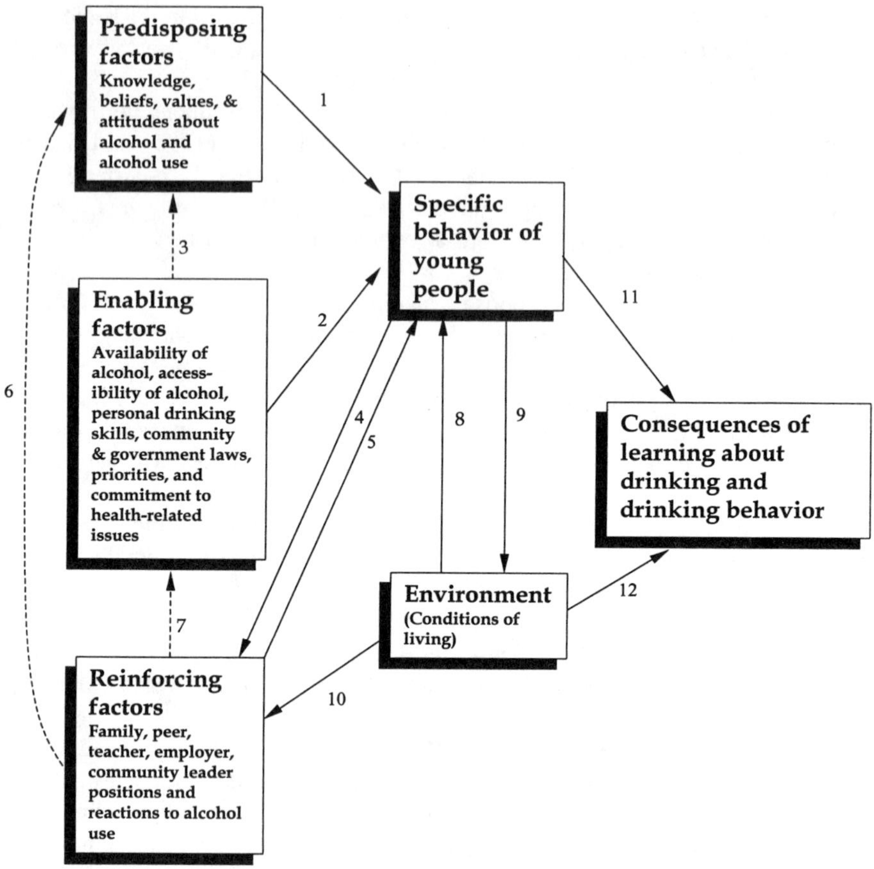

Figure 3 Relationships between multiple influences.

This section will examine these interrelationships through careful consideration of the model's key components.

First, the left-hand side of Figure 3 depicts predisposing factors. As mentioned previously, predisposing factors such as knowledge, attitudes, beliefs, and values affect behavior. This is true in terms of alcohol consumption patterns as with other behaviors. What one knows about alcohol and how one views it will very much determine consumption from the outset. Hence, predisposing factors directly affect specific behaviors as represented by Arrow 1.

Arrow 2 depicts the direct influence that enabling factors such as availability, access, and affordability exercise on behavior. For example, young people may have the initial impulse to drink and the motivation to carry out the impulse, but unless they have access to alcohol, and even the skill to know how to drink, they are unlikely to drink. Yet, as seen in Arrow 3, enabling factors also carry messages that influence predisposing factors.

If a young person has alcohol available, she or he may either opt to drink or not to drink. The likelihood that the person will repeat the action will depend on what reinforcement follows the initial experience of drinking or not drinking (Arrow 4). That feedback modifies future behavior (Arrow 5). The reinforcement could be physical, emotional, or social. Reinforcements enable and support predisposition (Arrow 6). Similarly, the feedback loops also act to reinforce those factors that enable specific behaviors (Arrow 7).

The physical and social environment provides reinforcement, both directly and indirectly. While the behaviors of other people are the principal reinforcing influences, the environment, or living conditions, also reinforces behavior patterns.

The environment in its totality affects behavior and behavior shapes the environment (Arrows 8 and 9). The environment can shape reinforcement (Arrow 10) and outcomes of behaviors as well as proscribe the consequences of behaviors (Arrow 11 and 12). The resulting consequences and behavior patterns are the products of the learning-about-drinking process.

Whether one agrees or disagrees with the order of these relationships, recognizing the existence of a complex web of influences is critical to beginning to understand the process of learning about drinking and the wide range of forces that shapes that process.

RISK AND PROTECTIVE FACTORS

At each point in the model depicted in Figure 3, risk factors and protective factors come into play. Risk factors are precursors to alcohol and other drug problems. Risk factors occur before actual abuse and are statistically associated with increased likelihood of abuse. Risk factor-based prevention programs seek to eliminate, reduce, or neutralize these precursors.

Among populations exposed to risk, however, significant subgroups are able to manage this exposure and successfully avoid associated problems (Werner, 1989). The difference in reaction is attributed to so-called protective factors, which reduce vulnerability to risk (Cowen & Work, 1988; Rutter, 1985; Werner, 1989) and which have only recently become the focus of systematic research (Brook et al., 1990). Labouvie and McGee (1986) noted that, for the concept of protective factors to be useful, they must be recognized as distinct from and not simply the opposite of risk factors.

Shedler and Block (1990), while not condoning the purchase or use of alcohol by minors, acknowledge that many young people use alcohol and other drugs without adverse outcomes and without putting themselves at excessive risk of developing alcohol-related addictions or dependencies. Hawkins, Lishner, and Catalano (1985) and Hawkins, Catalano, and Miller (1992) make a distinction between the risks of occasional use and the risks associated with abuse. They define abuse as frequent use in a manner that is problematic and dysfunctional. They suggest that the problematic outcomes be the defining variable and the focus of policymakers' and prevention program specialists' attention.

Risk factors associated with problematic alcohol use are seen as significant variables in how young people learn about drinking. Consideration of such factors is important and intriguing because they are associated with problematic use for some, but not for all young people exposed to them. Risk and protective factors, therefore, suggest a way to define "wider influences." However, as much of the risk factor research to date has focused on U.S. adolescents, its findings cannot be assumed to be applicable to the rest of the world, but rather it raises questions that can be asked of other cultures and societies. For example, in the U.S., low family bonding appears to be associated with early alcohol use by adolescents—a potential risk factor. Although the nature of the family and of bonding may differ from society to society, the U.S. research suggests the importance of questioning how family functioning affects the process of learning about drinking in other countries.

Two approaches to prevention implicitly recognize the role of risk and protective factors, individual behavior and environment in determining the consequences of drinking behavior. One of these approaches, risk reduction, focuses on such things as increasing knowledge about alcohol, clarifying attitudes toward alcohol, learning the contextual and temporal aspects of drinking (predisposing factor), developing skills for handling peer pressure (enabling factor), knowing and being able to handle personal limits (predisposing factor), and developing positive personal social support systems (reinforcing factor).

The second approach is frequently related to risk reduction and is referred to as the *harm reduction* approach. The harm reduction approach is based on the notion that it is possible to reduce the level of alcohol-related harm without necessarily reducing an individual's overall consumption. It seeks to do so by modifying, as much as possible, the environmental factors which further aggravate the negative outcomes of high-risk drinking. Supporters of this approach might, for example, campaign for changes in the design of automobiles and of roadside signs as a means of reducing harm caused by those driving under the influence. Designing smoother, padded interior surfaces in an automobile, safety belts, and road signs that easily break off all reduce the chances of occupant injury in the event of a crash.

Obviously nonuse represents the lowest level of risk, but there is also a considerable range of use that is low risk. Risk reduction and harm reduction strategies acknowledge that the outcomes of learning about drinking vary—even for moderate drinkers. And, while harm reduction programs clearly may not be possible in all settings for all drinkers, they do suggest ways of accommodating alcohol use which may be important to consider, particularly in the context of high-risk drinkers.

The focus that risk and harm reduction approaches bring to bear on the context of drinking *as it takes place* recognizes, however, only one side of the dual role played by the environment. The environment not only helps to shape the consequences of consumption, but it also influences the outcomes of the learning about drinking process and, thereby, the development of the very consumption patterns which are then addressed by risk and harm reduction strategies. Because of the difficulty in changing established patterns of behavior, the preferred option would involve preventing the development of harmful behaviors from the outset. Any attempt to shape the environment should, therefore, keep in mind that one group's behavior can factor in the environment of another and, in some cases, strongly influences the second group's learning experience.

IMPLICATIONS AND RECOMMENDATIONS

This chapter outlines the complexity of the influences involved in the process of learning about drinking. These influences are, in fact, so varied, numerous, and dynamic that they cannot be easily measured and represented in a simple statistical model. It is, therefore, not surprising that single or even multiple influence models explain only a small proportion of the variance in alcohol behavior and that programs which address only one or two influences prove to be relatively ineffective.

Furthermore, given that each influence is filtered through the individual's unique perspective, it is difficult for adults who seek to understand these influences to see them as young people do. Family, peer group, and community influences are seen and experienced by adolescents in a very different way than they are seen by adults. Therein lies the challenge for the adults who are developing policies and educational initiatives on behalf of young people and with the aim of "protecting" their welfare. It also suggests a need for further qualitative research that could shed light on how young people view the different influences which shape their learning about drinking experiences.

Most research efforts on young people to date have focused on high-risk drinking practices. Explanations of the precursors to these high-risk behaviors have tended to emphasize the linkage between predisposing factors and behavior, although recently attention has also been drawn to the role of enabling factors (e.g., refusal skills) and community organization (e.g., policies affecting availability and accessibility).

While numerous influences that shape the process of learning about drinking are common to many individuals, the interaction between these influences and individuals' unique characteristics produces highly variable patterns of drinking—from lifelong teetotaling to high-risk, problematic drinking. Recognizing this fact underscores the need to devote more attention to gaining a better understanding of low-risk, drinking adolescents, nondrinkers, and those who could be classified as problem drinkers during their later teens and early twenties but who later develop into and remain low-risk drinkers.

Indeed, reinforcing factors, which have attracted relatively little notice, might deserve further attention in this area. Probably the majority of young people enter adolescence as either nondrinkers or low-risk drinkers who have drunk only a few times, usually under supervision. Considering that such initial consumption patterns are desirable, much could be learned by studying the development of drinking patterns, and especially the role of reinforcement in maintaining low-risk patterns.

The complexity of influences on a young person learning about drinking should not be seen as an excuse not to explore these issues. As described by Wallace Stevens (1954), humanness is in its essence a process:

> And out of what one sees and hears and out
> Of what one feels, who could have thought to make
> So many selves, so many sensuous worlds

Recognizing this fact makes clear the need to explore old associations of influences while also identifying new ones.

REFERENCES

Atkin, C. K. (1990). Effects of televised alcohol messages on teenage drinking patterns. *Journal of Adolescent Health Care, 11*, 10–24.

Atkin, C. K. (1993). Effects of media alcohol messages on adolescent audiences. In V. C. Strasberger & G. A. Comstock (Eds.), *Adolescent medicine: State of the art reviews* (pp. 527–541). Philadelphia, PA: Hanley & Belfus.

Atkin, C. K., Hocking, J., & Block, M. (1984). Media effects on the young. Teenage drinking: Does advertising make a difference? *Journal of Communication, 34*, 157–167.

Bachman, J. G., Lloyd, D. J., & O'Malley, P. M. (1981). Smoking, drinking, and drug use among American high school students: Correlates and trends, 1975–1979. *American Journal of Public Health, 71*, 59–69.

Bandura, A. (1977). Self-efficacy: Toward a unifying theory of behavioral change. *Psychological Review, 84*, 191–215.

Blum, R. W., & Rinehart, P. M. (undated). *Reducing the risk: Connections that make differences in the lives of youth.* Minneapolis, MN: Division of General Pediatrics and Adolescent Health, University of Minnesota.

Brook, J. S., Brook, D. W., Gordon, A. S., Whiteman, M., & Cohen, P. (1990). The psychosocial etiology of adolescent drug use: A family interactional approach. *Genetic, Social, and General Psychology Monographs, 116*, 111–267.

Brown, J. D., & McDonald, T. (1995). Portrayals and effects of alcohol in television entertainment programming. In National Institute on Alcohol Abuse and Alcoholism (NIAAA) (Ed.), *The effects of the mass media on the use and abuse of alcohol* (Research Monograph No. 28, pp. 133–150). Washington, DC: NIAAA.

Brown, J. D., & Witherspoon, E. M. (1998, September). *The mass media and American adolescents' health.* Paper commissioned for Health Futures of Youth II: Pathways to Adolescent Health, sponsored by the Office of Adolescent Health in the Health Resources and Services Administration's Maternal and Child Health Bureau (MCHB), U.S. Dept. Of Health and Human Services, Annapolis, MD.

Bursick, R. J., Jr., & Webb. J. (1982). Community change and patterns of delinquency. *American Journal of Sociology, 88*, 24–42.

Connolly, G. M., Casswell, S., Zhang, J., & Silva, P. A. (1994). Alcohol in the mass media and drinking by adolescents: A longitudinal study. *Addiction, 89*, 1255–1263.

Cowen, E., & Work, W. (1988). Resilient children, psychological wellness, and primary prevention. *American Journal of Community Psychology, 16*, 591–607.

Evans, K. R., & Roche, A. M. (1998, February). *Learning about drinking*. Unpublished paper presented at a meeting of the Working Group on Learning about Drinking, International Center for Alcohol Policies, Washington, DC.

Green, L. W., & Kreuter, M. W. (1999). *Health promotion planning: An educational and ecological approach* (3rd ed). Mountain View, CA: Mayfield.

Grube, J. W., Wallack, L., & Madden, P. A. (1991, August). *The effects of television alcohol advertising on children*. Paper presented at the Annual Convention of the American Psychological Association, San Francisco, CA.

Hawkins, J. D., Catalano, R. F., & Miller, J. Y. (1992). Risk and protective factors for alcohol and other drug problems in adolescence and early adulthood: Implications for substance abuse prevention. *Psychological Bulletin, 112*, 65–105.

Hawkins, J. D., Lishner, D., & Catalano, R. F. (1985). Childhood predictors and the prevention of adolescent substance abuse. In C. L. Jones & R. J. Battjes (Eds.), *Etiology of drug abuse: Implications for prevention* (NIDA Research Monograph No. 56, DHHS Publication ADM 85-1335, pp. 75–126). Washington, DC: U.S. Government Printing Office.

Hilton, M. E. (1993). An overview of recent findings on alcoholic beverage warning labels. *Journal of Public Policy and Marketing, 12*, 1–9.

Hittner, J. B. (1997). Alcohol related outcome expectancies: Construct overview and implications for primary and secondary prevention. *Journal of Primary Prevention, 17*, 297–314.

International Center for Alcohol Policies (ICAP). (1997). *Health warning labels* (ICAP Reports No. 3). Washington, DC: ICAP.

International Center for Alcohol Policies (ICAP). (1998). *Drinking age limits* (ICAP Reports No. 4). Washington, DC: ICAP.

Kandel, D. B., & Andrews, A. (1987). Processes of adolescent socialization by parents and peers. *International Journal of the Addictions, 22*, 319–342.

Kelley, K. J., & Edwards, R. W. (1998). Image advertisements for alcohol products: Is their appeal associated with adolescents' intention to consume alcohol? *Adolescence, 33*, 47–59.

Kline, R. B., & Canter, W. A. (1994). Can educational programs affect teenage drinking? A multivariate perspective. *Journal of Drug Education, 24*, 139–149.

Labouvie, E. W., & McGee, C. R. (1986). Relation of personality to alcohol and drug use in adolescence. *Journal of Counseling and Clinical Psychology, 54*, 289–293.

Lerner, R. M. (1993). Early adolescence: Toward an agenda for the integration of research, policy, and intervention. In R. M. Lerner (Ed.), *Early adolescence: Perspectives on research, policy, and intervention* (pp. 1–13). Hillsdale, NJ: Erlbaum.

Lerner, R. M. (1995a). *America's youth in crisis: Challenges and options for programs and policies*. Thousand Oaks, CA: Sage.

Lerner, R. M. (1995b). Features and principles of effective youth programs: Promoting positive youth development through the integrative vision of family and consumer sciences. *Journal of Family and Consumer Sciences, 87*, 16–21.

Lerner, R. M. (1998). Theories of human development: Contemporary perspectives. In R. M. Lerner (Ed.), *The handbook of child psychology. Vol. 1: Theoretical models of human development* (5th ed., pp. 1–24). New York: Wiley.

Lerner, R. M., & Castellino, D. R. (1998, September). *Contemporary developmental theory and adolescence: Developmental system and applied developmental science*. Paper presented at the U.S. Department of Health & Human Services Invitational Conference on Health and the Future of Youth: Pathways to Adolescent Health, Annapolis, MD.

Luce, E. (1996, February 8). San Miguel growth held back at 9%. *Financial Times*, p. 22.

MacKinnon, D. P. (1995). Review of the effects of the alcohol warning label. In R. R. Watson (Ed.), *Alcohol, cocaine, and accidents* (pp. 131–161). Totowa, NJ: Humana Press.

Madrigal, E. (1989). Alcohol research in Latin America: A cup that is bubbling. *British Journal of the Addictions, 84*, 243–244.

Mathios, A., Avery, T., Bisogni, C., & Shanahan, J. (1998). Alcohol portrayal on prime-time television: Manifest and latent messages. *Journal of Studies on Alcohol, 59*, 350–310.

McDermott, D. (1984). The relationship of parental drug use and parents' attitudes concerning adolescent drug use to adolescent drug use. *Adolescence, 19*, 89–97.

McNeal, J. U. (1992). *Kids as customers: A handbook of marketing to children*. New York: Macmillan.

Montonen, M. (1997). Educational approaches. *Addiction, 92* (Suppl. 1), S121–S125.

Murray, D. M., Richards, P. S., Luepker, R. V., & Johnson, C. A. (1987). The prevention of cigarette smoking in children: Two and three-year follow-up comparisons of four prevention strategies. *Journal of Behavioral Medicine, 10*, 595–611.

Newman, I. M., Anderson, C. S., & Farrell, K. A. (1992). Role rehearsal and efficacy: Two 15-month evaluations of a ninth-grade alcohol education program. *Journal of Drug Education, 22*, 55–67.

Novelli, W. (1990). Controversies in advertising of health-related products. In C. Atkin & L. Wallack (Eds.), *Mass communication and public health* (pp. 78–87). Newbury Park, CA: Sage.

O'Malley, P., & Wagenaar, A. C. (1991). Effects of minimum drinking age laws on alcohol use, related behaviors, and traffic crash involvement among American youth 1976–1987. *Journal of Studies on Alcohol, 52*, 478–491.

Opposition to beer tax increases. (1993, March 13). *Manila Bulletin*, p. 12.

Perry, C. L., & Kelder, S. H. (1992). Models for effective prevention. *Journal of Adolescent Health, 13*, 355–363.

Perry, C. L., Grant, M., Ernberg, G., Florenzano, R. U., Langdon, M. C., Myeni, A. D., Waahlberg, R., Berg, S., Andersson, K., Fisher, K. J., Blaze-Temple, D., Cross, D., Saunders, B., Jackobs, D. R., Jr., & Schmid, T. (1989). W.H.O. collaborative study on alcohol education and young people: Outcomes of a four-country pilot study. *International Journal of the Addictions, 24*, 1145–1171.

Peterson, P. L., Hawkins, J. D., Abbott, R. D., & Catalano, R. F. (1994). Disentangling the effects of parental drinking, family management, and parental alcohol norms on current drinking by black and white adolescents. *Journal of Research on Adolescence, 4*, 204–227.

Regis, D., Bish, D., & Balding, J. (1994). The place of alcohol education: Reflection and research after Eiser et al. (1988). *Educational Research, 36*, 149–156

Rissel, C. E., Perry, C. L., Wagenaar, A. C., Wolfson, M., Finnegan, J. R., & Komro, K. A. (1996). Empowerment, alcohol, 8th grade students, and health promotion. *Journal of Alcohol and Drug Education, 41*, 105–119.

Room, R. (1988). The dialectic of drinking in Australian life: From the Rum Corps to the wind column. *Australian Drug and Alcohol Review, 7*, 413–437.

Rutter, M. (1985). Resilience in the face of adversity: Protective factors and resistance to psychiatric disorder. *British Journal of Psychiatry, 147*, 598–611.

Samuels, T., Schneider, M., & Everatt, D. (1998, February). *Learning about drinking: A report on how some youth in Southern Africa learn to drink*. Unpublished paper presented at a meeting of the Working Group on Learning about Drinking, International Center for Alcohol Policies, Washington, DC.

Sanchez-Sosa, J. J. (1998, February). *Culture and drinking patterns among Latin American adolescents: An exploratory study*. Unpublished paper presented at a meeting of the Working Group on Learning about Drinking, International Center for Alcohol Policies, Washington, DC.

Sargent, M. (1979). *Drinking and alcoholism in Australia: A power relations theory*. Melbourne: Longman Cheshire.

Shaw, R. A., Rosati, M. J., Salzaman, P., Coles, C. R., & McGeary, C. (1997). Effects on adolescent ATOD behaviors and attitudes of a 5-year community partnership. *Evaluation and Program Planning, 20*, 307–313.

Shedler, J., & Block, J. (1990). Adolescent drug use and psychological health: A longitudinal inquiry. *American Psychologist, 45*, 612–630.

Steele, J. R., & Brown, J. D. (1995). Adolescent room culture: Studying media in the context of everyday life. *Journal of Youth and Adolescence, 24*, 551–576.

Stevens, W. (1954). "Esthétique du Mal." In W. Stevens, *Collected poems* (p. 236). New York: Knopf.

Strickland, D. E. (1982). Alcohol advertising: Orientation and influence. *Journal of Advertising, 1*, 307–319.

Strickland, D. E. (1983). Advertising exposure, alcohol consumption and misuse of alcohol. In M. Grant, M. Plant, & A. Williams (Eds.), *Economics and alcohol: Alcohol consumption controls* (pp. 201–222). New York: Gardner Press.

Wagenaar, A. C., & Perry, C. L. (1994). Community strategies for the reduction of youth drinking: Theory and application. *Journal of Research on Adolescence, 4*, 19–345.

Werner, E. E. (1989). High-risk children in young adulthood: A longitudinal study from birth to 32 years. *American Journal of Orthopsychiatry, 59*, 72–81.

Chapter 9

Formal Education

David J. Hanson

This chapter examines the nature and origins of current alcohol educational efforts, details conflicting orientations on how best to reduce alcohol abuse, reports the empirical evidence of the effectiveness of differing approaches to alcohol education, discusses characteristics of effective programming, describes other curricular issues, and provides additional observations on enhancing effectiveness.[1]

CURRENT ALCOHOL EDUCATION

Current alcohol education programs in North America and many other parts of the world are a product of two major influences: the temperance education movement and the drug education movement. Both arose out of a concern for the damage to youth that could occur from substance abuse.

Temperance Education

In 1880, the Women's Christian Temperance Union (WCTU) in the U.S. established the Department of Scientific Temperance Instruction in Schools and Colleges with a former teacher, Mary Hunt, as its head. The dynamic Mrs. Hunt effectively promoted laws requiring mandatory temperance education in every state. More importantly, she developed guidelines for the content of that instruction. WCTU-approved texts had, for example, to stress that "a little drink creates an uncontrollable craving for more, illustrate the 'appalling effects of drinking

[1]The assistance of Andree van Emst, Puck Fillekes, Dwight Heath, Paul Lemmens, and Gerhard Schippers is gratefully acknowledged.

habits upon the citizenship of the nation,' and 'omit reference to the fact that doctors used alcohol for medicinal purposes' " (Tyack & Jones, 1985, pp. 517–518). Approved materials described alcohol as a poison and promoted the view that "any quantity of alcohol in any form was toxic and when consumed regularly produced inheritable disorders into the third generation" (Kobler, 1973, p. 40). The word "poison" was used repeatedly throughout approved texts, and the WCTU argued that consuming alcohol even in small quantities was the cause of physical problems and death.

The WCTUs Department of Scientific Temperance Instruction promoted as scientifically proved that:

- The majority of beer drinkers die from dropsy.
- It (alcohol) turns the blood to water.
- (Referring to invalids), a man who never drinks liquor will get well, where a drinking man would surely die (Kobler, 1973, p. 143).

Textbooks approved by the WCTU implicated psychological problems as well:

> Many people are made crazy by the use of alcoholic liquors. In some asylums where these people are kept, it has been found that nearly one-half of the crazy people were made crazy from this cause. Not all of these were drinkers themselves. It often happens that the children of those who drink have weak minds or become crazy as they grow older. . . .
>
> A noted murderer confessed that never, but once, did he feel any remorse. Then he was about to kill a babe, and the little creature looked up into his face and smiled. 'But,' he said, 'I drank a large glass of brandy, and then I didn't care' (Billings, 1903).

Because it taught that simply tasting alcohol created an insatiable desire for more, the very word "moderation" inflamed the WCTU, which insisted that, "It is the nature of alcohol to make drunkards" (Billings, 1903, pp. 30–31). Moderation was seen as the snare that entraps the unwary, who become "drunkards" by trying to drink in moderation.

By the time of her death in 1906, Mrs. Hunt had revolutionized education with her highly successful campaign for mandatory temperance education or "institutionalized prohibition propaganda" in every state (Clark, 1965). In a single year, 22 million children were exposed to systematic antialcohol education (Hunt, 1904). So-called Scientific Temperance Instruction laid the foundation for current alcohol education (Erickson, 1988), and some of the laws Mrs. Hunt had passed still remain (Garcia-McDonnell, 1993).

Drug Education

While Mrs. Hunt and the WCTU had an enormous impact on the nature of alcohol education, the other profound influence was the rapid rise of drug education beginning in the mid-1960's. This event was significant because education about alcohol (a legal substance) became a part of education about illicit drugs. To this day, alcohol is typically treated as a component in drug education courses. More importantly, the educational treatment given to alcohol is dominated by that given to illegal drugs.

By the mid-1960's, the American public had become alarmed at reports that illicit drug use was spreading rapidly into suburban and rural areas and that no place appeared safe from the perceived epidemic (Goldberg & Meyers, 1980). Increasingly, middle-class Americans felt threatened and demanded that something be done and be done quickly. In 1970, the President of the United States asserted that antidrug education, as a preventive measure of the highest national priority, must be provided to all publicly educated youth from kindergarten through the twelfth grade (Einstein et al., 1971). Subsequently, federal and state expenditures for antidrug education increased dramatically and by the early 1970's most of the school districts across the U.S. had implemented antidrug instruction (Zinberg, 1984).

Just as the temperance writers assumed that teaching the "evils of alcohol" in schools would frighten students into abstinence, it was now believed that teaching the evils of drugs would frighten young people into avoiding them.

THE CURRENT DEBATE IN ALCOHOL EDUCATION

The dominant orientation underlying alcohol education today is the control-of-consumption approach (more accurately called the reduction-of-consumption approach). It has a long history, and earlier advocates, including Mary Hunt and the WCTU, called for the total prohibition of alcohol. Today advocates typically call for more politically feasible measures to reduce rather than prohibit consumption. The approach is based on the assumption that the use of alcohol is the necessary and sufficient cause of alcohol abuse problems, the availability of alcohol determines the extent to which it will be used (and, hence, abused), the quantity of alcohol consumed (rather than the speed with which it is consumed, the purpose for which it is consumed, the social environment in which it is consumed, and so on) determines the extent of abuse, and social policy should promote reduction of use, if not abstinence.

An alternative approach is based on the cultural experience of peoples around the world who use alcohol extensively with relatively few problems. Such groups include Jews, Greeks, Italians, and Portuguese. These and other similarly successful groups tend to share three common keys to success. First, there is an absence of emotionality associated with alcohol, which is seen as a natural, normal part of life for those who choose to drink. It is seen as neither a poison on the one hand, nor as a solution to life's problems on the other. Second, there is little or no social pressure to drink. Abstaining and drinking in moderation are seen as equally desirable or acceptable choices. However, the abuse of alcohol is never tolerated by anyone for any reason. Third, young people learn at home from their parents and their parents' good example how to handle alcohol responsibly (Hanson, 1996b).

The sociocultural, or reduction-of-harm, approach assumes that it is the misuse of alcohol, rather than the substance of alcohol itself, that is the problem; that it is important to distinguish between alcohol use and alcohol abuse; and that alcohol abuse can be reduced by educating people either to abstain or to drink in moderation (Hanson, 1996a).

Reduction-of-consumption advocates frequently argue that it is inappropriate to teach moderation to young people. In the words of one leader, "We must reject the idea of teaching responsible use of alcohol; to do so is self-defeating and dangerous. Alcohol is illegal for underage people and there can be no responsible use of an illegal substance" (Horton, 1988, pp. 5–6). Of course, the unqualified assertion that alcohol is illegal for young people is clearly incorrect (Hanson, 1996b; International Center for Alcohol Policies, 1998). More importantly, teaching about responsible use does not require students to consume alcohol any more than teaching them world geography involves their visiting Nepal, or teaching them civics requires their voting for a president or running for governor. Such "programs would not encourage underage drinking, but would acknowledge the reality of alcohol experimentation. They would encourage thoughtful decisions and responsible behavior, incorporating information about drinking that an individual could use as an adult" (Engs & Fors, 1988, p. 27). Stated differently, "minors will soon be of legal drinking age, and should know how to be responsible drinkers before that time" (General Accounting Office, 1991, p. 62). On the basis of their study, Forney, Forney, and Ripley (1988) concluded that "efforts to educate youth about alcohol should incorporate acceptable uses as well as the negative aspects of drinking" (p. 194). They explained that

> Promoting responsible attitudes by alcohol-education efforts, we believe, should include information concerning the acceptable uses of alcohol. Emphasis on the unacceptable uses of alcohol alone does not appear to deter students from drinking. This finding is supported by our study showing that over half of our students in grades six through twelve are currently drinking, 18% of them frequently or heavily. We believe that efforts to curb frequent or heavy drinking among adolescents must focus on promoting responsible drinking behaviors and attitudes.
>
> Alcohol is part of our society and it seems clear that most adolescents will experiment with it. Leaving students to find out about alcohol on their own may lead to serious consequences. Effective sources of information should help students decide when and how alcohol use is acceptable (pp. 201–202).

As health educators St. Pierre and Miller (1986) emphasized,

> Alcohol education can provide the skills for adolescents and adults to abstain or to include alcohol as a part of the social situation. Through proper education, alcohol can be incorporated into the lifestyles of post-adolescent adults and older members of society without the traditional problems which [sometimes] accompany drinking in a social setting (p. 11).

Similarly, Carl May (1993) observed that

> Socialization about alcohol *use* is experienced almost entirely outside of the school. In the current climate, at least, it is not politically possible for school-based packages to stress 'harm reduction' as a desirable objective, although that may be precisely what the practical business of learning to drink is about. In this context, it is impossible not to echo O'Connor and Saunders' (1992, p. 180) argument that: "If educational activity is to persist then we will probably be better served by training our young people to drink safely." Given this, the question of where and how such education be delivered is important. A potential way of achieving this is by building on the existing educational efforts of parents (p. 163).

As Chng (1981) pointed out:

> The goal of abstinence implies that the school not only has primary responsibility for influencing behavior, but has full capacity for changing behavior as well. On the contrary, it is important to remember that much education does occur outside the school. The school is only one among many influences on the attitudes and behavior of the individual. Consequently, abstinence is an unrealistic, impractical goal because non-school influences sometimes may either nullify the effect of the school or render it unnecessary. The media, the peer group, and the family inevitably transmit their own form of "drug education" regardless of the intentions of the school. . . . It seems clear that drug education has not, and never will be able to accomplish this goal of abstinence. If it persists in retaining and promoting this goal, the cost of this "failure" may be severe (pp. 16–17).

Even religious groups theologically committed to abstinence are not highly successful in maintaining it among their members. For example, the Seventh-Day Adventist Church lists the "use, manufacture, or sale of alcoholic beverages" as grounds for expulsion from the church; it publishes two periodicals promoting abstinence among both elementary and high school students, and it operates an extensive system of schools and colleges "in order to provide an education in harmony with Adventist belief from kindergarten through graduate school" (Guthrie, 1986, pp. 8, 11). Yet in spite of the religious basis for abstinence, reinforced through education and strong social pressure, nearly 60% of seniors enrolled in a sample of Seventh-Day Adventist academies reported drinking (Guthrie, 1986, p. 79). The same is true for the Church of Jesus Christ of Latter-Day Saints ("Mormon" Church) and other religious groups that require and attempt to enforce abstinence (Hanson, 1995). Why should we expect secular alcohol education to reach even this low level of success?

There is absolutely no reason, either theoretically or empirically, to expect a no-use approach to be any more effective in alcohol education than it has been in other areas, such as human sexuality (Engs & Fors, 1988). The strict no-use approach was not effective in Mary Hunt's day and it is not effective today.

A narrow-minded insistence on abstinence as the only option will cause students to "turn off and tune out" of alcohol education (Spowart, 1982). "It is at odds with the prevailing norms of adult behavior" and it "diverts attention away from what is probably achievable to what is almost an impossibility" (O'Connor & Saunders, 1992, pp. 167–168). Furthermore, "there is little value in perpetuating a perspective that emphasizes *don't* but persuades few not to while simultaneously ignoring those who do" (O'Connor & Saunders, 1992, p. 178).

Over 30 years ago, Robinson (1969) noted that most alcohol education focused on the dire results and tragic consequences that could occur from alcohol misuse and made them appear almost inevitable. He stressed that:

> We have often failed to recognize the fact that the majority of young people who choose to drink do not end up dead, or in hospital, in jail, or pregnant. We usually fail to acknowledge that there are distinct pleasures and real benefits in drinking alcoholic beverages in an appropriate and non-damaging way. This one-sided, negative kind of teaching, which runs contrary to the experience of a great many young people as well as the experience of a majority of older social drinkers, substantially reduces the believability of all our teaching. Unless our teaching materials and our handling of this topic in the classroom present fairer statements of fact, balanced realistically between the rewards and punishments that do occur in the experience of alcoholic beverage users, the effectiveness of teaching on this topic cannot be increased (p. 3).

THE EVIDENCE

A recent worldwide study (Hanson, 1996b) examined the effectiveness of no-use compared to responsible-use oriented alcohol education programs as reported in materials published during the previous 15-year period. It analyzed in-school programs for general students (rather than high-risk students, students being punished for infractions, developmentally disabled students, etc.) that empirically assessed students' outcomes in alcohol knowledge, attitudes, and/or behaviors. The educational levels encompassed by the search extended from kindergarten through graduate school. Not examined were programs intended to educate drivers or those that merely examined the perceptions of effectiveness. In addition to books and articles, special efforts were made to identify relevant doctoral dissertations, master's theses, agency reports, and diverse fugitive literature.

The results clearly indicated that responsible-use alcohol education programs were demonstrably more effective than were no-use alcohol education programs (Hanson, 1996b). This superiority was systematic and dramatic. For example, on the very important variable of alcohol-related behavior, very few no-use programs demonstrated positive results and many were counterproductive. On the other hand, a large proportion of responsible-use programs yielded positive results and none were found to be counter-productive on behavior. But this is a very predictable finding. The reduction-of-consumption approach is based on highly questionable assumptions and has unrealistic goals.

EFFECTIVE ALCOHOL EDUCATION

Because the reduction-of-consumption orientation assumes that the problem is alcohol rather than the abuse of alcohol, it attempts to discourage or prevent people from consuming any alcohol rather than trying to prevent them from using alcohol irresponsibly. Under the direction of Ernest Noble, the U.S. National Institute on Alcohol Abuse and Alcoholism (NIAAA) adopted the reduction of consumption approach in the late 1970's. In Noble's opinion, "Alcohol is the dirtiest drug we have," and the institute's deputy director publicly asserted that there is no such thing as responsible drinking (Ford, 1988, p. 176). In its *Drug Prevention Education: A Guide to Selection and Implementation*, the U.S. Department of Education (1988) asserted that curricular materials should present a clear and consistent message that alcohol use is unhealthful and harmful. Educators selecting a curriculum were specifically warned that "Curricula which advocate 'responsible use' (of alcohol) should be rejected" (U.S. Department of Education, 1988, p. 10, emphasis in original). *Alcohol: the Gateway Drug*, New York State's curriculum guide, is consistent with federal policy: "Associated with the continued public acceptance of alcohol as a benign substance rather than a mind-altering, addictive drug is the concept of 'responsible drinking' " (New York State Division of Alcoholism and Alcohol Abuse, n.d., p. 2). The idea that people can use alcohol in moderation is even described by some reduction-of-consumption alcohol education writers as a deadly message that educators must avoid (Horton, 1989), a view held by Mary Hunt and the WCTU.

Alternatively, the harm reduction approach assumes that, because many individuals will choose to drink, moderate drinking norms should be taught and reinforced. Such efforts should present drinking in moderation (or abstaining) rather than drinking *per se* as a sign of maturity (Wilkinson, 1970). It is important that educational efforts present moderate drinking and abstinence as equally acceptable or appropriate choices for adults, and just as those who choose to drink should not force alcohol on abstainers, those who choose to abstain should not attempt to impose that choice on others (Education Commission of the States, n.d.).

Effective alcohol education requires a:

> realistic acceptance of certain facts. Alcohol is widely available and consumed in American society and teen-agers, as well as adults, must choose if, how and under what circumstances they will or will not drink. In a democratic society of which alcohol is a part, the only realistic, practical hope is that people will make choices about alcohol consumption that reduce their risk of alcohol-related problems. Alcohol education efforts should be focused on enabling people to adopt and maintain those low-risk choices.
>
> A definition of low-risk choices ... includes 1) the choice to abstain and for persons who do drink 2) the choice of a quantity and frequency of alcohol consumption that presents little, if any, risk for developing alcohol-related problems (Thompson, Daugherty, & Carver, 1984, p. 80).

GUIDELINES FOR RESPONSIBLE USE

The Education Commission of the States Task Force on Responsible Decisions about Alcohol (n.d., p. 4) identified guidelines for the responsible use of alcohol:

A. Situational responsibilities

1. Alcohol should not be the main focus of a gathering. Food and recreational activities should be available.
2. In serving beverage alcohol, measure correctly and do not push drinks.
3. Recognize the decision of others to drink or not to drink. Have beverages to accommodate both.
4. Recognize drunkenness as unacceptable behavior.
5. Recognize alcohol problems in yourself and others. Try to get or offer help.
6. Understand your own decision regarding the use of beverage alcohol.
7. Use alcohol in a relaxed setting and avoid drinking alone.
8. Recognize and make plans to promote the concepts of responsibility for the health and safety of others.

B. Health responsibilities

1. Stay within your limit when using beverage alcohol.
2. Recognize alcohol as a drug, do not combine its use with other drugs. It may combine unfavorably.
3. Recognize that alcohol cannot solve problems.
4. Recognize that for those who suffer from the disease alcoholism, the most responsible decision is to abstain.

C. Safety responsibilities

1. Avoid performing complex tasks such as driving a car, operating machinery, or engaging in physical activities while under the influence of alcohol.
2. Avoid riding with a driver who is under the influence.
3. Recognize that your behaviors and attitudes influence others, especially children.

At about the same time, the National Institute on Alcoholism and Alcohol Abuse issued a set of guidelines to assist teachers in educating about alcohol (Miller, 1982) and others have subsequently identified similar guidelines (Dolan, 1976; Hanson & Engs, 1994; Addiction Research Foundation of Ontario, 1998).

Guidelines for responsible hosting include:

1. Pass the drinks. Serve drinks at regular, reasonable intervals along with plenty of nonalcoholic beverages. A schedule of one alcoholic drink per hour is a good guide.

2 Have a responsible bartender. If you plan to have a friend act as bartender, make sure that the person is not a drink pusher.
3 Don't serve doubles. Many people count and pace their drinks. If you serve doubles, they will be drinking twice as much as they intended.
4 Push snacks. Make sure that people are eating along with drinking.
5 Don't push the drinks. Let the glass become empty before you offer a refill.
6 Be sure to serve nonalcoholic beverages also. Remember that one out of five college students chooses not to drink. Make sure that you have a reasonable selection of appealing nonalcoholic drinks to serve.
7 End the party properly. Decide, in advance, when you want your party to end. Before that time, stop serving alcohol and offer coffee and a substantial snack. This provides some nondrinking time before your guests leave. (Hanson & Engs, 1994, p. 178)

A responsible decision might be not to drink if any two of the following applies to the individual:

1 Gulps drinks for the effect that rapid drinking produces.
2 Starts the day with a drink.
3 Drinks alone to escape from reality, boredom, loneliness, or anger.
4 Frequently gets intoxicated.
5 Drinks to relieve a hangover.
6 Loses time from school or work because of drinking.
7 Drinks to lose shyness or build self-confidence.
8 Drinking adversely affects reputation.
9 Drinks to escape from worries.
10 Bothered if someone suggests he or she might drink too much.
11 Takes a drink in order to face a situation.
12 Experiences financial problems because of buying alcohol.
13 Has lost friends since beginning to drink.
14 Hangs around with a group that drinks a lot.
15 Drinks more than friends do.
16 Drinks until the bottle is empty.
17 Has had a loss of memory from drinking.
18 Has ended up in jail or hospital as a result of driving while intoxicated.
19 Gets annoyed with lectures or classes on drinking.
20 Thinks they have a problem with drinking (adapted from Hanson & Engs, 1994, pp. 178–179).

There is no lack of practical guidelines for moderate alcohol consumption. There is, however, a lack of courage to reject the failed "no use" approach in favor of others with the real possibility of reducing alcohol abuse. Defenders of "no use" often suggest that what is needed is *more* "no use" education; their solution is to offer more of the same. This approach is analogous to arguing that a dog chasing its own tail could catch it if only he would run faster.

OTHER CURRICULAR ISSUES

It is important that educational objectives be explicit, consistent with other objectives of the larger educational framework, and understood by those charged with achieving them. Unfortunately, objectives are often confusing to those not familiar with the curriculum in question. For example, the objective of teaching "responsible decisions regarding alcohol" often really means the objective of teaching students to decide not to drink. Similarly, "positive attitudes" often means negative attitudes toward alcohol and alcohol use (Cooper, 1989). Undefined value-laden terms, which are subject to multiple interpretations, such as "healthy attitudes," "rational choice," "positive self-concept," "proper behavior toward drugs," and the like, add further to the confusion. The goal of abstinence is sometimes concealed in vaguely enunciated program goal statements. It is only upon closer scrutiny of their respective methodologies and evaluation criteria that the goal of abstinence becomes clear (Chng, 1981).

There is evidence that alcohol education should be introduced in early childhood while beliefs, attitudes, and behavior patterns are in their formative period (Bradley, 1988; Tricker, 1985; Wilusz & Parker, 1982). Most alcohol education programs take place in schools, and while school students can be viewed as a single target population, they clearly are not a homogeneous group. The educational needs of children in kindergarten are different from those of college seniors, just as the needs of abstainers differ from those of chronic alcohol abusers (Brown, 1990).

Evidence also suggests that a school program on alcohol education should ideally be part of a total community effort, since students are also affected by the environment outside school. What is learned in school can then be reinforced (Benard, 1986; Flanigan, 1987; Durrell & Bukoski, 1985; Johnson, Amatetti, Funkhouser, & Johnson, 1988).

There is general agreement today that alcohol education should be comprehensive and should focus not only on the physiological and pharmacological aspects of alcohol use and abuse, but also on their psychological and emotional, legal, social, economic, political, and moral implications. While alcohol education has traditionally been located in health and physical education courses, some authorities argue that it should also be infused into other parts of the curriculum.

Belief in education as a major vehicle to reduce social problems receives widespread support in U.S. society as it does in other parts of the world. But neither confidence, laudable goals, diligent effort, nor the commitment of vast sums of money is adequate to ensure success (Nathan, 1983). Regardless of the objectives, target groups, content, or instructional methods, it is important to evaluate carefully the impact of alcohol education programs on students. Only in that way can we develop a secure foundation on which to base the design or selection of programs.

A leading alcohol educator has asserted that "We are throwing millions of dollars away on good faith efforts and programs that we *think* work. Little research is available on what actually works" (Gonzales, 1988, p. A35) because program evaluation is rarely conducted.

Furthermore, it is not enough merely to demonstrate that a program is effective, or doing some good. "Efforts have to be made to assess how much good, to whom, why, and at what cost" (Grant, 1985, p. 311). Another educator observed that, "It is often difficult to discontinue any program if it does not have the desired effect because time and money have typically been invested. Also there is often a feeling among presenters that 'at least we are trying to do something about the problem' " (Engs, 1977, p. 44) (see also Goodstadt, 1986). And "doing something" (almost *anything*) can protect administrators and school districts from law suits charging negligence (Baer, Kivlahan, Fromme, & Marlatt, 1994). On the other hand, increasing calls for accountability suggest the need to demonstrate successful educational efforts. More importantly, "All of the educating in the world concerning alcohol will be futile unless it is assured that the programs are effective" (Archibald, 1985, p. 27).

Not all countries are caught in the grip of temperance ideology and its consequences. For example, in the Netherlands, scientific research has heavily influenced the nature of the educational program. Earlier, alcohol education in the Netherlands consisted primarily of teaching knowledge, along with warnings about the potential dangers posed by the substance. However, research demonstrated that this approach had either no effect or even a negative effect (Trimbos Instituut, 1997).

A premise of current alcohol education in the Netherlands is that young people have a natural desire to experiment and that much experimental use eventually stops. This has led to the conclusion that it is better to steer the inevitable experimentation in the right direction by means of credible information and education. Education is based on facts and any exaggeration is avoided. Consequently, alcohol is stripped of its taboo image and of the sensationalism that actually acted as an attraction to young people. The emphasis now is on preventing any permanent harmful effects due to experimentation (P. Fillekes, personal communication, June 18, 1999).

Primary and secondary schools in the Netherlands include alcohol education within the health education curriculum. In addition to learning factual information about alcohol, students discuss norms, attitudes, and behaviors. They typically also learn social skills to avoid social pressure to drink through role-playing. The goal of these courses is not to prevent young people from drinking. In a society in which about 83% of adults drink alcohol, trying to create a large number of abstainers is viewed as naive and unrealistic (Garretsen & van de Goor, 1995). The aim is to prevent damage to health and society by promoting moderate drinking in general and abstinence in high-risk situations (Trimbos Instituut, 1997).

Research has demonstrated that it is relatively easy to transmit knowledge about alcohol, more difficult to change attitudes, and very difficult to change alcohol-related behaviors (Hanson, 1996b). Therefore, broad-based prevention programs are considered important in the Netherlands. The *Alcohol Voorlichtingsplan* (AVP) (Alcohol Education Plan) attempts not only to provide people with more information on the effects of alcohol and make them aware of problems caused by excessive drinking, but also to motivate them to drink only in moderation, in terms of both quantity and frequency of consumption. To this end, the AVP uses a four-pronged approach: it conducts national education campaigns; it provides public information; it conducts research; and it initiates a variety of educational projects. Reflecting its importance, the AVP is part of the National Institute for the Promotion of Health and Prevention of Illness (Trimbos Instituut, 1997).

The goals of alcohol education are being achieved in the Netherlands. For example, in 1995, young people aged between 15 and 25 who used alcohol consumed 6% less than in the year before. During the same period, the proportion of nondrinkers rose from 19% to 31% (Trimbos Instituut, 1997). And these results were obtained in a permissive environment promoting moderation. The approach to alcohol education used in the Netherlands has proven to be both realistic and successful.

TWO OBSERVATIONS

The word "drug" has negative connotations that are exploited when alcohol is called a drug and associated with cocaine and other illegal drugs. Stigmatizing alcohol as a drug may trivialize the use of illegal drugs and thereby inadvertently encourage their use. And, especially among the very young, it may create the false impression that parents who use alcohol in moderation are drug abusers whose good example should accordingly be rejected. Thus, this misguided effort to equate alcohol with illicit drugs is likely to be counterproductive. It is therefore essential that all attempts to stigmatize beverage alcohol as a "dirty drug," a poison, or inherently harmful should be abandoned. Instead of stigmatizing alcohol and trying to scare people into abstinence, one needs to recognize that it is not alcohol itself but rather the abuse of alcohol that is the problem.

When people believe that "everyone is doing it," abusive drinking increases as they try to conform to the imagined behaviors of others (Berkowitz, 1991; Hansen, Raynor, & Wolkenstein, 1991; Hanson & Graham, 1991). This is especially true among young people. Perceptions of the drinking behaviors of others strongly influence the actual drinking behavior of students (Graham, Marks, & Hansen, 1991; Prentice & Miller, 1993; Gruenewald, 1988; Vegega & Klitzner, 1989) and the exaggeration of alcohol abuse tends to create a self-fulfilling prophesy. The more young people believe heavy drinking occurs, the more heavily they tend to drink in order to conform (Perkins, 1996). Research has demonstrated that reducing misperceptions of alcohol abuse is an effective way to reduce actual abuse among adolescents (Haines, 1996; Hansen et al., 1991).

Individual students almost always believe that most others on campus drink more heavily than they do and the disparity between the perceived and the actual behaviors tend to be quite large. By conducting surveys of actual behavior and publicizing the results, reasearchers and educators can quickly and significantly reduce the extent of heavy drinking. The most carefully assessed such project demonstrated a 35% reduction in heavy drinking, a 31% reduction in alcohol-related injuries to self, and a 54% reduction in alcohol-related injuries to others (Haines, 1996).

CONCLUSION

The prevailing approach to alcohol education is based on temperance beliefs exemplified by the WCTU and Prohibition, as well as on the drug education panic beginning in the 1960's and exemplified by the U.S. campaign slogan "Just Say NO." In spite of the fervency with which this orientation is held by many, empirical evidence makes clear that a moderation approach is demonstrably more effective than is an abstinence approach, which is not only generally ineffective but is also sometimes counterproductive. This chapter explored a number of issues to be addressed in developing or selecting any alcohol curriculum, which, in every case, should be based on science and evidence rather than ideology and dogma.

REFERENCES

Addiction Research Foundation of Ontario. (1998, July). *Guidelines on low-risk drinking*. Available: http://sano.arf.org/apn/apn9708a.html

Archibald, N. (1985). *College administrator and student perceptions relative to probable effectiveness of alcohol education programs*. Unpublished doctoral dissertation, Texas Tech University, Lubbock, Texas.

Baer, J. W., Kivlahan, D. R., Fromme, K., & Marlatt, G. A. (1994). Secondary prevention of alcohol abuse with college student populations: A skills-training approach. In G. S. Howard & P. Nathan (Eds.), (pp. 83–108). Notre Dame, IN: University of Notre Dame Press.

Berkowitz, A. D. (1991). Following imaginary peers: How norm misperceptions influence student substance abuse. In G. Lindsay & G. Rulf (Eds.), *Project direction* (Module No. 2). Muncie, IN: Ball State University.

Benard, B. (1986). Characteristics of effective prevention programs. *Prevention Forum, 6*, 3–8.

Billings, J. S. (1903). *Physiological aspects of the liquor problem: Investigations made by and under the direction of U. O. Atwater, John S. Billings, and others. Subcommittee of the Committee of Fifty to Investigate the Liquor Problem*. Boston: Houghton, Mifflin.

Bradley, D. F. (1988). Alcohol and drug education in the elementary school. *Elementary School Guidance and Counseling, 23*, 99–105.

Brown, D. E. (1990). *A study of knowledge gain by at-risk middle school students participating in a drug and alcohol education program*. Unpublished master's thesis, Rhode Island College, Providence, RI.

Chng, C. L. (1981). The goal of abstinence: Implications for drug education. *Journal of Drug Education, 11*, 13–18.

Clark, N. H. (1965). *The dry years: Prohibition and social change in Washington*. New York: Norton.

Cooper, L. D. (1989). *The effectiveness of the Meeks-Heit drug and alcohol education curricular unit on sixth graders' attitude and behavior toward alcohol use*. Unpublished master's thesis, University of Kansas, Lawrence, KS.

Dolan, J. S. (1976). Observations about the responsible drinking theme and threshold. *Journal of Alcohol and Drug Education, 2*, 20–29.

Durrell, J., & Bukoski, W. (1985). Primary prevention of drug abuse: Major promising approaches. In International Congress on Alcoholism and Drug Dependence (Ed.), *Alcohol, drugs and tobacco: An international perspective—Past, present, and future. Proceedings of the 34th International Congress on Alcoholism and Drug Dependence*, Calgary, Alberta, Canada, August 4–10, 1985 (pp. 377–379). Calgary, Canada: Alberta Alcohol and Drug Abuse Commission.

Education Commission of the States. Task Force on Responsible Decisions about Alcohol. (n.d.). *Final report* (Booklet No. 2). Denver, CO: Education Commission of the States.

Einstein, S., Lavenhar, M., Wolfson, E., Louria, D., Quiones, M., & McAteer, G. (1971). The training of teachers for drug abuse education: Preliminary considerations. *Journal of Drug Education, 1*, 323–345.

Engs, R. C. (1977). Let's look before we leap: The cognitive and behavioral evaluation of a university alcohol education program. *Journal of Alcohol and Drug Education, 22*, 39–45.

Engs, R. C., & Fors, S. W. (1988). Drug abuse hysteria: The challenge of keeping perspective. *Journal of School Health, 58*, 26–28.

Erickson, J. B. (1988). Making king alcohol tremble: The juvenile work of the Women's Christian Temperance Union, 1874–1900. *Journal of Drug Education, 18*, 333–352.

Flanigan, B. (1987). The hidden subverter: A case study in community adolescent alcohol education. *Journal of Alcohol and Drug Education, 33*, 11–19.

Ford, G. (1988). *The benefits of moderate drinking: Alcohol, health, and safety*. San Francisco: Wine Appreciation Guild.

Forney, P. D., Forney, M. A., & Ripley, W. K. (1988). Alcohol and adolescents: Knowledge, attitudes, and behavior. *Journal of Adolescent Health Care, 9*, 194–202.

Garcia-McDonnell, C. L. (1993). *The effects of the Beginning Alcohol and Addictions Education Studies (BABES) prevention curriculum on the self-esteem and attitudes of junior high school students*. Unpublished doctoral dissertation, Wayne State University, Detroit, MI.

Garretsen, H. F. L., & van de Goor, I. (1995). The Netherlands. In D. B. Heath (Ed.), *International handbook on alcohol and culture* (pp. 190–200). Westport, CT: Greenwood.

General Accounting Office. (1991). *Drug abuse prevention: Federal efforts to identify exemplary programs need stronger design*. Washington, DC: General Accounting Office.

Goldberg, P., & Meyers, E. J. (1980). The influence of public understanding and articles on drug education and prevention. In Drug Abuse Council (Ed.), *The facts about drug abuse* (pp. 126–135). New York: Free Press.

Gonzales, G. M. Cited by Magner, D. K. (1988, November 9). Alcohol-related problems have not decreased on most college campuses survey indicates. *Chronicle of Higher Education*, A35, A37.

Goodstadt, M. S. (1986). Alcohol education and research practice: A logical analysis of the two realities. *Journal of Drug Education, 16*, 349–365.

Graham, J. W., Marks, G., & Hansen, W. B. (1991). Social influence processes affecting adolescent substance use. *Journal of Applied Psychology, 76*, 291–300.

Grant, M. (1985). Planning effective alcohol education. In N. Krasner, J. S. Madden, & R. J. Walker (Eds.), *Alcohol-related problems: Room for manoeuvre* (pp. 305–312). New York: John Wiley & Sons.

Gruenewald, P. (1988). An empirical examination of the assumptions underlying youth drinking/driving prevention programs. *Evaluation and Program Planning, 11*, 219–235.

Guthrie, R. S. (1986). *Abstinence and alcohol use among senior students enrolled in Seventh-day Adventist academies*. Unpublished master's thesis, University of Wisconsin, La Crosse, WI.

Haines, M. P. (1996). *A social norms approach to preventing binge drinking at colleges and universities*. Newton, MA: Higher Education Center for Alcohol and Other Drug Prevention.

Hansen, W. B., & Graham, J. W. (1991). Preventing alcohol, marijuana, and cigarette use among adolescents: Peer pressure resistance training versus establishing conservative norms. *Preventive Medicine, 20*, 414–430.

Hansen, W. B., Raynor, A. E., & Wolkenstein, B. H. (1991). Perceived personal immunity to the consequences of drinking alcohol: The relationship between behavior and perception. *Journal of Behavioral Medicine, 14*, 205–224.

Hanson, D. J. (1995). *Preventing alcohol abuse: Alcohol, culture, and control*. Westport, CT: Praeger.

Hanson, D. J. (1996a). Effectiveness of specific public policies on substance abuse prevention. *Current Opinion in Psychiatry, 9*, 235–238.

Hanson, D. J. (1996b). *Alcohol education: What we must do*. Westport, CT: Praeger.

Hanson, D. J., & Engs, R. C. (1994). Drinking behavior: Taking personal responsibility. In P. J. Venturelli (Ed.), *Drug use in America: Social, cultural, and political perspectives* (pp. 175–181). Boston: Jones & Bartlett.

Horton, L. (1988). The education of most worth: Preventing drug and alcohol abuse. *Educational Leadership, 45*, 4–8.

Horton, L. (1989). Don't let drug programs send deadly messages. *Education Digest, 54*, 38–39.

Hunt, M. H. (1904). *Reply to the Physiological Subcommittee of the Committee of Fifty* (Senate Document No. 171, pp. 578–586). Washington, DC: U.S. Government Printing Office.

International Center for Alcohol Policies. (1998). *Drinking age limits* (ICAP Reports No. 4). Washington, DC: International Center for Alcohol Policies.

Johnson, E. M., Amatetti, S., Funkhouser, J. E., & Johnson, S. (1988). Theories and models supporting prevention approaches to alcohol problems among youth. *Public Health Reports, 103*, 578–586.

Kobler, J. (1973). *Ardent spirits: The rise and fall of prohibition*. New York: G. P. Putnam's Sons.

May, C. (1993). Resistance to peer pressure: An inadequate basis for alcohol education. *Health Education Research, 8*, 159–165.

Miller, I. (1982). *The effects of two methodological approaches in alcohol education on the knowledge, attitudes, and behaviors of college students*. Unpublished doctoral dissertation, Pennsylvania State University, University Park, PA.

Nathan, P. E. (1983). Failures in prevention: Why we can't prevent the devastating effect of alcoholism and drug abuse. *American Psychologist, 13*, 459–467.

New York State Division of Alcoholism and Alcohol Abuse. (n.d.). *Alcohol: The gateway drug*. Albany, NY: New York State Division of Alcoholism and Alcohol Abuse.

O'Connor, J., & Saunders, B. (1992). Drug education: An appraisal of a popular preventive. *International Journal of the Addictions, 27*, 165–185.

Perkins, H. W. (1996). Scope of the problem: Misperceptions of alcohol and drugs. *Catalyst, 1*, 1–2.

Prentice, D. A., & Miller, D. T. (1993). Pluralistic ignorance and alcohol use on campus: Some consequences of misperceiving the social norm. *Journal of Personality and Social Psychology, 64*, 243–257.

Robinson, R. R. (1969). The prospect of adequate education about alcohol and alcoholism. *Journal of Alcohol Education, 14*, 1–4.

Spowart, A. C. (1982). *Teaching about alcohol abuse in a high school setting*. Educational Resources Information Center (ERIC) document number ED225046 (microfische).

St. Pierre, R., & Miller, D. N. (1986). Future directions for school-based alcohol education. *Health Education, 6*, 11–13.

Thompson, M. L., Daugherty, R., & Carver, V. (1984). Alcohol education in schools: Toward a lifestyle risk-reduction approach. *Journal of School Health, 54*, 79–83.

Tricker, R. (1985). *The evolution and documentation of the implementation of two drug and alcohol curricula in three Oregon school districts*. Unpublished doctoral dissertation, University of Oregon, Eugene, OR.

Trimbos Instuut. (1997). *Education and prevention policy: Alcohol and drugs* (Fact Sheet No. 5). Available: http://www.trimbos.nl/ukfsheet/fc5uk.html#0

Tyack, D. B., & James, T. (1985). Moral majorities and the school curriculum: Historical perspectives on the legalization of virtue. *Teacher College Record, 86*, 513–537.

U.S. Department of Education. (1988). *Drug prevention curricula: A guide to selection and implementation*. Washington, DC: U.S. Department of Education.

Vegega, M. E., & Klitzner, M. (1989). Drinking and driving among youth. *Health Education Quarterly, 16*, 373–338.

Wilkinson, R. (1970). *The prevention of drinking problems: Alcohol control and social influences*. New York: Oxford University Press.

Wilusz, J., & Parker, T. L. (1982). *Alcohol education: A study of high school students' knowledge and attitudes toward alcohol*. Unpublished master's project, California State University, Sacramento, CA.

Zinberg, N. E. (1984). *Drug, set, and setting: The basis for controlled intoxicant use*. New Haven, CT: Yale University Press.

Chapter 10

The Role of the Media

Janet E. Stockdale

SETTING THE SCENE

Few people would dispute the central role of the media in modern society, and yet their effects remain controversial. The extensive "effects" literature is based on the assumption that the media influence the way in which people think about their world, attitudes, and behavior. Most media researchers believe that the media have significant effects, even though they may be difficult to demonstrate. In particular, television has been seen as a pervasive and potentially powerful medium, both for social learning and for the transmission of sociocultural norms. Since the advent of television, concern about its effects has generated research to assess its impact and periodic evaluations of existing literature to guide public policy and legislation.

Alcohol also plays an integral role in many cultures and many people enjoy alcohol as part of their social and leisure lives. To pretend that young people will grow up without alcohol impinging on them is unrealistic. Not only do many young people personally encounter alcohol, but the media provide easy access to portrayals of alcohol and drinking. Alcohol-related information and images are provided through a wide range of media: television, music videos, the Internet, newspapers, magazines, posters/billboards, radio, films, books, and the theatre. While some of the portrayals of alcohol use and its consequences will be factual, others are fictional. Many appear in advertisements or television commercials, or arise from sponsorship, particularly of sports events.

It is often assumed that media representations are the most powerful influence on drinking behavior, especially among young people. This chapter questions that convenient but simplistic assumption. It argues that to blame the media for unacceptable alcohol consumption overstates the explanatory power of the traditional media effects model and underestimates the role of other factors in decisions about drinking alcohol and other lifestyle choices.

The chapter's initial focus is on media representations of alcohol and portrayals of drinking behavior. The images and symbolic values associated with alcohol in news reports, fictional accounts, and advertising have the potential to affect the views and expectations—both positive and negative—young people hold of alcohol and its impact. They have the capacity to influence young people's lifestyle choices, including decisions about alcohol. At the same time, exposure to media portrayals is often constrained by legislative frameworks and codes of practice which regulate the advertising and marketing of alcoholic drinks to young people.

The chapter then assesses how far empirical evidence supports the contention that the media play a major role in children's and young people's alcohol-related attitudes and behavior. The relevant research focuses on some key outcomes on which the media have been assumed to have an impact. These include the point at which children and young people start drinking alcohol, and what, how much, and how often they drink. A central issue in the impact assessment is how the media interact with other factors, such as peers, family/significant others, and personal values and beliefs, to affect attitudes and behavior. The chapter goes on to discuss the use of the media in countering alcohol misuse.

Finally, the chapter draws conclusions from this analysis of the role of the media in young people's drinking behavior. These provide the basis for recommendations about how the media—especially new, interactive forms of media—can be used to promote responsible, moderate drinking. The suggestions for future action highlight ways the media can help to empower young people to make appropriate decisions about alcohol use and help those who choose to drink to learn to do so safely.

There are significant difficulties in looking at the relation between the media and young people's drinking patterns. The majority of the relevant research evidence relates to young people under 18 years of age. However, there remains the problem of defining who or what young people are. For some, "young people" means those under 18 or even under 16 years of age. For others, it may mean those under 21 or even under 25 years of age. Young people, whatever their age range, are a heterogeneous group whose gender, ethnicity, religion, socioeconomic status, and a range of other attributes contribute to their diversity. This makes it very difficult to generalize about their attitudes and behavior even at a national level, let alone across different countries.

Further, the definition of "children" and its relation to "young people" are unclear (James & Prout, 1990; Moore & Kindness, 1998). While the United Nations Convention on the Rights of the Child defines a "child" as a person under 18 years of age, unless national laws fix an earlier age of majority, others restrict the use of the term to a younger age range such as the preteens. There is no clear division between child and young person, nor between child and adult.

The age at which children take on adult responsibilities varies, not only between and within cultures, but also between and within families. Moreover, the use of the different terms is context-dependent. For example, when preteenage drinkers are considered, or where, for whatever reason, a moralistic tone is adopted, the term "children" tends to be preferred. This reflects the traditional representation of children as separate, innocent, and vulnerably dependent (Hockey & James, 1993; Jenks, 1996).

In addition, there are major methodological problems associated with the measurement of alcohol consumption (over- and under-reporting, faulty recall, etc.) and the definition of different types of drinking behavior (e.g., light, medium, heavy). Cultural diversity in the sanctioning of drinking occasions poses problems for the identification of inappropriate patterns of consumption. There are technical difficulties associated with the assessment of media content and, to a lesser extent, media exposure (Gunter, 2000). Moreover, there is the problem of interpreting any observed link between young people's attitudes or behavior and media use (Livingstone, 1996).

Given the problematic nature of the exercise and its component steps, a brief overview cannot detail all the complexities of the analysis. What this chapter attempts to do is to highlight some of the major issues in the debate and provide some signposts. The aim is to add to our understanding of the role of the media in both reflecting and creating a world in which alcohol plays an integral part and in furthering the safe enjoyment of alcohol, if that is the lifestyle young people choose.

Media Use

The media, particularly television and other forms of electronic media, play an increasingly important role in the lives of children and young people. In contemporary society, the medium of television is ubiquitous; the television set has been described as just another piece of furniture or a slightly odd member of the family (Dorr, 1986). Television viewing is the primary leisure activity for much of the world's population (Huston et al., 1992). A wealth of studies in both the U.S. and Europe show that children typically watch between two and three hours of television each day (Condry, 1989; Livingstone, Holden, & Bovill, 1999). Estimates of the average length of children's viewing vary with a range of factors: the country under consideration; the child's age, class, and sex; the availability of alternative activities; the time of year and day; and, of course, the method of assessment.

Television viewing is not a unitary activity (Silverstone, 1990; Stockdale & Dockrell, 1995). It can range from total absorption in the program content to a mere background accompaniment to a primary activity, and can only be understood within the context of other activities. Furthermore, television and other traditional media are facing competition from newer media. The media environment experienced by children and young people is undergoing significant change with the integration of broadcasting, computing and video, and advances in computer games, the Internet, and other forms of interactive media.

A recent multidisciplinary, multinational project investigating the diffusion and significance of media and information technologies among young people aged 6–17 years in 12 European countries clarified the relative importance of both "new" and "old" forms of media in young people's lives (Livingstone et al., 1999). For example, the study showed that, while access to television had reached saturation across Europe, differences still existed in the amount of time that children and young people spend watching television. It ranged from around one-and-a-half hours in France, Germany, and Switzerland to over two-and-a-half hours in Denmark, Sweden, and the United Kingdom. Although Internet access at home is very variable from country to country—it is more common in Scandinavia, Israel, and Belgium than in larger European countries—the Internet is beginning to occupy a significant amount of young people's leisure time. There seems little doubt that the majority of children expect and do experience a multimedia, interactive environment. However, despite its increasing popularity, there is as yet scant research on how young people use the Internet and on its impact (Strasburger & Donnerstein, 2000).

MEDIA REPRESENTATIONS OF ALCOHOL

Fictional and Factual Portrayals

Alcohol use is a part of many people's everyday life. It would be surprising, therefore, if alcohol did not feature in all types of media (cf. Breed & DeFoe, 1984). There have been studies of the role of alcohol in literature (e.g., Kushnir, 1986; Montagne, 1988), films (e.g., Cook & Lewington, 1979; Herd, 1986; Herd & Room, 1982) and other media, including magazines and newspapers (Breed, DeFoe, & Wallack, 1984; Heiskala, 1988; Strickland, Finn, & Lambert, 1982). However, the major research focus has been on television. Television conveys a wealth of messages—some planned but others often unplanned—about lifestyle practices and their impact. Messages about alcohol are both frequent and consistent.

Analyses of drinking portrayals in entertainment programs in the U.S. have revealed a high rate of alcohol drinking compared to other beverages (DeFoe, Breed, & Breed, 1983; Garlington, 1977; Lowery, 1980). Greenberg, Fernandez-Collado, Graef, Kovzenny, and Aitken (1979) estimated that young people would be exposed to over 3,000 drinking acts per year assuming normal viewing patterns. Research in Great Britain confirmed the high frequency of alcohol consumption in television programs (e.g., Pendleton, Smith, & Roberts, 1991; Smith, 1985). Waxer's (1992) analysis of a range of programming (comedy, soap opera, drama, and police/detective programs) indicated that British television fiction had three times as much alcohol consumption as either U.S. or Canadian programming. When alcohol is consumed more than any other beverage on television

(Brown & McDonald, 1995), it is difficult to disagree with Greenberg's (1981) conclusion that viewers are likely to believe that everyone drinks alcohol and that it has positive rather than negative effects. Furthermore, given the way alcohol is used by the majority, these inferences reflect many people's personal experience (cf. Gerbner, 1995).

Although it is difficult to establish reliable trends in the frequency of alcohol portrayal (cf. Furnham, Ingle, Gunter, & McClelland, 1997), there are some indications that alcohol consumption in the media is not as dominant as it once was. In the past decade, some films and series produced in the U.S. have reflected the increasing popularity of water, especially with designer packaging, as a fashionable choice of drink. Moreover, some high-profile characters (e.g., Murphy Brown) have been explicitly portrayed as abstaining from drinking alcohol, without any obvious detrimental effect on their attractiveness or credibility. However, such portrayals remain the exception rather than the rule and abstinence is often a response to a problem rather than a positive choice. An extensive analysis of the frequency of alcohol portrayals on U.S. prime-time television (224 hours of programming across 276 programs on four major networks) showed that alcoholic beverages remain the most frequently portrayed food or drink (Mathios, Avery, Bisogni, & Shanahan, 1998).

Most portrayals of alcohol and drinking convey a consistent and coherent message. Many depict alcohol as an integral part of "normal" everyday life, and drinking is routinely shown as an enjoyable and sociable activity. Analyses of drinking contexts suggest that portrayals reflect society's general approval of alcohol (cf. Breed & DeFoe, 1980), the negative consequences of drinking rarely being acknowledged (DeFoe et al., 1983; Futch, Lisman, & Geller, 1984; Gerbner, Morgan & Signorielli, 1982; Montonen, 1986; Signorielli, 1987). Where drinking-related problems are addressed, the focus is most often on the short-term consequences for the individual (Wallack, Grube, Madden, & Breed, 1990).

All kinds of characters are shown drinking (DeFoe et al., 1983; Mathios et al., 1998). However, the evidence suggests that central program characters who drink are more likely to be "goodies" than "baddies" (Breed & DeFoe, 1978). For example, such characters have been depicted as upper class, attractive, and glamorous (Wallack et al., 1990) and as powerful, admirable, and smart (Mathios et al., 1998). Portrayals of drinking before driving or working and of underage drinking appear to be comparatively infrequent (Breed and DeFoe, 1981; DeFoe et al., 1983; Hansen, 1986; Neuendorf, 1985). However, Mathios et al. (1998) found higher rates of adolescent alcohol use on prime-time television than those found in earlier studies. The study also showed that adolescents portrayed as involved with alcohol displayed more negative personality characteristics than the older characters who drank. Alcohol consumption is portrayed in a variety of settings, but social drinking is depicted much more frequently than solitary drinking. Relaxation, dining, business, parties, and romance are typical triggers for consumption (Lowry, 1981). Such findings reinforce the perception of alcohol use as acceptable, commonplace, and for the majority, unproblematic.

Alcohol features in every genre but is particularly common in soap operas. These drama serials, which are screened on a regular basis, have a core set of characters and a story line that offers viewers the opportunity to become involved in the characters' lives. An early analysis of drinking in American soap operas found that one in three scenes contained visual or verbal references to alcohol (Lowery, 1980). This study also suggested that alcohol was most frequently used as a social lubricant, to cope with a crisis or to escape from reality. A more recent analysis of alcohol consumption in a sample of six soap operas on British television showed that 86% of all episodes contained verbal or visual references to alcoholic drinks (Furnham et al., 1997). On average there was one reference to alcohol in every 3.5 minutes of programming but few references to the hazards of alcohol consumption. Two of the most popular soap operas on British television (*Coronation Street* and *Eastenders*) revolve around public houses. Drinking alcohol is seen as an integral part of the characters' daily routine and the public house as a major focus of their social life and an important source of social support.

Successful soap operas have a number of key attributes (Gunter, 1997). In particular, they must be perceived as authentic and have characters with whom viewers can identify and become emotionally involved. They, therefore, offer unique role-modelling opportunities. Some of the most popular soap operas on British television have tackled the issue of alcohol dependence sensitively. Also, an analysis of drinking portrayals in a popular U.S. daytime soap opera indicated that the series provided several good role models for social drinking and abstinence (Wallack, Breed, & DeFoe, 1985). The portrayals highlighted some of the negative consequences associated with heavier or high-risk drinking, and presented an accurate overall depiction of drinking behavior and potential problems.

There are a number of different ways in which soap operas can take greater advantage of their audience figures and their privileged position in many people's lives. Soap operas can illustrate the negative consequences of other "scripts", such as binge drinking or the consistent use of alcohol to deal with personal problems or stress. In particular, their content can help to modify expectancies—people's beliefs about the effects of alcohol on behavior, mood, and emotions—which appear to be a key concept in explaining drinking behavior (Aas, Leigh, Anderssen, & Jakobsen, 1998; Grube, 1995; Killen et al., 1996; Kraus, Smith, & Ratner, 1994). Soap operas can also reinforce the "script" for responsible drinking which underlies much social interaction. They can provide believable characters whose enjoyment and success is not dependent upon excessive alcohol consumption. Characters can display a variety of drinking patterns, ranging from abstinence to sensible, moderate drinking. The story line can emphasize the acceptability of refusing alcohol because the character wants to, not because of an alcohol problem. This would help the choice of nonalcoholic drinks to be seen as a positive lifestyle decision rather than as a response to a failure of self-control. The endorsement of different options for using alcohol to enhance quality of life in soap operas would make them accessible to the many children and young people who enjoy such programs (Crouch, 1991).

Alcohol use is not uncommon in music videos, which are a popular form of entertainment for many young people. A content analysis of portrayals of alcohol and tobacco use in music videos across four television networks revealed that the lead performer was the person most often smoking or drinking (Du Rant et al., 1997). In all the videos, the use of alcohol was associated with a high degree of sexuality. This finding is congruent with earlier evidence which suggested that portrayals of alcohol and drinking in dramatic programs on U.S. prime-time television were more likely to be found in those involving sex and violence (Signorielli, 1987). The viewing preferences of many young people mean that they are likely to be exposed both to glamorized depictions of alcohol and to alcohol use linked with sexuality.

In contrast to the frequent portrayal of alcohol in entertainment programs, research by the Berkeley Media Studies Group suggests that, at least in the U.S., alcohol rarely appears as a main topic on television newscasts or in newspaper stories (Dorfman & Wallack, 1996). When it does appear, news portrayals tend to blame the drinker for the problem. The relative scarcity of mentions of alcohol in the news may serve to decrease the perceived salience of alcohol issues. Moreover, the way in which news stories about alcohol are framed, in particular the emphasis on personal responsibility rather than social accountability, will influence the way in which the public construes alcohol issues. In general, the amount and nature of the news coverage of alcohol issues does little to counter the portrayal of alcohol elsewhere in the media as acceptable and enjoyable, with few costs to either the individual or society.

In common with adults, young people like a mixed diet of television programs. Their viewing is not restricted to programs that might be expected to have a very limited alcohol content, such as children's shows or cartoons. Young people seek relaxation, enjoyment, and information and they like to watch soap operas, films, and other entertainment and news programs aimed at adult viewers. While these program preferences are not new, young people's access to and use of television and other media is undergoing radical change. Many households now own more than one television set and many young people have their own television—and often their own video recorder and computer—in their bedroom. The advent of satellite and cable television has provided many homes with access to multiple channels from countries with different regulatory frameworks. At the same time, there is an increasing emphasis on interactive communication. Many young people are familiar with interactive games and virtual reality scenarios, and are keen to experience interactive teletext, videophones, and video on demand. These changes in the media environment are accompanied, in many households, by a movement toward "parallel lifestyles." This means that children and young people frequently watch television and videos alone, with no adult to comment on or to interpret program content (Stockdale & Dockrell, 1995). Similarly, their use of the Internet is rarely monitored. In these circumstances, many children's exposure to alcohol-related information is neither regulated nor mediated by familial attitudes and values.

Advertising

Television advertisements for alcohol are relatively infrequent and viewers are far more likely to encounter alcohol in the course of their favorite soaps than in a commercial. However, the targeting of certain television audiences means that alcohol advertising is disproportionately represented in certain programs, such as sports programs (Madden & Grube, 1991). Thus, whereas alcohol commercials constitute 1.5% of all advertisements on prime-time television in the U.S., they comprise 7% of all advertisements in sports programs. In Great Britain, evidence was found that the frequency of alcohol advertising increased in the run-up to Christmas (Barton, 1989; Barton & Godfrey, 1988). The studies showed that alcohol advertisements were most frequent between 6 and 7 p.m., which was seen as an attempt to target underage viewers without apparently breaking the voluntary advertising code.

Alcohol advertising is also present in the print media where, typically, it is not restricted as it is on television. In the U.S., alcohol advertising features in many different types of magazine (cf. Breed & DeFoe, 1979; Cox, Huppner, Light, & Olsen, 1984; Minkler, Wallack, & Madden, 1987) and its presence in other countries' print media is similarly widespread. In Japan, for example, Okazaki and Higuchi (1995) noted the importance of weekly magazines as a medium for alcohol advertising, with over 50% of the 34 weekly magazines surveyed containing such advertisements. Billboard advertisements and electronic advertising displays are also used to promote a range of alcoholic beverages. The Internet offers a new advertising medium with increasing market penetration and minimal regulation.

The content of commercial portrayals depends upon the medium used. Print advertisements tend to be more product-oriented, while television portrayals of alcohol seek to exploit the medium's active features. Television advertisements, mainly for beer, often use models to provide images of activity, sociability, and masculinity. Although these and other messages may be identifiable, there is no clear consensus on how often certain themes occur or what they signify. For example, Atkin and Block (1981) contended that up to 43% of the televised beer commercials they analyzed contained excessive consumption appeals. In contrast, Finn and Strickland (1982, 1983) identified the same theme in less than 1% of such advertisements.

Whatever its content, alcohol advertising advocates the purchase and consumption of particular products and brands. According to the drinks industry, its advertising is not designed to make people drink more but to influence market share. Given this argument, it is understandable that younger adults, who are still establishing their drinking preferences, are often the target of much alcohol advertising. Some campaigns reflect evidence of diversity in both the appeal and the evaluation of alcohol advertisements, such as gender differences (e.g., Covell, Dion, & Dion, 1994; Slater et al., 1997). Some campaigns appear to target ethnic minority communities. Some marketing campaigns in the U.S. may be particularly salient to young African-Americans, Latinos, and Native Americans, many of whom may feel marginalized and socially and economically disadvantaged (cf. Wilson & Gutierrez, 1995). In the design of their marketing strategy, targeted campaigns frequently draw on the cultural system of the particular ethnic group at which the alcohol advertising is aimed. For example, Alaniz & Wilkes (1998) highlight the use of "power" and gang-related images to sell malt liquor to young African-Americans. In contrast, campaigns targeted at Latinos use relevant historical and cultural symbols.

It would be naive to accept the argument that advertising merely sells products and only promotes brand awareness and preference. Advertisements "sell" values, images, and lifestyles. They present images of happiness, achievement, sexuality, popularity, and normalcy. They tell us who we are, who we should be and, perhaps most importantly, who we could be—if we were to purchase the advertised product. Alcohol advertising often presents a direct equation between alcohol and happiness, success or some other desirable, but as yet unachieved, goal. It is all too easy for young people, many of whom are greatly engaged by alcohol advertising, to make the links between drinking alcohol and being attractive, athletic, or successful. Moreover, the use in beer advertisements (in the U.S.) of young adults who appear to be under 21 years of age may enhance the extent to which adolescents identify with their lifestyle and product choice (Slater et al., 1996a).

In order to process advertising, children need to be able to distinguish the commercial from the rest of the programming and understand its persuasive content. These abilities develop with age. Preschool children often cannot make even a nonverbal distinction between commercial and noncommercial content (Stephens & Stutts, 1982). By 7 to 8 years of age the majority of children can describe both the features that make television commercials different from programs and the purpose of commercials (Paget, Kritt, & Bergemann, 1984; Robertson & Rossiter, 1974; Rossiter & Robertson, 1974). Obviously, being aware of the aims of advertising does not necessarily offer protection against its effects (cf. Linn, de Benedictis, & Delucchi, 1982; Ross et al., 1984). Research does suggest that, as children mature, they pay less attention to commercials and become more skeptical of their claims (Robertson & Rossiter, 1974; Ward, 1972). However, commercials for alcoholic drinks seem to hold particular appeal for young viewers. There is considerable evidence that children and young people enjoy watching television commercials for alcoholic drinks and appreciate the style and content of such advertising.

Aitken, Leather, and Scott (1988) found that advertisements for alcoholic drinks became increasingly salient and attractive between 10 and 14 years of age. They concluded that campaigns for alcoholic drinks aimed at young adults present qualities that older teenagers find attractive. Interview data from young people aged 10–17 years indicated that young people are far more aware and appreciative of alcohol advertising than the majority of adults realize (Aitken, Eadie, Leather, McNeill, & Scott, 1988). The young people were particularly appreciative of television commercials for mass-produced lagers. There were differences between underage drinkers and nondrinkers, both in their ability to identify brand imagery in alcohol commercials and in their appreciation of such advertising. These differences suggested that, compared with nondrinkers, underage drinkers tended to pay more attention to and derived more pleasure from alcohol commercials. Of course, these results are merely indicative of an association between the processing of advertising content and drinking behavior. They do not necessarily mean that advertising plays a part in underage drinking.

The assumption of a causal link between advertising and alcohol consumption is one reason for imposing restrictions on alcohol advertising. These exist in most countries but they vary in both their scope and form (cf. Partanen & Montonen, 1988). Regulatory frameworks must be seen in terms of their societal context—particularly the cultural role of alcohol—and prevailing political perspectives on both alcohol and addiction (cf. Tether, 1989). In some countries there is a complete ban on alcohol advertising; in others the ban applies only to television advertising of all or some alcoholic beverages. In many countries, legislation is supplemented by self-regulation which restricts alcohol advertising in some or all of the mass media. In Great Britain, for example, there is a complex set of codes that regulates alcohol advertising and promotion in both broadcast and nonbroadcast media. While some of the codes have a statutory basis, most operate in a self-regulatory fashion.

Many of these codes explicitly recognize the perceived vulnerability of youth. The British Code of Advertising Practice, for example, which covers advertising in nonbroadcast media (newspapers, magazines, posters, brochures, leaflets, and also the cinema) stipulates that advertisements should not be directed at people aged under 18 years through the selection of media, style of presentation, content, or context in which they appear. Nor should they show drinking by anyone under 25. The regulations also state that advertisements should not suggest that any alcoholic drink can enhance mental, physical, or sexual capabilities, popularity, attractiveness, masculinity, femininity, or sporting achievements. Nevertheless, despite the restrictions that prohibit the targeting of minors, in many countries alcohol advertising is part of most young people's day-to-day world. The ubiquitous nature of alcohol advertising in a diverse range of media and indirect advertising through sponsorship, particularly of sport, mean that, even where restrictions exist, many young people are inevitably exposed to such material.

In developing countries, with a few notable exceptions (e.g., Mexico), there is less control of alcohol advertising. Examination of young people's attitudes to and use of alcohol in developing countries such as Lesotho, (cf. Meursing & Morojele, 1989), has led to concern about the potential impact of the marketing tactics used by the alcohol industry in emergent markets. There is particular disquiet about the effects of advertising that promotes Western cons patterns (Aitken, 1989; Amos, 1989).

Elsewhere, discussion of the regulation of alcohol advertising continues to reflect a variety of concerns about its nature and potential impact on young people. However, a major focus is the use of sport to promote alcohol. In many countries there is concern about the growth of indirect advertising of alcohol through the sponsorship of sports clubs, events, or competitors (cf. Reid, 1996). Concern about sponsorship is not new (Tether & Robinson, 1986), but there is increasing disquiet about the lack of controls. While many countries have codes governing tobacco industry sponsorship, or have banned such sponsorship, sponsorship by the alcohol industry is comparatively unregulated. Sponsorship has clear mutual benefits both for companies and for sporting organizations, many of which could not survive without such support. The benefits to the sponsoring company in terms of "free advertising" are particularly obvious when a sponsored event or sponsored teams receive television coverage. In many countries, guidelines have been introduced to try to limit this benefit, with varying degrees of success.

In Great Britain, drinks companies sponsor a variety of sports, ranging from horse and greyhound racing to yachting, angling, and darts, but football (soccer) is the primary focus. Brewers account for over 40% of football sponsorship and brand names are very visible at football grounds, on programs, and on the players' strip. There are obvious dangers inherent in the indirect advertising provided by sports sponsorship, and these may be more acute for the young. Alcoholic products may be seen to be associated with a healthy, active lifestyle, and to receive tacit endorsement from their favorite players, many of whom have the status of idols in the eyes of their young, often male, fans. The potential impact of sponsorship is illustrated by one of the few studies of its effects. Vaidya, Naik, and Vaidya (1996) found links between greater experimentation with tobacco and false associations between tobacco and sport among teenagers (aged 13–16 years) who had watched the tobacco-sponsored Indian national cricket team. Although this study related to tobacco rather than to alcohol, the implications for sponsorship by the alcohol industry are obvious. A study of 35 communications experts in New Zealand revealed major concern about both the appeal to the young of the macho imagery in alcohol advertising and the strong association between alcohol and sport (Thomson, Casswell, & Stewart, 1994). Similar disquiet exists in Europe. In 1995, European nongovernmental organizations that deal with alcohol problems called for greater control of indirect advertising deriving from sports sponsorship and other sources.

Virtually every report on the prevention of alcohol-related problems has called for greater controls over advertising (Harrison, 1989). In 1997, the American Society of Addiction Medicine stated its opposition both to the continued use of the airwaves to promote drinking and to the advertising of alcoholic beverages on radio and television. The society contends that the incidence of alcohol abuse and dependency is on the increase, especially among adolescents

(American Society of Addiction Medicine, 1997). Its strong stance on alcohol advertising reflects its belief that children and adolescents are strongly influenced by what they see on television (or hear on the radio) and that television (and radio) advertising of wine, beer, and distilled spirits is a major force in the promotion of alcohol use. Even if the empirical evidence supported the calls for strong action, both the process of globalization and technological developments have changed the nature of the debate. With greater access to multiple television channels via satellite or cable, and increasing use of the Internet, it is evident that advertising regulation is a supranational issue.

Effects Studies

Children know far more about alcohol, its consumption, and its effects than adults generally suspect. There is little doubt that the media, particularly television portrayals and advertising, are potential sources of information about alcohol (cf. Casswell, Gilmore, Silva, & Brasch, 1988; Fossey, 1994; Jahoda & Cramond, 1972; Jahoda, Davies, & Ragg, 1980; Spiegler, 1983). For example, interviews with a sample of New Zealand children aged 8 to 9 years revealed that they had firm ideas about alcohol and that television was a source of information for one in three (37%) of those interviewed. Parents and siblings were sources of information for one in four of the sample and one in five had witnessed the effects of alcohol they described. But, although the media may provide information about alcohol and its impact, the fundamental question is whether the media affect young people's drinking behavior and, if so, how.

The view that media representations, especially those used in advertising, affect alcohol consumption and are therefore related to the negative consequences of excessive use is widely held (cf. Flay & Sobell, 1983). Despite a wealth of empirical studies (e.g., Atkin, 1990; Atkin, Hocking, & Block, 1984) and a number of review papers (e.g., Dorn & South, 1983; Fisher, 1993; Partanen & Montonen, 1988; Smart, 1988), the findings are equivocal. However, many researchers retain their belief in the power of the media. Some, having failed to find an association between advertising and alcohol use, have discounted the results, resorted to counterarguments, or drawn unjustified conclusions (Fisher, 1993).

Evidence about the relation between the media and young people's use of alcohol has to be interpreted, at least in part, within the research framework adopted. As noted by Dorn and South (1983), the research questions asked and—perhaps more importantly—those suppressed, the types of findings and the resulting policy recommendations will depend upon the researcher's model of the media-audience relationship. Dorn and South identify four such models, of which the effects model is dominant. Research within this framework is quantitative rather than qualitative. It focuses on how, and to what extent, media messages affect the frequency of specific aspects of behavior. The essential question addressed within the effects framework is whether media messages about alcohol tend to increase or decrease the amounts that individuals drink (and, hence, the overall level of consumption).

Aitken et al. (1988) suggest that advertisements for alcoholic drinks might reasonably be expected to generate a number of specific outcomes:

- nondrinkers encouraged to drink;
- drinkers discouraged from giving up drinking;
- drinkers encouraged to increase their consumption;
- drinkers discouraged from reducing their consumption;
- drinkers encouraged to change or maintain their drink preferences; and
- drinkers encouraged to change or maintain brand preferences.

Obviously, their analysis is not restricted to the outcomes of commercial portrayals but can be applied to the outcomes associated with all types of media representations of alcohol and its use. However, the question of the relation between the media and drinking behavior has rarely been disaggregated to this extent. Although there is a wealth of relevant empirical work, data relating to specific outcomes are limited.

Fisher (1993) divides the relevant empirical work on the effects of advertising media into three content areas. Of these, econometric studies, which examine advertising variability and its relation to rates of consumption and abuse, do not provide any direct evidence on the role of the media in young people's drinking behavior. Moreover, econometric studies have failed to provide unequivocal support for either the claim that alcohol advertising increases consumption (van Iwaarden, 1983) or that restrictions on advertising have a significant or consistent impact on alcohol sales (Smart, 1988).

Both of the other two areas, when broadened to include all forms of media (not just advertising), may help to inform our understanding of young people's drinking behavior. Exposure studies examine the frequency and content of alcohol messages. The brief analysis of media portrayals of alcohol and alcohol advertisements in the two preceding sections indicated that depictions of alcohol consumption are commonplace and both reflect and reinforce many people's experience of alcohol as a routine, enjoyable activity. Experimental and quasi-experimental studies investigate the effects of the media on individuals. Although there are some studies that use the classic experimental paradigm (e.g., Lipsitz, Brake, Vincent, & Winters, 1993), many of these only examine short-term effects or offer limited generalizability. The majority use surveys to examine the relation between advertising, fictional portrayals, or some other aspect of the media, and alcohol-related attitudes or behavior. Such studies are correlational in nature and are, therefore, restricted to demonstrating an association between variables, which, of course, is not evidence of a causal link.

The effects model assumes that alcohol-related messages—whether or not to drink alcohol; how, when, and what to drink; and the outcomes of drinking—are ubiquitous in the environment. According to the model, media messages play a role in the learning process (cf. Bandura, 1977, 1986) which is assumed to underlie the onset and maintenance of alcohol consumption. Messages generated by the mass media are assumed not only to provide a normative context within which individual actions are validated and legitimized, but also to have the capacity to influence drinking behaviors directly. But, what is the evidence? How do children and young people respond to media messages about alcohol? Is the role of the media as pivotal as it is assumed to be? Does the impact of media messages outweigh the influence of peer and parental attitudes or expectations based upon the observation of others or derived from personal experience?

Although some research takes a broader perspective, much of the evidence derives from studies of the relation between young people's exposure to advertising and alcohol consumption. This evidence is mixed. Many of the early studies that did find some effect of alcohol advertising indicated that its impact was meager or very minor when compared with other factors, such as peer associations (cf. Smart, 1988). However, where advertising was shown to affect consumption, the effects applied to the whole class of products, not just to the brand advertised (Atkin, 1982). Studies in this area are fraught with methodological difficulties (cf. Wallack, 1983). Different analyses can lead to conflicting findings. Strickland (1983), for example, in his survey of some 1,000 teenagers and their families, found that television advertising had only limited effects on consumption level, and that these rarely translated into effects on alcohol problems. Interpersonal influences, especially peer association, did have significant effects—direct and indirect—both on alcohol consumption and the abuse of alcohol. However, a reanalysis of Strickland's data by Adlaf and Kohn (1989) suggested that televised alcohol advertising did have a direct effect on consumption and an indirect effect on abuse, but that these effects were small.

More recent research confirms the view that alcohol advertising can have an impact, but that it is limited. Any effects are generally small, and other factors appear to have a greater influence on young people's drinking. On the basis of their research in Scotland, Hastings, Mackintosh, and Aitken (1992) acknowledged the importance of a range of influences on children's drinking. They recognized that alcohol advertising was getting through to children and that by, 14 years of age, they were capable of sophisticated decoding of complex imagery. However, they argued that the effects of advertising should be kept in perspective, since both peer and parental attitudes towards alcohol seemed to be more important factors in young people's drinking.

Grube and Wallack (1994) examined the relation between televised beer advertising and drinking knowledge, beliefs, and intentions among children in grades 5 and 6 (aged 10–13 years). Their results suggested that greater awareness of televised beer advertising was related not only to more favorable beliefs about drinking and greater knowledge of beer brands and slogans, but also to increased intentions to drink as an adult. These findings were interpreted as indicating that alcohol advertising may predispose young people to drinking. In a study of adolescents, Slater et al. (1997) found that, although females responded less positively than males to televised beer advertisements, positive responses to such advertisements predicted planned alcohol use among both females and males.

However, again the importance of factors other than the media should not be overlooked. For example, in a survey of preadolescents, Austin and Meili (1994) found that children's intentions to drink were predicted by a range of factors, not all of which were media-related. Both the children's interpretation of television messages and their wish to emulate television characters who drink did play a role, but their perceptions of alcohol-related behaviors at home and their expectancies that drinking brings rewards were also important. These findings support the contention that, when reaching decisions about alcohol use, children make selective use of information from home as well as from television.

It is important for parents or other adults to be available to interpret media messages within the child's range of experience and to ground them within the child's value system. Austin and Nach-Ferguson's (1995) survey data showed that children aged 7–12 years in the U.S. possessed considerable general and brand-specific knowledge about alcohol. Use of the mass media as an information source predicted general knowledge of alcohol. More importantly, parental mediation of television viewing predicted brand-specific knowledge and this, together with liking for commercials, was associated with drinking. Even at this comparatively young age, nearly half the children sampled had tasted alcohol. Despite the acknowledged methodological problems with this study, the results suggest that even young school-age children are responsive to persuasive information about alcohol.

Using data from a longitudinal study in New Zealand, Connolly, Casswell, Zhang, and Silvia (1994) examined links between alcohol consumption at 18 years of age and alcohol-related media messages recalled at 13 and 15 years. The results were mixed. Men who had recalled more alcohol advertisements at 15 years of age drank larger quantities of beer at 18. However, no relationships were found between recall of commercial advertising and wine and spirit consumption among men and women. Also in New Zealand, Wyllie, Zhang, and Casswell's (1998a) cross-sectional study of a sample of 10- to 17-year-olds focused on their responses to alcohol advertisements and the relation between these responses and both current drinking behavior and future drinking expectations. Using structural equation modeling, the authors found tentative support for the hypothesis that positive responses to beer advertisements would increase the frequency of current and expected future drinking. Many of the young people sampled, especially 10- to 13 year-old males, felt that alcohol advertising encouraged young people to drink. The younger males were also most likely to agree that alcohol advertisements were realistic and that they got to know more about drinking from watching such advertisements. Casswell and Zhang (1998) also used structural equation modeling in a longitudinal study to examine the effect of televised alcohol advertising, and allegiance to specific brands of beer, on subsequent beer consumption and self-reports of aggressive behavior linked with drinking. The study provided some evidence that liking for televised alcohol advertising and brand allegiance at age 18 was linked to beer consumption and alcohol-related aggression at age 21. A further study by Wyllie, Zhang, and Casswell (1998b) indicated that liking of beer advertisements was related to the quantity of alcohol consumed on drinking occasions by young New Zealanders between 18 and 29 years of age. The effects, which were present after controlling for reciprocal effects, appeared to be both direct and indirect, via an influence on positive beliefs about drinking. Although these findings must be considered within the context of New Zealand, where alcohol advertising on television was not permitted prior to 1992 (cf. Wyllie, Casswell, & Stewart, 1989), they do suggest that alcohol advertising can have some influence on young people's behavior.

The results of a prospective cohort study of over 1,500 ninth grade students in California (mean age 14.6 years) add support to the idea that certain forms of increased media exposure are risk factors for the onset of alcohol use by adolescents (Robinson, Chen, & Killen, 1998). Among those who were nondrinkers at the start of the study, onset of drinking during the 18-month follow-up was significantly associated with hours of television, music video, and videotape viewing (controlling for age, sex, ethnicity, and other media use). Computer and video game use was not significantly associated with drinking onset. For those who were drinkers at the beginning of the study, there were no significant associations between past media use and maintenance of drinking.

Alcopops and Designer Drinks: A Case to Answer?

Since their introduction in the mid-1990s, alcopops—alcoholic lemonade and other sweet, flavored alcoholic sodas—have given rise to widespread criticism in many parts of the world, including Europe, Australia, New Zealand, and the U.S. The media were quick to voice concern about both the blurring of the distinction between soft drinks and alcoholic drinks and the potential appeal that sweet, fruit-flavored but alcoholic lemonades might have for young people, especially those under 16 years of age. But, while initially focused on the need to protect the young, the alcopops saga soon became a moral panic about modern youth (Brain & Parker, 1997).

Although young people are growing up in a complex and uncertain society, there is little evidence that young people are very different from in the past. As in previous generations, young people seek to establish their identity. Fashion decisions, music preferences, and choice of alcoholic drinks are just some of the mechanisms that can be used both to signal individuality and to endorse group membership. In Great Britain, young people display diverse and dynamic drinking profiles and choices (Brain & Parker, 1997). Taste, price, and strength appear to be the most important attributes in choosing what to drink. The image and style associated with particular products are also important to those who regularly drink in groups.

When alcopops were launched in Great Britain, designer drinks—especially premium cider, lager, and beer—were already established as the first choice for many young people (Hughes et al., 1997; McKeganey, Forsyth, Barnard, & Hay, 1996; Measham, 1996; Scottish Council on Alcohol, 1996). Alcopops have clearly made inroads into the youth drinking market, especially the under-15 sector (Brain & Parker, 1997; Goddard, 1997; Health Education Authority, 1997). However, the evidence that alcopops have played a significant role in changing drinking patterns among the young is limited. Goddard (1997) suggests that alcopops have merely extended the range of choices available to those who would have been drinking anyway. Also, alcopops are associated with light, occasional drinking and appear to be favored most by girls aged 13–14 years. Alcopops have limited appeal to many young male drinkers, who perceive them as offering poor value for money in terms of alcohol content and as a "girl's drink," incompatible with traditional images of masculine identity (Brain & Parker, 1997).

The labeling and imagery used to promote alcopops raises the question of whether the drinks industry is deliberately targeting teenagers (Alcohol Concern, 1997; McKibben, 1996). Typically the packaging uses vibrant colors and cartoon characters and the names are judged—usually by adults—to be rebellious or sexy or to be linked with illicit drugs commonly associated with the club scene. The Portman Group (established in 1989 by the leading companies in the United Kingdom alcohol beverage industry to promote sensible drinking) responded to the concerns about alcopops with a code of practice that covers the naming, packaging, and merchandising of all alcoholic drinks (Portman Group, 1996, 1997). The purpose of this code (introduced in 1996 and subsequently revised) was to try to ensure that alcoholic drinks are not aimed at—or perceived to be aimed at—under 18-year-olds. Out of the total of 92 complaints dealt with under the code up to September 2000, 60% were upheld (Portman Group, 2000).

Public concern over alcopops has clearly diminished. However, both the media reaction to their introduction and their continued presence in the marketplace still generate some disquiet. Media hype and exaggeration of young people's alcohol misuse can lead to a self-fulfilling prophecy by encouraging young people to conform to a norm that does not exist (Graham, Marks, & Hansen, 1991; Prentice & Miller, 1993). Questions remain about the imagery and marketing techniques associated not only with alcopops but with the broader category of designer drinks. Although not explicitly targeted at young people, the way many of these products are advertised is likely to appeal to just this group of consumers. For example, a recent United Kingdom advertising campaign, implying that drinking a particular premium beer was linked with breaking social conventions and proving that you are your own person, was likely to be attractive to many young people. The finding that advertisements for alcohol are recalled more easily and rated more positively than advertisements for other products by U.S. college students points both to the wide distribution of alcohol advertising and its potential appeal (Zinser, Freeman, & Ginnings, 1999). More specifically, the suggestion that adolescents prefer image or lifestyle advertising to product advertising, and that this preference may be linked to future drinking intention (Kelly & Edwards, 1998), merely serves to reinforce concern about the ethics of certain forms of advertising.

IMPACT ASSESSMENT

Myth More Than Reality

The belief that the media are responsible for the inappropriate levels of alcohol consumption among children and young people appears to be based more on myth than on reality. The media are just one of set of potential influences on beliefs about alcohol and on its use. The available evidence suggests that, compared with the influence of parental and peer behavior and each individual's normative environment, the impact of the media on young people's drinking behavior is relatively weak. There is some evidence of a positive relation between advertising awareness and recall and drinking, but the direction of this relationship is unclear. Although advertising does not appear to affect initial experimentation with alcohol, there appears to be a small but significant relationship between exposure and consumption. Also, there must be concern about the links between alcohol and sporting activity created by sponsorship, where the effects are likely to be subtle and insidious.

With respect to fictional portrayals, there is little or no evidence that they have either a direct or an indirect influence on attitudes to alcohol or on drinking behavior. There is some indication that media portrayals of alcohol can influence expectations of alcohol use. Also, there is little doubt that alcohol is portrayed as a frequent and enjoyable part of many people's lives. This "normalization" of alcohol has the potential to influence, and in some cases to reinforce, the acceptability of alcohol and the appropriateness of its use, thereby making the task of those involved in alcohol education more difficult.

Some Key Issues

What are the key inferences to be drawn from this analysis? First, although the effects model has dominated research in this area, it is not an appropriate representation of the relation between the media and young people's alcohol-related behavior. It is too simplistic to conceptualize the media as having straightforward effects on alcohol consumption. The relation between media messages and drinking practices cannot be understood in purely quantitative terms. More attention should be paid to the qualitative aspects of drinking behavior. Further information is needed on how children interpret media messages about alcohol and drinking and how such messages are integrated with other, often more immediate, sources of knowledge and social influence in making decisions about alcohol use. For example, there is a need to explore how media messages might modify young people's styles of drinking, the way in which they define drinking occasions and scripts, and the self-images of young drinkers and nondrinkers.

All of these have consequences for the construction and validation of drinking "careers."

Understanding the relation between the media and alcohol-related behavior demands an understanding of all the participants in the interaction. Not only do the complexities of the media and the audience need to be appreciated, but they also need to be contextualized. Discourses and images in the media are not value-free: "Information carries with it the ideology, values, and intentions of the communicator, and the interpretation reflects the recipients' understanding and biases, and the social and cultural environments to which they belong" (Stockdale, 1995, p. 31). Media portrayals of the consumption and effects of alcohol do not comprise a neutral, scientific reality but rather signify a network of social knowledge, value systems, and symbols. The audience is not a homogeneous entity. Young people, who are seeking to understand who they are and to establish their identity, are not only diverse, but also particularly receptive. The interpretation of media messages will depend on the characteristics and goals of the recipients, as well as the messages' content and symbolism. Moreover, media messages are interpreted within the framework provided by an individual's own experience, family and peer group attitudes, and the broader social and cultural setting (cf. Livingstone, 1990; Morley, 1992).

Exchanges between the media and their audiences are not unidirectional. The dominance of the effects model in early research on the use and impact of television resulted in children being depicted as passive recipients of televised images and information. However, much research stresses that young viewers should be seen not as passive but as active participants in the transaction between the viewer, the television, and the environment. Young people need to be regarded as dynamic viewers, who actively decode the messages to which they are exposed, their interpretations depending upon their level of development, and their experience of the medium (cf. Luke, 1985). Family mediation is also extremely important, both for the use children make of television and other media and for their decoding of messages. When watching television with their children, more involved, discursive, and argumentative parents can help their children to appropriate the medium and to make sense of program content.

Second, research horizons should be expanded and the need to include young age groups in any analysis of the factors that affect young people's drinking patterns acknowledged. Research on young people's relationship with alcohol has a restricted focus. This arises from the common assumption that the transitional stage from late childhood to early adolescence is the critical period in which the regular use of alcohol begins. The relative neglect of younger age groups has also been encouraged both by the belief that children are "innocent" with regard to alcohol and, more recently, by the concern that raising the topic may encourage earlier experimentation. However, the results of Fossey's (1994) study, which assessed young children's knowledge, attitudes and, to a lesser extent, behavior in relation to alcohol, supported the view that socialization to alcohol begins in early childhood. It is a continuous process, and an appreciation of young children's perceptions of alcohol and its effects is a prerequisite for understanding the drinking choices made by adolescents and young adults.

Third, the contribution of the media to young people's understanding and use of alcohol should not be dissociated from other sources of informational and normative influence (Deutsch & Gerard, 1955; Insko, Smith, Alicke, Wade, & Taylor, 1985). Understandably, young people look for "social proof" (Cialdini, 1993) and for confirmation of social acceptance, not only in the media but also through their interaction with others. Obviously the media, especially television, can provide role models for young people, as envisaged by social learning theory (cf. Bandura, 1986). Also, as suggested by "cultivation theory," viewers can learn a set of "facts" from television programs which influences the individual's broader world view, which in turn affects her or his own set of values and behavior (cf. Gerbner, Gross, Morgan, & Signorielli, 1986).

Children's knowledge of alcohol varies. In some cases, their knowledge may be simplistic or confused. In others, they have an accurate picture of the use and effects of alcohol. In many cases, their knowledge is based on personal experience of alcohol. Children and young people have the propensity and ability to learn about alcohol from an early age. But, the media are just one available source of information and influence. Young people's drinking behavior—whatever form it takes—reflects a portfolio of influences. These include expectations—positive and negative—about its effects, parental attitudes, ethnic and religious beliefs, gender norms, and societal and cultural influences (cf. Mathrani, 1998). The evidence suggests that children's and young people's information about alcohol and drinking is typically gained within the family context, usually well before they encounter any formal introduction to the subject (Alexander & Campbell, 1967; Barnes, 1977; Fossey, 1994; Kandel, Kessler, & Margulies, 1978). Parents and carers can provide both role models and a supportive environment in which young people can learn about alcohol (Foxcroft & Lowe, 1995; Foxcroft, Lowe, & May, 1994). The degree of family support and direction is linked not only to teenage drinking but also to other types of risk behavior (Nelson, Patience, & MacDonald, 1999; Plant & Plant, 1992).

The peer group is also important. In a qualitative study involving 144 10- to 17-year olds in the United Kingdom, friends and parents emerged as the most significant influences, with peer-group influence considerably more dominant than parental influence (Fox, 1997). Although the television and other media can be significant influences on young people's choices of clothing, music, and role models, these choices must be "approved" by their immediate circle of friends. Even advice from trusted sources was "validated" by the peer group and would not be followed unless it accorded with current practices among the peer group. Group membership is clearly a particularly powerful influence on young people seeking an identity. Those who are already experimenting with novel behaviors, such as using alcohol, are likely to choose to associate with those who share similar interests (May, 1993). But the issue is not just one of peer pressure. Young people are not only seeking acceptance by their peer group. They are also seeking to establish their independence and to live life to the full (Wyllie et al., 1998a). They are keen to join the adult world and the development of their values, attitudes, and behaviors with respect to drinking is an integral part of the process. In this context, media portrayals that emphasize the association between drinking and friendship, sociability, and having fun are likely to have a strong appeal (cf. Wyllie et al., 1998a).

Finally, there is a clear need for media literacy training to provide young people with the skills necessary to process messages effectively and to interpret their persuasive intent. Young people need to develop a portfolio of skills. They need to appreciate the principles and practices of advertising (Barons, 1980). They also need to develop critical skills, especially in relation to television. It is important that young people understand the medium, in terms of both its grammar and syntax and the values it endorses (Anderson, 1983). There is an increasing body of evidence that media literacy training can have immediate and longer-term effects on young people's use of media portrayals in making decisions about alcohol use (cf. Austin & Johnson, 1997a; Weintraub & Johnson, 1997). However, the training appears to be more effective when it is alcohol-specific rather than general (Austin & Johnson, 1997b). Also, discussion of alcohol advertising, when combined with alcohol education, can aid young people's cognitive resistance (counter-arguing) to such advertising (Slater et al., 1996b).

Using the Media in Initiatives to Combat Alcohol Misuse

The call for realistic educational initiatives to counter alcohol misuse by young people is not new (cf. Bagnall & Plant, 1987). But the reality of alcohol education has not always matched the rhetoric—an accusation that has been leveled at health promotion more generally (Parish, 1995). The dominant discourses in health education campaigns are those of risk, lifestyle, and individual responsibility. A discourse of risk is used to promote awareness of the dangers to health posed by lifestyle choices, such as drinking alcohol (Lupton, 1993). It is used to denote dangerous practices and groups susceptible to danger. Ideas about risk are closely associated with notions of accountability and responsibility and, implicitly, with moral judgements about lifestyle choices (cf. Beck, 1992). Risk, lifestyle, and individual responsibility are commonly linked, individuals being seen as responsible for choosing lifestyle options to protect themselves from risk (Peterson & Lupton, 1996).

However, alcohol use is not inherently risky. In fact, medical evidence suggests that moderate consumption of alcohol may be beneficial to long-term health. It is excessive or inappropriate use that can diminish an individual's quality of life or cause problems for society. Another issue is that risk has positive rather than negative connotations for many people, but especially for the young. Many young people drink precisely because of the perceived risk and the associated excitement. Faced with these paradoxes, it is tempting to let young people take their chance. Alternatively, ways of aiding young people in adopting a viable drinking lifestyle can be sought. This might mean endorsing nondrinking in the face of peer pressure and societal norms. Or it might mean helping those who wish to consume alcohol to do so in ways that maximize their enjoyment and minimize the likelihood of damage to themselves or to others. The essential question is what role, if any, do the media play in these scenarios.

Media campaigns that have attempted to change people's drinking habits have generally been judged to be ineffective at best and counterproductive at worst. Although this may be a rather harsh judgement, many early campaigns had obvious defects (cf. Miller & Ware, 1989). Campaigns frequently suffered from poor audience exposure and lack of targeting. "Universal" media campaigns have major flaws (cf. Gorman, 1995). Research in other fields of health promotion, such as safer sex advertising, has highlighted the importance of targeting and personalizing media messages. Members of the target population must see the messages as relevant to them if they are to reflect on their own behavior and its consequences (Dockrell & Stockdale, 1994; Stockdale, Dockrell, & Wells, 1989).

Early campaigns also paid scant attention to the key determinants of adolescent alcohol use (Flay & Sobell, 1983). Drinking behavior reflects a range of influences. Media campaigns must recognize the needs of young people and appreciate the various reasons why they drink (cf. Brain & Parker, 1997; Foxcroft & Lowe, 1995; Hughes et al., 1997). Research with young people in Great Britain suggests that 12- to 13-year-olds use alcohol to experience the adult world, because they are curious and they want to say they have tried alcohol. At 14 to 15 years of age young people like to test their own limits, while having fun, and they enjoy losing control occasionally and sharing the experience of being drunk with others. In contrast, 16- to 17-year-olds want to appear adult and sophisticated and to impress their girlfriends or boyfriends. A small minority of young people appears to drink with the main aim of getting drunk. Such "binge drinking" appears to be increasingly common, "getting wrecked" being seen as an enjoyable and acceptable experience (Measham, 1996).

Educational initiatives must build on young people's knowledge of alcohol (cf. Baillie, 1996; King, 1995) and an understanding of the practical and symbolic role alcohol plays in their lives (Hughes et al., 1997). Interventions designed to reduce binge drinking must understand its cultural meaning and recognize it as rational and legitimate consumption from the viewpoint of the immediate peer group (Brain & Parker, 1997; Haines, 1996). Similarly, media interventions that aim to promote moderate alcohol consumption or nondrinking must appreciate that many young people construe these drinking styles as unadventurous and unacceptable. The media have a vital role to play in "rebranding" moderate drinking and nondrinking as sophisticated and streetwise.

Many societies today continue to offer contradictory messages about alcohol. The ubiquitous media portrayal of the normality and positive sociability of drinking is reinforced by the fact that the majority of adults do drink alcohol and do so with friends. Moreover, in many countries the behavior of adults, the legislative framework governing the sale and use of alcohol, and media portrayals of drinking all convey the idea that alcohol consumption is the mysterious preserve of adults alone. This positive and multifaceted representation contrasts with alcohol education's typical reliance on health warnings that emphasize the negative outcomes of alcohol consumption. Although there is some suggestion that people may modify their beliefs in response to alcohol warnings (e.g., Slater & Domenech, 1995), the usefulness of such warnings in discouraging alcohol use remains controversial. For many people, media portrayals are likely to be a more salient and credible source of alcohol-related attitudes. The media can help to demystify alcohol consumption and to ensure that alcohol does not acquire the symbolism of forbidden territory.

Drinking behavior appears to be learned within the family environment and is supported within the peer-group context. Given the apparent primacy of these factors and the number of counter-influences—including alcohol advertising and media portrayals of drinking—campaigners must be realistic about what media-based interventions can be expected to achieve (Wallack, 1981). Media campaigns to encourage sensible drinking or to combat alcohol misuse should be seen as just one element in a portfolio of coordinated initiatives and should not be expected to be effective without other supporting action (cf . Miller & Ware, 1989; Wallack, 1983). All too often we expect too much from what are essentially weak, isolated interventions which have little perceived relevance to the lifestyles of those at whom they are aimed or which rely on patronising, dictatorial, or hypocritical messages. What is surprising is not that existing interventions have so little effect, but that they have any impact at all. Young people are keen to be seen as independent, self-directed, thinking individuals who make their own choices and decisions. Empowering young people, by involving them in the design, implementation and evaluation of interventions, will enhance the agency of young people and encourage their participation and commitment (Moore & Kindness, 1998). Thus, while it is unrealistic to expect media campaigns on their own to change drinking behavior, they may contribute to behavioral change when supported by other interventions, such as alcohol education in schools and other educational initiatives.

OVERVIEW

Conclusions

The evidence for a causal link between portrayals of alcohol in the media and young people's drinking patterns is equivocal. Research suggests that media portrayals are a source of information about alcohol and that they can influence young peoples' world-view and their behavioral choices. But the effects appear to be weak in comparison with familial context and peer relations. Young people learn to drink through a complex interaction of family, peer, and societal influences, including the media.

The ability to drink moderately and responsibly, or to be a nondrinker, implies access to information, credible role models and, when appropriate, "hands-on" experience. However, being healthy and "good" can seem boring—especially if you are young. Experimentation and novel experiences are inextricably part of youth culture and symbolize the perceived invulnerability of youth. Those who seek to promote moderate or minimal alcohol consumption have to appreciate the reasons why young people drink alcohol. It is vital to recognize the excitement and rewards offered by alcohol consumption and other "unhealthy" practices. Demonizing alcohol is likely to be counter productive. The media have a role to play in acknowledging the attractions of alcohol, while not portraying it as the panacea for all ills or as the pathway to personal success. In particular, the media have the potential to enrich young people's behavioral repertoire by legitimizing a range of drinking "scripts," including both nondrinking and moderate social drinking.

The media have to be seen as merely one element in the portfolio of influences that play a role in young people's lifestyle choices. Media messages alone are unlikely to change behavior. Moreover, any influence the media exert is likely to be subtle and insidious and to be mediated by the views of those in the young person's immediate family and social circle. These conclusions suggest an agenda for exploiting what power the media do have to enhance young people's quality of life.

An Agenda for Action

The media serve a diverse set of functions in society. They have a role in evaluating, interpreting, and disseminating information. But, by highlighting particular issues, the media also have a powerful agenda-setting function that should be exploited. The media facilitate and legitimize public debate, and thereby contribute both to setting research priorities and policy development. Focusing effort on evaluating these aspects of the media may be more fruitful than looking for simple media effects.

Cooperation between academic researchers, health professionals, and media and marketing practitioners is essential to devise appropriate portrayals, promotional materials, and codes of practice. However, constructive dialogue and evidence-based policy will require more than assertions about the role of the media. Most media researchers believe that the media make a significant contribution to reality, even though the evidence is less than convincing. Although the representation of alcohol in the media has generated a wealth of research, there have been few fruitful results (cf. Baillie, 1996). It is clear, therefore, that it is necessary to go beyond the simple effects model and construe media influences in their wider social and cultural context (Gunter, 2000; Livingstone, 1996). Instead of focusing on how the media make people act, research needs to focus on how the media contribute to making people who they are (Livingstone, 1996). This means understanding how the media contribute to the process of socialization, information provision and selection, and the way in which media consumers process and act on media messages. Only then will the role of the media in constructing and validating certain goals and lifestyle decisions, such as young people's choices concerning alcohol, be understood.

The media, particularly through the character development of key figures in popular entertainment and dramatic programs, can endorse a range of safe drinking options. They can also provide role models for parents and carers. Adults with a caring role need to be encouraged to participate in young people's lives and to provide them with the opportunity to live life to the full, so that alcohol is not seen as the primary source of excitement or relief from boredom. Also, when adults take a greater interest in what young people are thinking and doing, there is an opportunity for young people to interpret information about alcohol and to relate it to personal action. However, parents are not only facilitators or information sources. They also serve as behavioral models. If adults are a major influence on their children's drinking habits, then investment in modifying adult behavior may well be a productive route.

Alcohol socialization begins at an early age and both research and educational materials need to be focused on younger children. It should be recognized that children's knowledge of alcohol issues is often more sophisticated than many adults, especially parents, wish to believe. Educational initiatives need to be based on a clear understanding of how children think about and use alcohol. Researchers need to listen to children's views about how the media and other information sources lead them to develop their ideas about alcohol and the part it plays in people's lives. Educational initiatives must reflect their understanding and use their language, and their content must match the children's cognitive skills and emotional needs. More generally, there is a clear need to develop more imaginative, innovative, and streetwise educational initiatives that are appropriately targeted. Interventions that inform young people about alcohol need to be contextualized and related to other youth lifestyle issues (cf. Stockdale, 1998). The media have a role to play in such initiatives, but they must be supported by more immediate interventions and must exploit new technological advances.

Young people today have grown up not only with television but also with video and computer games, computers at home and in their schools, and the Internet. The young are a media-oriented generation with high expectations of the media in the future. The central role of the media in young people's lives, combined with advances in new technology and further market penetration, will change their personal and social environment. A key development is the increasing trend toward interactive communication between the media and the user. Such two-way communication includes interactive television, virtual reality scenarios, video-on-demand, and teleshopping. This trend is accompanied by the convergence of different forms of media, such as broadcasting, information services, telecommunications, and the Internet. Both of these developments are taking place against a backdrop of an ever-widening choice of television channels and the take up of the vast number of programming sources offered by the worldwide web via the Internet. These changes will not only mean new communication methods but also increasing access to individuals and markets.

The social and cultural world of young people in the 21st century is different from that of previous generations (cf. Eigen, 1996). The new media are a key part of the changes that are occurring; they offer both new opportunities and some dangers for young people. For example, interactive television affords some degree of program control to the audience as well as the producer so that, in principle, viewers can have some say over content, such as alcohol portrayals. Convergence of media and information technologies are likely to mean convergence of media uses, such as entertainment, information, and consumption, and of work, leisure, and maintenance activities. Also, globalization of media products and their distribution may mean less regulation and greater shared experience across national and cultural boundaries. Geographical communities are being eroded in favor of virtual spaces. This change, combined with demographic changes, may result in less social contact, which in turn may lead to alienation and stress. Decreased time spent on traveling, shopping, and other maintenance activities is likely to mean more time for leisure and consumption. Greater use of the Internet and teleshopping may lead to greater exposure to alcohol. Companies are already using the Internet to market alcohol products. Many of the marketing techniques used, such as colorful games, music, and interactive sites, are likely to appeal especially to children and young people (Center for Media Education, 1997). There is also increasing use of personalized advertising based on sophisticated market segmentation.

Some or all of these developments may contribute to greater use of alcohol, which offers a low cost-per-hour and convenient leisure option. The generation gap in technical expertise means that the degree to which adults can monitor and control young people's access to alcohol via the Internet or other media channels is limited. This lack of parental intervention is likely to be accentuated by the growth in parallel lifestyles and the increase in young people's access to their own media and information sources. If campaigns are to counter the increasing presence of alcohol promotion in cyberspace they will need not only to be innovative but also to exploit the new media. For example, chat rooms provide an ideal opportunity to access youth culture. These interactive facilities provide a means of accessing young people's views and concerns about alcohol and the opportunity for credible peer counselors to provide information and support. Moreover, the Internet has tremendous potential to provide a mentoring service to young people. A non-profit-making website already enables professionals in the U.S. to provide career advice to teenagers. The potential for providing information and guidance on alcohol consumption and other lifestyle issues is immense.

These and other creative interventions which exploit the opportunities afforded by the media—both traditional and new—can help to supplement the key contributions made by families and peers to young people's understanding of alcohol and their drinking behavior. If drinking is conceptualized as a skill, then the evidence suggests that young people should be given the opportunity to acquire this skill within an informed and supportive environment. The best model appears to be one in which family members and friends who wish to do so enjoy moderate consumption of alcohol within social and cultural norms. If alcohol is demonized, and young people are not provided either with the opportunity to experiment with the tastes and effects of alcohol or with appropriate role models within their immediate social circle, they are likely to seek their practical education about alcohol in more risky settings. The media do have a role to play in promoting the safe consumption of alcohol and in countering its misuse by young people. However, it is not the key influence on young people's drinking behavior. Young people's knowledge of alcohol and their drinking skills are mediated by the salience and management of alcohol in the family and peer group settings. The media, especially advertising, are perhaps blamed for young people's misuse of alcohol to distract attention from the essence of the problem—the way we drink.

REFERENCES

Aas, H. N., Leigh, B. C., Anderssen, N., & Jakobsen, R. (1998). Two-year longitudinal study of alcohol experiences and drinking among Norwegian adolescents. *Addiction, 93*, 373–384.

Adlaf, E. M., & Kohn, P. M. (1989). Alcohol advertising, consumption and abuse: A covariance-structural modelling looking at Strickland's data. *British Journal of Addiction, 84*, 749–757.

Aitken, P. P. (1989). Alcohol advertising in developing countries. *British Journal of Addiction, 84*, 1443–1445.

Aitken, P. P., Eadie, D. R., Leather, D. S., McNeill, R. E., & Scott, A. C. (1988). Television advertisements for alcoholic drinks do reinforce under-age drinking. *British Journal of Addiction, 83*, 1399–1419.

Aitken, P. P., Leather, D. S., & Scott, A. C. (1988). Ten- to sixteen-year-olds' perceptions of advertisements for alcoholic drinks. *Alcohol & Alcoholism, 23*, 491–500.

Alaniz, M. L., & Wilkes, C. (1998). Pro-drinking messages and message environments for young adults: The case of alcohol industry advertising in African American, Latino and native American communities. *Journal of Public Health Policy, 19*, 447–472.

Alcohol Concern. (1997). *Alcopops*. London: Author

Alexander, C., & Campbell, E. (1967). Peer influence on adolescent drinking. *Quarterly Journal of Studies on Alcohol, 28*, 444–454.

American Society of Addiction Medicine. (1997). Public policy statement on advertising. *Journal of Addictive Diseases, 16*, 104–105.

Amos, A. (1989). Use of alcohol among high school students in Lesotho: A health promotion perspective. *British Journal of Addiction, 84*, 1447–1449.

Anderson, J. A. (1983). Television literacy and the critical viewer. In J. Bryant & D. R. Anderson (Eds.), *Children's understanding of television: Research on attention and comprehension* (pp. 297–330). London: Academic Press.

Atkin, C. K. (1982). Television advertising and socialization to consumer roles. In D. Pearl, L. Bouthilet, & J. Lazar (Eds.) *Television and behaviour: Ten years of scientific progress and implications for the eighties. (Vol. 2): Technical reviews* (pp. 191–200). Washington, DC: U.S. Government Printing Office.

Atkin, C. K. (1990). Effects of televised alcohol messages on teenage drinking patterns. *Journal of Adolescent Health Care, 11*, 10–24.

Atkin, C. K., & Block, M. (1981). *Content and effects of alcohol advertising*. Report I: Overview and summary. Springfield, VT: National Technical Information Service.

Atkin, C. K., Hocking, J., & Block, M. (1984). Teenage drinking: Does advertising make a difference? *Journal of Drug Issues, 4*, 511–522.

Austin, E. W., & Johnson, K. K. (1997a). The immediate and delayed effects of media literacy training on third graders' ecision making for alcohol. *Health Communication, 9*, 323–349.

Austin, E. W., & Johnson, K. K. (1997b). Effects of general and alcohol-specific media literacy training on children's decision making about alcohol. *Journal of Health Communication, 2*, 17–42.

Austin, E. W., & Meili, H. K. (1994). Effects of interpretations of televised alcohol portrayals on children's alcohol beliefs. *Journal of Broadcasting and Electronic Media, 38*, 417–435.

Austin, E. W., & Nach-Ferguson, B. (1995). Sources and influence of young school-age children's general and brand-specific knowledge about alcohol. *Health Communication, 7*, 1–20.

Bagnall, G., & Plant, M. (1987). Adolescent drinking. *British Journal of Addiction, 82*, 829–830.

Baillie, R. K. (1996). Determining the effects of media portrayals of alcohol: Going beyond short term influence. *Alcohol and Alcoholism, 31*, 235–242.

Bandura, A. (1977). *Social learning theory*. Englewood Cliffs, NJ: Prentice Hall.

Bandura, A. (1986). *The social foundations of thought and action: A social cognitive theory*. Englewood Cliffs, NJ: Prentice Hall.

Barnes, G. (1977). The development of adolescent drinking behavior: An evaluative review of the impact of the socialization process within the family. *Adolescence, 12*, 571–591.

Barons, F. E. (1980). The nature of television advertising to children. In E. L. Palmer & A. Dorr (Eds.), *Children and the faces of television: Teaching, violence, selling* (pp. 273–286). New York: Academic Press.

Barton, R. (1989). Alcohol promotion on television. *World Health Forum, 10*, 181–185.

Barton, R., & Godfrey, S. (1988). Un-health promotion: Results of a survey of alcohol promotion on television. *British Medical Journal, 296*, 1593–1594.

Beck, U. (1992). *Risk society: Towards a new modernity*. London: Sage.

Brain, K., & Parker, H. (1997). *Drinking with design: Alcopops, designer drinks and youth culture*. Manchester, England: The Portman Group.

Breed, W., & DeFoe, J. R. (1978). Drinking on television: A comparison of alcohol use to the use of coffee, tea, soft drinks, water and cigarettes. *The Bottom Line, 2*, 28–29.

Breed, W., & DeFoe, J. R. (1979). Themes in magazine alcohol advertisements: A critique. *Journal of Drug Issues, 9*, 511–522.

Breed, W., & DeFoe, J. R. (1980). Mass media, alcohol and drugs: A new trend. *Journal of Drug Education, 10*, 135–143.

Breed, W., & DeFoe, J. R. (1981). The portrayal of the drinking process on prime-time television. *Journal of Communication, 31*, 58–67.

Breed, W., & DeFoe, J. R. (1984). Drinking and smoking on US television, 1952–1982. *Journal of Public Health Policy, 5*, 257–270.

Breed, W., DeFoe, J. R., & Wallack, L. (1984). Drinking in the mass media: A nine year project. *Journal of Drug Issues, 14*, 655–664.

Brown, J. D., & MacDonald, T. (1995). Portrayals and effects of alcohol in television entertainment programming. In *National Institute for Alcohol Abuse and Alcoholism, The effects of the mass media on the use and abuse of alcohol* (Research Monograph No. 28, Serial No. 95-3743, Chapter 9). Rockville, MD: U.S. Department of Health and Human Services.

Casswell, S., Gilmore, L. L., Silva, P., & Brasch, P. (1988). What children know about alcohol and how they know it. *British Journal of Addiction, 83*, 223–227.

Casswell, S., & Zhang, J. F. (1998). The impact of liking for advertising and brand allegiance on drinking and alcohol related aggression: A longitudinal study. *Addiction, 93*, 1209–1217.

Center for Media Education. (1997, March 6). *Alcohol and tobacco on the web: New threats to youth*. Washington, DC: Center for Media Education.

Cialdini, R. B. (1993). *Influence: Science and practice* (3rd ed.). New York: Harper Collins.

Condry, J. (1989). *The psychology of television*. Hillsdate, NJ: Erlbaum.

Connolly, G. M., Casswell, S., Zhang, J. F., & Silva, P. A. (1994). Alcohol in the mass-media and drinking by adolescents: A longitudinal study. *Addiction, 89*, 1255–1263.

Cook, J., & Lewington, M. (Eds.). (1979). *Images of alcoholism*. London: British Film Institute.

Covell, K., Dion, K. L., & Dion, K. K. (1994). Gender differences in evaluation of tobacco and alcohol advertisements. *Canadian Journal of Behavioural Sciences, 26*, 404–420.

Cox, W., Huppner, C., Light, C., & Olsen, T. (1984). Trends in the quality of alcohol and cigarette adverts in Psychology Today. *Bulletin of the Society of Psychologists in Addictive Behaviors, 3*, 109–112.

Crouch, C. (1991). The emergence of Soap: Primary school children's TV preferences in Northern Ireland, England and Australia. *Research in Education, 46*, 73–83.

DeFoe, J. R., Breed, W., & Breed, L. A. (1983). Drinking on television: A five year study. *Journal of Drug Education, 13*, 25–28.

Deutsch, M., & Gerard, H. B. (1955). A study of normative and informational influence upon individual judgement. *Journal of Abnormal and Social Psychology, 51*, 629–636.

Dockrell, J. E., & Stockdale, J. E. (1994). Advertising and HIV/AIDS. *British Journal of Sexual Medicine, 21*, 12–14.

Dorfman, L., & Wallack, L. (1996). *The news on alcohol - media advocacy strategies to promote prevention policy*. Paper presented at Alcohol Policy X, the 10th International Alcohol Policy Conference, Toronto, Canada.

Dorn, N., & South, N. (1983). *Message in a bottle*. Aldershot, England: Gower.

Dorr, A. (1986). *Television and children: A special medium for a special audience*. Beverley Hills, CA: Sage.

Du Rant, R. H., Rome, E. S., Rich, M., Allred, E., Emans, S. J., & Woods, E. R. (1997). Tobacco and alcohol use behaviors portrayed in music videos: A content analysis. *Journal of Public Health, 87*, 1131–1135.

Eigen, L. D. (1996). *The young and restless: Generation X and alcohol policy*. Paper presented at Alcohol Policy X, the 10th International Alcohol Policy Conference, Toronto, Canada.

Finn, T. A., & Strickland, D. E. (1982). A content analysis of beverage alcohol advertising. 2. Television advertising. *Journal of Studies on Alcohol, 43*, 964–989.

Finn, T. A., & Strickland, D. E. (1983). The advertising and alcohol abuse issue: A cross media comparison of the content of alcohol beverage advertising. In M. Burgeon (Ed.), *Communication yearbook* (pp. 850–872). Beverley Hills, CA: Sage.

Fisher, J. C. (1993). *Advertising, alcohol consumption and abuse: A world-wide survey*. Westport, CT: Greenwood Press.

Flay, B. R., & Sobell, J. J. (1983). The role of mass media in preventing adolescent substance abuse. In T. J. Glynn, C. G. Leukefeld, & J. P. Ludford (Eds.), *Preventing adolescent drug abuse: Intervention strategies* (NIDA Research Monograph No. 47, DHHS Publication No. ADM 83-1280). Washington, DC: U.S. Government Printing Office.

Fossey, E. (1994). *Growing up with alcohol*. New York: Routledge.

Fox, K. (1997). *Taskforce on underage alcohol misuse: Report of the under-18 panel meetings*. London: The Portman Group.

Foxcroft, D. R., & Lowe, G. (1995). Adolescent drinking, smoking and other substance use involvement links with perceived family life. *Journal of Adolescence, 18*, 159–177.

Foxcroft, D. R., Lowe, G., & May, C. (1994). Adolescent alcohol-use and family influences: Attributive statements by teenage drinkers. *Drugs Education, Prevention and Policy, 1*, 63–69.

Furnham, A., Ingle, H., Gunter, B., & McClelland, A. (1997). A content analysis of alcohol portrayal and drinking in British television soap operas. *Health Education Research, 12*, 519–529.

Futch, E. J., Lisman, S. A., & Geller, M. I. (1984). An analysis of alcohol portrayed on prime-time television. *International Journal of Addictions, 19*, 403–410.

Garlington, W. K. (1977). Drinking on television: A preliminary study with emphasis on method. *Journal of Studies on Alcohol, 36*, 2199–2205.

Gerbner, G. (1995). Alcohol in American culture. In S. E. Martin & P. Mail (Eds.), *Effects of the mass media on the use and abuse of alcohol* (Research Monograph No. 28, pp. 3–29). Bethesda, MD: National Institute on Alcohol Abuse and Alcoholism.

Gerbner, G., Gross, M., Morgan, M., & Signorielli, N. (1986). Living with television: The dynamics of the cultivation process. In J. Bryant & D. Zillman (Eds.), *Perspectives on media effects*. Hillsdale, NJ: Lawrence Erlbaum.

Gerbner, G., Morgan, M., & Signorielli, N. (1982). Programming health portrayals: What viewers see, say and do. In D. Pearl, L. Bouthilet, & J. Lazar (Eds.), *Television and behavior: Ten years of scientific progress and implications for the eighties* (Vol. 2, DHHS Publication No. ADM 82-1196, pp. 291–307). Washington, DC: U.S. Government Printing Office.

Goddard, E. (1997). *Young teenagers and alcohol in 1996: Volume 1*. London: Office for National Statistics.

Gorman, D. M. (1995). The changing role of the mass media in preventing excessive alcohol use. *Drugs Education, Prevention and Policy, 2*, 77–83.

Graham, J. W., Marks, G., & Hansen, W. B. (1991). Social influence processes affecting adolescent substance use. *Journal of Applied Psychology, 76*, 291–298.

Greenberg, B. S. (1981). Smoking, drugging and drinking in top rated TV series. *Journal of Drug Education, 11*, 227–233.

Greenberg, B. S., Fernandez-Collado, C., Graef, D., Kovzenny, F., & Aitken, C. K. (1979). Trends in the use of alcohol and other substances on television. *Journal of Drug Education, 9*, 227–234.

Grube, J. W. (1995). Television portrayals, alcohol advertising and alcohol expectancies among children and adolescents. In S. E. Martin & P. Mail (Eds.), *Effects of the mass media on the use and abuse of alcohol* (Research Monograph No. 28, pp. 105–121). Bethesda, MD: National Institute on Alcohol Abuse and Alcoholism.

Grube, J. W., & Wallack, L. (1994). Television beer advertising and drinking knowledge, beliefs and intentions among schoolchildren. *American Journal of Public Health, 84*, 254–259.

Gunter, B. (1997). An audience-based approach to assessing programme quality. In P. Winterhoff-Spurk & T. H. A. Little van der Voort (Eds.), *New horizons in media psychology* (pp. 11–34). Opladen, Germany: Westdeutscher Verlag.

Gunter, B. (2000). *Media research methods*. London: Sage.

Haines, M. P. (1996). *A social norms approach to preventing binge drinking at colleges and universities*. Newton, MA: Higher Education Center for Alcohol and Other Drugs Prevention.

Hansen, A. (1986). The portrayal of alcohol on television. *Health Education Journal, 45*, 127–131.

Harrison, L. (1989). The information component. In D. Robinson, A. Maynard, & R. Chester (Eds.), *Controlling legal addictions* (pp. 183–202). London: Macmillan.

Hastings, G. B., Mackintosh, A. M., & Aitken, P. P. (1992). Is alcohol advertising reaching the people it shouldn't reach? *Health Education Journal, 51*, 38–42.

Health Education Authority. (1997). *Young people and alcohol: A survey of attitudes and behaviour towards new types of alcoholic drinks in England*. London: Health Education Authority.

Heiskala, R. (1988). An exclusively male matter? Alcohol, gender and the family in Finnish general magazines and women's magazines in 1955 and 1985. *Alkoholipolitiikka, 53*, 199–209.

Herd, D. (1986). Ideology, melodrama and the changing role of alcohol problems in American films. *Contemporary Drug Problems, 13*, 213–247.

Herd, D., & Room, R. (1982). Alcohol images in American film 1909–1960. *Drinking and Drug Practices Surveyor, 18*, 24–35.

Hockey, J., & James, A. (1993). *Growing up and growing old: Ageing and dependency and the life course*. London: Sage.

Hughes, K., Mackintosh, A. M., Hastings, G., Wheeler, C., Watson, J., & Inglis, J. (1997). Young people, alcohol, and designer drinks: A quantitative and qualitative study. *British Medical Journal, 314*, 414–418.

Huston, A. C., Donnerstein, E., Fairchild, H., Feschbach, N. D., Katz, P. A., Murray, J. P., Rubenstein, E. A., Wilcox, B. L., & Zuckerman, D. (1992). *Big world, small screen: The role of television in American society*. Lincoln, NE: University of Nebraska Press.

Insko, C. A., Smith, R. A. Alicke, M. D., Wade, J., & Taylor, S. (1985). Conformity and group size: The concern with being right and the concern with being liked. *Personality and Social Psychology Bulletin, 11*, 41–50.

Jahoda, G., & Cramond, J. (1972). *Children and alcohol*. London: Her Majesty's Stationery Office.

Jahoda, G., Davies, J. B., & Ragg, S. (1980). Parents' alcohol consumption and children's knowledge of drinks and usage patterns. *British Journal of Addiction, 75*, 297–303.

James, A., & Prout, A. (Eds), (1990). *Constructing and reconstructing childhood: Contemporary issues in the sociological study of childhood*. Brighton, England: Falmer Press.

Jenks, C. (1996). *Childhood*. London and New York: Routledge.

Kandel, D., Kessler, R. C., & Margulies, R. S. (1978). Antecedents of adolescent initiation into stages of drug use: A developmental analysis. In D. Kandel (Ed.), *Longitudinal research in drug use: Empirical findings and methodological issues* (pp. 73–99). Washington, DC: Hemisphere-Wiley.

Kelly, K. J., & Edwards, R. W. (1998). Image advertisements for alcohol products: Is their appeal associated with adolescents' intention to consume alcohol? *Adolescence, 33*, 47–59.

Killen, J. D., Hayward, C., Wilson, D. M., Haydel, K. F., Robinson, T. N., Taylor, C. B., Hammer, L. D., & Varady, A. (1996). Predicting onset of drinking in a community sample of adolescents: The role of expectancy and temperament. *Addiction Behaviors, 21*, 473–480.

King, A. (1995). The ins and outs of alcohol education. *Health Education, 95*, 10–11.

Kraus, D., Smith, G. T., & Ratner, H. H. (1994). Modifying alcohol-related expectancies in grade-school children. *Journal of Studies on Alcohol, 55*, 535–542.

Kushnir, T. (1986). Smoking and drinking as psychological tools in stressful situations: Assumptions of fiction writers. *International Journal of Addictions, 21*, 1119–1123.

Linn, M. C., de Benedictis, T., & Delucchi, K. (1982). Adolescent reasoning about advertisements: Preliminary investigations. *Child Development, 53*, 1599–1613.

Lipsitz, A., Brake, G., Vincent, E. J., & Winters, M. (1993). Another round for the brewers: Television adverts and children's alcohol expectancies. *Journal of Applied Social Psychology, 23*, 439–450.

Livingstone, S. M. (1990). *Making sense of television: The psychology of audience interpretation*. Oxford, England: Pergamon.

Livingstone, S. M. (1996). On the continuing problem of media effects. In J. Curran & M. Gurevitch (Eds.), *Mass media and society* (2nd ed.). London: Arnold.

Livingstone, S. M., Holden, K. H., & Bovill, M. (1999). Children's changing media environment: Overview of a European comparative study. In U. Carlsson & C. von Feilitzen (Eds.), *Children and media: Participation and education. Yearbook from the UNESCO International Clearing House on Children and Violence on the Screen*. Göteburg, Sweden: Nordicom/UNESCO.

Lowery, S. (1980). Soap and booze in the afternoon: An analysis of the portrayal of alcohol use in daytime serials. *Journal of Studies on Alcohol, 41*, 829–838.

Lowry, D. T. (1981). Alcohol consumption patterns and consequences on prime-time network TV. *Journalism Quarterly, 58*, 3–8.

Luke, C. (1985). Television discourse processing: A schema theoretic approach. *Communication Education, 34*, 91–105.

Lupton, D. (1993). Risk as a moral danger: The social and political functions of risk discourse in public health. *International Journal of Health, 23*, 425–435.

Madden, P., & Grube, J. (1991, November). *Alcohol and tobacco advertising on sports and prime-time television*. Paper presented at the American Public Health Association Conference, Atlanta, GA.

Mathios, A., Avery, R., Bisogni, C., & Shanahan, J. (1998). Alcohol portrayal on prime-time television: Manifest and latent messages. *Journal of Studies on Alcohol, 59*, 305–310.

Mathrani, S. (1998). *Young people, alcohol and their social world: A qualitative study*. Health Education Authority and Research Works.

May, C. (1993). Resistance to peer pressure: An inadequate basis for alcohol education. *Health Education Research, 8*, 159–165.

McKeganey, N., Forsyth, A., Barnard, M., & Hay, G. (1996). Designer drinks and drunkenness amongst a sample of Scottish schoolchildren. *British Medical Journal, 313*, 401.

McKibben, M. (1996). *Pop fiction: The truth about alcopops*. London: Alcohol Concern.

Measham, F. (1996). The big bang approach to sessional drinking: Changing patterns of alcohol consumption amongst young people in North West England. *Addiction Research, 4*, 283–289.

Meursing, K., & Morojele, N. (1989). Use of alcohol among high school students in Lesotho: A health promotion perspective. *British Journal of Addiction, 84*, 1337–1342.

Miller, M. E., & Ware, J. (1989). *Mass-media alcohol and drug campaigns. A consideration of relevant issues* (Monograph Series No. 9). Canberra, Australia: National Campaign Against Drug Abuse.

Minkler, M., Wallack, L., & Madden, P. (1987). Alcohol and cigarette advertising in Ms. London magazine. *Journal of Public Health Policy, 8*, 164–179.

Montagne, M. (1988). The influence of literary and philosophical accounts on drug taking. *Journal of Drug Issues, 18*, 229–244.

Montonen, M. (1986). Alcohol and drinking on Finnish television. *Alkoholi Politiikka, 51*, 63–73.

Moore, H. L., & Kindness, L. (1998). Establishing a research agenda for the health and well-being of children and young people in the context of health promotion. In *Health Education Authority, Promoting the health of children and young people: Setting a research agenda*. (Report of a Expert Working Group, pp. 1–17). London: Health Education Authority.

Morley, D. (1992). *Television, audiences and cultural studies*. London: Routledge.

Nelson, B. V., Patience, T. H., & MacDonald, D. C. (1999). Adolescent risk behavior and the influence of parents and education. *Journal of the American Board of Family Practitioners, 12*, 436–443.

Neuendorf, K. A. (1985). Alcohol advertising and media portrayals. *Journal of the Institute for Socio-Economic Studies, 10*, 67–78.

Okazaki, N., & Higuchi, S. (1995). Alcohol beverage advertisements—Survey of weekly magazines. *Japanese Journal of Alcohol Studies and Drug Dependence, 30*, 23–32.

Paget, K. F., Kritt, D., & Bergmann, L. (1984). Understanding strategic interactions in television commercials: A developmental study. *Journal of Applied Developmental Psychology, 5*, 154–161.

Parish, R. (1995). Health promotion: Rhetoric and reality. In R. Bunton, S. Nettelton, & R. Burrows (Eds.), *The sociology of health promotion: Critical analyses of consumption, lifestyle and risk* (pp. 13–23). London: Routledge.

Partanen, J., & Montonen, M. (1988). *Alcohol and the mass media*. (EURO Reports and Studies No. 108). Copenhagen: WHO Regional Office for Europe.

Pendleton, L. L., Smith, C., & Roberts, J. L. (1991). Drinking on television: A content analysis of recent alcohol portrayal. *British Journal of Addiction, 86*, 769–774.

Peterson, A., & Lupton, D. (1996). *The new public health: Health and self in the age of risk*. London: Sage.

Plant, M., & Plant, M. (1992). *The risk takers: Alcohol, drugs, sex and youth*. London: Tavistock, Routledge.

Portman Group (1996). *The code report*. London: Portman Group.

Portman Group (1997). *The Portman Group code of practice on the naming, packaging and merchandising of alcoholic drinks*. London: Portman Group.

Portman Group (2000). *The code report 16*. London: Portman Group.

Prentice, D. A., & Miller, D. T. (1993). Pluralistic ignorance and alcohol use on campus: Some consequences of misperceiving the social norm. *Journal of Personality and Social Psychology, 64*, 243–256.

Reid, D. (1996). Teenage drug use: On the increase, and clear links with advertising and sports sponsorship. *British Medical Journal, 313*, 375.

Robertson, T. S., & Rossiter, J. R. (1974). Children and commercial persuasion: An attribution theory analysis. *Journal of Consumer Research, 1*, 13–20.

Robinson, T. N., Chen, H. L., & Killen, J. D. (1998). Television and music video exposure and risk of adolescent alcohol use. *Paediatrics, 102*, E541–E546.

Ross, R. P., Campbell, T., Wright, J. C., Huston, A. C., Rice, M. L., & Turk, P. (1984). When celebrities talk, children listen: An experimental analysis of children's responses to television adverts with celebrity endorsement. *Journal of Applied Developmental Psychology, 5*, 185–202.

Rossiter, J. R., & Robertson, T. S. (1974). Children's television commercials: Testing the defenses. *Journal of Broadcasting, 23*, 33–40.

Scottish Council on Alcohol (1996). *Young people and alcohol in Scotland: A survey of branded preferences of 15–17 year olds.*

Signorielli, N. (1987). Drinking, sex and violence on television: The cultural indicators perspective. *Journal of Drug Education, 17*, 254–260.

Silverstone, R. (1990). Television and everyday life: Towards an anthropology of the television audience. In M. Ferguson (Ed.), *Public communication: The new imperatives* (pp. 173–189). London: Sage.

Slater, M. D., & Domenech, M. M. (1995). Alcohol warnings in TV beer advertisements. *Journal of Studies on Alcohol, 56*(3), 361–367.

Slater, M. D., Rouner, D., Beauvais, F., Murphy, K., Domenech Rodriquez, M., & Van Leuven, J. K. (1996a). Adolescent perceptions of underage drinkers in TV beer ads. *Journal of Alcohol and Drug Education, 42*, 43–56.

Slater, M. D., Rouner, D., Beauvais, F., Murphy, K., Van Leuven, J. K., & Domenech Rodriguez, M. (1996b). Adolescent counterarguing of TV beer advertisements: Evidence for effectiveness of alcohol education and critical viewing discussions. *Journal of Drug Education, 26*, 143–158.

Slater, M. D., Rouner, D., Domenech Rodriguez, M., Beauvais, F., Murphy, K., & Van Leuven, J. K. (1997). Adolescent responses to TV beer advertisements and sports content/context: Gender and ethnic differences. *Journalism and Mass Communication Quarterly, 74*, 108–122.

Smart, R. (1988). Does alcohol advertising affect overall consumption? A review of empirical studies. *Journal of Studies on Alcohol, 49*, 314–323.

Smith, R. (1985). Booze on the telly. *British Medical Journal, 290*, 445–446.

Spiegler, D. L. (1983). Children's attitudes toward alcohol. *Journal of Studies on Alcohol, 44*, 545–552.

Stephens, N., & Stutts, M. A. (1982). Pre-schoolers' ability to distinguish between television programming and commercials. *Journal of Advertising, 11*, 16–26.

Stockdale, J. E. (1995). The self and media messages: Match or mismatch? In I. Markova & R. M. Farr (Eds.), *Representations of health and illness and handicap*. Chur, Switzerland: Harwood.

Stockdale, J. E. (1998). Health promotion for children and young people: Some social psychological perspectives. In *Health Education Authority, Promoting the health of children and young people: Setting a research agenda.* (Report of a Expert Working Group, pp. 33–35). London: Health Education Authority.

Stockdale, J. E., & Dockrell, J. E. (1995). *European children's understanding of television in the 1990s*. Paper presented at the IV European Congress of Psychology, Athens, Greece.

Stockdale, J. E., Dockrell, J. E., & Wells, A. J. (1989). The self in relation to media representations of HIV/AIDS—Match or mismatch? *Health Education, 48*, 121–130.

Strasburger, V. C., & Donnerstein, E. (2000). Children, adolescents and the media in the 21st century. *Adolescent Medicine, 71*, 51–68.

Strickland, D. E. (1983). Advertising exposure, alcohol consumption and misuse of alcohol. In M. Grant, M. Plant, & A. Williams (Eds.), *Economics and alcohol: Consumption and controls* (pp. 201–222). London: Croom Helm.

Strickland, D. E., Finn, T. A., & Lambert, M. D. (1982). Content analysis of beverage alcohol advertising. 1. Magazine advertising. *Journal of Studies on Alcohol, 43*, 655–682.

Tether, P. (1989). Legal controls and voluntary agreements. In D. Robinson, A. Maynard, & R. Chester (Eds.), *Controlling legal addictions* (pp. 203–220). London: Macmillan.

Tether, P., & Robinson, D. (1986). *Preventing alcohol problems: A guide to local action*. London: Tavistock.

Thomson, A., Casswell, S., & Stewart, L. (1994). Communication experts' opinion on alcohol advertising through the electronic media in New Zealand. *Health Promotion International, 9*, 145–152.

Vaidya, S., Naik, U. D., & Vaidya, J. S. (1996). Effects of sports sponsorship by tobacco companies on children's experimentation with tobacco. *British Medical Journal, 313*, 400.

van Iwaarden, M. J. (1983). Advertising, alcohol consumption and policy alternatives. In M. Grant, M. Plant, & A. Williams (Eds.), *Economics and alcohol: Consumption and controls* (pp. 223–237). London: Croom Helm.

Wallack, L. (1981). Mass media campaigns: The odds against finding behavior change. *Health Education Quarterly, 8*, 209–260.

Wallack, L. (1983). Alcohol advertising reassessed: The public health perspective. In M. Grant, M. Plant, & A. Williams (Eds.), *Economics and alcohol: Consumption and controls* (pp. 243–248). London: Croom Helm.

Wallack, L., Breed, W., & DeFoe, J. R. (1985). Alcohol and soap operas: Drinking in the light of day. *Journal of Drug Education, 15*, 365–379.

Wallack, L., Grube, W., Madden, P. A., & Breed, W. (1990). Portrayals of alcohol on prime-time television. *Journal of Studies of Alcohol, 51*, 428–437.

Ward, S. (1972). Children's reaction to commercials. *Journal of Advertising Research, 12*, 35–47.

Waxer, P. H. (1992). Alcohol consumption in television programming in three English-speaking cultures. *Alcohol and Alcoholism, 27*, 195–200.

Weintraub, A. E., & Johnson, K. K. (1997). Immediate and delayed effects of media literacy training on third graders' decision making for alcohol. *Health Communication, 9*, 323–349.

Wilson, C. C., II, & Gutierrez, F. (1995). *Race, multi-culturalism and the media*. London: Sage.

Wyllie, A., Casswell, S., & Stewart, J. (1989). The response of New Zealand boys to corporate and sponsorship alcohol advertising on television. *British Journal of Addiction, 84*, 639–646.

Wyllie, A., Zhang, J. F., & Casswell, S. (1998a). Responses to televised alcohol advertisements associated with drinking behaviour of 10–17 year olds. *Addiction, 93*, 361–371.

Wyllie, A., Zhang, J. F., & Casswell, S. (1998b). Positive responses to televised beer advertisements associated with drinking problems reported by 18 to 29-year-olds. *Addiction, 93*(5), 749–760.

Zinser, O., Freeman, J. E., & Ginnings, D. K. (1999). A comparison of memory for and attitudes about alcohol, cigarette and other product advertisements in college students. *Journal of Drug Education, 29*, 175–185.

Chapter 11

The Role of Government and the Law

Keith R. Evans and Ann M. Roche

Roizen (1997) argues that alcohol holds a unique position within most cultures in that, in spite of clear evidence of the powerful negative potential of the substance, it is bequeathed a special place of benign innocence, thereby avoiding the need for people to learn of ways to develop a "good" relationship with it. In this chapter it is argued that the need to learn (either as individuals or collectively as communities) how to use this substance with a minimum of risk takes precedence.

SETTING THE SCENE

For those living in countries in which the consumption of beverage alcohol is legally sanctioned, it is a rare event to be exposed to mass media reports addressing the question of alcohol misuse without seemingly ubiquitous reference to youthful drinking patterns. Concerns over the personal and social consequences of excessive drinking among young people are often cited as the rationale for decisions taken by political and community leaders to place increased restrictions on alcohol availability. These restrictions are commonly represented as being "in the public interest," and as a means of protecting our innocent youth from the seemingly inevitable negative consequences of their early relationship with beverage alcohol. Interestingly, young people are rarely if ever systematically taught to understand and appreciate the consumption of alcohol and safely integrate it into their lives. Where such an approach does occur it is likely to be in the context of the individual's family and not in any organized or structured manner.

It is increasingly recognized that alcohol consumption plays an important role in the overall health and well-being of the community (complex as this relationship may be). Concomitantly, there is also the need to recognize the ways in which alcohol differs from other consumer products and to determine what appropriate safeguards need to be in place to ensure maximum enjoyment and benefit from its use, while minimizing the potential for alcohol-related harm to the drinker.

The role of governments in exerting controls over the provision of alcohol has historically stemmed from a small number of key policy objectives. First, there is the obvious desire to raise revenue. Secondly, there is the desire to minimize the harmful effects of excessive alcohol consumption through regulatory measures. Thirdly, there is the desire to control market forces in relation to the provision of alcohol to the community.

In countries where alcohol is not legally and or culturally proscribed, there is considerable interest in and increasing debate over the relative importance and role of a wide variety of institutions and settings to determine how young people learn about drinking. This chapter considers the specific roles of government and the law as adjuncts to promoting low-risk drinking environments and responsible attitudes and personal behavior in relation to the consumption of alcohol. The chapter also examines contemporary activities of governments as they attempt to influence drinking practices and encourage sensible attitudes towards alcohol consumption, particularly with reference to young people. It will cover issues such as:

- the role of government in "shaping" drinking behavior;
- alcohol availability;
- mass media—especially as a tool for encouraging moderation in alcohol consumption;
- health education/public information;
- pricing/taxation;
- age of purchase and consumption; and
- drunk driving.

Consideration will also be given to answering the rather more intriguing question, "Where to from here?" Much of what has been attempted in the past to encourage sensible use of alcohol has clearly worked, given that the majority of the consuming public does so in moderation most of the time, with few or no negative consequences associated with their drinking practices.

However, it is also evident that we can improve our performance in teaching young people to better understand alcohol, with the goal of encouraging those who choose to drink to do so in moderation. In particular, there is untapped scope to delineate those occasions where "at-risk" drinking is associated with increased potential for harm at an individual and/or societal level.

A Time of Global Change

The role of governments and judiciaries in relation to alcohol needs to be considered in the widest geopolitical context. Currently, the global economy is undergoing rapid change as we enter the new millennium. Well-established political and trading alliances are being "re-engineered" so as to take advantage of new opportunities for economic growth afforded by geopolitical changes in regions such as Eastern Europe and Asia/Pacific. Standards of living are falling as many economies encounter a period of stagnation or, in some instances, negative growth, while demands from consumers for access to wider ranges of products available elsewhere show no signs of diminishing. Inevitably, expanded opportunities for exporters include an increased capacity to market alcohol. The globalization of the market place is occurring at the same time that access to information via an explosion in communications technology is achieving unprecedented levels. Any individual with access to a computer can join the cyber revolution.

Information on almost any subject is available virtually instantaneously. The latest "cocktail" craze in downtown New York is available to the "net surfer" in Delhi, Moscow, Nairobi, and Melbourne. The desire to communicate is universal and the capacity to communicate, expanding exponentially, seems limited only by our individual and collective imaginations. However, given this new global environment which provides little or no effective barrier to the free exchange of information, irrespective of its veracity or benefit to the recipient, the role and relative influence of traditional community values is under increasing pressure.

It is the youth of most societies who have taken to the cyber revolution with the greatest alacrity. Given the range of materials available through this new medium, it should come as no surprise that the knowledge of young people about alcohol products should in many cases far exceed that of their parents. While the Internet is by no means the principal source of information about alcohol, its capacity to reach directly into the computers of young people should not be underestimated or discounted. Attempts to censor the Internet have thus far been doomed to fail. The capacity of parents, guardians, and the government to filter the type of information accessed by young people is significantly less than the capacity of the Internet literate to circumvent attempts at censorship.

One's ability to use the same Internet platform to carry messages of moderation is largely untapped at present. If such attempts are to be successful, the methodology used to sell moderation needs to be of a high standard to compete with the other "noise" that pervades the Internet. Efforts to form partnerships with key bodies, including the beverage alcohol industry, to carry messages of moderation on its websites should be explored.

The cachet value associated with so many alcohol brands should not be underestimated. Knowledge of and exposure to the latest designer drinks is really not so different from the desire for designer labels on clothing. Given the problems associated with governmental attempts at blocking Internet access, one is experiencing a real revolution in information exchange technology. The material world is available at the touch of a button, no matter whose finger might be exerting the downward pressure. The age of the "surfer" is no limiting factor to her or his ability to access the brave new world of instant information.

Community and Social Values

The consumption of alcohol is largely, although not exclusively, a social activity. As such, it is shaped to a significant extent by social determinants of behavior. Traditionally, community values have strongly influenced the types of alcohol consumed and the manner in which it has been consumed. Social norms have exerted a very powerful influence over the use of alcohol. Clearly, over the past decades this situation has undergone enormous change, particularly in the developed world. Traditional beer-drinking countries such as the United Kingdom and Australia have also seen shifts towards greater consumption of wine at the same time as lager has dramatically increased in popularity in the traditional home of wine, France. This assimilation of nontraditional drinking patterns has been coupled with substantial changes in the manner in which communities as political units have been reengineered. This is not meant to diminish the continued influence of community in determining cultural norms and standards with regard to the use of alcohol. The advent of centralized decision-making (where the central locus of control is considerably removed from the community it seeks to influence/control) and attempts to have consistent laws in relation to alcohol between neighboring jurisdictions are examples of such changes. The European Union stands as a prime example of this "new reality" as it seeks to come to terms with the various models in place for the management of beverage alcohol within the borders of its member states.

Regardless of the perspective held about alcohol policies, there is widespread agreement that for any policy to be successful it must attract a reasonable level of community acceptance it. In recent years, there has been growing concern expressed by community organizations and individuals over (a) underage drinking; and (b) alcohol-related violence and social problems. These issues have been identified in developing as well as developed countries, in rural as well as urban settings.

In acknowledging the importance and centrality of these issues, government has to determine if the strategies it employs to promote its alcohol policy are capable of addressing the community's concerns. If not, government should be sufficiently flexible to be able to alter the policy mix in favor of alternative strategies that elicit public support. A deeper appreciation of the desires of the community with regard to reasonable access to alcohol, coupled with sensible measures aimed at reducing misuse, is required if the policy options chosen by government are to be effective and supported. Placing additional controls on the freedom of all drinkers to purchase and consume alcohol in order to influence the behavior of young and often new recruits to drinking is fraught with difficulty. While tolerance of such impositions is likely to be high at a time when public intoxication or publicly perceived alcohol-related violence is manifest, tolerance will diminish perceptibly in the absence of such phenomena.

It is the role of government to put in place the regulatory framework that provides for the maximum private and public benefit with the minimum burden on public-private decision-making. It is also the role of government to offer some degree of protection to the at-risk or vulnerable as well as to reflect community norms and values accurately. Further, government should play a proactive role in fostering community norms and attitudes with respect to beverage alcohol that are conducive to its use in a low-risk manner.

What Role for Government and the Law?

Drinking behavior is complex and is influenced by a multitude of factors. The complex array of determinants that may impinge on whether individuals drink, how much they drink, and where they choose to drink has been traditionally construed as being influenced by control issues such as:

- price, promotion, and access;
- law enforcement;
- public health pressures (e.g., anti-drunk-driving messages);
- cultural norms;
- religiosity and religious persuasion;
- individual factors (including socioeconomic status);
- psychosocial factors (such as drinking expectancies);
- economic factors.

Our individual and collective approach to alcohol, and the manner in which we learn about drinking, are inextricably linked to each of the factors highlighted above. A shift in focus away from a singular preoccupation with the harms associated with drinking and alcohol per se to a position whereby the positive and beneficial aspects of drinking are also acknowledged and meaningfully translated has not been a particular aspect of governmental strategy to date.

At one level, the question for governments to answer is a simple one. What are the key messages one wishes to offer to young people in regard to alcohol? It would appear on the basis of much that has been written regarding the development and implementation of alcohol policies that the dominant orientations to date have been:

- strategies aimed at discouraging alcohol consumption among young people below the legal age for purchase and or consumption of alcohol; and
- strategies aimed at highlighting the dangers associated with the consumption of alcohol.

Approaches utilized include mass media information campaigns, school-based alcohol education programs, legislation and local government regulation, and law enforcement strategies. The policies driving these strategies have largely been developed as a manifestation of the alcohol control policy model, which has dominated the alcohol legislative arena in most countries around the world over the past 10 to 20 years.

HEALTH, HARMS AND ALCOHOL CONTROL

The overt inclusion of health objectives in alcohol licensing legislation is a relatively recent phenomenon. Previously, legislation tended to have safeguarding the interests of the alcohol and hospitality industries as its primary focus. However, in more recent years there has been growing recognition of the association between excessive alcohol consumption and a wide range of health and social problems.

Alcohol-Related Harms

Traditionally, alcohol-related harms have been perceived as those types of problems resulting from long-term chronic heavy alcohol use. Not unexpectedly, much of the alcohol control research literature has also focused on strategies designed to protect heavy drinkers or those who are alcohol-dependent. Scant attention had been focused on other patterns of drinking until relatively recently. It is now widely recognized that attention needs to be directed to intoxication and other acute effects, dependence, and regular use.

The appropriate forms of control and prevention strategies that are most effective for these three categories of alcohol-related problems are potentially different. For instance, strategies to minimize intoxication (e.g., service refusal, server liability) may be quite different from strategies to minimize problems of dependence (e.g., early opening hours and hours of extended trading). Increasing interest has been directed to the issue of intoxication as a major contributor to public health problems and to overall levels of community safety. A key public health message today is to avoid intoxication and, when at risk of intoxication, to take extra safety precautions (Roche, 1997).

This is especially important in relation to young people, as surveys suggest that alcohol use may be associated with risky sexual behavior and increased vulnerability to coercive sexual activity. Among adolescents surveyed in New Zealand, alcohol misuse was significantly associated with unprotected intercourse and sexual activity before the age of 16 (Fergusson & Lynskey, 1996). Among sexually active Massachusetts teenagers, 44% said that they were more likely to have sexual intercourse if they had been drinking, and 17% said they were less likely to use condoms after drinking (Strunin & Hingson, 1992). These findings have important public health implications, especially in communities where alcohol consumption levels among teenagers are particularly high (and also given their propensity to and overt intentions of drinking to achieve intoxication). The outcome to be sought by government in this area should be to reduce the likelihood of young people consuming alcohol in such a manner as to increase the potential for risky sexual behavior.

Positive alcohol-related expectancies[1] have also been identified as risk factors for adolescent drinking. Positive expectancies about alcohol have been found to increase with age (Miller, Smith, & Goldman, 1990) and to predict the onset of drinking and problem drinking among adolescents (Christiansen, Smith, Roehling, & Goldman, 1989; Smith, Goldman, Greenbaum, & Christiansen, 1995; Smith & Goldman, 1994). Certain expectancies are related not only to earlier and more frequent drinking, but also to the potential for violence. Governments can play a role in fostering positive and low-risk expectancies around alcohol. These issues are examples of some as yet relatively new and uncharted waters to be explored.

TRADITIONAL GOVERNMENTAL APPROACHES

To canvass the range of options available to governments in relation to managing alcohol, the following section of this chapter outlines some of the traditional responses that have been taken. The underlying concepts and precepts on which many of these approaches have been based are also highlighted.

Availability Theory

Most alcohol policies in developed countries over the past two to three decades have been predicated on the "availability theory" of consumption. This theory in essence holds that:

1. increased availability results in increased consumption;
2. increased consumption results in increased alcohol-related problems.

The corollary of this position is that in order to reduce alcohol-related problems in a community, control policies are required which reduce access to and consumption of alcohol. This orientation toward alcohol has driven alcohol control policies and most prevention strategies for the last several decades, although there are now alternative models and growing opposition to unduly simplistic availability theories and their uncritical application in policy.

Traditional alcohol control theory has been limited in its focus and has not widely addressed the full range of issues that have an impact on alcohol use and

[1] Alcohol expectancies are essentially the beliefs that individuals hold about the effects of alcohol on their behavior, moods and emotions. They are seen to be an important factor in the early motivations that underlie drinking behavior.

on alcohol-related harms and potential strategies for minimizing such harms. Factors that have been identified as exerting an impact on alcohol consumption and levels of alcohol-related harms, and over which there is a scope for government intervention, include the following:

- alcohol content of beverages;
- density of alcohol outlets;
- minimum drinking age;
- responsible beverage service;
- server liability;
- hours and days of sale;
- alcohol advertising/marketing strategies; and
- alcohol beverage labeling practices.

Holder and Edwards (1995) have described how public policy has been used as a tool to reduce problems involving alcohol. Governments in most industrialized societies have outlawed or limited private production of alcohol and thus have made alcohol a legal product that must either be supervised by government or actually produced and distributed by government. As a result, alcohol products have probably been the most regulated legal commodity in most industrialized countries today. Questions arise as to whether this degree of government regulation is appropriate or excessive, necessary for the public good, or a hindrance to individual freedom of choice.

It is also important to note the degree to which such regulation is actually enforced. There is strong evidence to indicate, for instance, that there is extreme reluctance on the part of many law enforcement officers or liquor licensing authorities to actively enforce compliance with the relevant legislation. Hence, while many control strategies are successful revenue-generating techniques, they frequently fail to act as adequate public health strategies because of a lack of enforcement at the point of delivery (Jeffs & Saunders, 1983). Failure to implement laws available on the statute books to inhibit access to alcohol or reduce the likelihood of overconsumption inevitably leads to the flouting of the laws by the young people that the legal frameworks have been established to protect. If young people know that there is little chance that they will be discovered and/or penalized for underage drinking, then the greater the likelihood is that they will engage in this disapproved of behavior.

On the basis of the evidence, it is the view that overall availability of alcohol (the central strand of much international alcohol policy) is too blunt and insensitive a measure to be used in isolation to determine or guide the development of alcohol policies. The number of outlets and hours of trading are not always strong and consistent predictors of problems, with some important exceptions, such as remote and geographically isolated areas or in concert with certain socioeconomic circumstances (e.g., high unemployment levels, lack of social restraints).

Price

Price remains one of the consistent measures and predictors of alcohol consumption in general terms. At specific points in time, pricing and other strategies (e.g., free drinks, cheap drinks), which encourage excessive consumption and intoxication with the potential for obvious harmful consequences, are strongly contraindicated.

Licensed Environment

The nature of the licensed environment is highly predictive of problems. Recent studies have demonstrated the extent to which such environments are amenable to problem reduction. A wide range of problem reduction and problem containment strategies now exist that are highly supported by empirical evidence (Homel, 1997; McKnight & Streff, 1994; Saltz, 1987).

Substantial scope, therefore, exists for governments and other key players to more fully utilize the potential in the licensed environment to minimize harms associated with alcohol use. Emphasis should be placed on the nature of the licensed premise and enforcement of the regulations, rather than simply the regulation of the number and density of outlets.

Improved controls to prevent sales to underage drinkers and intoxicated patrons are of increasing importance, with evidence of need to improve compliance in this area. Ease of access to alcohol for young and very young drinkers is highly predictive of problems (Wagenaar et al., 1996). As these drinkers do not usually frequent on-license premises, there are important implications here for the provision of alcohol through off-license premises such as supermarkets, convenience stores, and petrol stations. There is a good basis for curtailing the sale of alcohol through these outlets, or at the very least, requiring sales staff to be of legal drinking age and registered and trained to sell alcohol.

Enforcement strategies have been demonstrated to have great potency but are generally underutilized. Lack of enforcement needs to be treated seriously and addressed in a systematic manner at a structural level.

Internationally, there has been increasing interest in the introduction of educational and facilitative roles for liquor licensing authorities. It is evident that many providers of alcohol are unaware of many aspects of the liquor licensing legislation in force. The likelihood of achieving compliance is therefore substantially compromised. This can be easily remedied and licensing authorities provide an obvious vehicle through which this could be achieved. Examples of proactive strategies on the part of licensing authorities include:

- voluntary or compulsory training programs for managers and staff of licensed premises;
- regular communications to licensed premises on the nature of changes to legislation and particular activities of the licensing authority aimed at ensuring compliance;

- updates on revocation of licenses for outlets that fail to observe the regulations; and
- regular meetings with representatives of the commercial and retail sectors of the industry to promote a partnership approach to reduce on-premise problems.

Simplicity in Alcohol Legislationpoint to identifies the importance of clear and simpler liquor laws. This is needed both for ready comprehension by the general public and also to facilitate enforcement. To date, confusing and convoluted laws have served only to befuddle the public and impede enforcement. Public acceptance of strategies has been repeatedly found to be essential for the successful implementation of and compliance with alcohol laws. Experience around the world suggests that consultation with the general public is essential in any revision of alcohol legislation (Holder & Edwards, 1995).

Given the highly variable and situation-specific nature of much of the evidence about alcohol availability and harms, it is desirable that changes to existing legislation be implemented in an incremental and step-wise fashion. In this way, major changes are not introduced which later prove to be both unsatisfactory and difficult to amend or revoke.

Legal Age of Consumption

The legal age for consumption of alcohol varies considerably from country to country. The rationale often stated to justify the imposition of a minimum age for purchase and/or consumption of alcohol is that younger people are neither physically nor emotionally ready for the use of a psychoactive substance such as alcohol. It is well recognized that high-risk behaviors generally (Strunin & Hingson, 1992), and drinking to intoxication in particular, are more common among young people, and especially among young males (National Drug Strategy, 1996; Wyllie, Millard, & Zhang, 1996).

Recent Australian data indicate that young people are drinking more at an earlier age and that more of them are drinking at hazardous or harmful levels (National Drug Strategy, 1996) as defined by the National Health and Medical Research Council (Pols & Hawks, 1992). There is also substantial evidence that younger drinkers are more likely to sustain acute alcohol-related harms than older drinkers (Casswell, Zhang, & Wyllie, 1993).

Surveys from the U.S. undertaken prior to the enactment of uniform drinking age laws showed that adolescents from states with higher drinking ages were more likely to abstain from drinking and less likely to be heavy drinkers (Maisto & Rachal, 1980). They also reported fewer incidents of drinking and driving and less frequent intoxication.

Other studies have also shown a significant relationship between early drinking and later heavy drinking and alcohol-related problems (Chou & Pickering, 1992; Fillmore, Harka, Johnstone, Leino, Motoyoshi, & Temple, 1991). Studies on the effects of changes in drinking age laws have substantiated these findings. Such studies have routinely found that lowering the drinking age increases adolescent drinking and driving, whereas raising the drinking age decreases adolescent drinking and driving (e.g., Arnold, 1985; Cook & Tauchen, 1984; Saffer & Grossman, 1987; Smith, Hingson, Morelock, Heeren, Mucalel, Mangione, & Scotch, 1984; Wagenaar, 1986a, 1986b).

Table 1 (International Center for Alcohol Policies, 1998) summarizes the minimum drinking and purchasing age laws in 54 countries. The disparity between various countries shown in this table reflects cultural as well as historical and geopolitical realities.

Underage Purchasing

Studies of underage purchasing consistently confirm the ease with which young people can buy alcohol (Hingson et al., 1983; Preusser & Williams, 1992; Wagenaar et al., 1996). In a number of studies in the U.S., nearly 50% of alcohol sales in off-sale outlets were sold to apparent minors (Forster, McGovern, Wagennar, Wolfson, Perry, & Anstine, 1994, 1995). Off-license wine markets and supermarkets have been found to be principal sources of alcohol supply for youth aged 14 to 17 years (Wyllie, et al., 1996). Given the increased levels of consumption among younger teenagers and their increased propensity to drink to intoxication, this is an area warranting close attention, especially as enforcement of sales to minors is commonly lax (Wagenaar & Wolfson, 1995).

Warning Labels on Beverage Alcohol Containers

The requirement for labels carrying information to warn consumers of risks associated with drinking alcohol in certain circumstances is mandated in at least nine countries (International Center for Alcohol Policies, 1997). Such messages cover the full spectrum of advice from the generic to the specific.

The impact of warning labels on the consumption intentions of young people has not been specifically analyzed. However, there is little evidence to support the view that warning labels on their own have any impact on drinking behavior (MacKinnon, 1995). A review of the likely impact of warning labels carried out for the Alcohol Advisory Council of New Zealand (Evans, 1991) concluded that there were three main criticisms of the approach:

- Small size of the product warning information is a major impediment to its utility.
- Definitive evidence supporting its effectiveness in achieving behavior change is lacking.
- There is potential for immunization against the impacts of warning statements.

Governments have a responsibility to provide accurate and timely advice to young people as they reach a point in their lives where the legal consumption of

Table 1 Minimum drinking and purchasing age laws—March 1998

Country	Minimum drinking age (MDA)	Minimum purchasing age (MPA)	Notes
Argentina	18	—	
Australia	18	18	State and territory laws prohibit the sale or serving of alcohol to those under 18.
Austria	—	16, 18 in some cases for spirits.	On-premises consumption of alcohol is subject to provincial regulation. In general, the MDA is 16. Some provinces also prohibit the consumption of spirits for those under 18.
Azerbaijan	No MDA	No MPA	
Belgium	16	16	The law prohibits anyone under 16 (unless married or accompanied by a parent or guardian) from entering a "dance hall" where fermented beverages are sold.
Brazil	18	—	
Canada	In Alberta, Manitoba, and Quebec, it is 19; in all other provinces, 19	All provinces have their own legal MPA.	Drinking by minors under adult supervision is permitted in licensed premises in provinces of Manitoba and New Brunswick and at home in Prince Edward Island, Alberta, British Columbia, Ontario and Saskatchewan.
Chile	18	—	
China	No MDA	—	
Colombia	18	—	
Czech Republic	18	—	
Denmark	—	18	There are no age restrictions on sales for off-license consumption.
Estonia	18	—	
Finland	18	18, 20	The MDA for on-premises consumption of all alcoholic beverages is 18; for off-premises consumption the MPA for beverages up to 21% alcohol by volume is 18. The MPA for spirits is 20.
France	16	16	
Georgia	No MDA	No MPA	

Germany	16, 18	16, 18	The MDA and MPA is 16 for beer and wine and 18 for spirits.
Hong Kong	18	No MPA	
Hungary	18	—	
Iceland	20	—	
Indonesia	—	16	
Ireland	18	18	Individuals under 18 are allowed in bars, but those under 15 must be accompanied by a parent or guardian.
Israel	18	—	
Italy	16	16	
Japan	20	20	
Korea (Rep. of)	21	—	21 years of age; or a college student, if under 21.
Latvia	18	—	
Lithuania	18	—	
Luxembourg	17, 18	18	The on-premises MDA is 17 if accompanied by an adult.
Malaysia	21	—	
Mexico	18	—	
Moldova	18	18	
Mongolia	18	18	Parents and guardians may not offer alcohol beverages to their children under 18.
Netherlands	—	16, 18	The MPA for spirits is 18, 16 if accompanied by an adult. The MPA for beer and wine is 16.
New Zealand	20 (with some exceptions)	20 (with some exceptions)	In designated areas alcohol may be sold to those between 18 and 20 who are having a meal or are accompanied by their parent, guardian, or spouse aged over 20.
Norway	18, 20	18, 20	The MPA for spirits is 20. For beer and wine the MPA is 18.
Peru	18	—	
Poland	—	18	The MPA for alcoholic beverages (more than 4.5% alcohol by weight) is 18. There is no minimum purchasing age for beverages under 4.5% ABV.
Portugal	No MDA	No MPA	
Russia	—	21	
Slovakia	18	—	
Slovenia	18	18	"Applies only to buying or drinking in public places such as bars or discos."

(continued)

Table 1 (*Continued*)

Country	Minimum drinking age (MDA)	Minimum purchasing age (MPA)	Notes
South Africa	18	18	
Spain	16	16	Those under 16 may purchase beer and wine if accompanied by their parents.
Sweden	18	18, 20	Class 1 beer is non-alcoholic and no age restrictions apply. Off-license purchases have different age limits: the MPA for buying beer from food stores is 18, the MPA for buying other alcohol beverages at Systembolaget stores is 20.
Switzerland	14–18	14–18	Federal law prohibits supplying spirits to those under 18. The MDA and MPA for beer and wine are controlled by the cantons and vary between 14 and 16.
Thailand	No MDA	—	
Turkey	—	18	
Turkmenistan	18	18	
Ukraine	21	21	
United Kingdom	18	18	In bars and off-licensed premises the MDA and MPA are 18. The MPA for beer and cider is 16 when purchased for consumption with meals (except when in a bar). Children over 5 may consume alcoholic beverages at home with a parent's consent.
United States	21*	21**	*In 19 states alcohol consumption by youth under 21 is not specifically illegal. **Exceptions to the 21 law in some states include possession for religious purposes when accompanied by a parent, spouse, or legal guardian; medical reasons; in private clubs or establishments; and in the course of lawful employment by a duly licensed manufacturer.
Uruguay	18	—	
Venezuela	18	—	

alcohol becomes a reality. Warning labels on alcohol containers do not provide a useful means of furthering the knowledge or understanding of young people beyond what they already have.

Compliance and Enforcement of Laws

There is substantial international evidence that many alcohol laws suffer from inadequate enforcement. In some instances, this is held to be because the laws themselves are too complex (note, for example, caveats that exist for legal drinking ages) and open to subjective interpretation (for example, the assessment of intoxication). As a result, the laws are frequently inadequately enforced. This has especially been found to be the case for off-license premises, an important source of supply for young drinkers.

In an effort to simplify and thereby improve the probability of effective enforcement, some jurisdictions are opting for simplified liquor laws. In New Zealand, it has recently been proposed that the legal age for drinking be based solely on the criterion of age in contrast to the overly complex, confusing, and difficult to enforce laws that previously governed legal consumption. The New Zealand Government has passed legislation reducing the minimum purchase age for alcohol to 18 years. Prior to this change, the nominal age for purchase was 20 years. However, there were a large number of exceptions to the purchase age. For all practical purposes, the legal age was 18. Research also indicates that compliance with legislation can be achieved through greater threat and expectation of prosecution. Strategies that have demonstrated improved compliance with the legislation have included increased police visibility and successful local prosecutions (Jeffs & Saunders, 1983; Stockwell, 1993). Some argue that licenses should be easier to obtain, but also vastly easier to lose, than they are at present.

Licensed Environments and Harms

With the recent and growing adoption of harm minimization over availability control approaches, a variety of new strategies have taken on greater significance. Extensive research has now identified a range of features of the physical and social environments of bars and other drinking environments that may help to reduce the rates of aggression, or limit the harm caused by aggressive incidents that are often associated with them (Hauritz, Homel, McIlwain, Burrows, & Townsley, 1998). Identified features include: attractive, nicely furnished, well-maintained bars, and comfortable, uncrowded surroundings that promote enjoyment and do not irritate or frustrate people; a social atmosphere with clear rules and limits; practices that discourage drinking to intoxication and foster a positive social atmosphere; and the employment of trained, peace-loving bar workers and security staff (Hauritz et al., 1998).

Crowding has also been identified as one among a number of key factors that acts as a major contributor to violence on licensed premises (MacIntyre

& Homel, 1997). Other practical harm minimization considerations involve elements of the drinking environment. The use of tempered (toughened) glass, for instance, in place of conventional annealed glass in bars and pubs is increasingly being urged (McClean, Sheperd, Brann, & Westmoreland, 1997).

Responsible Server Programs

Host responsibility and responsible management practices are increasingly seen as the key to improving the drinking environment (Saltz, 1987; Single, 1994). Bar staff who continue to serve "obviously intoxicated" patrons have also been identified as a predictor of harm (Stockwell, Lang, & Rydon, 1993). Thus, on-license premises offer important opportunities for effective prevention and enforcement efforts (McKnight & Streff, 1994; Room, 1984).

Responsible server programs have become a common way to reduce alcohol-related harms over the past decade. Such approaches have been found to be quite effective, especially if combined with enforcement (Putnam, Rockett, & Campbell, 1993; Saltz, 1987; Stockwell, 1997). Server training, now mandatory in some states in the U.S., educates alcohol servers to alter their serving practices, particularly with underage customers and those who show obvious signs of intoxication. Server training explains the effects of alcohol, applicable laws, how to refuse service to obviously intoxicated patrons, and how to assist customers in obtaining transportation as an alternative to driving. Some, but not all, studies report more interventions with customers after server training than before. One evaluation of the effects of Oregon's mandatory server-training policy indicates that it had a statistically significant effect on reducing the incidence of traffic crashes in that state (Holder & Wagenaar, 1994).

It has been argued that prevention involves a shift from thinking in terms of offenders and their motivations to offenses and their settings, which in the case of licensed premises implies a focus on management practices that give rise to unsafe environments (Hauritz et al., 1998).

Aspects of safe environments include:

- alcohol serving practices;
- physical design;
- selection and training of security staff;
- the permissiveness of the social climate in venues; and
- hidden deals between managers and police.

Situational theory has been applied to the drinking environment and includes:

- rule setting (through codes of practice);
- stimulating conscience (by encouraging managers to regard themselves as responsible businessmen);

- controlling disinhibitors (by controlling alcohol through server intervention); and
- facilitating compliance (by creating a regulatory environment in which it is financially worthwhile for licensees to adhere to the code of practice) (Hauritz et al., 1998).

Local Initiatives and Community Actions

Achieving compliance with existing alcohol licensing legislation has mostly proved challenging. A number of projects have been undertaken both in Australia and overseas to determine ways to facilitate compliance. One such approach was the Queensland Surfers Paradise Safety Action project, conducted over several years from the early 1990s, which was based on self-regulation informally monitored by the local community.

Homel (1997) reports that this approach worked well in the short term, with a marked reduction in violence in and around licensed premises. But success was followed by a return within 2 years to preproject levels of alcohol-related violence and aggression.

Policies Can Create Problems as Well as Alleviate Them

It has been argued that alcohol-related problems associated with licensed drinking environments not only exist because of the inherent nature of many such environments and because of the psychoactive properties of alcohol, but that this potentially volatile mix can be further exacerbated. Hauritz et al. (1998) hold that certain antecedent conditions, such as a political environment emphasizing deregulation of liquor licensing, leads to problem behaviors, such as cut-throat competition between venues and irresponsible drinks promotion. That is, the existence of certain types of policy positions, or the perception of certain policy positions, can actually create alcohol-related problems. Such extreme circumstances are held to have contributed to the ground-swell of interest in community mobilization and community development as alternative strategies to enforcement in addressing out-of-hand situations, as the Surfers Paradise situation was seen to be.

CONTROL POLICIES VERSUS HARM MINIMIZATION APPROACHES

In recent years, there have been a number of challenges to the traditional precepts underpinning alcohol control policies. One argument is that reduced alcohol consumption is not necessarily required to reduce problems associated with alcohol.

Empirical evidence to support this position is found in the data on the reduction of alcohol-related road trauma and random breath testing (RBT) in

Australia. The evidence of the efficacy of RBT is probably the most persuasive of any form of community intervention and prevention approaches (Homel, 1993). Significant improvements were achieved with respect to alcohol-related road trauma, including both morbidity and mortality, without changing (or even attempting to change) the overall level of alcohol consumption among the targeted communities.

> In many countries, public emphasis regarding responses to the alcohol question has come to be laid more and more on education, information, and treatment, in recent decades. In addition, market forces and economic considerations have increasingly overshadowed preventive policies, and in some countries a strengthening of liberal attitudes has led to a stress on individual responsibility and a denial of the justification of any control measures. Accordingly, limiting the physical availability of alcoholic beverages or imposing high taxation as a means to control consumption and related harmful effects, are nowadays regarded by an increasing number of people as an archaic patchwork of laws and as irrelevant to contemporary life (Österberg, 1995).

Therein lies the current dilemma. Contemporary trends are in the direction of deregulation, free markets, and individual responsibility of consumers. Underlying contemporary public policy is a much broader view of alcohol-involved problems. Alcohol problems are now described by most countries and the World Health Organization (WHO) as public health concerns. The mid-1970s saw a major shift in focus away from an exclusive orientation to the problems of the relatively few alcohol-dependent individuals towards an emphasis and concern for the population overall.

Community Views and Acceptance of Alcohol Policies

For any government-imposed or initiated alcohol policy aimed at ameliorating the impacts of alcohol-related harms to be effective, there needs to be a high level of community support. Indeed, there tends to be widespread agreement, regardless of the perspective held about alcohol control policies, that for any policy to be successful there must be a reasonable level of community acceptance. Public support and compliance are essential to prevent policies from being circumvented (Edwards et al., 1994). Many potentially efficacious interventions have low community acceptance. An example of this would be raising the drinking age in Australia to 21 years, as in the U.S.

The National Drug Strategy household survey of 1995 (1996) reported general support for a range of policy initiatives designed to reduce the harm caused by alcohol. The most frequently supported (by more than 90% of the population) were policies aimed directly at drunk persons, including stricter enforcement of the law against serving customers who are already drunk, and more severe penalties for drunk drivers. The least popular policy, not unexpectedly, was increasing the price of alcohol, supported by just 33% of respondents.

It is important to note that in successful community interventions projects, such as that undertaken by Holder et al. (1997) in the U.S., there is speculation that at least some of the success of the projects was attributable to increased levels of community awareness and community debate about strategies such as responsible beverage service (Saltz & Stanghetta, 1997).

DIRECTIONS FOR THE NEW MILLENNIUM

In the text box, a summary is provided of the traditional governmental controls exercised over alcohol as described by Giesbrecht (1995).

Traditional Government Controls on Alcohol

- Facilitate the distribution and sale of alcoholic beverages in a manner that does not increase social, health, or safety risks to consumers or other citizens.
- Provide a wide range of alcohol in a convenient and responsible manner to legitimate customers, with information available to the customers about the products as well as the risks of inappropriate or excessive consumption.
- Display and sell these products in safe and pleasant venues.
- Ensure quality control of the products sold so that the products do not contain poisons or toxins (other than alcohol), or at levels above acceptable public health standards.
- Provide a pricing structure and support for or implementation of other control measures that ensure that consumption rates and risky use patterns do not increase.
- Prevent the sale of alcoholic products to persons who are below the legal drinking age, or are under the influence of alcohol.
- In collaboration with police, liquor inspectors, customs officials, and others, monitor and curtail the smuggling of alcoholic products from elsewhere, the bootlegging of alcoholic products, and the illegal production and sale of alcoholic products.
- Provide the state with revenues in a cost-effective manner.
- Continually be aware of the need for balancing a multiple agenda and demands: revenue generation, retail distribution and sales, customer service, and public health and safety concerns.
- Work collaboratively with appropriate agencies and institutions in achieving that revenue generating, retail/commercial, consumer service, and public health and safety agenda, and ensure that there is a balanced, diverse, and arm's length arrangement in contacts with agencies, interest groups, and organizations representing a wide range of perspectives and agendas.

Future models for government and lawmakers also need to be predicated on promoting a sense of personal responsibility in terms of alcohol consumption, while simultaneously balancing the needs of communities to exercise moderation and some degree of control over this product. Examples of approaches can include those outlined below.

Low-Risk Drinking Guidelines

One of the greater challenges for government is to establish low-risk drinking guidelines without fear that this is an attempt to encourage excessive drinking, but rather as an attempt to provide the general public and consumers with clear and accurate information. Such guidelines should recognize community standards and be provided in an accessible and meaningful format. Furthermore, consideration should be given to the use of multimedia avenues to disseminate information in a balanced and appropriate manner that maximizes the probability of the consumer interpreting the guidelines so as to reduce any risks associated with their drinking.

Alcohol and Harm Minimization

Considerable potential exists for governments to apply harm minimization principles and practices, largely developed for application in the illicit drug area, to reduce harms associated with risky alcohol consumption. Strategies aimed at risk reduction and harm containment have been well received and adopted in a number of settings. A shift in emphasis away from mean consumption to patterns of consumption provides an opportunity for the application of strategies which have a capacity to reduce the level of alcohol-related harm without necessarily altering the overall alcohol consumption level of an individual, community, or society (Heather, 1993). One of the principal platforms of harm reduction is the importance of shifting emphasis away from *consumption* per se to the consequences of consumption—that is, not how much we drink, but rather the way in which we drink. When alcohol consumption is viewed from a harm reduction perspective the focus shifts away from the question of use (regardless of level) to more telling concerns addressing any consequences of use. It is recommended that this be a guiding principle for governments in years to come.

Finally, it is important to pay attention to the "context" in which alcohol is consumed, to situate such consumption in the beliefs and social practices of particular communities and to understand the meaning that alcohol has for consumers. Rehm, Ashley, Room, Single, Bandy, Ferrence, and Gresbrecht (1996) suggests that

> [we] need to make fewer value judgements about alcohol as a substance and talk more about the consequences of mixing alcohol use with behaviors such as workplace tasks, driving a car, or leisure activities—that have an element of danger (p. 5).

REFERENCES

Arnold, R. D. (1985). *Effect of raising the legal drinking age on driver involvement in fatal crashes: The experience of 13 states* (DOT HS 806-902). Washington, DC: Department of Transportation, National Highway Traffic Safety Administration.

Casswell, S., Zhang, F. F., & Wyllie, A. (1993). The importance of amount and location of drinking for the experience of alcohol-related problems. *Addiction, 88*, 1527–1534.

Chou, S. P., & Pickering, R. P. (1992). Early onset of drinking as a risk factor for lifetime alcohol-related problems. *British Journal of Addiction, 87*(8), 1199–1204.

Christiansen, B. A., Smith, G. T., Roehling, P. V., & Goldman, M. S. (1989). Attitudes, expectancies, and adolescent drinking behaviour after one year. *Journal of Consulting and Clinical Psychology, 57*(1) 93–99.

Cook, P. J., & Tauchen, G. (1984). Effect of minimum drinking age legislation on youthful auto fatalities, 1970–1977. *Journal of Legal Studies, 13*, 169–190.

Edwards, G., Anderson, P., Babor, T., Casswell, S., Ferrence, R., Giesbrecht, N., Godfrey, C., Holder, H., Lemmons, P., Makela, K., Norstrom, T., Osterberg, E., Romelsjo, A., Room, R., Simpura, J., Skog, O. J. (1994). *Alcohol policy and the public good.* Oxford, UK: Oxford University Press.

Evans, K. (1991). *Health messages on alcohol containers.* Position paper prepared for the Alcoholic Liquor Advisory Council, New Zealand.

Fergusson, D. M., & Lynskey, M. T. (1996). Alcohol misuse and adolescent sexual behaviours and risk taking. *Paediatrics, 98*, 91–96.

Fillmore, K. M., Hartka, E., Johnstone, B. M., Leino, E. V., Motoyoshi, M., & Temple, M. T. (1991). A meta-analysis of life course variation in drinking: The Collaborative Alcohol-Related Longitudinal Project. *British Journal of Addiction, 86*, 1221–1268.

Forster, J. L., McGovern, P. G., Wagennar, A. C., Wolfson, M., Perry, C. L., & Anstine, P. S. (1994). Ability of young people to purchase alcohol without age identification in northeastern Minnesota, USA. *Addiction, 89*(6), 699–705.

Forster, J. L., Murray, D. M., Wolfson, M., & Wagennar, A. C. (1995). Commercial availability of alcohol to young people: Results of alcohol purchase attempts. *Preventive Medicine, 24*(4), 342–347.

Giesbrecht, N. (1995, November). *Proposed privatisation of retail alcohol sales in Ontario: Health, social, economic and safety implication.* Paper presented at the Information Symposium on Alcohol Privatisation/Deregulation, Addiction Research Foundation, Toronto, Canada.

Hauritz, M., Homel, R., McIlwain, G., Burrows, T., & Townsley, M. (1998). Reducing violence in licensed venues through community safety action projects: The Queensland experience. *Contemporary Drug Problems, 25*, 511–551.

Heather, N. (1993). Application of harm-reduction principles to the treatment of alcohol problems. In N. Heather, A Wodak, E. A. Nadelmann, & P. O'Hare (Eds.), *Psychoactive drugs and harm reduction: From faith to science* (pp. 168–183). London: Whurr Publishers.

Hingson, R. W., Scotch, N., Mangione, T., Meyers, A., Glantz, L., Heeren, T., Lin, N., Mucatel, M., & Pierce, G. (1983). Impact of legislation raising the legal drinking age in Massachusetts from 18 to 20. *American Journal of Public Health, 73*, 163–169.

Holder, H., & Edwards, G. (1995). Research as a basis for rational policies on alcohol consumption. In H. Holder & G. Edwards (Eds.), *Alcohol and public policy: Evidence and issues.* New York: Oxford University Press.

Holder, H., & Wagenaar, A. C. (1994). Mandated server training and reduced alcohol-involved traffic crashes: A time series analysis of the Oregon experience. *Accident Analysis and Prevention, 26*, 89–97.

Holder, H. D., Saltz, R. F., Grube, J. W., Boas, R. B., Grunewald, P. J., & Treno, A. J. (1997). Community prevention trial to reduce alcohol-involved accidental injury and death: Overview. *Addiction, 92* (Suppl. 2), 155–171.

Homel, R. (1993). Random breath testing in Australia: Getting it to work according to specifications. *Addiction, 88* (Suppl.), 27S–33S.

Homel, R. (1997). Editor's introduction. Policing for prevention: Reducing crime, public intoxication and injury. In R. V. Clarke (Series Ed.) & R. Homel (Vol. Ed.), *Policing for prevention: Reducing crime, public intoxication and injury*. Monsey, NY: Criminal Justice Press.

International Center for Alcohol Policies (ICAP). (1997). *Health warning labels* (ICAP Reports No. 3). Washington, DC: ICAP.

International Center for Alcohol Policies (ICAP). (1998). *Drinking age limits* (ICAP Reports No. 4). Washington, DC: ICAP.

Jeffs, B. W., & Saunders, B. (1983). Minimising alcohol-related offences by enforcement of the existing licensing legislation. *British Journal of Addiction, 78*, 67–77.

MacIntyre, S., & Homel, R. (1997). Danger on the dance floor: A study of interior design, crowding and aggression in nightclubs. In R. Homel (Ed.), *Policing for prevention: Reducing crime, public intoxication and injury. Crime Prevention Studies* (Vol. 7). New York: Criminal Justice Press.

MacKinnon, D. P., & Woodward, J. A. (1986). The impact of raising the minimum drinking age on drive fatalities. *The International Journal of Addictions, 21*(12), 1331–1338.

Maisto, S. A., & Rachal, J. V. (1980). Indications of the relationship among adolescent drinking practices, related behaviors, and drinking age laws. In H. Wechsler (Ed.), *Minimum-drinking-age laws* (pp. 155–176). Lexington, MA: Lexington Books.

McClean, W., Sheperd, J. P., Brann, C. R., & Westmoreland, D. (1997). Risks associated with occupational injury in bar staff with special consideration of hepatitis B infection. *Occupational Medicine, 47*, 147–150.

McKnight, A. J., & Streff, F. M. (1994). The effect of enforcement upon service of alcohol to intoxicated patrons of bars and restaurants. *Accident Analysis and Prevention, 26*, 79–88.

Miller, P. M., Smith, G. T., & Goldman, M. S. (1990). Emergence of alcohol expectancies in childhood: A possible critical period. *Journal of Studies on Alcohol, 51*, 343–349.

National Drug Strategy. (1996). *Household Survey: Survey Report 1995*. Canberra: Commonwealth Department of Health.

Österberg, E. (1995). Do alcohol prices affect consumption and related problems? In H. Holder & G. Edwards (Eds.), *Alcohol and public policy: Evidence and issues* (pp. 145–163). New York: Oxford University Press.

Pols, R., & Hawks, D. V. (1992). *Is there a safe level of daily consumption of alcohol for men and women*. Canberra: Australian Government Publishing Service.

Preusser, D. F., & Williams, A. F. (1992). Sales of alcohol to underage purchasers in three New York counties and Washington, DC. *Journal of Public Health Policy, 13*, 306–317.

Putnam, S. I., Rockett, I. R., & Campbell, M. K. (1993). Methodological issues in community-based alcohol-related injury prevention projects: Attribution of program effects. In T. K. Greenfield & R. Zimmerman (Eds.), *Experiences with community action projects: New research in the prevention of alcohol and other drug problems* (CSAP Prevention Monograph No. 14, pp. 31–42). Rockville, MD: Center for Substance Abuse Prevention.

Rehm, J., Ashley, M. J., Room, R., Single, E., Bondy, S., Ferrence, R., & Giesbrecht, N. (1996). On the emerging paradigm of drinking patterns and their social and health consequences. *Addiction, 91*(11), 1615–1621.

Roche, A. M. (1997). The shifting sands of alcohol prevention: Rethinking population control approaches. *Australian and New Zealand Journal of Public Health, 21*, 621–625.

Roizen, J. (1997). Epidemiological issues in alcohol-related violence. In M. Galanter (Ed.), *Recent developments in alcoholism* (Vol. 13, pp. 7–40). New York: Plenum Press.

Room, R. (1984). Alcohol control and public health. *Annual Review of Public Health, 5*, 293–317.

Saffer, H., & Grossman, M. (1987). Beer taxes, the legal drinking age, and youth motor vehicle fatalities. *Journal of Legal Studies, 16*, 351–374.

Saltz, R. (1987). The roles of bars and restaurants in preventing alcohol-impaired driving: An evaluation of server training. *Evaluation in Health Professions, 10*, 5–27.

Saltz, R., & Stanghetta, P. A. (1997). A community wide Responsible Beverage Service program in three communities: Early findings. *Addiction, 92* (Suppl. 2), S237–S249.

Single, E. (1994). *What can we do about problematic drinking environments? Licensing initiatives in Canada*. Paper presented to the Perspective for Change Conference, Rotorua, New Zealand.

Smith, R. A., Hingson, R. W., Morelock, S., Heeren, T., Mucatel, M., Mangione, T., & Scotch, N. (1984). Legislation raising the legal drinking age in Massachusetts from 18 to 20: Effect on 16 and 17 year-olds. *Journal of Studies on Alcohol, 45*(6), 534–539.

Smith, G. T., & Goldman, M. S. (1994). Alcohol expectancy theory and the identification of high-risk adolescents. *Journal of Research on Adolescence, 4*, 229–247.

Smith, G. T., Goldman, M. S., Greenbaum, P. E., & Christiansen, B. A. (1995). Expectancy for social facilitation from drinking: The divergent paths of high-expectancy and low-expectancy adolescents. *Journal of Abnormal Psychology, 104*, 32–40.

Stockwell, T. (1993). Influencing the labelling of alcoholic beverage containers: Informing the public. *Addiction, 88* (Suppl.), 53–60.

Stockwell, T., Lang, E., & Rydon, P. (1993). High risk drinking settings: The association of serving and promotional practices with harmful drinking. *Addiction, 88*(11), 1519–1526.

Stockwell, T. (1997). Regulation of the licensed drinking environment: A major opportunity for crime prevention. In R. Homel (Ed.), *Policing for prevention: Reducing crime, public intoxication and injury* (pp. 7–33). Monsey, NY: Criminal Justice Press.

Strunin, L., & Hingson, R. (1992). Alcohol, drugs, and adolescent sexual behavior. *International Journal of the Addictions, 27*, 129–146.

Wagenaar, A. C. (1986a, January). Youth, alcohol, and traffic crashes. In: *Research issues in the prevention of alcohol-related injuries: Background draft papers* (pp.1–18).

Wagenaar, A. C. (1986b). The legal minimum drinking age in Texas: Effects on an increase from 18 to 19. *Journal of Safety Research, 17*, 165–178.

Wagenaar, A. C., & Wolfson, M. (1995). Deterring sales and provision of alcohol to minors: A study of enforcement in 295 counties in four states. *Public Health Reports, 110*, 419–427.

Wagenaar, A. C., Toomey, T., Murray, D. M., Short, B. J., Wolfson, M., Jones-Webb, R. (1996). Sources of alcohol for underage drinkers. *Journal of Studies in Alcohol, 57*, 325–333.

Wyllie, A., Millard, M., & Zhang, J. F. (1996). *Drinking in New Zealand: A national survey, 1995*. Auckland: Alcohol and Public Health Research Unit.

The Beverag Industry and Learning About Drinking

Gary Max and Graham Willersdorf

This volume looks at the influences by which communities learn or acquire their drinking patterns. Such drinking patterns are dynamic and have altered tremendously in the last three decades. In the so-called developed economies, alcohol consumption peaked in the mid to late 1970s and has steadily declined since that time. This fall, which occurred while economic output was generally growing and restrictions to alcohol availability were becoming more relaxed, can be partly explained by a growing concern with community health generally and specific programs to reduce the social, health, and economic costs of alcohol misuse more particularly. This has resulted in increased levels of education about drinking and the impact of alcohol.

The learning process is important for the young as they develop understanding of the familial, social, legal, health, and cultural environments in which drinking takes place in their community. It is also important for adults, who have demonstrated their capacity to change drinking patterns substantially, particularly in response to changes in attitudes to personal and community health and well-being.

A significant number of interventions have been employed to reduce misuse of alcohol by encouraging and/or prescribing more moderate consumption patterns. Many of these interventions have been initiated and implemented by governments (but, as this chapter demonstrates, not exclusively so). They can be broadly divided into three categories:

1 Controls over supply. This includes, for example, legislation governing hours for selling, sale of licenses, price manipulation and, in the extreme, product bans. As already noted, many of these controls have been generally relaxed in developed countries since the 1970s.
2 Legislative controls over unacceptable alcohol-related behavior. This incorporates penalties for drinking and driving, drunk and disorderly behavior, etc. The ability to detect and effectively penalize drivers who have consumed more than a prescribed legal amount of alcohol has had a major impact on drinking behavior, and this in turn has had a major impact on the drinking patterns of adults as well as the young.
3 Education to encourage more responsible use of alcohol. Educational programs cover a broad spectrum and now rarely reflect a temperance view; rather they reflect a change in attitude that accepts a harm minimization approach instead of attempting to prevent all consumption. That approach recognizes that alcohol consumption per se need not be harmful, and it is here that a common understanding between the alcohol beverage industry and the broader community (and its regulators) has fostered industry's contribution to education.

The alcohol beverage industry has become a significant contributor to programs in the third category, often reflecting a cooperative approach which provides benefits for industry as well as the community. This chapter offers a sample of some of the many programs the beverage alcohol industry has sponsored in partnership with a variety of actors, including government, universities, and research institutions, to educate young people about the safe, low-risk use of alcohol.

INDUSTRY AS PARTNER

The alcohol beverage industry is a vast array of competing companies, whose main interests lie in making a profit, although many of them recognize their obligation to be good corporate citizens and have developed their own social, environmental, or community-related programs. Clearly, making a profit is not unique to the alcohol beverage industry but is common to all private sector enterprises. Despite a climate of fierce competition between companies, however, there also exists a set of common beliefs that transcend this competition. Two are relevant to this chapter. First, the beverage alcohol industry members acknowledge that, although their products can offer considerable personal pleasure and social benefit, they can also cause serious personal and social harm if consumed irresponsibly. Secondly, preventing misuse of its products is in a company's long-term strategic interest and is therefore consistent with its economic objectives.

This latter point is sometimes viewed cynically because of the erroneous assumption that the alcohol beverage industry is willing to sell its products under any circumstances. Apart from its genuine desire to be socially concerned, reckless drinking, irresponsible advertising, or inappropriate promotional activities can have very serious consequences for the alcohol beverage industry in the form of more restrictive government regulation. The sponsors of the International Center for Alcohol Policies (ICAP) take pride in the products they produce, many of which have long and distinguished histories, and wish to have as free a reign as possible in making them available to those in the public who wish to consume them and are legally allowed to do so. Similarly, the responsible service of alcohol to consumers is vital for the health of businesses that retail alcoholic beverages. Both shareholders and corporate management know that turning a blind eye to misuse is ultimately bad for business.

The obvious question to be raised is, "What has the alcohol beverage industry done to contribute to minimizing risks associated with its products?" This chapter will now explore industry's contribution to the range of social and cultural factors that have an impact on particular patterns of alcohol use. Such contributions have ranged from wider social involvement down to the specific level of educating young people about the risks of alcohol beverages. It is recognized here that the range of factors that contribute to the experience of learning about alcohol is very diverse, and that diverse responses are also required on the part of the industry.

DEVELOPMENT OF SOCIAL ASPECTS ORGANIZATIONS

The involvement of the alcohol industry in alcohol education and social policy has quite a long history. In the 1930s, for example, Joseph E. Seagram and Sons, a leading U.S. and Canadian distiller, was running extensive advertising campaigns counseling moderation. Some of the advertisements stressed the importance of having parent-to-child discussions about alcohol or showed the connection between responsible consumption by an adult and youth behavior. Thus, the important role of the parent in shaping a young person's drinking behavior was being promoted even in the 1930s. More recently, Coors, Miller Brewing, and Anheuser-Busch, the leading U.S. brewers, have also been active in promoting moderation campaigns over the last two decades.

While these and other individual company initiatives continue, in the late 1980s a number of major international drinks companies began to take a broader look at the way the industry responded to alcohol issues, and particularly to issues affecting young people such as underage drinking and drinking and driving. The goal was to find a way forward that would not penalize the vast majority of drinkers who drink responsibly, but that would demonstrate real success in tackling alcohol misuse. The key to this new approach was the idea of "partnerships."

Those concerns led to the creation of social aspects organizations (SAOs), as these industry groups came to be called. They represent a contemporary approach on the part of the beverage alcohol industry to the promotion of responsible drinking and the reduction of alcohol misuse. Similarly, they reflect its desire to play a more dynamic and proactive role in the area of alcohol-related social policy. Social aspect organizations also reflect the industry's desire for a balanced policy debate to be conducted on the role of alcohol in society as well as the measures taken to address the potential for misuse.

In 1989, four SAOs existed. The first was Stichting Verantwoord Alcoholgebruik (STIVA), located in the Netherlands. Its views on industry involvement are as follows: "The alcohol industry wishes to make an active contribution to achieving a balanced policy on alcohol. It will do so by self-regulation, promoting scientific research, and by information provision and prevention" (Phoa, 1994, p. 12). It is the oldest SAO, incorporated in 1959, and has been active and taken seriously in policy and alcohol education discussions in the Netherlands for decades. The Industry Association for Alcohol (ARA) in South Africa, formerly known as the Social Aspects of Alcohol Committee, was established in 1986. It was founded to coordinate and direct the alcohol industry's efforts "to reduce and prevent the abuse of its products" (Social Aspects of Alcohol Committee of the South African Liquor Industry, n.d., p. 5). The Portman Group in the United Kingdom was set up in 1989 as was Educ'Alcool in Canada. The Portman Group's role is reflected in the current director's comment on the occasion of its tenth anniversary:

> When the UKs leading drinks companies set up The Portman Group in 1989, they showed they meant business about promoting sensible drinking and helping to prevent alcohol misuse. Cynics might argue that self-interest is a powerful factor, but others will work out that it's in everyone's interest to be part of the anti-misuse solution. The industry has benefited from The Portman Group's role in helping to drive up standards in marketing and promotion (Portman Group, 1999, p. 3).

Today over 30 SAOs exist, centered mainly in Europe and North America, but also in parts of Australasia and Africa. One of the newest SAOs is the SASPI set up in India in 1999. Society for alcohol social policy initiative's views on alcohol reflect a complex social environment. As posited in its introductory brochure, alcohol-related ". . . problems are rooted in the ethos of each society." Critical factors in the sensible and rational use of alcohol "are the availability of shelter, nutrition, productive employment and public health facilities" (Society for Alcohol and Social Policy Initiative, 1998, p. 1).

While the focus and specific activities are different in each country, often reflecting cultural differences, generally speaking the activities of SAOs address four main topics:

- delivering better education to young people (those in their teens to early 20s) and promoting greater understanding of alcohol and sensible drinking;
- discouraging drinking and driving;

- disseminating the sensible drinking idea for those who choose to drink; and
- developing and enhancing mechanisms for providing a level of self-regulation of industry marketing practices.

The partnerships that have developed over the years are a testament to how seriously these organizations and, indeed, the alcohol beverage industry more generally, have been taken. Partnerships include those with the Swedish Government, the Ministry of Public Health in Thailand, the University of Melbourne in Australia, Canada's College of Family Physicians, the University of Illinois in the U.S., the German and British Departments of Transport, the Ford Motor Company in Germany, the Spanish Association of Public Affairs, and the Institute of Traffic Safety in the Netherlands, to name but a few.

The activities of SAOs have covered substantial ground in the last decade, but individual companies and trade associations are also active partners in preventing alcohol abuse.

PARTNERSHIPS IN ACTION

While the anti-misuse activities sponsored by the alcohol beverage industry cover a range of topics, the lion's share of its efforts are focused on young people. There is no disputing that the transition from child to adolescent to adult can be a tricky period for many young people. The desire to be independent, with the feelings of invincibility that characterize adolescence, can be acted out in varied and potentially risky ways. It is a time of immense social learning, figuring out relationships, testing new ground, and it is incumbent upon all who make up their community to do their part in helping their passage be the safest possible. This requires not proscribing every potentially harmful item from their view, but rather equipping them with good decision-making skills and providing an environment that reduces the potential for harm but still allows them to learn, make decisions, and take ownership of their lives.

The partnerships that have developed from industry-sponsored programs support these kinds of goals, but in different ways around the world.

Young People

While drinking and driving is the main topic addressed by industry-sponsored programs, the larger issue of drinking by youth, in general, is also covered in many countries. Many of the current programs stress a message of moderation but also of responsibility—individual responsibility, peer group responsibility, and to a certain degree parental responsibility. In most cultures where drinking is a part of the social fabric of a country, there is a need to be consistent with the messages given to young people through informal social learning and to make the message appropriate to the age group (Plant & Plant, 1992; Russac

& Weaver, 1994). In most countries in Europe, for example, where drinking alcohol is very much a part of the culture, some alcohol education programs try to provide young people with factual information about drinking so that when they choose to drink, they can do so responsibly.

This is where the focus on parents' drinking behavior is paramount. As other chapters in this volume make clear (see, for example, Chapters 2, 3, 4, and 8), the family is a highly influential variable in a young person's early exposure to alcohol. Many industry-sponsored programs target adults, not only urging them to talk with their youngsters about alcohol but also discussing the influence that their drinking behavior has on young people.

The Portman Group, for example, developed a leaflet called *Discussing Drinking with Your Children*. This was distributed through doctors' surgeries, parent-teacher associations, and health promotion agencies in the United Kingdom. Gode Alkoholdninger (GODA), the SAO in Denmark, has produced a book entitled *Unge, Alkohol og Fester* (Young People, Alcohol, and Parties), which urges parents, teachers, and other adults responsible for young people to cooperate in making rules for the young people with regard to parties and alcohol.

In the U.S., The Century Council produced a video in collaboration with Boys & Girls Clubs of America called *Ready or Not—Talking with Kids about Alcohol* aimed at parents and adult supervisors of middle-school-age children (aged 10–14 years). The video illustrates five key steps in talking to children about alcohol. It is accompanied by a facilitator's guide and promotion materials, which are also available in Spanish. An independent evaluation conducted in Michigan, by the Pacific Institute for Research and Evaluation, found that out of the 130 parents who participated in the project, two-thirds were motivated to talk with their children about alcohol in the 4–6 weeks following the program. Of those parents, two-thirds found the program helpful in deciding what to say (Pacific Institute for Research and Evaluation, 1995). The Century Council has followed up with another program aimed at parents of first-year university students called *Parents: You're not done yet*. The brochure encourages parents to discuss college drinking with their children before they leave home.

Entreprise & Prevention, a French SAO, supported a program called *Soif de Vivre* (Thirst for Life) aimed at 14 to 20 year-olds. The purpose of the program was to give accurate information on alcohol and its effects, without being moralistic, and to encourage responsible use of alcohol. The Century Council in the U.S. sponsors a program called *Cops in Shops*, which aims to curtail underage drinking by making it difficult to purchase alcohol under the minimum drinking age. The Portman Group in the United Kingdom launched a program called *Prove It*, a proof-of-age card scheme for those seeking to make purchases of alcohol beverages on licensed premises. The card is received through an application process that must be sponsored by a responsible adult and the age of every applicant is verified. The program helps licensees to protect their licenses and prevents underage youths from buying alcohol. The Australian Associated

Brewers, through the Australian Brewers Foundation, supports a program called *Rethinking Drinking: You're in Control*, a secondary school alcohol education curriculum that focuses on harm minimization (see text box). The Beer Institute in the U.S. has been active in a number of programs aimed at college students.

Social aspects organizations and trade associations that sponsor alcohol education programs do not, of course, necessarily agree that messages to young people have to be negative. Life skills education is an example of a positive approach, and one that is used in a variety of countries by nonindustry funded groups as well. Its purpose is to equip young people with the kinds of skills they need to make responsible decisions about their lifestyle. The ARA in South Africa sponsored a life skills program for primary school children that was not specifically about alcohol, but used several issues to illustrate the kinds of decisions for which young people need to prepare.

Stichting Verantwoord Alcoholgebruik (STIVA) in the Netherlands also funds life skills education in schools. Gode Alkoholdninger produced high school educational materials on alcohol that were used to educate pupils in the historical and cultural dimensions and the social and psychological aspects of alcohol. Other countries that have used similar approaches include France, Germany, Spain, and the United Kingdom. Coors, a brewer based in the U.S., sponsors a program in the U.S. called *An Apple a Day*, which aims to build literacy and critical thinking skills in young people and parents. Coors has also supported the Grow Girl program for 10 to 12 year-old girls, which aimed to decrease high-risk behavior, including underage drinking, by providing a forum where the girls could discuss the changes and difficulties associated with growing into young women.

FORUM, which represents the spirits and wine companies in Belgium, initiated a program in Flemish schools aimed at 16 to 18 year-olds called *The Development of Taste*. Its objective is to help to develop young people's sense of taste as a means of helping them to appreciate quality by promoting a sense of well-being in what they eat and drink. The Century Council is piloting an interactive CD-rom program called *Alcohol 101* in partnership with the University of Illinois in the U.S., aimed at first year university students. Students can experience a variety of simulated situations concerning alcohol issues without ever leaving their computer. It has proven to be a fun but informative way to educate young people about responsible and irresponsible drinking behavior. ADIGRAM in Spain conducted an advertising campaign based on the concept of responsibility.

Drinking and Driving

The overrepresentation of young people in serious road crashes, including crashes associated with alcohol use, has received much attention since the late 1970s in many countries. Governments' major interventions have taken the form of policing and enforcement: the introduction of random breath testing with sig-

Rethinking Drinking

Rethinking Drinking is a secondary school curriculum aimed at students in grades 9 and 10, the 14 to 16 year age range. The project to develop and distribute the curriculum was funded by the Australian Brewers Foundation (ABF), an arm of the Australian Associated Brewers, which has a long history of funding medical research related to alcohol problems. The work was undertaken by the Youth Research Centre at Melbourne University.

The curriculum is now delivered to more than 40% of students in the age range in Australia each year. More than 2,300 teachers, police, and youth workers have been trained to deliver the materials and approximately 1,700 schools across the country use Rethinking Drinking or adaptations of the materials.

The novel partnership of industry and school curriculum professionals was well managed through an agreement established by the Youth Research Centre. It was vital to establish the integrity of the curriculum with teachers, students, parents, community groups, and government. There is clear understanding that Rethinking Drinking was developed by professional educators and that the funders have neither determined the content, nor overtly branded it as an industry product. The ABFs position has quite clearly been to see effective education programs developed to tackle the problems of misuse rather than see the imposition of restrictions which inconvenience consumers and damage the liquor industry generally.

The project commenced in 1993 with research that found that there was a range of materials dealing with health and alcohol but with no clear implementation or single approach to the issues related to alcohol. The research also found that there was a definite need for professional development of teachers delivering alcohol programs. The teaching of abstinence from alcohol was a usual approach in schools, yet the National Campaign Against Drugs and Alcohol has been based on a harm minimization theme since the mid-1980s. Although harm minimization recognizes that abstinence is a choice, the central aim is to inform so that wise choices can be made without prescription.

Following the initial research, the curriculum was then written and developed, with early reference to schools and teachers, by teachers with experience in health issues with middle secondary school students. There is a particular emphasis on student participation and students relating their own experiences or knowledge of alcohol use. The program underwent pilot studies in 1994 and was then adjusted before national distribution took place in 1995 and 1996.

(*continued*)

Rethinking Drinking (*Continued*)

Two other factors have been key to the success of the program. The first has been the provision of in-depth professional development training for teachers managing the program at their schools. This ensures full understanding of the harm minimization approach and the importance placed on student contribution and interaction on the subject matter.

The second factor is the provision of information explaining the program to parents and other teachers at participating schools. It is important to provide understanding and a level of acceptance in teaching what has traditionally been a very sensitive issue.

Rethinking Drinking curriculum materials include:

- A video, "Taking the hiccups out of alcohol education," to explain the harm minimization approach which is targeted at a broad audience so that parents, students, and other teachers understand the aims of the program;
- A booklet to assist the responsible teacher in introducing the program to these broader audiences;
- A teacher's manual with a course overview and eight structured lesson plans;
- A student workbook providing for students to record their own experiences or knowledge of alcohol and their reactions to the lessons;
- Videos portraying drinking situations students could relate to and discuss in group sessions; and
- A computer model allowing students to learn the effects of drinking different combinations of drinks in various situations.

Since 1997, the curriculum has been distributed by the Australian Council for Health, Physical Education, and Recreation.

nificant penalties, the reduction of legal blood alcohol levels to almost zero for probationary licensed drivers, together with a high level of enforcement in many countries. Learner drivers are provided with anti-drink driving material in the introductory road rule booklets in some countries (e.g., Australia), and may be asked questions about the drink driving law in their compulsory written test.

An aspect that is frequently addressed by industry-sponsored programs is finding innovative ways to approach drinking and driving issues. The response has been a variety of strategies to appeal to their target audiences.

In Germany, for example, a disproportionate number of young drivers between 18 and 25 years were involved in car accidents after leaving discotèques. The industry-sponsored Deutsche Initiative zur Förderung eines verantwortungsvollen Umgangs mit alkoholhaltigen Genußmitteln (DIFA FORUM), the German SAO, teamed up with Ford Motor Company, the Department of Police, and other businesses to develop a program to address this problem. The approach was to educate young people on sites such as discos by using an electronic simulator to show them first-hand what driving under the influence is like. DIFA FORUM (n.d.) reports that there was a 10% reduction in alcohol-related accidents in the program area during the period of the program. A similar program was carried out by GODA in Denmark, in which a sober subject had to cope with various traffic situations and then drive with a simulated BAC level of 1.0.

Another approach of making the learning process as interactive and realistic as possible was initiated by DIFA FORUM and replicated by a number of industry-sponsored groups in Belgium, Ireland, France, Austria, Spain, and Denmark. These programs were funded in part by the Amsterdam Group, a Pan-European SAO and the European Road Safety Federation. The approach involved selecting a group of young people to participate in a driving experiment. The young adults drove a car on a short test track: once before each driver had anything to drink, and then again after consuming alcohol. They were asked after having nothing to drink how they thought they would drive after a few drinks. Most thought they would drive better and were surprised at the outcome. The whole experiment was taped and made into a video called *Teste de Conduite pour Jeunes:, Alcool au Volant* (Driving Test for Young People: Alcohol at the Wheel). Adaptation of this video is being undertaken in Thailand with support from the Asia-Pacific Alcohol Policy Forum, an Asian SAO.

Other approaches have included using testimonials to relay the message about the hazards of drinking and driving, as was tried by The Century Council in the U.S. One such program that has been especially well received by audiences throughout the country, according to the council, is *Brandon Tells His Story*. Through the use of video and live presentations, Brandon, a young man who was permanently disabled in an alcohol-related crash, speaks to high school students and their parents about what his life was like before and after the crash.

There are also a number of SAOs in different countries that sponsor taxi-cab services from bars and restaurants as well as designated driver programs. In the United Kingdom, for example, the Portman Group sponsored a campaign called *If You Drink, Let Others Drive* together with the Ministry of Transport. The campaign message appeared on taxis, car stickers, buses, and beermats, in railway stations and on posters. Éduc'Alcool in Canada sponsored a campaign in 1995, urging drivers to make an agreement with a loved one so that a drinker would be picked up by the sober partner to the deal. This was run as a competition and more than 105,000 drivers took part. A similar program was run in Australia called "*Home Safely*." Sponsored by the Distilled Spirits Industry Council of Australia, the Australian Brewers Foundation and the Registered and Licensed Clubs Association of Australia, the program was based on a "Contract for Life" to agree ground rules for getting home safely and encouraging parents/adults to provide a suitable role model (see text box).

Home Safely

Home Safely is a national campaign which aims to reduce the incidence of teenagers involved in alcohol-related road trauma. The program is an initiative of the Distilled Spirits Industry Council of Australia and was supported by the Australian Brewers Foundation and the Registered and Licensed Clubs Association of Australia. The campaign commenced in 1986, received significant drive during 1993–1995, in particular, and is ongoing.

Home Safely is designed to encourage discussion between young people, their families, and other adults in positions of responsibility. The program also encourages teenagers and their parents (or another responsible adult) to take positive action by signing an agreement known as the "Contract for Life," which commits them to taking steps to avoid being in a vehicle if they or the vehicle's driver have had too much alcohol to drive.

Under the agreement teenagers commit to:

- Calling home from any place and at any time for assistance and/or transportation to get home safely; or
- Arranging for another person who has not been drinking alcohol to drive them home safely whenever they or any other person who is driving them have been affected by alcohol.

Parents or the responsible adult commit to:

- Coming to pick up or arranging transport to get the teenager home safely from any place at any time when called for assistance; and
- Arranging safe transport with someone who has not been affected by alcohol to bring the teenager home safely whenever the adult or another person who has been driving them has consumed too much alcohol.

This simple program has been widely promoted through schools, community service groups, youth groups (including sporting bodies and activity groups such as scouts and guides), road safety groups (including driving schools, police, and community road safety groups), and municipal governments. It is estimated that 1.3 million "Contracts for Life" have been distributed to Australian families since the program commenced in 1986.

(*continued*)

Home Safely (*Continued*)

Evaluation of the program showed strong support from teachers and parents. Indeed, although promotional support is not current, strong interest from teachers and community group continues to demand distribution of kits. There is significant anecdotal evidence that most young people, particularly in metropolitan and large regional centers, do make arrangements to avoid drinking and driving. This should not be attributed solely to Home Safely when there are a range of powerful interventions to deter drunk driving among young drivers, e.g., loss of driver's license and a strong likelihood of detection. Nevertheless, the program has played a role in encouraging discussion of the issue among new drivers and providing approval for making safe choices.

BROADER PROGRAMS

The programs cited above are some examples of industry-sponsored alcohol education efforts in different countries aimed at reducing harm and improving knowledge. The alcohol beverage industry is committed to improving its programming and increasing its partnerships in developed and developing countries. Some of these programs have been evaluated, with largely positive results (Houghton, 1998). But the process of evaluation is a difficult and complex field which poses challenges for industry-sponsored and public health-supported programs alike (Grant, 1984; Houghton, 1998; Kayser, Schippers, & van der Staak, 1995; May, 1991). However, it is fair to say on such issues as drinking and driving the industry has certainly made a contribution to the significant reductions in driving fatalities in a number of countries.

Self-Regulation

As mentioned in the introduction to this chapter, the alcohol beverage industry is committed to broader policies that aim to influence the environment in which drinking takes place, some of which affect youth and two of which deserve mention here.

They are self-regulation and server training. The development of advertising codes and self-regulatory mechanisms allows the industry to police itself in terms of how its products are portrayed to the public. This has been particularly successful in the United Kingdom, where the Portman Group has issued a Code of Practice on the Naming, Packaging, and Merchandising of Alcoholic Drinks. The Portman Group's code was launched in 1996 and then strengthened in 1997 to include a new independent complaints panel. The industry is committed to taking steps to encourage the development and enforcement of self-regulatory bodies where they do not currently exist, especially in emerging markets. STIVA also has such a code, as does the ARA in South Africa and industry groups in a number of other countries. Trade associations such as the Beer Institute and the Distilled Spirits Council of the United States also have codes, as do many individual companies.

As is stated in the *Geneva Partnership on Alcohol: Towards a Global Charter*, a document agreed to by an international partnership of public health, government, research bodies, and the alcohol beverage industry in May 2000:

> Advertising and promotional activities should not, for example, create an impression that the drinking of alcohol is a requirement for success, or present a negative portrayal of those who abstain; nor should they be targeted at children or those who do not have the legal right to buy or consume alcohol (International Center for Alcohol Policies, 2000, p. 3).

Server Training

The second issue is that of promoting and training hospitality staff, whether in bars or restaurants. This idea of responsible server training is not new. For example, the Arthasastra, an Indian text, some 2000 years old, tells us:

> The appointment of a "superintendent of liquor," not only to control the sale and consumption of alcoholic drinks but also to organise their manufacture... Tavern keepers are to be instructed to make their establishments well-furnished and comfortable, and to prevent their patrons from over-indulgence... (Basham, 1977, p. 217, as cited in Allsop, Martin, Sweeney, & Leitner, 1996).

In Australia, the industry licensing scheme is a self-regulating code of conduct introduced in the state of Victoria by the Australian Hotels and Hospitality Association (Victoria) and the Licensed Clubs Association of Victoria. These associations cover a large proportion of venues, other than restaurants, where alcohol is sold for consumption on the premises. The voluntary licensing scheme, which is endorsed by the relevant minister and the government's formal liquor licensing authority, aims to raise the awareness of venue management and staff of their responsibilities under public liability law and as service providers to customers to reduce alcohol-related harm in the community. Around 2,000 businesses have signed on to the scheme since its launch in April 1998.

This voluntary licensing scheme is an extension and formalization of existing voluntary codes of practice, particularly those relating to the responsible service of alcohol. A major impetus to formalize such codes has been the threat of legal action relating to failures to exercise a proper duty of care, particularly under regulations pertaining to alcohol service to intoxicated people and to underage drinkers, and the consequent skyrocketing of insurance costs. Although such legal actions in Australia have been limited, the experience in North

America has demonstrated to the Australian industry the need to be proactive in improving its programs and obtaining formal recognition for their implementation.

In the U.S., the Training for Intervention Procedures (TIPS) program is sponsored by Anheuser-Busch, Coors Brewing Company, UDV North America, and Miller Brewing Company. It is the most widely recognized alcohol server training program in the U.S., with the aim of educating and training all facets of society in the responsible sale and consumption of alcohol. According to the program literature, there are over 500,000 TIPS-certified servers and 18,000 trainers in the U.S. Training for intervention procedures-trained servers are also active in 22 countries including Canada, Japan, the Netherlands, and the United Kingdom.

CONCLUSION

While the alcohol beverage industry has made substantial progress in educating the community against harmful drinking, there is clearly more work to be done. Building and maintaining cooperation and trust with government and community agencies is the foundation for industry's involvement in community education and in implementing effective self-regulation. Strengthening and maintenance of these relationships must be consciously pursued.

Where strong industry involvement is well established, closer cooperation in research, policy formulation, and joint programs will evolve. In Australia, industry has been involved over the last 2 years as a partner in the development of a National Alcohol Strategy, which has included community research focused on youth drinking habits and the development of a targeted community campaign. This evolution from industry-managed programs to joint programs can benefit communities by improving research knowledge through cooperative funding and oversight, and improved evaluation of education programs.

Underpinning the development of industry involvement and acceptance in education about drinking choices is the recognition by governments and the community that moderate consumption patterns are a desirable community goal. Industry too has developed a stronger appreciation of its roles and responsibilities as a marketer of alcohol. Learning how to drink and to understand the consequences of drinking behaviors has an important bearing on a community's alcohol problems, and responsible and cooperative education play a vital role in influencing more positive outcomes.

Whether or not to drink is but one of many decisions a young person will confront. The sponsors of ICAP believe that a full understanding of the influences that have an impact on this decision is important and should shed light on education efforts regarding alcohol. Effectively equipping young people for the many responsibilities of being an adult requires the ingenuity and imagination of all parties involved in their community, including the alcohol beverage industry. As one strives to provide an environment that reduces the potential for harm, one must remember that this environment must also provide young people with the freedom to learn, make their own decisions, and take ownership of their lives.

REFERENCES

Allsop, S., Martin, P., Sweeney, R., & Leitner, A. (1996). *Responding to alcohol-related harm in and around licensed premises*. Queensland, Australia: National Centre for Education and Training on Addiction with Queensland Police Services, National Police Research Unit, and Drug and Alcohol Services Council.

DIFA FORUM. (n.d.). *Alkohol und Verantwortung: Deutsche Initiative zur Förderung eines verantwortungsvollen Umgangs mit alkoholhaltigen Genußmitteln* (Brochure). Wiesbaden, Germany: DIFA.

Grant, M. (1984). The moderating influence: A review of trade-sponsored alcohol education programmes. *British Journal of Addiction, 79*, 275–282.

Houghton, E. (1998). A comparative analysis of alcohol education programs sponsored by the beverage alcohol industry. *Journal of Alcohol and Drug Education, 43*, 15–33.

International Center for Alcohol Policies. (2000). *The Geneva partnership on alcohol: Towards a global charter*. Washington, DC: ICAP.

Kayser, R. E., Schippers, G. M., & van der Staak, C. P. F. (1995). Evaluation of a Dutch educational "driving while intoxicated (DWI)" prevention program for driving schools. *Journal of Drug Education, 25*, 379–393.

May, C. (1991). Research on alcohol education for young people: A critical review of the literature. *Health Education Journal, 50*, 195–199.

Pacific Institute for Research and Evaluation. (1995). 8201 Corporate Drive, Suite 220, Landover, MD 20785 (Michigan branch): Pacific Institute for Research and Evaluation.

Phoa, K. L. (1994). *Towards a balanced policy on alcohol: Background and views*. Rotterdam, Netherlands: Stichting Verantwoord Alcoholgebruik.

Plant, M. A., & Plant, M. L. (1992). *Risk-takers: Alcohol, drugs, sex and youth*. London: Tavistock/Routledge.

Portman Group. (1999). *Ten years and counting: A review of progress towards sensible drinking*. London: Portman Group.

Russac, R. J., & Weaver, S. T. (1994). Fine-tuning the prevention message: A developmental perspective. *Journal of Alcohol and Drug Education, 39*, 46–55.

Social Aspects of Alcohol Committee of the South African Liquor Industry. (n.d.). *SAAC advertising, packaging and promotions code* (Brochure). Cape Town, South Africa: SAAC.

Society for Alcohol & Social Policy Initiative (1998). (Program Brochure). New Delhi, India.

Chapter 13

Conclusion

Eleni Houghton

"How can we muster shock or surprise if people who have never been taught fail to exercise a discernment that must be learned? Don't we have a moral responsibility to educate them before we attempt to hold them responsible for their actions?"

Edward W. Schneider, PhD
Chairman
American Council on Alcoholism

Adolescence can be characterized as a period of "rapid physical growth, significant physical and psychological changes, and evolving personal relationships" (Scheidt, Overpeck, Wyatt, & Aszmann, 2000, p. 24). Teenagers are at the height of experimenting with life and taking risks, and seem to have limitless energy to engage in both. One of many potentially risky activities that is likely to cross their path during these years is drinking alcohol. For many cultures the consumption of alcohol during adolescence is not a particularly noteworthy event. For others, drinking—and particularly drinking to get drunk—is practically a rite of passage. What does a young person in Italy know where young people experience relatively few problems, for example, that many young people in the U.S. do not?

The International Center for Alcohol Policies (ICAP) was interested in what generated these different patterns of drinking by young people and specifically how they were learning about drinking in the first place. ICAP commissioned five regional papers, covering Australasia, China, Europe, Latin America, and southern Africa, that sought to explain the primary influences on how a young person learns about alcohol. The papers revealed generally that family, peers, and culture were dominant influences on young people, usually in that order. At an international meeting hosted by ICAP to discuss the papers, it was noted that whether or not there is a conscious effort by parents or society to teach young people about alcohol, young people learn about alcohol nonetheless.

In this book, the authors have looked at the influences that come to bear on a young person's decision to drink or not. They have addressed how these influences interact with one another, in the belief that if one understands these influences and relationships one can better teach young people to avoid harm that can be associated with reckless drinking. This concluding chapter will draw out some of the major findings and implications of the preceding chapters and offer some suggestions for future work.

DRINKING OVER THE LIFESPAN

In order to focus on major influences on youthful patterns of drinking, it was thought essential to begin the book by offering some perspectives on a "normal" pattern of drinking over the life course. Roche (Chapter 1) explores the most common human encounters with alcohol, how they are first experienced and how they change over time and throughout one's life. While Roche fully acknowledges that for some adolescents problematic drinking during adolescence does continue into adulthood, for the majority of youth it does not (Johnstone, Leino, Ager, Ferrer, & Fillmore, 1996).

Alcohol is an integral part of most cultures and has been so for centuries (Heath, 2000). How, why, when, what, and with whom people consume alcohol has a rich history, and yet it goes largely unexplored. With alcohol's potential for harm, some may balk at the notion of promoting it further, arguing that this is more than adequately accomplished by the alcohol beverage industry. But, in fact, most people, as Roche points out, do not incur harm from alcohol over the life course. Most people who consume alcohol do so because they find it pleasurable (Peele & Grant, 1999). This is an important point because it is a reflection of societal norms, which in turn affect drinking patterns of young people. Young people need to understand both the positive and negative consequences of alcohol and yet, as many authors in this volume point out, alcohol education tends to focus almost exclusively on the negative.

LEARNING

Young people learn about alcohol in a variety of ways, many of which are explored in this book. The complexity of the learning process should not be underestimated, especially when it comes to learning about alcohol. While some of the more dominant influences such as family and peers, the media, religion, and government are addressed in separate chapters, it is really the interaction of all these influences combined that "teach" a young person about alcohol, in the broadest sense. Newman (Chapter 8) addresses this complexity in his review of multiple influences, but he acknowledges that we can never fully understand the complex interaction of forces that influence behavioral decisions. In addition, given that these influences are filtered through the individual's unique perspective, it can be difficult for adults to see them as young people do. Still it is useful in focusing our thinking when developing alcohol education strategies to consider the total environment in which the young person exists.

Acknowledging the complexity of learning about alcohol and the influences that come to bear on a young person does not preclude a discussion of how learning in general terms takes place. Looked at from an educational perspective, it includes providing information in a nonthreatening way, and allowing individuals the opportunity to practice what they have learned and to participate responsibly in the process of learning (Rogers—cited in Roche's chapter, p. 5).

Consider, for example, the amount of attention we give to teaching a young person to drive a car. We explain the purpose of the different parts of the car, how to conduct oneself on the road, how to hold the steering wheel, the meaning of different signs and safety measures. Most countries provide a "learning" period to develop driving skills, and in some countries there are written and practical exams that a young person must pass before actually acquiring a license. We take such care with teaching young people to drive a car because of the potential for harm if they did not have such instruction. In most countries, this privilege of driving is granted at the age of 16 or 18 years.

When it comes to drinking alcohol, most cultures do not have a formal learning process. While many European societies expose children to alcohol in the home, this is not the case, for example, in much of North America. A major theme in this book—and indeed its basic premise—is that drinking behavior is learned, and so is learning to drink responsibly. Drinking responsibly can be viewed as a competence. Competence, as Schippers and colleagues explain in Chapter 2, reflects a person's ability to solve problems, which might relate, for example, to development or to new opportunities or challenges such as drinking alcohol. Learning to drink responsibly can be seen as a part of the process of developing an identity in which exploration and commitment are important dimensions. They point out that even experimenting with drinking heavily on some occasions can be seen as part of the normal development of nonproblematic drinking.

Schippers and colleagues explore in detail two theories underpinning this notion. The first is social learning theory, which focuses on issues concerned with modeling, reinforcing, and imitating behavior (Bandura, 1977), and the second is socialization theories, which examine parenting styles and the relationship between parents and peers (Baumrind, 1991). Their view is that effective prevention of problematic drinking should concentrate not only on preadolescent children but on their parents as well. "By addressing the familial environment, focusing on the establishment of an affectionate and nonconflictual relationship in which the children identify with their parents, prevention programs can influence the development of responsible drinking habits" (Chapter 2, p. 51).

ROLES AND RESPONSIBILITY

A recurring theme in this book is the degree of responsibility one ascribes to different actors, whether they be government, schools, families, the alcohol beverage industry, religious establishments, the media, or the young people themselves. Some cultures believe more strongly in the rights of individuals, while others prize the collective will of society. These beliefs also vary within cultures, and can lead to confusing or mixed messages with respect to alcohol consumption.

In relation to young people and alcohol, each of the actors discussed in this book has a role to play and a concomitant responsibility. What those responsibilities are and what roles each should play, unfortunately, are not so clear-cut in many countries. Indeed, some of the actors are sometimes believed to cause more harm than good with respect to alcohol and youth. Both the media and the beverage alcohol industry have faced criticism in some countries, as have overpermissive or overcontrolling parents. In general, it seems that problems occur least often when all the actors work together in informal partnerships. Those cultures where there is a common approach among diverse actors stand a better chance of educating their young people about alcohol with relatively few problems.

Hanson (Chapter 9), in discussing formal education, notes that cultures where alcohol is consumed extensively but where social problems related to alcohol are relatively few, such as Greece, Italy, and Portugal, have three elements in common. First, there is an absence of emotionality associated with alcohol, which is seen as a normal part of life for those who choose to drink. Secondly, there is little or no social pressure to drink, and abuse of alcohol is not tolerated. Thirdly, young people learn at home from their parents and their parents' example of how to handle alcohol responsibly.

The benefits of sending clear messages to young people through example and education is further highlighted in Weiss's remarks (Chapter 5) on the influence of religion and what it can teach us about drinking. The research she presents, much of which is based on studies conducted in Israel, indicates that prescriptive religions can be effective in the promotion of moderate consumption of alcohol, as evidenced by the relatively low consumption rates of Jews. In Judaism, moderate drinking practices are an integral part of life, and the gradual introduction of children to alcohol in the family setting can result in a low prevalence of intoxication and harm.

Family

The importance of family is further elaborated upon by Sanchez-Sosa and Poldrugo in Chapter 3 and Milgram in Chapter 4. Without question, the strongest initial influence on a young person's drinking behavior is parents and family. This holds true across all countries and cultures. It is the drinking patterns of one's parents that young people are apt to model initially, and perhaps even ultimately.

Sanchez-Sosa and Poldrugo emphasize that in many societies, primitive and contemporary families have adopted celebrations whose social histories include the use of alcohol. Families influence many aspects of individual behavior. "Drinking, as traditional custom, as part of daily eating routines or as a sign of dysfunctional relations is also a human activity that starts within the family." (Chapter 3, p. 57). As these authors point out, acculturation patterns end up in either healthy or problem drinking as a function of parenting styles, family attitudes, values, and models. In general, children have a positive attitude towards drinking alcohol if no alcohol-related problems arise in their families.

While Milgram also recognizes the long history that has characterized alcohol in most cultures, she notes that public attitudes towards its use are often confused and paradoxical in some cultures, and predominantly focused on excessive use and related problems. In cultures such as the U.S., where the family unit is often not a focal point or a conspicuously influential element for a young person after the early teens, being involved in a young person's life is more difficult for parents, but no less important.

Milgram also points to the mixed messages that a young person receives from parents, peers, and school, particularly in the U.S., which render many harm prevention efforts out of touch with a young person's reality. She describes parents and siblings as the principal and most influential role models regarding when, where, how often, and to what extent alcohol is consumed.

Family, particularly parents, have an important role to play in educating young people about alcohol. Regardless of whether parents drink or not, they have enormous influence in shaping young people's attitudes toward alcohol both negatively and positively.

Other Influences

Though parents can play a role, during the teen years, peers tend to become more influential, though as some research notes it depends on the nature of the relationship between parent and child (Costa, Jessor, & Turbin, 1999; Scheidt et al., 2000; Chapter 2). Milgram (Chapter 4) explores the influence of peers, noting that peers can serve as models of behavior and provide the context in which drinking takes place. Two issues which she highlights concern the perception of friends drinking and the notion of peer pressure. Perception, whether accurate or not, has been shown to be a strong influence on youth drinking. Peer pressure is also believed to be a strong influence. However, it is not at all clear whether adolescent drinking is the result of peer pressure or peer preference. Milgram notes that young people who wish to drink may select friends who "accept, encourage, and support drinking" (Chapter 4, p. 97).

Other actors play important though arguably not dominant roles in a young person's education about alcohol.

Media There is little question that the media play a central role in most societies. Much has been made of the effect that the media have on young people, whether through television, the Internet, newspapers, radio, or film. Stockdale (Chapter 10) explores media representations of alcohol and portrayals of drinking behavior. She then goes on to assess how far empirical evidence supports the contention that the media play a major role in young people's alcohol-related attitudes and behavior. She concludes that while the media are a source for information about alcohol and can influence young people's view of the world, their "effects appear to be weak in comparison with familial context and peer relations" (Chapter 10, p. 231).

The media have the potential to be a positive influence if they are credible. Stockdale suggests, for example, that chat rooms on the Internet provide an ideal opportunity to access youth culture and be an effective means for credible peer counselors to provide information and support. Many groups, including the alcohol industry, are supporting interactive situational games on the Internet to help young people to explore various lifestyle issues for themselves, including drinking alcohol.

Government Evans and Roche (Chapter 11) examine the role of government and how its programs and legal framework concerning alcohol policy affect young people. The specific roles of government generally concern issues regarding alcohol availability, public information, drinking and driving, and age of legal purchase/consumption. For government policies to be successful there must be widespread agreement with the goals of the policy and a reasonable level of community support and acceptance. In addition, government policies need to be enforced if they are to succeed.

Concerns over the personal and social consequences of risky drinking among young people are often cited as justification for decisions taken by government and community leaders. The variation in minimum age for the purchase/consumption of beverage alcohol in different countries has been highlighted in a number of chapters. In fact, this provides a good example of how governments reach different conclusions ostensibly with the same goal in mind. For example, to decrease traffic road fatalities in the U.S., the minimum legal purchase age was raised in 1987 from 18 to 21years. Traffic fatalities then did decrease substantially in the U.S.—by 57% for the period 1982–1998 for this age group. It has been argued by many that the change in legislation was the principal reason for this reduction. However, significant decreases in traffic fatalities have also occurred in the United Kingdom and Australia, where the minimum purchase age has remained 18 years. In New Zealand, the minimum age for consumption was recently (2000) lowered from 20 to 18 years because, in part, it was felt that the higher drinking age was being flouted so extensively that the limit was out of step with societal norms (New Zealand Advisory Committee, 1996). While there may be a variety of reasons these decreases have occurred, it is worth noting that the drinking age may not be the sole reason.

Alcohol Beverage Industry Traditionally, there are tensions around the issue of the role that the beverage alcohol industry can and should have, and specifically whether the industry has sincere interest in reducing young people's drinking. Questions also arise about the role of the industry in relation to its contribution to minimizing harms associated with the use of alcohol. As Max and Willersdorf (Chapter 12) point out, the industry takes the misuse of its products very seriously and has worked hard—most particularly over the past decade—to support effective programs that seek to minimize harm that can be associated with reckless drinking. Their work is supported through trade associations, social aspects organizations, and individual companies, and in partnership with a wide variety of actors that include government, the private sector, education authorities, and NGOs.

Formal Education For better or worse, the responsibility of educating young people about alcohol in some cultures falls on the shoulders of schools. Hanson (Chapter 9) outlines the history of alcohol education in formal educational settings, mostly from the perspective of the U.S., which has traditionally focused on a no-use approach. Schools, however, are often limited by funding and time, rendering many of their programs ineffective in changing behavior.

Nevertheless, most countries still make use of the school curriculums to promote alcohol education. Hanson highlights The Netherlands, for example, which recognizes that young people have a natural desire to experiment and that much of this experimentation eventually stops. Such a realization has led the government to include alcohol education as a part of the school curriculum in primary and secondary schools. It also ensures that its messages to young people about alcohol are factually accurate, informative, and appealing to the target audience. In addition, the program is a good example of effective partnerships between the alcohol beverage industry, government, and public health in working to prevent alcohol-related harm.

MOVING AHEAD

Alcohol Education Programs

The most promising approaches for alcohol education appear to be those that are comprehensive and evidence-based (Williams, Perry, Farbakhsh, Veblen-Mortenson, 1999). There have been some promising programs in the U.S. and Australia, for example, which have taken a holistic approach to alcohol education by involving the community, parents, teachers, and students. Again, the key seems to be the establishment of effective and functioning partnerships.

The School Health and Alcohol Harm Reduction Project (SHAHRP) in Australia is an evidence-based intervention research study that aims to reduce alcohol-related harm by enhancing students' abilities to identify and deal with high-risk drinking situations. The study is unusual in that its primary aim is harm minimization rather than nonuse or delayed use. It has shown some promising results in terms of influencing behavior by young people (McBride, Midford, Farringdon, & Phillips, 2000).

Project Northland, implemented in a small town in the U.S., has different objectives. Rather than harm minimization the objectives are to delay initial use and/or prevent drinking before the legal age of consumption. Using a variety of approaches, including intensive parental involvement, the program has provided evidence that using this comprehensive approach can reduce early adolescent behavior in rural and small town communities (Williams et al., 1999). The project is now in Phase II, where the same group of students will be tracked during the high school years.

While both programs focus on evidence-based approaches, the SHAHRP program's goal of minimizing harm as opposed to "just say no" approaches is gaining currency among public health educators in many countries. The contents of this book should challenge us in new ways to make us—parents, educators, communities, businesses, governments—more effective in educating young people about alcohol.

Setting an Example

It would appear that much more work needs to be done in encouraging parents to teach young people about alcohol in cultures where such education is absent. Since formal alcohol education programs, even when they are available, are obviously not sufficient in teaching young people about drinking, a major responsibility still rests with parents. This includes teaching parenting skills, informing parents how young people model behavior, and the importance of setting a good example. Teaching young people about alcohol may mean trying to get a message across not to drink before it is legal to do so, or it may mean explaining through word and deed how to drink responsibly. Some advice for parents is discussed by Hanson in Chapter 9. Archie Brodsky has also offered advice, as outlined in the text box. Milgram (Chapter 4) stresses the importance of staying involved in young people's lives all through the teen years and gives suggestions for how this might be done. It might also be helpful, as Sanchez-Sosa and Poldrugo suggest in Chapter 3, for parents who are particularly effective in educating young people about alcohol to serve as role models for other parents.

The Message

Whether focused on young people or adults, in communicating about drinking behavior, a central component is having a clear message to convey. The message that each culture will communicate is of course different. Ragnar Waahlberg, former Chairman of the Alcohol Education Section of the International Council on Alcohol and Addictions (ICAA), described during the international meeting that resulted in this book the importance for adults and young people in many

Guidelines for Parents

1 Establish a positive drinking atmosphere in your home. Probably nothing influences the way people drink more than the way they see people around them drink. Model the following attitudes, beliefs, and practices:

- Drinking **in moderation** is one of life's little pleasures, binding people together in an atmosphere of relaxation and conviviality.
- Alcohol is not a magic potion, for good or for ill.
- There are good and bad ways of drinking, and it is essential to know the difference. Good drinking is done for pleasurable reasons, in moderation, with people of both genders and all ages, and as an accompaniment to other positive activities (celebrations, holiday, meals, etc.).
- People are expected to behave appropriately when they drink, and those who do not are to be corrected. Those who misbehave persistently should be avoided when possible.
- When visiting friends and relatives, when observing people on the street and in restaurants, point out people who use alcohol in pleasurable, responsible ways, as well as those who drink in ugly, abusive, or dangerous ways. Show by your approval and disapproval the kind of people your kids should emulate and the kind they should avoid.

2 Nurture positive values. Drinking behavior does not occur in a vacuum. People don't act destructively when they enjoy a purposeful and engaged life. Among the core values that protect both adolescents and adults from excess and addiction of any kind are:

- self-control and moderation;
- accomplishment and competence;
- awareness of oneself and one's environment;
- health;
- self-respect; and
- connectedness with others, with a community, and with society.

In other words, people tend to drink in a beneficial manner when their lives are grounded in positive satisfactions, skills, and strong relationships with and responsibility towards others.

3 Compensate for drinking problems if these exist in your family. Nonabusing family members can support this resilience and improve the child's chances of overcoming the problem by doing the following:

- Maintain family rituals such as consistent dinner times and holiday celebrations.

(*continued*)

Guidelines for Parents (*Continued*)

- Don't excuse the parent's alcohol abuse and its consequences, but also don't blame it for everything that goes wrong in the family.
- Don't handicap your child by acting as if he/she is doomed to repeat the parent's behavior.
- Help provide—or encourage your child to discover—models of positive drinking patterns outside the home.

4 Provide guidance as the teenager enters high-risk environments:

- When your child enters any new peer-oriented drinking environment, talk about the risks ahead of time. Remind this emerging adult of the values she has developed that may set her apart from some of her peers.
- Instead of taking absolute, *a priori* stands, meet your child on his own ground. Let him talk through with you his reasoning about drinking decisions in terms of his own values, goals, and motivations.
- Talk about activities and events to avoid (those built around excessive, irresponsible drinking) and suggest alternative ways of making friends and enjoying a full social life.
- Equip your child with drink avoidance/refusal strategies to limit consumption in high-risk situations. These can range from simply saying "No, thank you—I'm driving" (assertiveness) to refilling a mixed drink throughout a party with only the mixer (a behavioral technique) to conjuring up vivid images of the painful consequences of past excesses (a cognitive technique). Some strategies utilize prior contracting and social support, like agreeing in advance to take a drink at a party only when a light-drinking partner does so.
- Keep a line of communication open that allows your child to give you ongoing feedback about her alcohol use away from home and to share any dilemmas that arise for her. You can't do much to help a child who feels she has to lie and conceal.

5 Avail yourself of realistic alcohol education programs at the college level and encourage the adoption of such programs.

Source: Brodsky (1998).

Scandinavian countries of knowing that different patterns of drinking exist besides simply drinking to get drunk. As he pointed out, "If young people learn more about different ways of drinking, then it is possible for future generations to change their drinking patterns to patterns associated with less harm."

In Canada, a very successful partnership called Educ'Alcool has emerged in Quebec between the public and private sector, including the alcohol beverage industry whose main message is "La modération a bien meilleur goût," "Moderation is always in good taste." Hubert Sacy, Educ'Alcool's Executive Director, who is also Chairman of the ICAA Alcohol Education Section, argues that prevention programs should not limit themselves to the harms of excessive drinking but should also promote the moderate consumption of alcohol for those who choose to drink. "Our main goal is to eliminate the myths and prejudices surrounding alcohol and ensure its rightful place in human activities, which in most cases relates to conviviality, relaxation, and good taste. In doing this, we will be able to convey the values we want to promote throughout those activities that our society [engages in]" (Sacy, 1996).

Research on Drinking Patterns

In the last several years much research has emerged on the importance of studying patterns of drinking. Studying beneficial and problematic patterns of drinking allows researchers and practitioners to understand and prevent abuse more effectively (Grant & Litvak, 1998). Research has focused on harm rather than the substantial numbers of young people who do not drink in a problematic way and what factors facilitate the nonproblematic uses of alcohol.

In the U.S., Michael Haines is working with Northern Illinois University on changing the perception of what "normal" drinking on university campuses is, because research has shown that students think other students drink far more than they actually do. Haines has stated that "The vast majority of students don't harm themselves or others as part of their drinking behavior, and that's the best kept secret in the country" (Gose, 1997). His strategy of changing this perception has yielded positive results in terms of both changing perceptions and lowering alcohol consumption by students (Haines & Spear, 1996).

There is much to learn from young people who drink moderately, and even from young people who do not drink at all. Other important areas for research are addressed by Engs in Chapter 7.

Risk and Responsibility

Risk and experimentation are inevitable features of youth. Mixing these features with a sense of invincibility makes a potent combination. How these attributes manifest themselves varies from individual to individual. Alcohol can be part of risky behavior for young people but experimentation is not necessarily all negative. Plant (Chapter 6) explores the dimensions of experimentation and risk and notes that experimentation can play a positive role for young people.

While it is true that experimentation may involve a degree of risk, it is also an essential part of learning. Some cultures may try to overprotect youth. But young people cannot fully develop as mature independent adults without testing limits and engaging in some risky behavior. The transition from adolescence to adulthood involves choices, responsibilities, and risks. Removing the ability to make those choices, within reason, does not teach responsibility, it hinders it. Understanding the dimensions of risk and how it is communicated warrants further exploration (Leigh, 1999).

This book at its core is a reminder that young people can—and most do—learn to drink alcohol responsibly. It addresses how young people learn about alcohol, which factors seem to influence their learning most, at what time and what lessons one can draw from this knowledge. If beverage alcohol is an enjoyable part of life for most adults, one should not be shy about encouraging responsible drinking and fully exploring mechanisms and pathways by which that may be achieved.

REFERENCES

Bandura, A. (1977). *Social learning theory*. Englewood Cliffs, NJ: Prentice–Hall.

Baumrind, D. (1991). Parenting styles and adolescent development. In R. Lerner, A. C. Peterson, & J. Brooks-Gunn (Eds.), *The encyclopedia on adolescence* (pp. 746–758). New York: Garland.

Costa, F. M., Jessor, R., & Turbin, M. S. (1999). Transition into adolescent problem drinking: The role of psychosocial risk and protective factors. *Journal of Studies on Alcohol, 60*, 480–490.

Gose, B. (1997, October 24). Colleges try to curb excessive drinking by saying moderation is okay. *The Chronicle of Higher Education, 44*, A61–A62.

Grant, M., & Litvak, G. (Eds.). (1998). *Drinking patterns and their consequences*. Washington, DC: Taylor & Francis.

Haines, M. S., & Spear, S. F. (1996). Changing the perception of the norm: A strategy to decrease binge drinking among college students. *Journal of American College Health, 45*, 134–140.

Heath, D. (2000). *Drinking occasions: Comparative perspectives on alcohol and culture*. Philadelphia, PA: Brunner/Mazel.

Johnstone, B. M., Leino, E. V., Ager, C. R., Ferrer, H., & Fillmore, K. M. (1996). Determinants of life-course variation in the frequency of alcohol consumption: Meta-analysis of studies from the collaborative alcohol-related longitudinal project. *Journal of Studies on Alcohol, 57*, 494–506.

Leigh, B. (1999). Peril, chance, adventure: Concepts of risk, alcohol use, and risky behavior in young adults. *Addiction, 94*, 371–383.

McBride, N., Midford, R., Farringdon, F., & Phillips, M. (2000). Early results from a school alcohol harm minimization study: the school health and alcohol harm reduction project. *Addiction, 95*, 1021–1042.

New Zealand Advisory Council. (1997). *Report of the advisory committee on the liquor review*. The Advisory Committee Liquor Review, 1996, Ministry of Justice, Wellington, New Zealand.

Peele, S., & Grant, M. (Eds.). (1999). *Alcohol and pleasure: A health perspective*. Philadelphia, PA: Brunner /Mazel.

Sacy, H. (1999). The ideology, programs and results of the Québec experience: How Éduc'alcool helps people make responsible decisions about drinking. Presentation to the Foundation of Oberoende Alkoholsaurarbetet, Stockholm, Sweden. October 4.

Scheidt, P., Overpeck, M. D., Wyatt, W., & Aszmann, A. (2000). Adolescents' general health and well being. In C. Currie, K. Hurrelmann, W. Settertobulte, R. Smith, & J. Todd (Eds.), *Health policy for children and adolescents: Issue 1. Health and health behaviour among young people* (EUR/ICP/IVST 06 03 05(A), pp. 24–38). Copenhagen: World Health Organization.

Williams, C. L., Perry, C. L., Farbakhsh, K., Veblen-Mortenson, S. (1999). Project Northland: Comprehensive alcohol use prevention for young adolescents, their parents, schools, peers and communities. *Journal of Studies on Alcohol* (Suppl. 13), 112–124.

Index